Lecture Notes
in Business Information Processing 474

LNBIP reports state-of-the-art results in areas related to business information systems and industrial application software development – timely, at a high level, and in both printed and electronic form.

The type of material published includes

- Proceedings (published in time for the respective event)
- Postproceedings (consisting of thoroughly revised and/or extended final papers)
- Other edited monographs (such as, for example, project reports or invited volumes)
- Tutorials (coherently integrated collections of lectures given at advanced courses, seminars, schools, etc.)
- Award-winning or exceptional theses

LNBIP is abstracted/indexed in DBLP, EI and Scopus. LNBIP volumes are also submitted for the inclusion in ISI Proceedings.

Shaofeng Liu · Pascale Zaraté ·
Daouda Kamissoko · Isabelle Linden ·
Jason Papathanasiou
Editors

Decision Support Systems XIII

Decision Support Systems in An Uncertain World:
The Contribution of Digital Twins

9th International Conference on Decision
Support System Technology, ICDSST 2023
Albi, France, May 30 – June 1, 2023
Proceedings

Springer

Editors
Shaofeng Liu (iD)
University of Plymouth
Plymouth, UK

Daouda Kamissoko (iD)
University of Toulouse 1 - IMT Mines Albi
Albi, France

Jason Papathanasiou (iD)
University of Macedonia
Thessaloniki, Greece

Pascale Zaraté (iD)
University of Toulouse Capitole - IRIT
Toulouse, France

Isabelle Linden (iD)
University of Namur
Namur, Belgium

ISSN 1865-1348   ISSN 1865-1356 (electronic)
Lecture Notes in Business Information Processing
ISBN 978-3-031-32533-5   ISBN 978-3-031-32534-2 (eBook)
https://doi.org/10.1007/978-3-031-32534-2

This Springer imprint is published by the registered company Springer Nature Switzerland AG
The registered company address is: Gewerbestrasse 11, 6330 Cham, Switzerland

EURO Working Group on Decision Support Systems (EWG-DSS)

The EWG-DSS is a Euro Working Group on Decision Support Systems within EURO, the Association of the European Operational Research Societies. The main purpose of the EWG-DSS is to establish a platform for encouraging state-of-the-art high-quality research and collaboration work within the DSS community. Other aims of the EWG-DSS are to:

- Encourage the exchange of information among practitioners, end-users, and researchers in the area of decision systems
- Enforce the networking among the DSS communities available and facilitate activities that are essential for the start-up of international cooperation, research, and projects
- Facilitate the creation of professional, academic, and industrial opportunities for its members
- Enhance the development of innovative models, methods, and tools in the field of decision support and related areas
- Actively promote interest in decision systems in the scientific community by organizing dedicated conferences, mini-conferences, workshops, and seminars, as well as editing special and contributed issues in relevant scientific journals

The EWG-DSS was founded with 24 members, during the EURO Summer Institute on DSS that took place in Madeira, Portugal, in May 1989, organized by two well-known academics of the OR community: Jean-Pierre Brans and José Paixão. The EWG-DSS group has grown substantially through the years. Currently, we have over 400 registered members from around the world.

Through the years, much collaboration among the group members has generated valuable contributions to the DSS field, which resulted in many journal publications and collaborative projects. Since its creation, the EWG-DSS has held annual meetings in various European countries, and has taken an active part in the EURO Conferences on decision-making-related subjects. Starting from 2015, the EWG-DSS established its own annual conference, namely, the International Conference on Decision Support System Technology (ICDSST).

The current EWG-DSS Coordination Board comprises six passionate scholars in the DSS field: Shaofeng Liu (UK), Boris Delibašić (Serbia), Isabelle Linden (Belgium), Jason Papathanasiou (Greece), Pavlos Delias (Greece), and Ana Paula Cabra (Brazil). The Coordination Board is supported by an Advisory Board (chaired by Pascale Zaraté) and a Board of Assistants (potential future Coordination Board members).

Preface

This thirteenth edition of the EWG-DSS Decision Support Systems published in the LNBIP series presents a selection of high-quality papers from the 9th International Conference on Decision Support System Technology (ICDSST 2023), held in Albi, France, during May 30 – June 1, 2023, with the main theme "Decision Support Systems in An Uncertain World: The Contribution of Digital Twins". This event was organized by the Euro Working Group on Decision Support Systems (EWG-DSS) in collaboration with the University of Toulouse 1 – IMT Mines Albi.

The EWG-DSS series of International Conferences on Decision Support System Technology (ICDSST), starting with ICDSST 2015 in Belgrade, were planned to consolidate the tradition of annual events organized by the EWG-DSS in offering a platform for European and international DSS communities, comprising the academic and industrial sectors, to present state-of-the-art DSS research and developments, to discuss current challenges that surround decision-making processes, to exchange ideas about realistic and innovative solutions, and to co-develop potential business opportunities.

The scientific topic areas of ICDSST 2023 include:

- Decision Support Systems: Advances and Future Trends
- Multi-Attribute and Multi-Criteria Decision Making
- Knowledge Management, Acquisition, Extraction, Visualisation, and
- Decision Making
- Multi-Actor Decision Making: Group and Negotiated Decision Making
- Collaborative Decision Making and Decision
- Discursive and Collaborative Decision Support Systems
- Mobile and Cloud Decision Support Systems
- GIS and Spatial Decision Support Systems
- Data Science, Data Mining, Text Mining, Sentiment Analysis, and Process Mining
- Big Data Analytics
- Imaging Science (Image Processing, Computer Vision, and Pattern Recognition)
- Human-Computer Interaction
- Internet of Things
- Social Network Analysis for Decision Making
- Simulation Models and Systems, Regional Planning, Logistics, and SCM
- Business Intelligence, Enterprise Systems, and Quantum Economy
- Machine Learning, Natural Language Processing, Artificial Intelligence
- Virtual and Augmented Reality
- New Methods and Technologies for Global Crisis Management
- Analytics for Mitigating the Impact of Pandemics
- Intelligent DSS for Crisis Prevention
- Innovative Decision Making during Global Crises
- New DSS Approaches for Post-Crisis Recovery of Economy
- Decision Making in Modern Education

- Decision Support Systems for Sports
- Immersive Analytics for Decision Making
- Digital Twins for Decision Making
- General DSS Case Studies

This wide range of topics allowed us to present various solutions regarding the decision-making process and decision support in a great number of domains, and to highlight the main trends and research evolution. This EWG-DSS LNBIP Springer edition includes contributions selected via a double-blind evaluation process, maintaining the society's high-quality profile. Each selected paper was reviewed by at least three internationally known experts from the ICDSST 2023 Program Committee. Through its rigorous review and revision, 21 out of 65 submissions were selected for publication in this 13th EWG-DSS Springer LNBIP Edition, which represents a 32% acceptance rate.

The selected papers are representative of the current and recent DSS research and application advancements. The papers are topically organised in four sections:

(1) DSS models, methods, and tools. The five papers in this section present innovative decision models, methods, and tools. The first paper, written by Boris Delibašić, Draženko Glavić, Sandro Radovanović, Andrija Petrović, Marina Milenković, and Milija Suknović, discusses the multi-actor VIKOR method for highway selection in Montenegro, followed by a tool to support decisions for the trace clustering problem with a non-compensatory approach from Nikolaos Zapoglou and Pavlos Delias. Papers 3 and 4 propose two important DSS models: an asset-based causal loop model (authored by Romain Ben Taleb, Matthieu Lauras, Mathieu Dahan, Aurelie Montarnal, and Romain Miclo) and a time-aware optimisation model by Herwig Zeiner. The last paper in this section provides a comprehensive study of emerging technologies for prevention and detection of network attacks, authored by Tauheed Khan Mohd, Paul Addai, Ryan Freas, Elnatan Mesfin Tesfa, and Max Sellers.

(2) DSS solutions for improving business performance and engaging stakeholders. This section includes six papers focusing on the provision of DSS solutions to improve different aspects of business performance and stakeholders' engagement. Firstly, the paper by Emna Masmoudi, Laurent Piétrac, and Séverine Durieux analyses the impact of Industry 4.0 on OEE improvement. Then, the paper from He Huang, Shiqi Sun, Lina Liu, Koen Mommens, and Cathy Macharis provides a data-driven stakeholder-based decision-support system that considers uncertainties. George Tsakalidis, Nikolaos Nousias, and Kostas Vergidis developed a BPR Assessment Framework staging business processes for redesign using cluster analysis. This section includes two papers discussing the role of knowledge in DSS: the paper of Jiang Pan, Shaofeng Liu, Sarah Tuck, and Aira Ong explores Lean Knowledge Management Processes for improving the performance of manufacturing supply chain decisions, and the paper of Charikleia Karakosta, Zoi Mylona, Jason Papathanasiou, and John Psarras integrates existing knowledge to accelerate building renovation rates in Europe. The last paper in this section explores equity-based allocation criteria for water deficit periods with a case study in South Africa.

This paper is authored by Sinetemba Xoxo, Jane Tanner, Sukhmani Mantel, David Gwapedza, Bruce Paxton, Denis Hughes, and Olivier Barreteau.

(3) DSS applications for sustainability: health, energy and transportation. The third section is about DSS applications to achieve sustainability ambitions in various areas. The first paper, by Aikaterini Papapostolou, Charikleia Karakosta, Filippos Dimitrios Mexis, and John Psarras, tackles financing issues in green energy projects. The second paper, from Sarra Samet and Ridda Laouar, deals with health sustainability issues through building risk prediction models for diabetes decision support systems. The last three papers in this section all address sustainability issues in transportation. Jean Baptiste Rakotoarivelo 's paper applies AHP method to the evaluation of costs and pollution emitted by combined means of transport. The paper by Eva Petitdemange, Sam Ban, Matthieu Lauras, and Srang Sarot evaluates the potential of the physical internet for last-mile delivery in developing countries. Finally, the paper of Xiaofang Wu, Shaofeng Liu, Shaoqing Hong, and Huilan Chen focuses on port sustainability assessment.

(4) DSS users and successful adoption. The final section is formed by five papers on DSS users and successful adoption of DSS systems and technologies. The first paper investigates cloud ERP adoption using technology-organisation- environment (TOE) and diffusion of innovation (DOI) theories, authored by Sin Ting Cheung, Uchitha Jayawickrama, Femi Olan, and Maduka Subasinghage. The paper from Christer Carlsson and Pirkko Walden provides insights into young elderly DSS users - some reasons for successful adoption. The third paper presents behavioral studies for the use of visualization in holistic evaluation for multicriteria decision problems decision. The paper is authored by Evanielle Barbosa Ferreira, Tarsila Rani Soares de Vasconcelos, Lucia Reis Peixoto Roselli, and Adiel Teixeira de Almeida. Sean Eom's paper discusses digital distance learning critical success factors for conducting learning analytics research. Finally, the paper from Peter Keenan and Ciara Heavin elicits past trends and future opportunities for scientific authorship in DSS research.

We would like to thank many people who greatly helped the success of this LNBIP book. First of all, we would like to thank Springer for giving us the opportunity to guest edit the DSS book, and we especially wish to express our sincere gratitude to the Springer staff who have provided us with timely professional guidance and advice during the volume editing process. Secondly, we need to thank all the authors for submitting their state-of-the-art work to be considered for the LNBIP volume. All selected papers are of high quality. It was a hard decision for the guest editors to select the best 21. Thirdly, we wish to express our gratitude to all reviewers, who volunteered to help with the selection and improvement of the papers.

We believe that this EWG-DSS Springer LNBIP volume has selected a collection of high-quality and interesting research papers addressing the conference's main theme and related topics. We hope the readers will enjoy the publication!

March 2023

Shaofeng Liu
Pascale Zaraté
Daouda Kamissoko
Isabelle Linden
Jason Papathanasiou

Organization

Reviewing Committee

Adiel Teixeira de Almeida	Federal University of Pernambuco, Brazil
Alberto Turón	University of Zaragoza, Spain
Alexander Smirnov	Russian Academy of Sciences, Russia
Alexis Tsoukias	Université Paris Dauphine, France
Alok Choudhary	Warwick University, UK
Ana Paula Cabral Seixas Costa	Federal University of Pernambuco, Brazil
Andy Wong	University of Strathclyde, UK
Ben C. K. Ngan	Worcester Polytechnic Institute, USA
Bertrand Mareschal	Université Libre de Bruxelles, Belgium
Boris Delibašić	University of Belgrade, Serbia
Carlos Henggeler Antunes	University of Coimbra, Portugal
Christian Colot	University of Namur, Belgium
Daouda Kamissoko	IMT Mines Albi, France
Dragana Bečejski-Vujaklija	Serbian Society for Informatics, Serbia
Emilio Larrodé	University of Zaragoza, Spain
Fátima Dargam	SimTech Simulation Technology/ILTC, Austria
Femi Olan	University of Essex, UK
Festus Oderanti	Liberty University, USA
Fernando Tricas	University of Zaragoza, Spain
Francisco Antunes	Beira Interior University, Portugal
George Aretoulis	Aristotle University of Thessaloniki, Greece
George Tsaples	University of Macedonia, Greece
Gloria Phillips-Wren	Loyola University Maryland, USA
Guoqing Zhao	Swansea University, UK
Guy Camilleri	Toulouse III University/IRIT, France
Hing Kai Chan	University of Nottingham Ningbo China, China
Isabelle Linden	University of Namur, Belgium
Jan Mares	University of Chemical Technology, Czech Republic
Jason Papathanasiou	University of Macedonia, Greece
Jean-Marie Jacquet	University of Namur, Belgium
Jelena Stankovic	University of Niš, Serbia
João Lourenço	Universidade de Lisboa, Portugal
Jorge Freire de Sousa	Engineering University of Porto, Portugal
José Maria Moreno-Jiménez	University of Zaragoza, Spain

Juan Carlos Trujillo	University of Alicante, Spain
Kathrin Kirchner	Technical University of Denmark, Denmark
Karim Soliman	Arab Academy for Science, Technology, and Maritime Transport, Egypt
Konstantinos Vergidis	University of Macedonia, Greece
Manuel Salvador	University of Zaragoza, Spain
María Teresa Escobar	University of Zaragoza, Spain
Marc Kilgour	Wilfrid Laurier University, Canada
Marko Bohanec	Jozef Stefan Institute, Slovenia
Md Asaduzzaman	Staffordshire University, UK
Michael Madas	University of Macedonia, Greece
Nikolaos Matsatsinis	Technical University of Crete, Greece
Panagiota Digkoglou	University of Macedonia, Greece
Pascale Zaraté	IRIT/Toulouse University, France
Pavlos Delias	Kavala Institute of Technology, Greece
Rita Ribeiro	UNINOVA – CA3, Portugal
Rudolf Vetschera	University of Vienna, Austria
Sandro Radovanovic	University of Belgrade, Serbia
Sean Eom	Southeast Missouri State University, USA
Sergio Pedro Duarte	University of Porto, Portugal
Shaofeng Liu	University of Plymouth, UK
Stefanos Tsiaras	Aristotle University of Thessaloniki, Greece
Stelios Tsafarakis	Technical University of Crete, Greece
Theodore Tarnanidis	University of Macedonia, Greece
Loukas Tsironis	University of Macedonia, Greece
Uchitha Jayawickrama	Loughborough University, UK
Wim Vanhoof	University of Namur, Belgium
Xiaofang Wu	Jimei University, China

Contents

DSS Applications for Sustainability - Health, Energy and Transportation

DSS Users and Successful Adoption

DSS Models, Methods and Tools

Multi-actor VIKOR Method for Highway Selection in Montenegro

Boris Delibašić[1(✉)] [iD], Draženko Glavić[2] [iD], Sandro Radovanović[1] [iD],
Andrija Petrović[1] [iD], Marina Milenković[2] [iD], and Milija Suknović[1]

[1] Faculty of Organizational Sciences, University of Belgrade,
Jove Ilića 154, Belgrade, Serbia
boris.delibasic@fon.bg.ac.rs
[2] Faculty of Transport and Traffic Engineering, University of Belgrade,
Vojvode Stepe 305, Belgrade, Serbia

Abstract. Nowadays, decision-making systems in modern infrastructural planning greatly impact everyday life. This paper proposes a novel modification of the multi-criteria decision analysis (MCDA) method VIKOR that can be successfully applied to infrastructural decision-making systems. Our contributions are twofold: We first solve a highway section selection on the Montenegro A1 highway. Secondly, we modify the VIKOR method for the multi-actor (MA) setting. Although the original VIKOR method recognized multi-actor preferences through the selection of the value of the compromise parameter v, it did not explicitly include multiple actors in the decision-making process. Moreover, we show how the multi-actor (MA) VIKOR method can serve as a decision support system for making important infra-structural decision problems, improve the transparency of the decision-making process with the rising need to include citizens in the decision-making process, and how it successfully solves the distortion in social choice problem.

Keywords: MCDA · VIKOR · highway selection · multi-actor

1 Introduction

Huge infrastructure projects influence a country's economy, and building them involves including multiple actors, i.e., stakeholders. Usually, these stakeholders have different points of view, and bringing those views together to select the best alternative is challenging. Here, we analyze a highway section selection decision problem with the use of the MA-VIKOR method.

This paper analyzes two motorway alternatives for a 49 km long section through Montenegro highlands with a 682 and 629 million EUR estimated value (2019 estimate), i.e., 13.9 and 12.8 million EUR per kilometer. For a country with 600.000 inhabitants, and a public depth of 83% of GDP this project represents an additional, yet necessary burden, as it is a critical part of the envisioned pan-European corridor XI, a motorway/ferry corridor linking Bari (Italy), Bar

---

The original version of this chapter has been revised. The city name was updated to Berane. A correction to this chapter can be found at
https://doi.org/10.1007/978-3-031-32534-2_22

S. Liu et al. (Eds.): ICDSST 2023, LNBIP 474, pp. 3–14, 2023.
https://doi.org/10.1007/978-3-031-32534-2_1

(Montenegro), Belgrade (Serbia) and Bucharest (Romania). As the more expensive alternative has been chosen, we show a transparent decision analysis of the best alternative selection.

To this end, we modify the existing VIKOR method [9] and propose the multi-actor VIKOR method (MA-VIKOR) that can work with multiple stakeholders (actors). Until now VIKOR has not been explicitly defined for a multi-actor setting, although it was implicitly used through the v parameter. Also, VIKOR has not been used before for a small number of alternatives, as the original normalization it uses is not suitable for a small number of alternatives. Still, we are confident that in real-life decision-making, the decision-making process boils often down to selecting among two or a small number of alternatives.

Compared to other MCDA methods VIKOR includes some favorable features. These are:

1. It has a stability analysis of the best-ranked alternative with clearly defines conditions needed for an alternative to be ranked better than a competing alternative.
2. VIKOR includes the parameter v, which can take values in the [0,1] interval, where 1 means a democratic stakeholder setup (each stakeholder's vote is equal), and 0 where there is a possibility of a single stakeholder strongly influencing the decision outcome.
3. VIKOR also has a long history of being used for the evaluation of critical infrastructure projects (e.g. water dams, motorways, highways, and railroads).

The here proposed MA-VIKOR method is able to:

– Work with a small number of alternatives,
– Work with multiple stakeholders (i.e.) actors, and
– To alleviate the distortion in social choice.

The remainder of the paper is organized as followed. The related research is presented in Sect. 2. To introduce the proposed approach, we first explain the method VIKOR in Sect. 3. Once the main concepts are introduced, the authors introduce the proposed MA-VIKOR in Sect. 4. The main conclusions as well as limitations of the proposed approach are explained in the Sect. 6.

2   Related Research

Multi-actor or multi-stakeholder MCDA is getting more and more attention in the literature than regular MCDA as it allows explicit stakeholders to be involved in the decision-making process. Macharis and Bernardini [11] reviewed multiple MCDA methods for the evaluation of transport projects and identified among the first the need for a multi-actor approach. In Sun et al. [18] a multi-actor multi-criteria analysis approach is recommended for the selection of a low-carbon transport policy. Jiang et al. [9] evaluated the city readiness for connected and autonomous vehicles using a multi-stakeholder multi-criteria analysis with the analytic hierarchy process method. Perera and Thompson [16] used the multi-actor multi-criteria analysis for selecting optimal toll schemes.

MCDA has been widely used in highway decision-making. Radzi et al. [17] made a systematic review of existing decision-making research in highway construction projects. They emphasized the application of MCDA in four areas: feasibility, conceptual, detailed scope, and detailed design. In Antoniou and Aretoulis [2] multi-criteria decision-making methods were applied to two case study projects with different characteristics and awarding authorities' needs to choose between seven different contract types based on nine selection criteria. In Kalamaras et al. [10] multicriteria decision analysis was used to select the best high-way section. In Ellis et al. [8] technical, environmental/ecological, social/community, and economic cost factors are identified as the most important sustainability criteria in assessing long-term cost-effective drainage operations on highways. In Ortiz-Garcia et al. [15] multicriteria decision analysis is suggested as an appropriate decision-making tool for setting road maintenance standards. Four methods were analyzed: utility theory, goals programming, several outranking methods, and the analytic hierarchy process (AHP) method. El-Rayes and Kandil [7] presents a multi-objective optimization model that supports decision-makers in performing the selection of innovative contracting methods to improve construction quality. The traditional two-dimensional time-cost trade-off analysis is transformed into a three-dimensional time-cost-quality trade-off analysis. The model and its capabilities are validated by generating and visualizing optimal tradeoffs among construction time, cost, and quality.

VIKOR is one of the MCDA methods that is widely used in infrastructure and traffic decision processes. Opricović [13] published a university course book (in the Serbian language) where he explained several case studies he participated in and applied the VIKOR method for water management systems (system Gornjak-Mlava, Foča-Goražde), road planning (Major road construction in Belgrade, High-velocity railroad between Novi Sad and Inđija, Road maintenance construction), construction works (selection of construction mechanization, selection of methods and technologies for construction, selection of construction materials). Babashamsi et al. [3] used a hybrid fuzzy AHP and VIKOR methods to prioritize pavement maintenance activities. Malik et al. [12] used an AHP - Entropy weighting and BORDA-VIKOR method for ranking roadside units positioning. Bakioglu and Atahan [4] used a hybrid AHP weighting and TOPSIS and VIKOR methods with Pythagorean fuzzy sets to prioritize risks in self-driving vehicles. Belošević et al. [5] used a fuzzy VIKOR method for the early-stage evaluation of infrastructure projects.

3   VIKOR Method

VIKOR is an MCDA method, which specificity is that it introduces:

1. A compromise solution (Q) between two aggregation methods S and R:
   (a) S (expressing average alternatives' goodness regarding all the criteria - weighted sum), and

(b) R (expressing the weakest alternatives values across the criteria - $MINIMAX$ solution).

2. Conditions needed for an alternative to outrank another alternative:
   (a) Sufficient advantage, and
   (b) Sufficiently stable position.

The compromise solution is a weighted sum between the S and R aggregations, where parameter $v \in [0, 1]$ and the values of v indicate several decision situations, $v = 0.5$ being the default value. A v close or equal to zero indicates a situation where a decision committee member has the right to veto voting, and there is no possibility of discussion between committee members. A v close to or equal to 1 indicates a situation where each committee's member vote has the same weight and there is a possibility for discussion between committee members [14].

Regarding the conditions needed for an alternative to being ranked single at the first position, the sufficient advantage defines a threshold an alternative a' Q (compromise) value should have over other alternatives' $a"$ Q. The first condition is that $Q(a') - Q(a") \geq DI$, $DI = min(0.25, 1/(J - 1))$, where J is the number of alternatives, and DI the difference interval. This condition is tested under the condition that $v = 0.5$. The first condition means that an alternative has a value of Q better than any other alternative, but also better by a defined amount of utility (DI). The second condition states that the first position has to be maintained in one of the following cases:

- $v = 0$,
- $v = 0.25$ and $v = 0.75$, or
- $v = 1$.

The second condition asks for an alternative $Q(a')$ to maintain the first rank position on a minimum on half of the v interval, i.e. [0, 0.5], [0.25, 0.75], or [0.5, 1] as depicted in Fig. 1.

The VIKOR method consists of several steps. Let A be the decision matrix $A = [a_{ij}]_{mxn}$, where i is the number of alternatives $i = 1, .., m$, and j is the number of attributes/criteria $j = 1, .., n$, and a_{ij} are values of the ith alternative and the jth criterion. A^N is the normalized matrix A that uses the max-min normalization (1):

$$a_{ij}^N = \frac{(a_{ij} - a_j^{min})}{(a_j^{max} - a_j^{min})} \tag{1}$$

where a_j^{min} represents the worst value of jth criterion and a_j^{max} represents the best value of jth criterion. It is worth noting that the worst and the best values depend on the type of the criterion, i.e., whether the criterion is a benefit (a higher value is better) or a cost criterion (a lower value is better). We modified the original formula for (1) in order to achieve that the best values are closer to 1, and the worse values are closer to 0. The original method uses the opposite logic, as it regards 0 as the ideal solution, which means that there is no distance

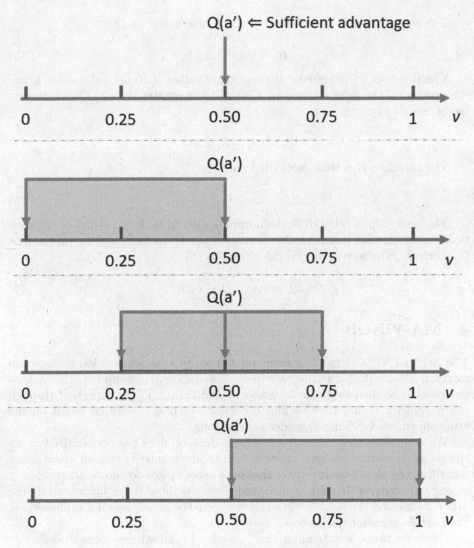

Fig. 1. Sufficient advantage and sufficiently stable position.

to the optimal solution. By applying the modification we did not change the outcome of the results but achieved that the results are comparable to other MCDA methods.

VIKOR is using weights w for expressing the importance of criteria, where $\sum w_j = 1, j = 1, .., n$.

The aggregation S is calculated for each alternative as (2):

$$S_i = \sum_{i=1}^{m} w_j a_{ij}^N \qquad (2)$$

The aggregation R is calculated for each alternative as (3):

$$R_i = min(w_j a_{ij}^N) \qquad (3)$$

The R values are modified if the minimum values of R_i are not unique, i.e., if the number of the same minimums is equal to or greater than 2. The correction factor equals (4):

$$r_i = (S_i - R_i)/100 \qquad (4)$$

The modified R is than calculated as (5):

$$R_i = min(w_j a_{ij}^N) + r_i \qquad (5)$$

The next step in VIKOR is the normalization of both the S and R aggregations using the max-min normalization shown in (1) with S_i and R_i values. The final compromise aggregation is calculated as (6):

$$Q_i = vS_i + (1 - v)R_i \qquad (6)$$

4   MA-VIKOR

The original VIKOR method assumed the setup that all decision-makers can work on a single decision table, where a constellation of a group (whether a decision should be democratic or favorable to individuals [6]) is expressed through the parameter v that tries to find the most acceptable solution based on the group openness for democratic decision-making.

We emphasize that the outcome of the decision does not necessarily remain the same in contexts where multiple actors are involved, and all criteria are considered by all actors. It implies that each actor makes decisions independently (using only criteria that are available to them), without being influenced by the other actors, and thus may act in a self-interested or greedy manner while making the best decision for themselves.

Here, we propose extending this capacity by allowing various stakeholder views (agents) to participate in the decision-making process. We also allow these various agents to use disjunctive, partially overlapping, or the same criteria for decision-making. In real-life settings, as we will see in the case study (Sect. 5), it is not realistic that all agents are interested in the same decision criteria. Although this is usually regulated by ruling out criteria with small weights assignments, here we allow agents to select their own set of criteria for decision-making.

After selecting decision criteria, each agent uses the VIKOR method for ranking the alternatives. As we are here interested in using a small number of alternatives, i.e., < 4, we utilize a different normalization than the VIKOR original normalization. The originally proposed one is not suitable for a small number of alternatives, due to the fact that at least two alternatives for each criterion take the values 1 and 0 for the maximum and minimal value for each criterion.

We propose to use the L_1 normalization, as in the hierarchical additive weighting method (HAW), which actually shows the percentage of each alternative's criteria in the criteria values sum.

So, we transform the original VIKOR A^N matrix to $A^N_{L_1}$ matrix using the L_1 normalization. We apply on the $A^N_{L_1}$ matrix the VIKOR methodology and extract S, R, and Q (for the setting of $v = 0.5$). We use the default value of v, as it is necessary for calculating the stability of the first rank condition, and later in the process, we check the stability also with other v, i.e. $v = \{0, 0.25, 0.75, 1\}$.

After each agent produces their VIKOR generated Q values for each alternative we merge all these Q's from various agents in a single column and use the VIKOR normalization method in order to test the stability of the first rank position using VIKOR methodology. Here we produce at least 4 alternatives (two actors, and two alternatives), so we can safely proceed using the VIKOR method. The whole workflow of the method is shown in Fig. 2.

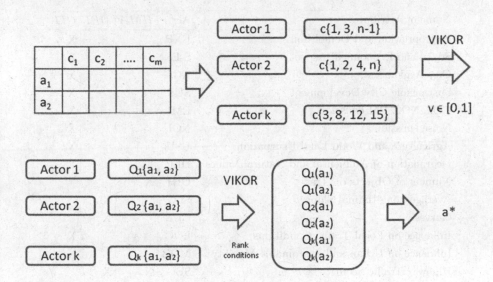

Fig. 2. MA-VIKOR workflow.

In the next section, we apply the proposed MA-VIKOR method to the case study for choosing the most appropriate route for the Berane-Boljare high-way section.

5   Highway Section Selection (Case Study)

One of the biggest infrastructure projects on the Balkan Peninsula has many challenges, one of them is choosing the appropriate trace. We here focus on a 49 km long section on the E763 highway in the Republic of Montenegro. The main difference between the two analyzed alternatives is whether a bypass should be built through the town of Berane bypass or the highway should be built through the city.

We argue that using standard MCDA methods could not reveal clear results of the outcome. We, therefore, propose using the MA-VIKOR method where high-way section alternatives from each individual decision maker were aggregated and the best alternative is identified.

Three actors were involved in the decision-making process: the citizens (CIT), the end users, i.e. drivers (DRI), and the highway managing authority (HMA).

The decision criteria, their abbreviations, and appurtenance to the actors are given in Table 1. Although all actors are aware of all attributes, they were solely interested in the attributes which best allow fulfilling their own goals.

Table 1. List of attributes, their abbreviations, and interestingness for actors.

Name of Attribute	Acr.	HMA	DRI	CIT
Expropriation and Demolition	EXP			X
Social and Economical Aspect	S-E			X
City Agglomeration	AGG			X
Sustainable City Development	SUS			X
COx, NO2, PM emission	EMI			X
Noise emission	NOI			X
Agriculture and Wood Land Usurpation	USU			X
Degradation of Ambiental and Natural Values	DEG			X
Number of Objects on Trace	OBJ	X		
Average Longitudinal Slope	SLO		X	
Curves	CUR		X	
Influence on Local Traffic Conditions	LOC		X	
Influence on Urban and Sustainable Mobility	MOB			X
Highway Traffic Security	SEC	X	X	
Costs of Project Realization	COS	X		
Costs for Highway User	USE		X	
Operative and Periodical Costs of Maintenance	EXP	X		

It can be noticed from Table 1 that only the criteria SEC affects two actors, namely DRI and HMA, while all other attributes are of interest to only one actor (decision perspective).

The decision alternatives are:

1. Highway through the city of Berane (THR), and
2. Berane bypass (BYP).

In this case study, all criteria weights were given the same weight, as the selected decision criteria were conjunctive and the values of these criteria are clearly in favor of one or the other alternative. In Tables 2 through 4 normalized values for the three actors are given. In Table 5 all the Q's are integrated, so the set of alternatives is six, where all actors have various values of these alternatives, as well as the integrated multi-actor alternatives normalized with the IKOR normalization (formula 1). Based on this table it is now possible to test the conditions for stable ranking of the first alternative.

The authors acknowledge that using the same weights for criteria and actors is not always realistic in real-world decision-making scenarios. However, the purpose of the paper is not to propose a one-size-fits-all solution, but rather to demonstrate the effectiveness of a particular decision-making method in a specific context. In this case, the authors chose to use the same weights for criteria and actors to simplify the problem and highlight the capabilities of the proposed method. They recognize that in practice, decision-makers may assign different weights to criteria and actors based on their relative importance. Nonetheless, the authors believe that the proposed method can be adapted to address similar decision-making problems in the future, with different weightings assigned to criteria and actors as deemed appropriate by the decision-makers. The key takeaway from the paper is the usefulness and applicability of the proposed method, rather than the specific weightings used in this particular example.

Table 2. HMA normalized decision table with extracted Q values from VIKOR method

Alt.	OBJ	SEC	COS	MAI	S	R	Q
THR	0.589	0.600	0.520	0.600	0.577	0.565	0.571
BYP	0.411	0.400	0.480	0.400	0.423	0.435	0.429

Table 3. DRI normalized decision table with extracted Q values from VIKOR method

Alt.	SLO	CUR	SEC	DRI	S	R	Q
THR	0.549	0.496	0.600	0.508	0.538	0.554	0.546
BYP	0.451	0.504	0.400	0.492	0.462	0.446	0.454

The authors are aware of the limitations of the normalization method used for Table 5 and recognize the potential for alternative approaches. The authors have chosen to focus on a specific aggregation method for their case study, but the authors plan to explore other aggregation approaches in future work. This will provide a more comprehensive analysis and may lead to more insightful results. The authors acknowledge the limitations of the proposed aggregation

Table 4. CIT normalized decision table with extracted Q values from VIKOR method

Alt.	EXP	SOC	AGG	SUS	EMI	NOI	USU	DEG	TRA	MOB	S	R	Q
THR	0.442	0.167	0.286	0.286	0.286	0.333	0.396	0.400	0.167	0.167	0.293	0.230	0.261
BYP	0.558	0.833	0.714	0.714	0.714	0.667	0.604	0.600	0.833	0.833	0.707	0.770	0.739

Table 5. Integrated aggregated decision alternatives from HMA, DRI, and CIT

Alt.	Q	
THR-CIT	0.2615	1.0000
BYP-CIT	0.7385	0.6495
THR-HMA	0.5713	0.5965
BYP-HMA	0.4287	0.4035
THR-DRI	0.5460	0.3505
BYP-DRI	0.4540	0.0000

method and will continue exploring alternative approaches in order to improve our understanding and decision-making processes.

The best-ranked alternative is the BYP alternative proposed by the citizen ac-tor. The second best alternative is the highway through the city (THR) proposed by the highway managing authority. It can be noticed that both the sufficient advantage and the sufficient stable position were maintained so the alternative BYP was clearly advantageous over the THR alternative. This alternative guarantees the most satisfaction among decision-makers and the least regret.

On the other hand, if we would analyze the voting of actors in Tables 2 through 4 it is clear that both the HMA and DRI are in favor of the THR alternative, where only the actor CIT is in favor of the bypass around Berane. However, if we would consider the average Q of the actors it can be noticed that the THR alternative achieved an average of 46% among the actors, while the BYP alternative achieved a 54% average Q among the actors. This is an example of distortion in social choice [1], where we are getting different outcomes if we consider the votes and preferences of the actors.

On the other hand, the proposed method MA-VIKOR succeeds in achieving to find the most appropriate alternative and showing it achieves a clear advantage. In real-life, this alternative was also finally chosen, and the highway will go around the city of Berane.

6   Conclusion

The paper proposes a novel modification of the MCDA method VIKOR that can be successfully applied to infrastructural decision-making systems. The proposed multi-actor (MA) VIKOR method is an improvement over the original VIKOR method, which recognized multi-actor preferences through the selection of the value of the compromise parameter v but did not explicitly include multiple actors in the decision-making process.

The study validated the proposed MA-VIKOR method through a real-life case study for the selection of a highway route in Montenegro with two alternatives, where it successfully found the most appropriate solution. The method improves the transparency of the decision-making process by incorporating citizens' preferences in the decision-making process. The proposed method is also useful for solving the distortion in social choice problems. The method's success in the real-life case study shows that it can be applied to solve similar decision-making problems in the future. The method's ability to include multiple actors in the decision-making process improves the transparency of the decision-making process and increases citizens' trust in the decision-making system, which is crucial in the modern world where citizens demand to be included in the decision-making process.

Although the study's findings are encouraging, further research is necessary to validate the method in more real-life cases and setups with more than two alternatives. Nonetheless, the paper proposes some possible improvements and applications of the VIKOR method in the multi-actor setting.

The authors are aware of the limitations of the normalization method used for Table 5 and recognize the potential for alternative approaches. The authors have chosen to focus on a specific aggregation method for their case study, but the authors plan to explore other aggregation approaches in future work. This will provide a more comprehensive analysis and may lead to more insightful results. The authors acknowledge the limitations of the proposed aggregation method and will continue exploring alternative approaches in order to improve our understanding and decision-making processes.

Acknowledgements. The authors do not have any funding to disclose other than their affiliation.

References

1. Anshelevich, E., Filos-Ratsikas, A., Shah, N., Voudouris, A.A.: Distortion in social choice problems: the first 15 years and beyond. arXiv preprint arXiv:2103.00911 (2021)
2. Antoniou, F., Aretoulis, G.N.: Comparative analysis of multi-criteria decision making methods in choosing contract type for highway construction in Greece. Int. J. Manag. Decis. Mak. **17**(1), 1–28 (2018)
3. Babashamsi, P., Golzadfar, A., Yusoff, N.I.M., Ceylan, H., Nor, N.G.M.: Integrated fuzzy analytic hierarchy process and VIKOR method in the prioritization of pavement maintenance activities. Int. J. Pavement Res. Technol. **9**(2), 112–120 (2016)
4. Bakioglu, G., Atahan, A.O.: AHP integrated TOPSIS and VIKOR methods with Pythagorean fuzzy sets to prioritize risks in self-driving vehicles. Appl. Soft Comput. **99**, 106948 (2021)

5. Belošević, I., Kosijer, M., Ivić, M., Pavlović, N.: Group decision making process for early stage evaluations of infrastructure projects using extended VIKOR method under fuzzy environment. Eur. Transp. Res. Rev. **10**, 1–14 (2018)
6. Dodevska, Z., Petrović, A., Radovanović, S., Delibašić, B.: Changing criteria weights to achieve fair VIKOR ranking: a postprocessing reranking approach. Auton. Agent. Multi-Agent Syst. **37**(1), 9 (2023)
7. El-Rayes, K., Kandil, A.: Time-cost-quality trade-off analysis for highway construction. J. Constr. Eng. Manag. **131**(4), 477–486 (2005)
8. Ellis, J.B., Deutsch, J.C., Mouchel, J.M., Scholes, L., Revitt, M.: Multicriteria decision approaches to support sustainable drainage options for the treatment of highway and urban runoff. Sci. Total Environ. **334**, 251–260 (2004)
9. Jiang, L., Chen, H., Chen, Z.: City readiness for connected and autonomous vehicles: a multi-stakeholder and multi-criteria analysis through analytic hierarchy process. Transp. Policy **128**, 13–24 (2022)
10. Kalamaras, G., Brino, L., Carrieri, G., Pline, C., Grasso, P.: Application of multicriteria analysis to select the best highway alignment. Tunn. Undergr. Space Technol. **15**(4), 415–420 (2000)
11. Macharis, C., Bernardini, A.: Reviewing the use of multi-criteria decision analysis for the evaluation of transport projects: time for a multi-actor approach. Transp. Policy **37**, 177–186 (2015)
12. Malik, R., et al.: Novel roadside unit positioning framework in the context of the vehicle-to-infrastructure communication system based on AHP-Entropy for weighting and Borda-VIKOR for uniform ranking. Int. J. Inf. Technol. Decis. Mak. **21**(04), 1233–1266 (2022)
13. Opricović, S.: Višekriterijumska optimizacija sistema u građevinarstvu. Građevinski fakultet Univerzitet u Beogradu (1998)
14. Opricovic, S., Tzeng, G.H.: Extended VIKOR method in comparison with outranking methods. Eur. J. Oper. Res. **178**(2), 514–529 (2007)
15. Ortiz-Garcia, J., Snaith, M.S., Costello, S.B.: Setting road maintenance standards by multicriteria analysis. In: Proceedings of the Institution of Civil Engineers-Transport, vol. 158, pp. 157–165. Thomas Telford Ltd. (2005)
16. Perera, L., Thompson, R.G.: Multi-stakeholder acceptance of optimum toll schemes. Res. Transp. Bus. Manag. **41**, 100654 (2021)
17. Radzi, A.R., Rahman, R.A., Doh, S.I.: Decision making in highway construction: a systematic review and future directions. J. Eng. Des. Technol. (2021). (ahead-of-print)
18. Sun, H., Zhang, Y., Wang, Y., Li, L., Sheng, Y.: A social stakeholder support assessment of low-carbon transport policy based on multi-actor multi-criteria analysis: the case of Tianjin. Transp. Policy **41**, 103–116 (2015)

A Tool to Support the Decisions for the Trace Clustering Problem with a Non-compensatory Approach

Nikolaos Zapoglou[1](✉) [iD] and Pavlos Delias[2] [iD]

[1] Department of Computer Science, International Hellenic University, Kavala, Greece
xizapog@cs.ihu.gr
[2] Department of Accounting and Finance, International Hellenic University,
Kavala, Greece
pdelias@af.ihu.gr

Abstract. Process Discovery and Trace Clustering are used to extract business process-related knowledge from event logs and create models of processes. A non-compensatory approach, involving concordance and discordance settings, can be used to assess trace similarity and form groups. Previous research demonstrated the effectiveness of that approach, but it is time-consuming and requires a deep understanding of the technique's parameters and desired outcomes. To make the process more efficient, we developed a software tool to assist with parameter definition and analysis of results. The tool provides a user-friendly interface, visual aids, and the ability to adjust parameters to ensure the solution reflects user preferences, allowing users to make more informed decisions. The publicly available tool combines the power and versatility of the R language with the friendly interfaces implemented using the Shiny libraries.

Keywords: Trace Clustering · Shiny applications · Non-compensatory · Process Mining

1 Introduction

Process discovery is a major function of Process Mining that is used to extract information from event logs and create a model of how the process actually operates. However, this can be difficult for complex processes or for processes that have many possible variations, leading to "spaghetti" process models that are hard to understand. Trace clustering is a method for addressing this issue by dividing the event log into groups and creating a separate model for each group, intending to produce more comprehensible results. This approach aims to facilitate knowledge discovery and support decision-making by identifying coherent groups of process behaviors when there is big variability.

Using only one criterion to cluster traces is equivalent to ignoring certain aspects of the process being studied. It also risks imposing a subjective perspective as objective truth [20]. To achieve effective clustering, it is necessary to use a set of criteria that retain the original meaning of the similarities between objects being analyzed. This helps to provide a more comprehensive understanding of the process.

In previous research [4], we demonstrated that a non-compensatory approach can produce effective results for the trace-clustering problem. Specifically, we argued that using a multiple-criteria approach is necessary to consider all relevant aspects of the context and that using a set of criteria with heterogeneous scales allows for a more comprehensive analysis. To assess the similarity between pairs of traces, we used a non-compensatory approach that involves concordance and discordance settings. The concordance setting requires that a sufficient number of criteria be in agreement with the similarity, while the discordance setting ensures that no criterion conflicting with the similarity is present among those that are not in agreement. This non-compensatory approach was used to aggregate the contributions of individual criteria to the overall similarity, and the resulting similarity metric was then used in an agglomerative hierarchical clustering step to form groups of traces. Furthermore, in [5] we extended that idea by providing additional clustering techniques and by allowing decision-makers to customize the solution to better reflect their preferences, via the introduction of additional thresholds.

While the approach described in [4,5] has shown to be effective in analyzing and clustering process behaviors, it demands a remarkable amount of effort from the decision maker. This involves defining a range of parameters (criteria weights, preferences thresholds), some of which may not have a clear or predictable impact on the final result. The process of selecting and adjusting these parameters can be time-consuming and require a deep understanding of the data and the desired outcomes. In order to support the decision maker in this process and make it more efficient, a software tool that can assist with the parameter definition and analysis of the results would be beneficial. This would allow the decision-maker to focus on the important aspects of the analysis and make informed decisions, rather than being bogged down by the technical details of the process. By automating certain tasks and providing visualizations and other aids, such a tool could significantly improve the efficiency and effectiveness of the trace clustering process.

To this end, we have developed a software tool that allows decision analysts and decision-makers to adjust the parameters of the analysis. This tool guides users through the workflow of the algorithm step-by-step, providing visualizations of the solutions and allowing analysts and decision-makers to experiment with multiple configurations. By providing a user-friendly interface and visual aids, our tool helps users to understand the results of the analysis and make informed decisions. Additionally, the ability to adjust the parameters and experiment with different configurations allows analysts and decision-makers to ensure that the final solution reflects their preferences. Overall, our tool aims to make the trace clustering process more accessible and efficient for analysts and decision-makers, enabling them to make more informed and effective decisions. The tool has been developed with Shiny [13], an R package that allows to easily create interactive web apps, and it is openly available.

The rest of this paper is organized as follows. In Sect. 2 an overview of the methodology for non-compensatory trace clustering is described. Section 3 includes the general architecture of the shiny app as well as software availability and data requirements. In Sect. 4, a description of an example/case study step-by-step, including the interpretation of the results is presented and finally, Sect. 5 gives a brief discussion of recommended use cases and general limitations, and future work.

2 Background

2.1 The Trace Clustering Problem in Process Mining

In a process mining context, the purpose of process discovery is to represent event log data in the form of a process model, but these models, due to overwhelming complexity, can often fall short of understandability. Process trace clustering is a well-established and effective method to deal with this issue. Existing trace clustering approaches start from an event log to generate features (either relevant to the control-flow perspective, or more generally relevant to the context perspective), to prepare the inputs for the clustering technique. Most approaches use a distance/similarity metric to create a pairwise similarity matrix for all traces [25].

The first approaches used bag-of-activities trace representation where a trace is transformed into a vector, each dimension of the vector corresponding to an activity, and the values are the activities' frequencies in each trace [3]. In order to take into account different process perspectives, trace profiles [22], have been proposed, each measuring a number of features from a specific perspective (case and event attributes, performance, etc.). Features of multiple perspectives are also used in [4], where a multiple criteria method is proposed to create a pairwise similarity matrix. Since in approaches that are taking into account multiple features, the "significance" weight of each feature is an important factor for the final solution, [11] focused on defining the optimal weighting of each perspective in the distance measure used by the clustering. For a more elaborated overview of the wealth of existing trace clustering techniques, a recent survey can be found in [25].

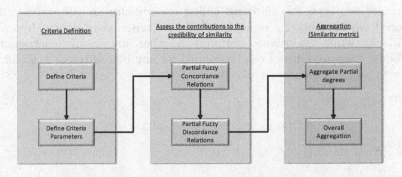

Fig. 1. Flow chart of the methodology [4].

2.2   Principles of the Classical Non-compensatory Trace Clustering

Let us first present the principles of the non-compensatory trace clustering, as it was introduced in [4]. Figure 1 depicts the flow chart of the methodology. We shall start from the preparatory step of *Criteria Definition*: A criterion i is defined as a function $g_i : A \to \Re/\alpha \to g_i(\alpha)$ where $g_i(\alpha)$ is the evaluation of the *alternative* $\alpha \in A$ over the criterion g_i (in our case an alternative is a pair of traces and A is the universe of all the possible pairs of traces). This function must fulfill the monotonicity property, namely for two alternatives $\alpha, \beta \in A$, $g_i(\alpha) > g_i(\beta)$ implies that α outranks β. Some (indicative) criteria that are common in a trace clustering project are common activities between two traces, common ordering of the activities, case attributes, etc. Next, for every two objects (traces), we define a set of pairwise relations to represent the similarities between two objects $(x, y) : x\mathcal{S}y \Leftrightarrow x$ and y are strongly similar; $x\mathcal{Q}y \Leftrightarrow x$ and y are weakly similar; $x\mathcal{I}y \Leftrightarrow x$ and y are indifferent with respect to their similarity; and $x\mathcal{R}y \Leftrightarrow x$ and y are disparate.

Then, to account for the impact of imperfect knowledge [19] on the trace clustering process, we have designated three thresholds for each criterion g_j: a *similarity* threshold s_j that indicates strong similarity between two traces, a *veto* threshold v_j that reflects the ability of the criterion to nullify the similarity, and an *indifference* threshold q_j that indicates neither strong similarity nor strong dissimilarity. These thresholds are defined with the following relations in an increasing order (without any loss of generality) and are used to establish the discrimination power of the method:

$$s_j \leq g_j(x,y) \Leftrightarrow x\mathcal{S}^j y \tag{1}$$

$$q_j \leq g_j(x,y) < s_j \Leftrightarrow x\mathcal{Q}^j y \tag{2}$$

$$v_j < g_i(x,y) < q_j \Leftrightarrow x\mathcal{I}^j y \tag{3}$$

$$g_j(x,y) \leq v_j \Leftrightarrow x\mathcal{R}^j y \tag{4}$$

where the superscript index j on the pairwise relations indicates a partial (with respect to the current criterion) relation.

Then, the next step assumes assessing the contributions of criteria to the credibility of similarity. In order to evaluate the similarity between two traces, we consider two types of conditions called *concordance* and *discordance*. Concordance looks at whether a sufficient number of criteria support the hypothesis of similarity, while discordance examines whether any criteria contradict the hypothesis. These conditions can be defined for any pair of traces x, y and with respect to each criterion g_j as follows:

$$c_j(x,y) = \begin{cases} 1, & \text{if } j \in J^\mathcal{S} \\ \frac{g_j(x,y) - q_j}{s_j - q_j}, & \text{if } j \in J^\mathcal{Q} \\ 0, & \text{else} \end{cases} \tag{5}$$

and

$$d_j(x,y) = \begin{cases} 1, & \text{if } j \in J^{\mathcal{R}} \\ \frac{q_j - g_j(x,y)}{q_j - v_j}, & \text{if } j \in J^{\mathcal{I}} \\ 0, & \text{else}. \end{cases} \quad (6)$$

where $J^{\mathcal{S}}$ is the set of criteria that support the strict similarity; $J^{\mathcal{Q}}$ the set of criteria that support only the weak similarity; $J^{\mathcal{I}}$ the set of criteria that are indifferent; and $J^{\mathcal{R}}$ the set of criteria that pose a veto to the assertion of the similarity.

Then, moving to the *Aggregation* step, and following established literature [8,21], to get the overall concordance index, we can aggregate the partial concordance degrees using a weighted sum:

$$C(x,y) = \sum_{j=1}^{n} w_j c_j(x,y) \quad (7)$$

We should notice at this point that the weight w_i reflects a criterion's voting power when it contributes to the majority that is in favor of the similarity between two objects (traces). There are a few ways to specify this particular parameter. One could just assess it directly neglecting the risks from such an arbitrary action, or follow more formal procedures like Simos [7], using assignment examples [17], generating ordered weighted averaging operator weights via rank-based weighting functions [1], or an aggregation/disaggregation method [12]. A detailed description of this kind of methods is out of the scope of this work.

Then, to get the overall discordance index, we can use the following disjunctive operator:

$$D(x,y) = 1 - \prod_{j \in J \setminus d_j > c_j} \frac{1 - d_j(x,y)}{1 - c_j(x,y)} \quad (8)$$

Finally, to measure the overall similarity between two traces x and y the following formula is used:

$$s(x,y) = \min\{C(x,y), 1 - D(x,y)\} \quad (9)$$

Eventually, this overall similarity metric is used as the core input for the clustering techniques that are to be applied. The tool provides the option to choose between agglomerative hierarchical clustering and spectral clustering. Agglomerative clustering, also known as a bottom-up approach or hierarchical agglomerative clustering is a method of cluster analysis that starts with each element as a singleton cluster and progressively merges clusters until all elements belong to a single cluster or a stopping criterion is reached. This clustering algorithm does not require us to pre-specify the number of clusters. Spectral clustering is a method of cluster analysis that uses the eigenvectors of a similarity matrix of the data to derive a lower-dimensional representation of the data, and then clusters the data in this lower-dimensional space. It is often used when the structure of the clusters is not clearly defined, the clusters are not convex in the original space, or the clusters are not linearly separable.

3   Engineering the Tool

3.1   General Architecture and Workflow Logic

Despite the effectiveness of analyzing and clustering the traces of the process execution using the methodology described in [4,5], adjusting the definition of parameters (criteria weights, preference thresholds) can be time-consuming and require a deep understanding of the data. To overcome these barriers, a software tool has been implemented to help define parameters and analyze the results. This tool can significantly improve the efficiency and effectiveness of the trace clustering process by automating certain tasks and providing visualizations and other aids. By providing a user-friendly interface and visual aids, the tool helps users to understand the analysis results and make informed decisions. For these reasons, we use Shiny to develop the tool.

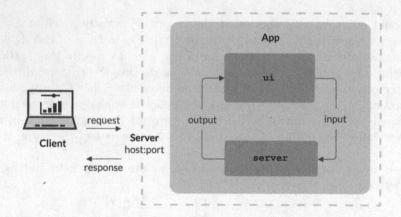

Fig. 2. General architecture of a shiny app.

Shiny is a web application framework developed in R. Unlike a regular web page, a web application typically connects multiple programming environments and supports more complex interactions, such as the exchange of information between multiple machines. Shiny apps typically consist of a single R script that implements the User Interface (UI) and Server functions, two essential components, in a straightforward structure. The UI controls the display, takes input from users, and then proceeds to the server function. The Shiny architecture enables the exchange of data between the UI and the server by calculating the output and returning it to the UI for rendering. The server function also defines the code to be executed in R. Shiny has built-in functions for creating server components and UI widgets, which are interactive controls that affect the application. The Shiny app consists of the UI and server components. Figure 2 illustrates the architecture of a general application. Thanks to their straightforward app structure, creating, distributing, and hosting Shiny applications is easy.

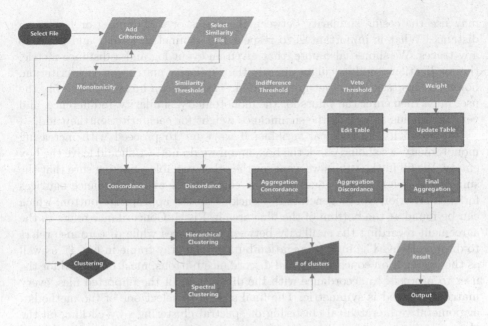

Fig. 3. Logical workflow

Shiny is designed with a reactive programming model. Reactive Programming is a programming approach that focuses on calculations and transactions that evolve over time. Shiny only recalculates reactive R expressions when a user changes an input value in UI widgets after the application has been initialized. The UI then displays the recalculated output of the Server function in response to the user's actions. Shiny is a great option for creating interactive visuals, as its reactive programming model optimizes the application's execution path. It also enables users to view results through interactive dashboards. In order to run the R scripts when sharing the application, users must be in an R environment. Web-based access to the Shiny application can now be provided to a wider audience by hosting it on the R Shiny Server without requiring any software to be installed on the client's device. Data scientists often utilize the open-source stack to expedite the analysis and visualization of results, motivated by the time-to-value offered by Shiny and R.

The workflow logic of the tool is depicted in Fig. 3. Initially, the user must select the file they want to upload (as seen in the "Choose your csv file" section in Fig. 4). However, due to issues with back-end programming, this step is currently being skipped and is planned for the future. The purple frame panel in Fig. 4 is reserved for the user to import the similarity file for each criterion. The similarity file for a criterion i is expected to be a comma-separated values (csv) file containing a symmetric numerical matrix with the pairwise similarities of traces in its cells (with traces existing in both its rows and columns) and it stands for g_i according to the methodology described in Sect. 2.2. Our approach is agnostic to the way that the similarity file is constructed, for instance, users may use the cosine similarity between the traces or a Hamming or Euclidean distance. What is important is to respect the symmetric format and not skip any traces. We should also note, that given an event log and a distance metric, the application could calculate directly the similarity matrix for each criterion, however, this task is not yet implemented. Then, as can be seen in Fig. 5b, the user must then enter the values for the monotonicity, similarity, indifference, and veto thresholds as well as the significance weight for each criterion they add.

Monotonicity is a logical variable; if we want to proceed with increasing monotonicity, we should check the box, and if we do not, we should leave the box empty. We fill in the values we want for the other variables, making sure that the sum of the weights must equal one. The concordance and discordance matrices for each criterion can be generated by clicking on the appropriate button, which can be found at the bottom of the blue area in Fig. 4. Concordance refers to the agreement regarding the similarity between two traces while discordance refers to disagreement. The final aggregation button (the gray frame in Fig. 4), as well as the aggregation concordance and discordance buttons, must be clicked for the user to proceed. In accordance with the dimensions of the imported files, every matrix produced is symmetric. The final step is to select one of the methods - agglomerative hierarchical clustering or spectral clustering - by clicking on the clustering button (located in the gray panel in Fig. 4) and entering the desired number of clusters (in the red panel of Fig. 4). Figures 8a and 8b show the results as a table and a dendrogram, respectively.

3.2   Components and Requirements

The tool we have developed is available on the shinyapps.io server at https://nza poglou.shinyapps.io/r-tool/ and can be launched as a Shiny app in any web browser. Figure 4 shows the main components of our tool. On the left side of the figure, we can see the panel for importing our csv data file. The area where we import the similarity files and add the criteria is marked with a purple color and is numbered 1. The region marked with a blue hue casing (enumerated as "2") is where we fill in the variables, update or modify our table, and construct concordance and discordance matrices. The aggregation lane and clustering selection are represented by the number 3 in a gray tint on the upper right of the diagram. Number 4 in a green hue is the location where our updated table is displayed (as seen in Fig. 6). The area marked with a yellow shade and numbered 5 is where the navigation panel, created by the aforementioned files, is displayed. A plot based on the user's data is shown in an orange hue in the sixth frame. The desired number of clusters should be inserted in the seventh frame in red blush. Finally, press the eighth frame, which is painted brown. Let us examine some of the aforementioned sections in more detail. Figure 5a shows the lane where we can add the criterion and import its similarity file, while Fig. 5b shows the area where we fill in the necessary variables for the next step. The outcome is shown in Fig. 6 after the preceding procedure has been completed. The imported data in our example has 25 traces, so the resulting matrix is 25×25 because the matrices in question are symmetric.

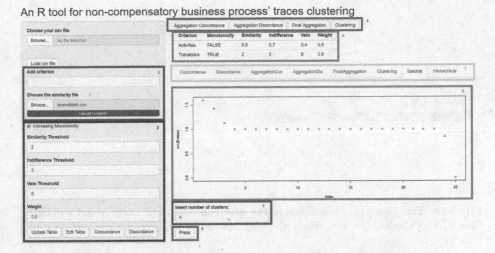

Fig. 4. Components of the proposed shiny app: Each individual panel of the application is marked with a different color. Panel 1, framed in a purple hue, depicts the "Add criterion" and "Choose the similarity file" panels. Panel 2, painted blue, presents the area where we can enter the appropriate values and the buttons to create tables and matrices. Panel 3, which is encased in gray, contains the buttons of the aggregation lane. Panel 4, which is green, displays the table created from Panels 1 and 2. Panel 5 has a yellow-tinted frame and presents the navigation panel for the created matrices. Panel 6, shown in an orange box, displays the plots and tables. Panel 7, which has a red hue, depicts the "Insert number of clusters" panel. Panel 8, shown in a brown shaded frame, displays the button for the final results. (Color figure online)

We have relied on several packages to achieve our objectives and execute the method in the R environment. First, the user interface was implemented using the *Shiny* package [13]. We then used an opinionated collection of R packages designed for data science, namely *tidyverse* [10]. All packages share an underlying design philosophy, grammar, and data structures, such as the *dplyr* and *ggplot2* packages. To flexibly restructure and aggregate data we added the *reshape2* [9] package. We also utilized the *data.table* [15] format for its potential to quickly aggregate large amounts of data. To manage sparse matrices, we included the *qlcMatrix* [16] package. Some of its functions are generally revealed, while others are highly specific for a particular data format used for quantitative language comparison. To calculate pairwise string distances between two elements, we used the *stringdist* [14] package. To take advantage of the potential of simulating correlated data, we also included the *NCmisc* [18] package. We implemented *ShinyFiles* [24] because it provides the functionality for client-side navigation of the server-side file system in Shiny apps. File selection, folder selection, and file saving are also available. We added the *sClust* [6] package for its utility as an R toolbox for unsupervised spectral clustering and the hierarchical spectral clustering algorithm, as well as its cluster-containing methods for cluster analysis. To extract and visualize the output of multivariate data analyses from different

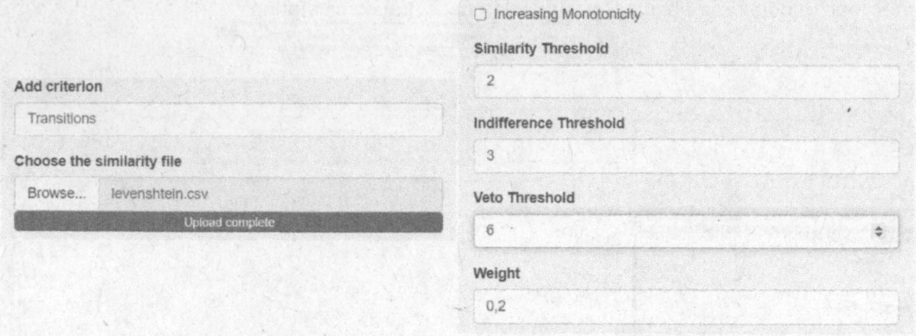

(a)   (b)

Fig. 5. a: This panel represents where the user can add their criteria and similarity files. b: This depicts the area where the user fills in the required information.

R packages including functions for simplifying some clustering analysis steps, we used the *factoextra* [2] package. We also used the *dendextend* [23] package, which offers a set of functions for extending "dendrogram" objects in R, allowing us to visualize and compare trees of "hierarchical clustering".

4   Use Case

Assuming a business process related to the customer service desk of a company, two service lines are defined; one for high-class customers and one for lower-tier customers, which will be referred to as gold and normal customers, respectively. When a normal customer calls, activity A is performed first, followed by activities C and D to resolve the issue, and then activity E is carried out to verify if the resolution was successful. If there is no resolution, activities C, D, and E must be repeated until a resolution is achieved. When a gold customer calls, activity B is performed to resolve the issue, followed by activity E to check if the resolution was successful. If there is no resolution, the gold customer will also go through activities C, D, and E until a resolution is achieved. At the end of the process, the company categorizes the customer as either high or low. In this example, we assume 25 imaginary customers with the profile presented in Table 1 as defined in the event log file.

Let us begin by defining the criteria. We have established four criteria for similarity. (i) Common Activities: We have set this attribute equal to the Cosine similarity of two vectors that correlate with two traces. The Cosine similarity will yield higher values for pairs of traces that have more elements in common. (ii) Common Transitions: We used the Edit (Levenshtein) distance hypothesizing the traces of the customers as strings and determining the difference between two traces as the minimum number of single-character edits (insertions, deletions or substitutions) necessary to transform one trace into the other. (iii) Status: A binary variable to indicate whether two customers reside in the same tier (gold

Table 1. Profile of input data (event log file)

Case.ID	Activity	Timestamp	Status	Satisfaction
1	B	0:01:00	GOLD	High
1	E	0:02:00	GOLD	High
2	B	0:01:00	GOLD	High
2	E	0:02:00	GOLD	High
⋮	⋮	⋮	⋮	⋮
22	D	0:06:00	NORMAL	Low
⋮	⋮	⋮	⋮	⋮
25	E	0:03:00	GOLD	High

or normal) or not. (iv) Satisfaction: A binary variable to specify if two customers have the same level of satisfaction (high or low) or not.

Table 2. Similarity matrix. This is a square matrix with all the case IDs at the rows as well as at the columns. The values at the cells indicate the pairwise similarity for the corresponding criterion.

Case ID	Case 1	Case 2	Case 3	Case 4	⋯	Case 25
1	1	0.8017837	0.3535534	0.3922323	⋯	0.8164966
2	0.8017837	1	0.7559289	0.8386279	⋯	0.6546537
3	0.3535534	0.7559289	1	0.9707253	⋯	0.5773503
4	0.3922323	0.8386279	0.9707253	1	⋯	0.4803845
⋮	⋮	⋮	⋮	⋮	⋯	⋮
25	0.8164966	0.8728716	0.5773503	0.6405126	⋯	1

The table in Fig. 6 depicts the parameters of the criteria. It is important to note that setting a veto threshold at -1 on a binary-scaled criterion, such as Status or Satisfaction, effectively indicates that there is no veto. Lastly, we assume that the four natural clusters - high and low satisfaction customers, and gold and normal customers - are the ones we want to target.

In order to proceed, we need to add criteria to our application, select and upload the appropriate similarity file for each criterion, and fill in the parameters as shown in Fig. 5a. As shown in Fig. 5a, for example, we can include the common transition criterion and upload the appropriate similarity file, such as the levenshtein.csv file. The morphology of a similarity file can also be observed in Table 2. After that, we complete the table by adding the specified variables. We choose decreasing monotonicity for our paradigm, fill in the similarity, indifference, and veto thresholds, and weight the prices 2, 3, 6, and 0.2, as shown in

Criterion	Monotonicity	Similarity	Indifference	Veto	Weight
Activities	TRUE	0.8	0.7	0.4	0.2
Transitions	FALSE	2	3	6	0.2
Status	TRUE	1	0	-1	0.3
Satisfaction	TRUE	1	0	-1	0.3

Fig. 6. Users can create a table by adding their criteria and filling in the variable values.

Fig. 5b, respectively. To save our data in a table, we can click on the "Update Table" button (located at the bottom of the blue frame in Fig. 4) after entering all of the required information. We can edit the data by clicking on the "Edit Table" button, which is next to the update table button, if we want to change or edit the elements for the current cells. We must press the appropriate buttons to display the concordance and discordance relations for each criterion as partial indices of the criteria. Concordance suggests that the similarity theory must be compatible with a sufficient number of criteria. Discordance, on the other hand, implies that none of the criteria that are not in agreement must be in opposition to the similarity theory. In the end, we will obtain a table that is comparable to the one shown in Fig. 6.

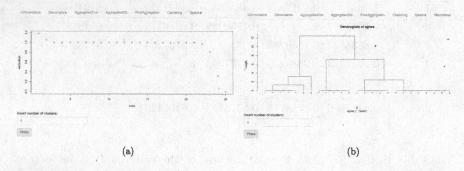

(a)   (b)

Fig. 7. a: This shows the eigenvalues for the pre spectral clustering procedure. b: This depicts the dendrogram of agnes for the pre agglomerative hierarchical clustering process.

Subsequently, we proceeded to the concordance and discordance aggregation matrices, before continuing to the final aggregation matrix. By pressing their respective buttons (as underlined in the gray frame in Fig. 4), it creates the aggregation matrices, following the proposed procedure. The final step is to choose which clustering method to proceed with, either spectral clustering or agglomerative hierarchical clustering. By selecting the first method, spectral clustering, a plot is displayed in a new tab, according to the imported data, as

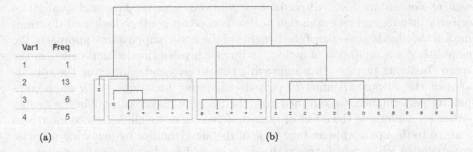

Var1	Freq
1	1
2	13
3	6
4	5

(a)   (b)

Fig. 8. a: The table shows the results of the spectral clustering method, with the first column indicating the number of clusters and the second column indicating the number of elements in each cluster. b: The final dendrogram is depicted using the agglomerative hierarchical clustering procedure.

depicted in Fig. 7a. This plot has been created to help us decide which number of clusters is most suitable for our data. By choosing the latter method, agglomerative hierarchical clustering, another plot is created in a new tab, as shown in Fig. 7b, based on the given information. This plot helps us to determine the recommended number of clusters for our data. As mentioned, after specifying the clustering technique we continue and select the correct number of clusters for our imported data, in our example the number is four. When we enter the number of clusters, we obtain the optimal results. For the spectral clustering method, the final outcome is a table as depicted in Fig. 8a, where we can also see the number of participants for each of the clusters. For the agglomerative hierarchical clustering approach, the result is a dendrogram as is clarified in Fig. 8b.

5 Discussion

In this paper, we introduce a software tool as an algorithmic procedure to guide the configuration of parameters, such as defining criteria weights, adjusting thresholds and setting values, to further support decision-makers. This application guides users through the algorithm's workflow step-by-step, eliminating the need for coding skills, and provides visualizations of the results, allowing analysts and decision-makers to experiment with various configurations. Our solution helps users comprehend the results of the study and make sound decisions by offering a user-friendly interface and visual aids. Furthermore, decision-makers and analysts can ensure that the final solution meets their preferences by experimenting with multiple configurations and adjusting the parameters as necessary. The ultimate aim of our solution is to enhance the trace clustering process for analysts and decision-makers, allowing them to make more informed and effective decisions.

The similarity metric enables a multiple criteria non-compensatory logic to address the clustering challenge through a set of discriminating thresholds, as well as concordance and discordance conditions. Quantitative and qualitative criteria, heterogeneous evaluation scales, non-compensatory logic and discrimination thresholds are some of the benefits of the non-compensatory approach. We established a compilation of actions to further involve the decision-maker in the trace clustering process, thus improving the process and addressing the robustness of the outputs. Aiming to provide clustering techniques with more compelling performance, we outlined how the decision maker can guide the results either by reinforcing the effect of their preferences, or by allowing a counter-veto feature to the non-compensatory logic of the algorithm, or by declaring pairwise constraints such as which traces should or should not be clustered together.

During the development of the tool and following the instructions from previous papers for the non-compensatory trace clustering process, undesirable and unresolved messages emerged. Concerning the "Choose your csv file" stage where the user should upload their file to start the clustering methodology from the beginning, due to source code obstacles, both back-end and front-end, this step was skipped and is designated as a future aspect. In that case, a similarity file could be calculated by the system. This improvement will help the functionality of the tool and make it easier for the user to upload their data file and get the desired results. Furthermore, the final table of the spectral clustering method should have included two additional columns (penetrating elements) to produce even more thorough results and provide the user with a deeper analytical understanding. This supplementary information helps us to clearly understand the input, especially when dealing with large data files. An additional future ambition is to implement a more transparent approach (white box) in the application. Although the current approach has identified and implemented several necessary steps for non-compensatory trace clustering, there are multiple solutions available for each step, each with its own set of assumptions and outcomes. In the future, the application could offer users the ability to iteratively choose options for each step while simultaneously informing them of the associated assumptions and consequences of each choice. This would provide the decision-maker with greater flexibility and a wider range of trace clustering procedures to choose from. Ultimately, this would lead to a more comprehensive and accurate understanding of the clustering process.

Acknowledgment. This work was supported by the MPhil program "Advanced Technologies in Informatics and Computers", hosted by the Department of Computer Science, International Hellenic University, Kavala, Greece.

References

1. Ahn, B.S., Choi, S.H.: Aggregation of ordinal data using ordered weighted averaging operator weights. Ann. Oper. Res. **201**(1), 1–16 (2012). https://doi.org/10.1007/s10479-012-1169-3
2. Kassambara, A., Mundt, F.: Factoextra. https://cran.r-project.org/web/packages/factoextra/index.html

3. Bose, R.P.J.C., van der Aalst, W.M.P.: Context aware trace clustering: towards improving process mining results. In: Proceedings of the SIAM International Conference on Data Mining, SDM 2009, Sparks, Nevada, USA, 30 April–2 May 2009, pp. 401–412. SIAM (2009). https://doi.org/10.1137/1.9781611972795.35

4. Delias, P., Doumpos, M., Grigoroudis, E., Matsatsinis, N.: A non-compensatory approach for trace clustering. Int. Trans. Oper. Res. **26**(5), 1828–1846 (2019). https://doi.org/10.1111/itor.12395. https://onlinelibrary.wiley.com/doi/10.1111/itor.12395

5. Delias, P., Doumpos, M., Grigoroudis, E., Matsatsinis, N.: Improving the non-compensatory trace-clustering decision process. Int. Trans. Oper. Res. itor.13062 (2021). https://doi.org/10.1111/itor.13062. https://onlinelibrary.wiley.com/doi/10.1111/itor.13062

6. Poisson-Caillault, E., et al.: sClust. https://cran.r-project.org/web/packages/sClust/index.html

7. Figueira, J., Roy, B.: Determining the weights of criteria in the ELECTRE type methods with a revised Simos' procedure. Eur. J. Oper. Res. **139**(2), 317–326 (2002)

8. Figueira, J.R., Greco, S., Roy, B., Słowiński, R.: ELECTRE methods: main features and recent developments. In: Zopounidis, C., Pardalos, P.M. (eds.) Handbook of Multicriteria Analysis, vol. 103, pp. 51–89. Springer, Heidelberg (2010). https://doi.org/10.1007/978-3-540-92828-7_3

9. Wickham, H.: Reshape2. https://cran.r-project.org/web/packages/reshape2/index.html

10. Wickham, H.: Tidyverse. https://cloud.r-project.org/web/packages/tidyverse/index.html

11. Jablonski, S., Röglinger, M., Schönig, S., Wyrtki, K.M.: Multi-perspective clustering of process execution traces. Enterp. Model. Inf. Syst. Architect. (EMISAJ) Int. J. Conceptual Model. **14**(2), 1–22 (2019). https://doi.org/10.18417/emisa.14.2

12. Jacquet-Lagrèze, E., Siskos, Y.: Preference disaggregation: 20 years of MCDA experience. Eur. J. Oper. Res. **130**(2), 233–245 (2001)

13. Kasprzak, P., Mitchell, L., Kravchuk, O., Timmins, A.: Six years of shiny in research - collaborative development of web tools in R. Technical report. arXiv:2101.10948 [cs, stat] (2021)

14. van der Loo, M., et al.: stringdist. https://cran.r-project.org/web/packages/stringdist/index.html

15. Dowle, M., et al.: data.table. https://cran.r-project.org/web/packages/data.table/index.html

16. Cysouw, M.: qlcMatrix. https://cran.r-project.org/web/packages/qlcMatrix/index.html

17. Mousseau, V., Figueira, J., Naux, J.P.: Using assignment examples to infer weights for ELECTRE TRI method: some experimental results. Eur. J. Oper. Res. **130**(2), 263–275 (2001). https://doi.org/10.1016/S0377-2217(00)00041-2. https://www.sciencedirect.com/science/article/pii/S0377221700000412

18. Cooper, N.: NCmisc. https://cran.r-project.org/web/packages/NCmisc/index.html

19. Roy, B., Vincke, P.: Pseudo-orders: definition, properties and numerical representation. Math. Soc. Sci. **14**(3), 263–274 (1987)

20. Roy, B.: Mulcriteria Methodology for Decision Aiding. Kluwer, Dordrecht (1996)

21. Słowiński, R., Vanderpooten, D.: Similarity relation as a basis for rough approximations. In: Wang, P.P. (ed.) Advances in Machine Intelligence & Soft-Computing,

vol. 4, pp. 17–33. Duke University, Department of Electrical Engineering, Durham, NC (1997)

22. Song, M., Günther, C.W., van der Aalst, W.M.P.: Trace clustering in process mining. In: Ardagna, D., Mecella, M., Yang, J. (eds.) BPM 2008. LNBIP, vol. 17, pp. 109–120. Springer, Heidelberg (2009). https://doi.org/10.1007/978-3-642-00328-8_11

23. Galili, T., et al.: dendextend. https://cran.r-project.org/web/packages/dendextend/index.html

24. Pedersen, T.L., et al.: shinyFiles. https://cran.r-project.org/web/packages/shinyFiles/index.html

25. Zandkarimi, F., Rehse, J.R., Soudmand, P., Hoehle, H.: A generic framework for trace clustering in process mining. In: 2020 2nd International Conference on Process Mining (ICPM). IEEE (2020). https://doi.org/10.1109/icpm49681.2020.00034

An Asset-Based Causal Loop Model to Improve Corporate Value

Romain Ben Taleb[1]([envelope]), Matthieu Lauras[1], Mathieu Dahan[2], Aurélie Montarnal[1], and Romain Miclo[3]

[1] Center of Industrial Engineering, University of Toulouse, IMT Mines Albi, Albi, France
{romain.ben_taleb,matthieu.lauras,
aurelie.montarnal}@mines-albi.fr
[2] School of Industrial and Systems Engineering, Georgia Institute of Technology, Atlanta, GA, USA
mathieu.dahan@isye.gatech.edu
[3] AGILEA1, Toulouse, France
romain.miclo@agilea-group.com

Abstract. Assessing a company's value is an important leverage for decision-making. Indeed, all decisions made within a company are generally aimed at maximizing the company's value. In accounting, almost all models for assessing the value of a company are related to the amount of cash the company is able to generate. As a result, maximizing the value of a firm is usually about maximizing cash flow. However, beyond the usual accounting models, several recent initiatives have highlighted the key role of managing all assets, and not only the ones considered by the general accountability, in decision making and cash generation. Unfortunately, these methods are currently limited to conceptual and qualitative proposals that do not lead to a real decision support system thus far. This paper proposes a first step of formalization aiming at providing tools for these asset-oriented decision support approaches. The contribution is a Causal Loop Diagram to Support Decision-Making in order to maximize the value of companies. Based on a dedicated literature review, we design an asset-based causal loop model that formalizes the qualitative results of the literature review. We then develop an instantiation on an illustrative case via simulation in order to verify the relevance of the proposal and to show how such a model can be used in practice for decision making. This will support next research to develop an asset-based decision support system to maximize value of companies.

Keywords: Assets · Causal-Loop Model · Decision Support · Corporate Value

1 Introduction

To be competitive and sustainable, any company has to maximize its value. However, the corporate value is something difficult to get and various formula can be used. The current methods for valuation rely on financial statements, particularly based on a cashflow perspective, which are produced after financial operations have taken place and have

S. Liu et al. (Eds.): ICDSST 2023, LNBIP 474, pp. 31–44, 2023.
https://doi.org/10.1007/978-3-031-32534-2_3

been recorded and presented according to reporting standards. This process is time-intensive and resource-intensive, and often only provides a retrospective view of the company's performance. In addition, only few assets of the company are considered in those models as demonstrated in [14] and [17].

Few authors like [2] have demonstrated the importance of including all of the company's assets in the decision-making process to improve the company's performance. According to accounting standards, assets are the resources controlled by a company and that can generate income [25]. Most of the assets are allowed to be accounted in balance sheet that is one of mandatory annual financial statements. Nevertheless, accounting provides guidelines to specific assets, notably immaterial assets such as Brand that valuation is difficult to assess and gives rules that exclude a large scope of resources from the recognition as assets [25]. However, only qualitative and conceptual approaches seem to have been proposed for the moment in the perspective of asset-based company modelling [2]. At the same time, [13] analyzed the use of simulation techniques for solving accounting and financial questions over the last 50 years. They showed that existing models never considered the company in a systemic way and that only some of accounting assets are usually examined. Obviously, system models have been used to evaluate different dimensions of a company's operational performance [17] but never to evaluate or predict its financial performance [13], and therefore its value. Authors such as [14] proposed models that include external and internal influences on the firms performance, but not with an asset-oriented perspective. On their side, [17] modeled with a resource perspective the case of a single manufacturing production unit. While it is asset-oriented, this model is far from considering all the assets of a company. Consequently, we believe that there is room for improvement by seeking to list exhaustively all the accounting and non-accounting assets of a company and by seeking to link them in terms of cause-and-effect relationships with respect to their impact on cash flow. The current research work aims to identify and formalize the causal links that exist between the different assets of a company in order to maximize its overall value. The ultimate ambition of this research work is to allow practitioners to instrument ex-post and ex-ante valuation models of the simulation or optimization type.

Finally, the expected benefits of this proposal are both to provide a prediction on the company's ability to generate cash flow and to be able to predict the state of the company's assets over time. This method will provide all the information needed to calculate the valuation of companies with performance forecasts that are undoubtedly more reliable, precise and above all dynamic than existing methods. Ultimately, this is the first step in a process aimed at establishing an asset-oriented decision support system to maximize the value of a company.

The remainder of the paper breaks down as follows. First, we will present the research methodology adopted. Then, the proposed model will be developed based on a selection of studied state-of-the-art and an application case will be described in order to underline the scope of the proposal and to discuss its limits. Finally, a quick conclusion and several research perspectives will be developed.

2   Research Methodology

The first step of our research methodology intends to answer the next questions:

1. Which types of assets are identified in the literature?
2. How are these assets connected in companies to complete value creation?

To answer the first question, we first referred to the existing assets in accounting standards [25]. Then we searched on the Scopus database for articles containing the keywords "asset" OR "resource-based theory" to explore the literature. The first step of the process is to distinguish and exclude articles that only deals with financial assets namely company's shares, options, obligations and all the scope of financial assets that value is based on the performance of an underlying company. The goal of this research is to find in the literature the occurrences of the term "asset" that enlarges the accounting concept meaning that it is a resource used by a company to create value. We then identified the list of assets of any company, through a categorization process, to group the different resources into specific categories. To complete this process and strengthen the literature review, we then processed several queries with the following structure "{asset type} is an asset" to confirm that the literature contains this statement (Table 1). Thus, we tested these assumptions each time a category of asset was identified by the previous qualitative analysis. Results of the tests confirmed each category of assets.

Table 1. Methodology for assets' identification

#	Request in Abstract, Title and Key Words	Articles	Results
1	"customer portfolio" AND asset	20	7
2	"human resources as an asset"	4	4
3	"information technology" PRE/2 asset)	100	10+
4	"innovation" PRE/1 asset	93	5+
5	"material asset"	265	10+
6	"organization as an asset"	3	1
7	"product portfolio" PRE/2 asset	2	1
8	"reputation is an asset"	4	4
9	"stock is an asset"	2	2
10	"supply network" PRE/2 asset	8	6
11	"cash flow cycle" AND asset	2	1

Table 1 provides the precise requests done in Scopus, the number of articles returned by Scopus, and the results columns that counts (at least if there is a +) how many of these responses correspond to the definition of asset that we aim at understanding.

In our research the term asset as "a resource that can generate income" is not necessarily "controlled" as required by the accounting standards. Human resources are not assets for IFRS because the contracts that bind them to the company are not (and are not willing to be) ownership contracts. Moreover, the criterion of recognition of an asset "that generates income" is admitted in accounting only when the cash flow of is processed. The findings highlight that resources in a system can participate to generate income or cash flow indirectly by impacting other assets.

Regarding the second question, reading the articles selected for question #1 allowed us to find some relationships between certain types of assets. We also queried Scopus by the specific term "impact" between two types of assets. For example, we searched for "impact of reputation on customers."

For analyzing the results of these queries, we used two types of inferences to conclude to a result. On one hand, some articles directly provided a result to the research question, as for example in: *"In fact, most corporate annual reports boldly state that the firm's people are its most important asset."* [1]. On the other hand, results were deduced by inference from the original text, as for example in: *"Therefore, the certification can become a resource that interacts with the capabilities of the firm, expressing complementarities that stimulate the formation of dynamic capabilities"* [23]. In this example the original text did not use the term "asset," but we could deduce that "certification" in this context is an organizational resource.

The second step of the research methodology consisted in modeling the literature analysis findings as a causal loop model or causal loop diagram [7]. A causal loop model is a causal diagram that helps visualize how different variables in a system are related to each other. This type of model fits with the qualitative findings from the literature review that assets of the company impact each other. Causal feedback loops are very important features of this type of model and this step intended to identify them for our problem. A link marked "+" indicates a positive relationship where an increase in the causal variable leads, all else equal, to an increase in the effect variable. A marked link "–" indicates a negative relationship where an increase in the causal variable results leads, all else equal, to a decrease in the effect variable. A positive causal link can be said to result in a change in the same direction, and an opposite link can be said to result in a change in the opposite direction, i.e., if the starting variable of the link increases, the other variable decreases and vice versa [7].

The third and final step was a verification of our proposed model. Practically, following the suggested causal-loop diagram, we modeled a fictive company and its basic management rules. Then, we instantiated this use case through a Systems Dynamics simulation approach. The results were discussed to highlight benefits and limits.

3 Proposal

This section develops the asset-based causal loop model we designed to improve the value of a company. It is divided into 3 sub-sections: (i) accounting and non-accounting assets' identification, (ii) causal relationships' identification and (iii) asset-based causal loop modeling.

3.1 Assets' Identification

Based on the definition that an asset is a resource used by the companies to create value, we categorized them and the following categories.

Clients: [21] or [14] consider clients as an asset for any company. They consider customer relationships as a resource that explains the business performance of the company. [14] identifies "customer relationships or brand equity" as a critical factor in the market value of firms. [21] highlights that investments for customer satisfaction and customer loyalty support firm performance.

Human Resources: Human resources are directly identified as a company asset in [1] and [3]. [3] explains that knowledge derived from "the collective intelligence and skills of employees" is a key resource for companies. Furthermore, [1] explains that "reports state boldly that the company's people are its most important asset".

Information Technology: IT is clearly stated as a core corporate asset by [9] and that IT assets support other business assets.

Innovation: Innovation is an asset that merges different forms of investments in new processes, new resources or new products. It can take various forms such as prototypes or patents. [12] also considers the innovation capability of a company's resources as the key explanation of innovation in pharmaceutical companies.

Material Resources: These are all the materials needed for production, from short-term consumables to long-term equipment such as machinery, land, vehicles as we extract from [24]. For example, [19] consider manufacturing units as assets for firms.

Organization: ISO 9001 or 14000 certifications are management methods that provide an advantage to the company and its Organization [4]. Thus [11] and [4] discuss management certifications as company's assets. We infer from several definitions that management methods are an index to identify the organization as a specific asset. [24] defines sales and operations planning methods as a process that provides strategic capabilities to decision makers. Management certifications become a resource for the company's ability to create value.

Products: [10] considers the requirement of specific investments in assets to create products. This allows products and the products portfolio to be considered as an asset. [6] proposes the application of portfolio management to electrical installations in the energy sector. Thus, we conclude that the products that the firm owns or can produce (portfolio) can be considered as assets for the firm.

Reputation: [5] identifies brand as a market-based asset. [8] explains that reputation has an impact on the price of products. [18] informs about the impact of employer brand on employee loyalty. By deduction, the reputation of the company can be identified as an asset that impacts other assets and the value of the company.

Stocks: Stocks identification refers to the definition of inventories in international accounting standards and more precisely IAS 2 [25].

Supply Network: [16] confirms the supply network as an asset for a company and emphasizes the importance of accounting for supply relationships as intangible assets.. The supply chain asset is also influenced by environmentally friendly certifications that reduce risk and manage behavioral uncertainty among supply chain members [28].

Cash Flow: Cash flow (CF) is the last type of asset encountered in the literature. Definitions of cash flow can be found both in the academic literature and in international accounting standards. IAS 7 [25], which standardizes the "Statement of Cash Flows", gives the definition of cash flow as followed: "cash flow is the sum of all sales less all costs of other assets". According to [22], cash flow influences and is influenced by all other assets. The most important positive cash flow is the sum of sales to clients, but assets that belong to the company can be sold, if they are owned by the company, such as material resources (e.g., a machine). Moreover, most of documented methods to compute a company's valuation are based on past and forecasts of Cash Flow.

   Thus, we have identified eleven types of assets existing in all companies, namely: Clients, Human Resources, Information Technology, Innovation, Physical Resources, Organization, Products, Stocks, Supply Network, and Cash Flow. These are assets in a broader definition of the concept than that found in accounting standards. It is by acting on all these assets that companies manage to influence their performance, and their value. The challenge now is to understand the causal links that exist between these assets, particularly with respect to cash flow, the source of the company's value.

3.2 Causal Relationships' Identification

To identify the relationships between the assets, we used the keyword "impact" in the requests. This term is commonly used to indicate that a variable has an effect on another one. With requests formatted as ["{type of asset}" and "impact*" and "{other type of asset}] we identified at least the following relationships between the assets in the literature even if not exhaustive.

Clients (from and to): Reputation and Innovation have a direct impact on customers, as explained in [7]. For example, [7] indicates that reputation has a positive impact on product price. Moreover [7] demonstrates the positive impact of brand and customer relationships on the market value of the firm. Customers, through sales, have a direct impact on cash flow as explained in IFRS 15 [25].

Human Resources (from and to): Human Resources are needed to produce products [24], and can increase innovation or reputation [12].

Information Technology (from and to): [15] summarizes the role of IT tools as it distinguishes four functions in companies: (a) "Technology as Labor Substitution Tool," (b) "Technology as Productivity Tool," (c) "Technology as Information Processing Tool," (d) "Technology as Social Relations Tool." Based on [15] IT can have a positive impact on Material Resources and Human Resources as a Productivity Tool or negative impact as a Labor Substitution Tool. It can also influence Organization by improving management capabilities as stated in [9].

Innovation (from and to): According to [12], Human Resources can have a positive impact on Innovation. Moreover, [20] identifies other sources of Innovations: from materials, products, marketing, processes, or organization. Thus, Innovation can increase or decrease in regards of other assets such as IT or Organization [8, 9].

Material Resources and (from and to): [24] Material Resources and Stocks can be purchased from Suppliers Network or produced in the company. They can be produced by the Human Resources who manufacture the company's Products using other Material Resources. Material Resources increase when they are acquired or produced and decrease when they are used (amortization and depreciation [25]) or sold.

Stocks (from and to): Material Resources and Products in storage, before they are used or sold, are considered as a Stock asset [24, 25]. The quantities in Stock evolve in the same way as Material Resources and can be sold to Clients.

Organization (from and to): Organization can improve the Supply Network by reducing risks and uncertainty [23]. It can improve company's ability in Innovation [20] and customers management [21]. Organization can also be improved by Information Technology such as Business Intelligence or ERP systems [9].

Products (from and to): can be managed as a portfolio that is acquired directly from the Supply Network or is the positive result of Innovation [20]. They are produced by employing Material and Human Resources in order to be sold to Clients [22, 25]. Basically, sales operations increase the Cash Flow [22].

Reputation (from and to): [8] explains that reputation impacts the price of the products. [8] highlights the sensitivity reduction of customer price connected to products' reputation. [18] informs about the positive impact of employer brand on employees' loyalty. Reputation is increased by work of Human Resources and by Innovation.

Supply Network (from and to): The Supply Network can be positively impacted by the Organization of the company. It provides Material Resources (increase) at a cost paid with Cash Flow (decrease) [24].

Cash Flow (from and to): Cash Flow (CF) is the sum of all the sales minus all the cost of the other assets. All the other assets can impact Cash Flow. Getting new assets is considered as investment that are different from fixed costs due to the assets' ownership or use. The most important positive flow of Cash Flow is the sum of the sales to Clients, but some assets that are owned by the company can be sold, such as Material Resources (a machine for example) or Stocks [22].

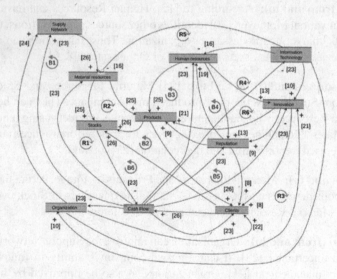

Fig. 1. Complete causal loop model

At this step of the research, we have only identified these relations between the assets by a qualitative methodology and qualitative links. Next step of our article is to highlight how these connections can be formally analyzed thanks to a causal loop diagram methodology and later, to highlight how this analysis can support companies modelling and value-oriented decision-making.

3.3   Asset-Based Causal Loop Model

Table 2.   Main causal loops identified regarding the cash flow perspective.

Type of Loop	Description	Assets involved
R1 – Reinforcement	Diminishing CF to increase Material Resources diminishes CF, increasing Stocks and diminishing CF	Material Resources (+) Stocks (−) CF (−)
R2 – Reinforcement	Diminishing CF to increase Organization increases Supply Network that increases Material Resources that increase Stocks that reduce CF	Organization (+) Supply Network (+) Material Resources (+) Stocks (−) CF (−)
R3 – Reinforcement	Diminishing CF to increase Organization increases Innovation that increases Products that increase Stocks that reduces CF	Organization (+) Innovation (+) Product (+) Stocks (−) CF (−)
R4 – Reinforcement	Diminishing CF to increase Information Technology reduces Human Resources that increase Products that increase Clients that increase CF	Information Technology (−) Human Resources (+) Product (+) Clients (+) CF (−)
R5 – Reinforcement	Diminishing CF to increase Information Technology reduces Material Resources that increase Products that increase Clients that increase CF	Information Technology (−) Material Resources (+) Product (+) Clients (+) CF (−)
R6 – Reinforcement	Innovation increases Reputation that increases Human Resources that increase Innovation	Innovation (+) Reputation (+) Human Resources (+)
B1 – Balance	Diminishing CF to increase Supply Network increases Material Resources that increase Stocks that diminish CF	Supply Network (+) Material Resources (+) Stocks (+) CF (−)
B2 – Balance	Diminishing CF to increase Material Resources increases Products that increase Clients that increase CF	Material Resources (+) Products (+) Clients (+) CF (−)
B3 – Balance	Diminishing CF to increase Human Resources increases Products that increase Clients that increase CF	Human Resources (+) Products (+) Clients (+) CF (−)

(continued)

Table 2. (*continued*)

Type of Loop	Description	Assets involved
B4 – Balance	Diminishing CF to increase Human Resources increases Reputation that increases Clients that increase CF	Human Resources (+) Reputation (+) Clients (+) CF (−)
B5 – Balance	Diminishing CF to increase Human Resources increases Innovation that increases Clients that increase CF	Human Resources (+) Innovation (+) Clients (+) CF (−)
B6 – Balance	Diminishing CF to increase Material Resources increases Products that increase Clients that increase CF	Material Resources (+) Products (+) Clients (+) CF (−)

The view of the complete Causal Loop Diagram (Fig. 1) emphasizes the difference between Causal Loop links that are financial, material, informational or work flows. This next model is a Causal Loop Diagram that highlights the dynamics inside the companies with an asset perspective. This Causal Loop Diagram will be able to support simulation modeling to estimate companies' performance and value. Twelve loops directly influencing the cash flow, and so the value of the company, have been identified in Table 2. 6 Loops correspond to the definition of reinforcement loops and 6 Loops correspond to balancing Loops. The reading of these loops gives an overview of the decisions that can be taken on the company's assets and that have an impact on its performance via its Cash Flow and therefore its valuation.

4   Illustrative Example

4.1   Description of the Fictive Company

An entrepreneur wants to start a company that would create and distribute boardgames to customers. The entrepreneur wants to set up a simulation to estimate the future financial performance of his company. To do so, he defined a set of assumptions and rules for the assets to simulate decisions. The company starts with a single human resource who is the creator of the company. When the cash flow is positive, he recruits other employees for 10% of this amount. These employees remaining in the company their cost persists even when the treasury is negative. All human resources devote a part of their working time to the creation of new games (Innovation) and to commercial promotion activities (Reputation). The more employees there are, the more cash the company can generate but also the more it spends (loops). Other constraints, such as the maximum cost invested in game events or a constraint on the rate of recruitment in the game, which cannot exceed 0.5 employee/month, impose constraints on the system.

4.2   The Simulation Model

The proposed Causal Loop Diagram has been instantiated via a System Dynamics type of simulation model in Anylogic software. Following the System Dynamics oriented simulation standards, custom equations have been defined for all concerned stocks to model assets, flows to model relationships and variables to set values (see Table 3). They have been used to compute the simulation results and translate the Causal Loop model representations. The equations account for the impact of assets on other assets and define the rules and constraints that link them. One rule is to hire new employees when cash flow is positive at 10% of free cash flow. One constraint is that the company will not spend more than 100,000 units of money per period to promote games through the events network or hires at maximum 0.5 employee/month.

The time step chosen for the simulation is one month. The simulation was run over forty steps (months) to analyze the performance of the company.

4.3   Results

The cash flow units generated in the simulation, which are needed for processing the evaluation of the company in further research, are presented in Fig. 2. In this paper, we mainly focused on the B1, B3 and B5 loops identified in Table 2 as they are the more basic ones. Basically, we simply consider that Human Resources are employed to create new games (Products) and promote them (Reputation). These new games allow increasing the demand of the Clients which increase the turnover of the company, and so the Cash Flow. But, at a same time, Human Resources, Material Resources and Supply Networks have costs that reduce Cash Flow. We can notice that B3 and B5 have a net positive impact on the Cash Flow of this company as it overtakes the effect of the constraints. The first plateau where the cash flow is negative is explained by the initial decrease in cash flow related to human resources costs. However, because the initial cash flow was positive, the company hired the time equivalent of one employee. During this period, the cost of the employee is not sufficient to sell enough games to generate positive cash flow. However, there are enough human resources to create new games, which also increases demand. After the 12th month, the company's assets are sufficient to generate positive cash flow. The second downward slope in period 28–32 corresponds to the effect of a constraint on the acceptable costs to maintain the distribution network (Customers) that produces a decrease in cash flow. But loop B4 overcomes this constraint from period 33 onwards because the employees manage to sell enough games. We also remark that the cash flow trend for this company takes an exponential shape that is a limit of this example because we did not include life cycle constraints.

Table 3. Complete description of the illustrative example

Type	Name	Description	Rule	Equation
Flow	buysEv	counts games sold in Events	represents 5% of Clients. Max = 200	min(0.05*Clients,200)
Flow	buysSpe	counts games sold in Shops	represents 90% of Clients	0.9*Clients
Flow	craft	number of games crafted	crafts the demand + 5% of stock	(distribSpe+distribEv)*1.05
Flow	create	account for creator's wages spent in R&D	100% of creator's wage is R&D	wageCreator
Flow	develop	account for employee's wages spent in R&D	20% of spendings in wages	0.2*Employees*wageEmp
Flow	distribEv	counts products sold in Events	based on Client's demand	buysEv
Flow	distribSpe	counts products sold in Shops	based on Client's demand	buysSpe
Flow	enablestoCraft	not used. Boolean variable meaning at least one game is created	not used	0
Flow	pays	financial flow for supplier payment	supplier is payed based on a unit prod. cost	prodCost*craft
Flow	paysCr	wage of creator	fixed	Creator*wageCreator
Flow	paysEmp	wage of employees	when treasury is > 0, 10% of treasury is invested in additive workforce from new employees	max(0.10*Treasury,0)
Flow	paysgame	turnover	Demand * Price	buysSpe*gameprice+buysEv*gameprice
Flow	produces	R&D to create games. Accounted in GamesPortfolio's formula	not used	0
Flow	promote	employees generate new clients	employees' work is to generate clients	Employees*cliperemp
Stock	Clients	number of clients. Initial Value = 100	depends on number of employees that promote games and on number of games in portfolio	0*(paysgame+buysSpe+buysEv)+promote*min(GamesPortfolio*2,300/(GamesPortfolio+1))
Stock	Creator	number of creator. Initial Value = 1	one single entrepreneur has founded the company and works in it	0-(0*paysCr)+(0*create)
Stock	Employees	number of employees	depends on how much the company spends in wages - when possible 10% of treasury - but maximum hire is 0.5 new employees per month	min(paysEmp/2000,0.5)-0*(develop+promote)
Stock	EventsNetwork	number of events participated	depends on the ratio of Clients from events	buysEv/avgSales-0*distribEv
Stock	GamesPortfolio	number of games the company can make craft and sell	new games are not linearly produces. Assumption is new games are created fastly at beginning, less fast after, but controlled by the average cost of R&D for a game	Math.log(1+ResearchDevelopement/avgCostRD)+0*produces-0*enablestoCraft
Stock	GamesCrafter	total of cost to pay to supplier for crafting	supplier is payed based on a unit prod. cost	(enablestoCraft+craft)*0+pays
Stock	GamesStock	number of games in safety stock	5% of the demand	0.05*(distribSpe+distribEv)-0*craft
Stock	ResearchDevelopement	amount of the part of wages cumulated in R&D	Adds costs of R&D	develop+create-0*produces
Stock	SpecialShops	number of shops to sell to	number of retailers to sell to the average demand for a retailer	buysSpe/avgSales-0*distribSpe
Stock	Treasury	amount of Cash owned by the company. Initial Value = 10000	Result between turnover and all costs including retailers margin (8)	-paysEmp-paysCr-pays-costEv+paysgame-distribSpe*8
Variable	avgCostRD	average cost of R&D required to finish one new game	fixed value representing the average cost of developement for one new game	30000
Variable	avgSales	average number of product sold in a shop or an event	average number of product sold in a shop or an event	30
Variable	cliperemp	average number of new client generated by employees	average number of new client generated by employees	wageEmp/400
Variable	costEv	cost of participating to events	cost of participating to events. Maximum 100.000	min(1500*EventsNetwork,100000)
Variable	gameprice	average sale price of a game for final customer	average sale price of a game for final customer	40
Variable	prodCost	cost of production of one game	cost of production of one game	10
Variable	wageCreator	wage of the Creator	wage of the Creator	3000
Variable	wageEmp	wage of an employee	wage of an employee	2000

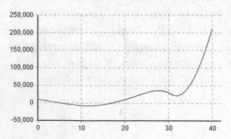

Fig. 2. Outputs of cash flow by simulation

5 Conclusion

The goal of any company is to maximize its value in order to be competitive and sustainable. The traditional methods of valuation, which are based on financial statements and a cashflow perspective, are time-intensive and limited in scope. They only consider a few assets of the company and provide a retrospective view of its performance. There was a room for improvement in terms of identifying and formalizing the causal links between different assets of a company and linking them to their impact on cash flow. The current research work aimed to do just that, with the ultimate goal of establishing a decision support system to maximize the value of a company. Our proposal was to model the causal relationships that exist between all the assets of a company and to identify the main associated causal loops able to influence the cash flow of this company. Finally, as demonstrated in the illustrative case, this contribution should make it possible in the near future to provide a more reliable, precise, and dynamic prediction of the company's ability to generate cash flow. The benefits of this proposal are significant, and it is the first step in a process aimed at maximizing the value of a company.

While this research work remains in its infancy, several research perspectives will have to be developed in the coming years. Notably, develop a metamodel that embeds this Asset-Based Causal Loop Diagram to provide a complete view of the companies as systems led by the strategy to create value. The next step in our work should be to validate the model with a real-world case based on historical business data. Then we will examine and apply accepted business valuation methods to these simulation results. Finally, this causal diagram can solve decision support problems thanks to the levers of action it mobilizes (the assets) and the output of the system it dynamically predicts: the cash flow and the valuation of the firm. Mainly, this model can support the use of optimization methods to maximize the value of companies.

References

1. Barney, J.B., Wright, P.M.: On becoming a strategic partner: the role of human resources in gaining competitive advantage. Hum. Resour. Manag. **37**(1), 31–46 (1998). https://doi.org/10.1002/(SICI)1099-050X(199821)37:1%3c31::AID-HRM4%3e3.0.CO;2-W
2. Ben Taleb, R., et al.: Toward an innovative risk- and opportunity-oriented system for SMEs' decision-makers. In: Actes du congrès CIGI QUALITA 2021, Grenoble, France, pp. 450–457 (2021)
3. Bollinger, A.S., Smith, R.D.: Managing organizational knowledge as a strategic asset. J. Knowl. Manag. **5**(1), 8–18 (2001). https://doi.org/10.1108/13673270110384365
4. Botterweck, G., Pleuss, A.: Evolution of software product lines. In: Mens, T., Serebrenik, A., Cleve, A. (eds.) Evolving Software Systems, pp. 265–295. Springer, Heidelberg (2014). https://doi.org/10.1007/978-3-642-45398-4_9
5. Delgado-Ballester, E., Luis Munuera-Alemán, J.: Does brand trust matter to brand equity? J. Prod. Brand Manag. **14**(3), 187–196 (2005). https://doi.org/10.1108/10610420510601058
6. Devinney, T.M., Stewart, D.W.: Rethinking the product portfolio: a generalized investment model. Manag. Sci. **34**(9), 1080–1095 (1988). https://doi.org/10.1287/mnsc.34.9.1080
7. Dhirasasna, N., Sahin, O.: A multi-methodology approach to creating a causal loop diagram. Systems **7**(3), 42 (2019). https://doi.org/10.3390/systems7030042

8. Erdem, T., et al.: The impact of brand credibility on consumer price sensitivity. Int. J. Res. Mark. **19**(1), 1–19 (2002). https://doi.org/10.1016/S0167-8116(01)00048-9

9. Fink, L., et al.: Business intelligence and organizational learning: an empirical investigation of value creation processes. Inf. Manag. **54**(1), 38–56 (2017). https://doi.org/10.1016/j.im.2016.03.009

10. Georgiopoulos, P., et al.: Optimal design decisions in product portfolio valuation. Presented at the ASME 2002 International Design Engineering Technical Conferences and Computers and Information in Engineering Conference, IDETC/CIE2002 (2002)

11. Hart, S.L., Dowell, G.: A natural-resource-based view of the firm: fifteen years after. J. Manag. **37**(5), 1464–1479 (2011). https://doi.org/10.1177/0149206310390219

12. Hess, A.M., Rothaermel, F.T.: When are assets complementary? Star scientists, strategic alliances, and innovation in the pharmaceutical industry. Strateg. Manag. J. **32**(8), 895–909 (2011). https://doi.org/10.1002/smj.916

13. Leitner, S., Wall, F.: Simulation-based research in management accounting and control: an illustrative overview. J. Manag. Control. **26**(2–3), 105–129 (2015). https://doi.org/10.1007/s00187-015-0209-y

14. Nalchigar, S., Yu, E., Easterbrook, S.: Towards actionable business intelligence: can system dynamics help? In: Frank, U., Loucopoulos, P., Pastor, Ó., Petrounias, I. (eds.) PoEM 2014. LNBIP, vol. 197, pp. 246–260. Springer, Heidelberg (2014). https://doi.org/10.1007/978-3-662-45501-2_18

15. Orlikowski, W.J., Iacono, C.S.: Research commentary: desperately seeking the "IT" in IT research - a call to theorizing the IT artifact. Inf. Syst. Res. **12**(2), 121–134 (2001). https://doi.org/10.1287/isre.12.2.121.9700

16. Philippart, M.: Les fournisseurs comme capital immatériel: une solution pour aligner la contribution des achats à l'innovation sur les objectifs des actionnaires. Presented at the Vers Les Achats 4.0: Quelles Compétences Développer Pour Être Plus Performant, Lausanne, Switzerland, 10 October (2018)

17. Rahimifard, A., Weston, R.H.: A resource-based modelling approach to support responsive manufacturing systems. Int. J. Adv. Manuf. Technol. **45**(11), 1197 (2009). https://doi.org/10.1007/s00170-009-2025-8

18. Rai, A., Nandy, B.: Employer brand to leverage employees' intention to stay through sequential mediation model: evidence from Indian power sector. Int. J. Energy Sect. Manag. **15**(3), 551–565 (2021). https://doi.org/10.1108/IJESM-10-2019-0024

19. Rippel, M., et al.: Building blocks for volume-oriented changeability of assets in production plants. Presented at the Procedia CIRP (2016). https://doi.org/10.1016/j.procir.2015.12.009

20. Schumpeter, J.: Business Cycles. A Theoretical, Historical and Statistical Analysis of the Capitalist Process

21. Smith, M., Chang, C.: The impact of customer-related strategies on shareholder value: evidence from Taiwan. Asian Rev. Account. **17**(3), 247–268 (2009). https://doi.org/10.1108/13217340910991947

22. Soenen, L.A.: The concept of cash flow: techniques for speeding up the flow of cash. Manag. Decis. **11**(5), 314–322 (1973). https://doi.org/10.1108/eb001031

23. Stranieri, S., et al.: Adopting environmentally-friendly certifications: transaction cost and capabilities perspectives within the Italian wine supply chain. Supply Chain Manag. **27**(7), 33–48 (2022). https://doi.org/10.1108/SCM-12-2020-0598

24. ASCM Supply Chain Dictionary | ASCM. https://www.ascm.org/learning-development/certifications-credentials/dictionary/. Accessed 04 Dec 2022

25. IFRS - Conceptual Framework for Financial Reporting. https://www.ifrs.org/issued-standards/list-of-standards/conceptual-framework.html/content/dam/ifrs/publications/html-standards/english/2021/issued/cf/. Accessed 03 Dec 2022

Time-Aware Optimisation Models
for Hospital Logistics

Herwig Zeiner(✉) [iD], Roland Unterberger[iD], Julia Tschuden[iD],
and Mohammad Yusuf Quadri[iD]

JOANNEUM RESEARCH Forschungsgesellschaft mbH,
Steyrergasse 17, 8010 Graz, Austria
{herwig.zeiner,roland.unterberger,
julia.tschuden,yusuf.quadri}@joanneum.at
http://www.joanneum.at

Abstract. Our healthcare system must become more efficient! Cost
reduction in the medical sector usually means lowering the quality of
patient care, which is socially unacceptable. Therefore, we need to identify areas of the healthcare system where cost reductions can be achieved
without compromising on patient care. One area with significant potential for savings is hospital logistics, which still has far-reaching possibilities for optimization, especially in the planning and implementation
of patient transport. The systems currently used for planning transport operations are mostly semi-automated and provide useful solutions
for simple standard situations. However, such systems are incapable of
exploiting the optimisation potential of complex logistics problems or of
reacting independently to emergencies and combining patient transports
in an optimal way. These disadvantages lead to the under-utilization
of existing transportation capacities (vehicles, personnel) and delays in
transport handling, which disrupt transportation logistics resources. In
this paper, we present a novel, scale-able scheduling algorithm for patient
transport in healthcare facilities and hospitals. We consider the time-
aware aspects (e.g. short lead times in planning and opening hours of
the stations).

Keywords: transport scheduling · time-awareness · robust
implementation

1 Introduction

1.1 Initial Situation in Hospitals

Hospitals are increasingly becoming performance-oriented organisations that are
evaluated according to performance criteria or evaluate themselves accordingly.
This development poses great challenges for many healthcare organisations and
hospitals. For example, more and more hospitals find themselves in a situation
that is almost impossible to cope with: They have to guarantee high-quality

S. Liu et al. (Eds.): ICDSST 2023, LNBIP 474, pp. 45–55, 2023.
https://doi.org/10.1007/978-3-031-32534-2_4

patient care with ever-decreasing financial resources. One of the most important logistic supply processes, patient transport, is particularly impacted by the increase in hospital expenses. A large number of different departments of medical facilities and functional areas such as x-rays are linked to the quality of patient transport. This has a direct impact on the productivity of the hospital's medical services. Despite a decreasing length of stay in the hospital, services are provided in ever shorter periods of time. It is therefore necessary to receive the right patient in the right medical and nursing condition and then transport them even faster to the right place at the right time. In the hospital, a wide range of different players are involved in the provision of services to patients: Nurses, doctors, and carriers must give their best every day - and work together as efficiently as possible. Again and again, hospitals are intensively searching for sensible optimisation possibilities that do not have a negative impact on the quality of patient care despite cost savings. The optimisation of patient transport, including external patient transport, is particularly relevant for reducing the operating costs of hospitals.

1.2   Challenges in Hospital Logistics

Fully automated process optimisation systems require the integration of numerous subsystems that provide solutions for various logistics processes in hospitals. Depending on the logistics process, different optimisation algorithms are required and these must be combined into an intelligent overall system. In order to optimally design the examination and therapy of patients in the hospital, patients often have to be transported several times a day to various locations within the hospital area. Patient transport is subject to a multitude of different characteristics: They include walking, sitting, or lying patients and it includes individual or collective transports which take place on a long-term basis or increasingly at very short notice. Basically, patient transports should be distinguished from object transports because patients expect additional services such as a customer-friendly approach.

Today, the organisation of a transport service usually depends on the size, layout, (building)history, and route structure of a hospital. From a size of approx. 200 beds upwards, a central organisation, which is responsible for the central acceptance, control, and disposition of the transports, is almost always appropriate. Overall, patient logistics has great potential for optimisation through intelligent automation, and this is where this research project aims to tap. The optimisation algorithms that such intelligent automation is based on must be able to respond flexibly to different designs, hospital sizes, and processes, as well as quickly account for possible structural changes. For the optimisation itself, the loading and travel times as well as the waiting times of patients are relevant variables.

In this paper, flexible and powerful algorithms for the dynamic planning of combined patient transports including external patient transport in hospitals are developed. The proposed system is designed to support as many different types of hospital construction (e.g., pavilion style, central construction, and mixed style), processes in patient transport, and organizational forms as possible. Real-life situations for spontaneously occurring events in the interaction between patient and transport resources (e.g. vehicle) must be optimally supported and, if possible, solved automatically without any human intervention.

1.3   Structure of This Work

The rest of the paper is organised as follows. Section 2 describes the corresponding work. In Sect. 3 we present the model description. In Sect. 4 we describe how we implemented it. The assessment of the implemented approach is described in Sect. 5. In Sect. 6 we highlight the main conclusions and describe possibilities for future work.

2   Related Work

Previously available systems, including their underlying algorithms, could not or could only partially take into account the above-mentioned aspects. For example, such algorithms work satisfactorily in so-called "normal times", where no spontaneous events requiring a lot of interactions occur. However, if many ad hoc situations (i.e. "stressful times") occur, previous systems provide very little assistance to the internal dispatching center. The situation then requires extensive manual interaction by the dispatchers and carriers themselves, who perform according to subjective experience. However, each individual action taken by a carrier can cause significant disruption and delay to the overall system of all transport orders, resulting in further delays. The optimisation problems arising from practical application requirements have received little attention in the literature to date and cannot be solved by adapting and extending classical optimisation algorithms. Therefore, a considerable amount of basic research is necessary to prepare and examine the problems in a generally valid form and then to design usable algorithms for hospital logistics. The general question of the present logistics disposition can be presented as a special case of a dial-a-ride problem, for which there are numerous amounts, especially from the field of collective taxi transport for the disabled (e.g. [1,3,9,13,14,16]). The specific question of hospital logistics has also been dealt with in specialist literature (e.g. [2,4–6,10,11]), but always tailored to the specific situation of an individual hospital with all its special conditions. In addition, two requirements were identified, which appear in different forms in numerous practical cases, but are only considered in the literature on hospital logistics as isolated special cases. Firstly, from an optimisation point of view, the question of the permissible load of a vehicle must be considered. Previous applications only allowed for the combination of lying, sitting, or wheelchair-bound patients, resulting in a relatively small number of permissible loading patterns that can typically be "tested" by complete enumeration. Furthermore, it has always been assumed that a selected loading pattern is maintained until the vehicle returns to the base ([2,12,15,18]). Secondly, a further new requirement concerns the robustness of the dispatching system against unexpected events or emergencies. This can be a sudden request for a vehicle as a result of an emergency or a reaction to a vehicle failure (e.g. defect, or mobile communication device defect). Such aspects are known as disruption recovery, rerouting, or rescheduling in the literature, and have been considered primarily in classical transport problems, such as the delivery of goods (e.g. [7,8,17,19]). However, it is clear that patient transport, such as overly scheduled examinations for equipment with a high workload, necessitates more planning than package delivery.

3   Dynamic Time-Aware Model Description

This section describes the time-aware model. Time-awareness is relevant in many type of applications, as discussed in [20]. In this work, we develop an algorithm that takes new transport orders or order changes into account in an adequate way. In order to provide the transport personnel at all times with up-to-date information on the tasks that need to be completed, technical aids are required for optimum communication. The described model is most closely related to a dynamic dial-a-ride problem. On the one hand, the application of meta-heuristics is only possible to a limited extent despite ever-improving computer performance. On the other hand, the computing time of these algorithms is still relatively high and the use of these methods requires considerable optimisation knowledge of the users (e.g. hospital staff).

The task of automated optimisation is to independently allocate the recorded transport orders to the available transport resources (carriers, vehicles). The calculations leading to this allocation are carried out at regular intervals and at least as often as necessary, to take into account all new and short-term transport orders. In each of these optimisation runs, all available transport resources are considered, and open transport orders are allocated as optimally as possible.

There are a number of transport orders, each order involving the transport of a patient between two departments of a hospital (Tables 1 and 2).

Table 1. Description of a transport order

Name	Description
Pick-up place	This is the place A for the transport order from A to B
Delivery place	This is the place B for the transport order from A to B
Transport type	This describes the transport type
Priority	indicates the urgency of the transport

The vehicles are located at one or more depots, where place $s(v)$ is the starting depot and $d(v)$ is the destination depot of the vehicle v. Usually $s(v) = d(v)$. The vehicles of a hospital are equipped differently (heterogeneous fleet), i.e. each vehicle has a certain capacity for different types of transport. The capacity of

Table 2. Description of a transport resources (e.g. vehicle)

Name	Description of the capacity	Example
Car 1	Max. capacity: 4 persons sitting, 2 persons lying, 1 wheel chair	2 persons sitting
Car 1	Max. capacity: 2 persons lying or 2 wheel chairs	1 wheel chair
Car 1	Max. capacity: 6 persons sitting or 3 persons lying	4 persons sitting
Car 1	Max. capacity: 4 persons sitting or 2 wheel chairs	2 persons sitting

vehicle v for transport type m considers different loading variants such as, for example, maximal 2 persons lying in the vehicle.

Different **transport resource**s are available (vehicles, bed teams, porters, etc.), each of which can transport one or more patients. In concrete terms, the available transport resources must fulfill the orders on hand in a timely manner. For each transport order the transport resource that completes the order has to be decided on, as well as the transport's starting time (i.e. time of pickup of the patient at the starting point) and its finishing time (i.e. time of delivery of the patient). Additionally, the route covered to complete the transport job for each transport resource should be specified as well. Vehicles transporting patients may only wait at a collection point if they arrive before the requested collection time. It is also common practice for empty vehicles to return to their depot to avoid idle time at the pick-up node.

The following, most relevant **constraints** should be taken into account when creating the best schedule for the transport orders:

- Each pick-up and delivery point should only be visited once.
- Transport resource capacities for patients must be taken into account.
- Pick-up and delivery nodes of an order must be approached by the same transport resource.
- Each patient must first be picked up before they can be transferred.
- The time between pick up and delivery place must not exceed a specified value.

The **optimisation** is not only to minimise costs but also to develop a reliable and stable system that provides viable solutions even in difficult operating situations, taking into account both customer satisfaction and the minimisation of logistics costs, particularly in the case of patient transport. Key factors for customer satisfaction are e.g. the waiting period of patients at pick-up and delivery stations.

Due to the different opening hours of different hospital departments, there are also optimisation targets depending on the day of the week and the time of day. Since the number of transport orders to be completed during normal opening hours (weekday mornings) is significantly higher than those at weekends or at night, it makes sense to assume different optimisation targets for these periods. In the case of a high load order, attention should be paid to the optimum and highest possible utilisation of transport resources with the associated minimum time expenditure.

The number of possible solutions to the optimisation task is limited by a number of restrictions that apply to orders and/or transport resources. Each order and transport resource, as well as potential start and destination locations, are characterised by a number of (hospital-dependent) properties, which are included in the optimisation as constraints. For transport resources, capacity (especially in the case of vehicles), working hours, and breaks must be followed, and capabilities for handling special transports must be considered. The transport orders themselves are distinguished by factors such as the transport service patient or the mode of transport (for patients: lying, wheelchair, walking).

4   Implementation of the Scale-able Scheduling Service

This section describes the implementation of the chosen approach. The aim of this implementation is to be as universally applicable as possible, with extensive configuration options, in order to move from a tailor-made individual solution to a general and scale-able implementation. The presented algorithm goes beyond proposed variants e.g. from [2] in several ways. First, the loading pattern of the vehicles can be changed at run-time, because the vehicles can be modified at run-time. Second, a time window is defined for loading or unloading the patient. In our case, the violation of the time window depends on the order type. Furthermore, in this work, we focus on the patient loading nodes rather than the critical loading nodes first. The improvement of the insert heuristic is the focus of this work. This is similar to the work of [12]. The following are the main differences between her works. This work takes into account various vehicle occupancy levels. Furthermore, we do not assume the mandatory adherence to predefined time windows and maximum transport time.

The four steps of heuristics are described in more detail below:

Step 1 - Initialisation Phase for the Scheduling Service:

- The routes of the vehicles are initialised according to their service period, which is defined by the work plans of the transport personnel.
- The transport personnel determines crew assignment to the transport resources in advance.

- The depot is the first and last vehicle stop; transport orders can only be entered within these two stops.
- Scheduled breaks are inserted as special transport orders in the initial route. The "pickup node" is the critical node.

Step 2 - Combine Transport Orders in the Neighborhood: To combine orders, "neighbourhoods" are required, which are defined in both temporal and spatial dimensions. The proximity of two orders is defined by the spatial and temporal proximity of their critical nodes. The neighbourhood $Np(i)$ of a not yet assigned order i is the set of all critical nodes which are close to the critical node of order i. The proximity is measured by the spatial proximity of p1 stops and by the temporal proximity of p2 stops, where p1 and p2 are user-defined parameters with $p1 + p2 = p$. Each subset $Npk(i)$, $k = 1,2$, is additionally subdivided into predecessor $Npk-(i)$ and successor $Npk+(i)$ of the critical node of order i. To measure the spatial proximity between i1 and i2, the shortest path between the two critical nodes is determined. The temporal proximity of the two tasks is defined by the compatibility of the time windows of their critical nodes. The time windows (or planning horizon) depend on the building structure. A typical value is for example 30 min. Within t, you consider the transport for an assignment.

Step 3 - Insertion Phase: New transport orders must be assigned to a vehicle as quickly as possible and inserted into the vehicle's existing route. In order to minimise the computing effort, only those new orders are assigned whose planned end time lies within a certain time window. When inserting new orders, only permissible solutions are allowed. Using the spatial and temporal distance measurements from phase 2 a list of neighbouring nodes, that occur as planned stops in the existing routes, is generated for the critical node of a job to be inserted. This list, which is ordered by ascending (temporal and spatial) distance, is then processed to check and evaluate the corresponding insertion positions. In the worst-case scenario, the insertion adds two new stops to an existing route; in the best-case scenario, no additional stop is required. The recalculated routes are evaluated using the previously mentioned cost function. A new order is added to the route in the best possible position to result in the lowest costs. In this cost function, we consider several parameters. First, the travel time to the start location of the transport order is taken into account and also the travel time to fulfill the orders including loading and unloading times. Third, we calculate the time delay for the pickup at the start location or delivery node of each order. Fourth, we take also the waiting time at the starting point or destination for each order. This is compared to the saved time, if we execute the transport orders in separate tasks.

Step 4 - Improvement Phase: If there is enough time between the insertion phase and the arrival of a new order, an attempt is made to improve the existing solution and thus the currently planned routes. For this purpose, shifts of orders between two routes (inter-route) or the shift of an order within a route (intra-route) are considered. The iterative calculation of such possible shifts is generally started with the order that has the greatest delay based on the current planning. Possible shifts of orders are generated until new orders arrive, or a predetermined maximum number of iterations is reached. A new solution is adopted if it outperforms the existing solution in terms of the cost function.

5   Evaluation

In the evaluation process, two test scenarios were considered, which take into account the different construction methods of hospitals. These test scenarios, including their most important characteristics, are described in the following two sections. In both scenarios, a specific transport is defined by some fixed transport characteristics, which are either considered as restrictions in the optimisation or are included in its objective function. Anonymous artificially generated data was generated for the tests. The number of reports varied from 1,000 to 10,000. The composition of the vehicles was created by using data based on a typical patient in a hospital.

For the first test scenario, the **pavilion construction** method of a hospital, which is still very common, was selected, in which the individual stations and outpatient clinics are in different buildings. The different buildings are connected by roads. In our test example, there are about 40 buildings, and the different floors within a building (pavilion) are not differentiated. In some cases the routes between the buildings are directed, i.e. the distances between the buildings are not symmetrical (distance A->B may be unequal to distance B->A). The transports, which in this test scenario are exclusively patient transports, take place within the hospital premises between the individual buildings and are all carried out with vehicles. A certain number of transport resources (vehicles) with different possible loading variants are available. These loading variants can be configured by defining corresponding maximum capacities and are very diverse in the present test case. The test scenario is characterised by relatively long transport routes which can be handled very quickly with the help of vehicles. The stopping times (loading and unloading times) are relatively long in relation to the travel times, so that - apart from minimising travel - a major objective of optimisation is to minimise necessary stops. It is therefore desirable to combine such orders in one vehicle, which has as many common starting points or destinations as possible.

In the second test scenario, we assume that transports within the hospital are concentrated in a large building with several wings and several floors, where the individual wards and outpatient departments are located. The relatively short distances are covered exclusively on foot or by elevator, and the transport resources are called runners or porters. Depending on the type of transport, different "loading variants" are possible, although the maximum capacity of a runner is usually limited to one patient. Optimisation is less about a combination of transports to be carried out simultaneously by one runner, but rather about the most favourable order placement possible. One objective here is, for example, to minimise the empty distances between the individual orders, which is particularly important when the load order is high. In the case of a low overall load, it is important to ensure that the runners experience capacity as evenly as possible. It must therefore be ensured that even runners that are located in a relatively remote station receive orders again and do not "stick" to a remote location.

The results for the two evaluations with both construction methods can be summarised as follows:

- Numerous optimisation runs were carried out with different modifications of the input data. The effects on logistics costs as well as on customer satisfaction were checked. The results show that transport paths are optimized and thus patient waiting times are reduced. In this way, patient satisfaction is improved. Furthermore, the runs always delivered a result. Thus, the solution can be used in fully automated operations.

- The computing times of the individual optimisations will not be discussed, as the differences in computing time for different parameter choices were small. The test was carried out on a standard laptop. The computing time was always less than 10 s. This means that the solution can also be used on larger computing units or in the cloud.
- Furthermore, it was tested how well the algorithm scales with different numbers of transports. This test also delivered usable results for higher numbers (e.g. 10,000 transports). In this case, the computing time was higher. However, it was still within 60 s. This was a key requirement for the involved hospitals.

6   Conclusion

There are several essential factors that have a significant influence on the optimisation results for this type of problem. The most important points and related conclusions are briefly summarised again here.

Firstly, the dynamic aspects of patient transport are a critical factor and significantly impact the selection of algorithms. A few hours can be assumed for the planning horizon, which depends on the geographical structure and organisational culture of the hospitals. It is also clear that in this environment it is rarely possible to work with hard time frames. Due to the highly dynamic nature of the issue, in many situations the violation of time windows is necessary (e.g. when extremely short-term emergency transports occur), as the rejection of transport orders is not an alternative in most cases.

Secondly, time-awareness plays a significant role. Especially in order to achieve meaningful and practicable automated transport optimisation, realistic time estimates for loading and unloading times as well as travel times are of major importance. The optimisation results are only plausible if the underlying time estimates are also realistic and have a practical value. For a practical system, it is important that these time estimates are adjusted during operation. This requires regular and reliable feedback from the transport staff on the time of patient pick-up, patient handover, the start of the actual journey, the end of the actual journey, etc. It is, therefore, necessary to store these times in an appropriate database and finally to carry out a regular evaluation of the data including a determination of the statistical distribution of the driving and loading times.

Thirdly, fast response times are of central importance. It is therefore necessary to choose solution methods that provide workable solutions very quickly. In our test examples, very short response times of less than 1 s were consistently achieved. However, it is foreseeable that in practical implementation the optimisation algorithm can also be used with the usual number of transports in a hospital. This number depends on the size of the hospital and the number of patients. Significant progress and improvements can be achieved here through higher computer performance and parallel solution procedures.

Finally, we contributed to the advancement of dynamic loading variants and capacities. In general, several vehicle types with different loading options or capacities are used. As there are several different loading patterns for each vehicle, the capacities of the vehicles have to be adjusted at run-time. For example, one vehicle can transport two lying patients and three sitting patients, or eight sitting patients. With our approach, it is also possible to change the transport capacity of the vehicle during operation. According to our current state of knowledge, this problem has not been scientifically addressed with a scale-able implementation in this environment.

Acknowledgement. This work was partly funded by the K-Project DeSSnet which is funded within the context of COMET - Competence Centers for Excellent Technologies by the Austrian Ministry for Transport, Innovation, and Technology (BMVIT), the Federal Ministry for Digital and Economic Affairs (BMDW) and the federal states of Styria and Carinthia. The program is conducted by the Austrian Research Promotion Agency (FFG). The authors are grateful to the institutions funding the DeSSnet project and wish to thank all project partners for their contributions. Furthermore, this work was partially funded by project FAIRWork (grant No 101069499 of the European Commission).

References

1. Agatz, N., Erera, A., Savelsbergh, M., Wang, X.: Optimization for dynamic ride-sharing: a review. Eur. J. Oper. Res. **223**(2), 295–303 (2012)
2. Beaudry, A., Laporte, G., Melo, T., Nickel, S.: Dynamic transportation of patients in hospitals. OR Spectr. **32**(1), 77–107 (2010)
3. Berbeglia, G., Cordeau, J.F., Laporte, G.: Dynamic pickup and delivery problems. Eur. J. Oper. Res. **202**(1), 8–15 (2010)
4. Hanne, T., Melo, T., Nickel, S.: Bringing robustness to patient flow management through optimized patient transports in hospitals. Interfaces **39**(3), 241–255 (2009)
5. Kallrath, J.: Vehicle routing problems in hospital transportation. i models and solution approaches. In: Online Storage Systems and Transportation Problems with Applications: Optimization Models and Mathematical Solutions, pp. 57–120 (2005)
6. Kergosien, Y., Lente, C., Piton, D., Billaut, J.C.: A tabu search heuristic for the dynamic transportation of patients between care units. Eur. J. Oper. Res. **214**(2), 442–452 (2011)
7. Li, J.Q., Borenstein, D., Mirchandani, P.B.: A decision support system for the single-depot vehicle rescheduling problem. Comput. Oper. Res. **34**(4), 1008–1032 (2007)
8. Li, J.Q., Mirchandani, P.B., Borenstein, D.: Real-time vehicle rerouting problems with time windows. Eur. J. Oper. Res. **194**(3), 711–727 (2009)
9. Madsen, O.B., Ravn, H.F., Rygaard, J.M.: A heuristic algorithm for a dial-a-ride problem with time windows, multiple capacities, and multiple objectives. Ann. Oper. Res. **60**(1), 193–208 (1995)
10. Parragh, S.: Ambulance routing problems with rich constraints and multiple objectives. Ph.D. thesis, uniwien (2009)

11. Parragh, S.N.: Introducing heterogeneous users and vehicles into models and algorithms for the dial-a-ride problem. Trans. Res. Part C: Emerg. Technol. **19**(5), 912–930 (2011)
12. Parragh, S.N., Cordeau, J.F., Doerner, K.F., Hartl, R.F.: Models and algorithms for the heterogeneous dial-a-ride problem with driver-related constraints. OR Spectr. **34**(3), 593–633 (2012)
13. Parragh, S.N., Doerner, K.F., Hartl, R.F.: Variable neighborhood search for the dial-a-ride problem. Comput. Oper. Res. **37**(6), 1129–1138 (2010)
14. Pillac, V., Gendreau, M., Guéret, C., Medaglia, A.L.: A review of dynamic vehicle routing problems. Eur. J. Oper. Res. **225**(1), 1–11 (2013)
15. Schmid, V., Doerner, K.F.: Examination and operating room scheduling including optimization of intrahospital routing. Transp. Sci. **48**(1), 59–77 (2014)
16. Toth, P., Vigo, D.: Heuristic algorithms for the handicapped persons transportation problem. Transp. Sci. **31**(1), 60–71 (1997)
17. Wang, X., Ruan, J., Shi, Y.: A recovery model for combinational disruptions in logistics delivery: considering the real-world participators. Int. J. Prod. Econ. **140**(1), 508–520 (2012)
18. Wong, K.I., Bell, M.G.: Solution of the dial-a-ride problem with multi-dimensional capacity constraints. Int. Trans. Oper. Res. **13**(3), 195–208 (2006)
19. Wu, Y., Zheng, B., Zhou, X.: A disruption recovery model for time-dependent vehicle routing problem with time windows in delivering perishable goods. IEEE Access **8**, 189614–189631 (2020)
20. Zeiner, H., Unterberger, R.: Time-aware data spaces-a key computing unit in the edge-to-cloud continuum. In: 2021 8th International Conference on Future Internet of Things and Cloud (FiCloud), pp. 250–255. IEEE (2021)

Prevention and Detection of Network Attacks: A Comprehensive Study

Paul Addai, Ryan Freas, Elnatan Mesfin Tesfa, Max Sellers,
and Tauheed Khan Mohd$^{(\boxtimes)}$ (iD)

Department of Math and Computer Science, Augustana College,
Rock Island, IL 61201, USA
{pauladdai19,ryanfreas19,elnatanmesfintesfa20,maxsellers20,
tauheedkhanmohd}@augustana.edu

Abstract. Cybersecurity is currently a topic of utmost significance in tech sectors. The ever-evolving landscape of this field makes it particularly difficult to navigate. This paper aims to help the reader understand the complexity of network attacks and also show how we may never 'solve' the problem of cyber attacks. Our paper may be accessible to the layman, but a basic understanding of networking fundamentals would be desirable. Computer security, cybersecurity, or information technology security may all be used interchangeably throughout the paper. An 'attack' will refer to a breach in security to an online system that may cause (but is not limited to) the following: unauthorized information disclosure, theft of technology, or disruption of services.

Keywords: cybersecurity · network · system · attack · security

1 Introduction

The field of cybersecurity has become more and more critical in recent years due to our increasing dependence on modern technology; having a deep understanding of the prevention and detection of cyber attacks is crucial due to how data is being used in this modern era. The network connects and controls almost everything around us, including the internet of things (IoT), self-driving cars, social media, payments, etc. Ensuring data privacy, system integrity, and protecting large networks that can host millions of people are all things that fall under the branch of cybersecurity. From shutting down a power grid to disrupting air trafficking systems, one minor breach in a network can have worldwide repercussions. This is why network security is so heavily studied. This field is changing so rapidly that it is no longer sufficient for consumers to pay for software to protect their computers. Instead, it is necessary to start buying subscriptions that constantly update to protect against any new threats that may emerge. Preventing and detecting network attacks can be costly but very important since a

S. Liu et al. (Eds.): ICDSST 2023, LNBIP 474, pp. 56–66, 2023.
https://doi.org/10.1007/978-3-031-32534-2_5

breach in a network system can allow hackers to take over the systems, which can cause harm to both the company and the customers. The data and scientific literature about cyber security are continuously being updated and expanded upon. Previous research in cyber security offers a comprehensive view of the many different types of attacks that may occur and a detailed analysis of the different prevention techniques at our disposal. The research also discusses what makes a computer susceptible to attacks. The research article talks about the prevention and detection of network attacks; we are trying to find out different types of attacks and how to mitigate such risks in the network using AI and various machine learning algorithms.

2   Related Work

Research conducted on network attacks focuses on an attack called a "wormhole," which is challenging to safeguard. In the paper, they explained that even if the attacker has not compromised any hosts and even if every communication is valid and secret, the wormhole attack is still feasible. The wormhole attack involves the attacker capturing packets (or bits) at one point in the network, tunneling them (perhaps selectively) to another, then retransmitting them into the network from that point. In wireless networks, the wormhole attack poses a severe risk, particularly to several ad hoc network routing methods and location-based wireless security solutions. Without a technique to protect against the wormhole attack, for instance, most current ad hoc network routing systems would be unable to identify routes longer than one or two hops, drastically impairing communication.

For identifying and countering wormhole assaults, they provided a generic technique termed "packet leashes," which can be implemented using the TIK protocol [1].

Detecting and preventing network attacks can be tedious and would require some form of automation. A research article focuses on the use of artificial intelligence. They focus on deep learning models, in particular, to detect network attacks [2]. In their research, they provided an end-to-end early intrusion detection system to guard against network attacks before they might further harm the system that is already under attack and to avoid unplanned downtime and disruption. For assault detection, they used a deep neural network-based classifier. Instead of depending on a manual feature selection procedure like other previous systems, the neural network is trained in a supervised manner to extract pertinent characteristics from raw network traffic data. Additionally, they provided a brand-new statistic termed "earliness" to measure how quickly their suggested technique picks up on attacks. They empirically tested their strategy on the CICIDS2017 data set (Intrusion Detection Evaluation Data-set). The outcomes demonstrated that their method worked effectively and got an overall balanced accuracy of 0.803. When put into context, this is an impressive accuracy rating.

3 Types of Cyber Attacks

One of the most common forms of cyber attacks is called Distributed Denial of Service attack, or a DDOS attack. A DDoS (distributed denial-of-service) attack aims to shut down a machine or a network, rendering it unavailable to its intended clients. With these attacks, it is important to act quickly as the level of these attacks can increase. When these attacks spread, it is hard to handle, and it sometimes needs to be analyzed to detect them. With DDoS attacks, they are attacked by intruders that are either a part of the network or outside the network which creates the conflict of false "traffic" or the amount of data packets in the network.

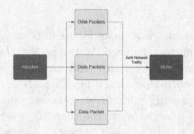

Fig. 1. Example of how DDos attack works

3.1 DDoS Attacks

This false traffic can be quite hard to detect, and there are many different approaches to try to detect them. There are a few approaches that looked very interesting way to approach. Researchers created an algorithm based on the immune system when discussing a network as shown in Fig. 1. Interesting parameters in the study were the speed of the detection, false alarms, and the time of detection [21]. Another exciting algorithm was a school bus routing system which included the parameters of data packet loss ratio and data packet delivery ratio. These algorithms proved to be suitable, but a different approach was found that proved to be a more optimized approach in both detection and energy. This model was created to enhance security. The parameters for this algorithm include sensor devices that examine the environment of the network, a control center that collects the data, DDoS Attacker nodes that attack the improper data, nodes to capture valid data as well to make traffic easier to read, an energy monitoring unit, a unit that measures bandwidth, and a unit that detects an attacker's behavior [22].

The parameters for this algorithm include sensor devices that examines the environment of the network, a control center that collects the data, DDoS Attacker nodes that attack the improper data, a commander node that commands the DDoS attacker the falsified data, nodes to capture valid data as well to make traffic easier to read, a energy monitoring unit, a unit that measures bandwidth, and a unit that detects an attacker's behavior [22].

3.2 Brute Force Attack

A brute force assault involves the use of trial-and-error techniques by attackers to access a target account. Depending on the circumstance, this can entail getting information like a password or personal identification number. The majority of brute force attacks are automatic; therefore there is a considerable diversity of targets or categories of victims. Attackers can gain unauthorized access to websites that contain vital information thanks to brute force techniques. They can use this technique to entirely shut down the website or access user accounts. The Kali Linux operating system uses Patator, an application approach with a modular design and flexible structure, for brute force attacks. Attacks using the Secure Shell (SSH) and File Transfer Protocol (FTP) can be carried out using this technique [10].

3.3 Cross Site Scripting

An attack known as cross-site scripting (XSS) or cross-code execution (CCE) involves an attacker putting malicious code into a victim's online application that would damage the browser of another user. XSS flaws typically give an attacker access to the user's data and the ability to perform any action the target user could perform. The attacker can manage the control of the application as a target and have complete control over the data if the target user has access within the program [15]. There are numerous XSS attack techniques. A malicious script that is executed by the target user can perform XSS. The target may be seeing a false page or a form page that contains a link and asks for the user's credentials. An XSS attack may be launched against websites that contain adverts that the target displays or against users or communities that receive malicious emails.

3.4 Man-in-the-middle Attacks

Man-in-the-middle (MITM) attacks are a type of denial-of-service attack that target networks by monitoring communication between two connections, collecting data, or monitoring communication while enacting a variety of changes. MITM allows for the interruption of two-way communication or the creation of deceptive communication. This attack can be summed up as network packet manipulation and capture. The target and network elements' communication can be overheard by the attacker (server, switch, router, or modem). They can intercept data packets that are freely moving via the communication network, local network, or remote network in this assault. This assault has become riskier as IoT devices become increasingly prevalent. Different strategies have been devised for the attack's detection and prediction. Intrusion detection methods based on machine learning are starting to achieve increasingly successful outcomes [11].

3.5   Injection Attack

By forcing a web application to execute particular commands, an attacker who uses an injection attack can affect the execution of the application. A web server may get totally compromised or have data exposed or damaged as a result of an injection attack. Such attacks are conducted by taking advantage of flaws in an application's code that permits unauthenticated user input [6]. Cross-site scripting and SQL injection are the most frequent types of injection attacks.

3.6   Other Network Attacks

Other network attacks were also focused on mobile ad hoc applications. The collection of mobile devices that connect to one another wirelessly, such as computers, smartphones, sensors, etc., without a central access point creates a mobile ad-hoc network. This type of network connection is very vulnerable to a lot of different attacks [18]. These attacks include; Black-Hole, Gray-Hole, Jellyfish, Cooperative Black-Hole, Worm-Hole, HELLO Flood, Man in Middle, etc. These indicate that there is a high probability that this type of connection is part of the top 5 most vulnerable network connections [19].

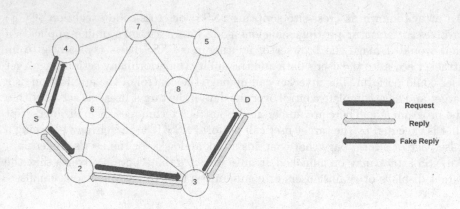

Fig. 2. Example of how Black Hole Attack works [16].

Black Hole Attacks. Black Hole Attacks are one of the major attacks in the Mobile Ad Hoc Network (MANET). These attacks happen when a node consumes all of the routes in the MANET. Attackers do this by responding to requests and updating messages with fake replies. These attackers might add errors followed by updates to it. They created a Black Hole attack confirmation system that finds and confirms the attacks in MANET with a honeypot. This honeypot system finds the type of black hole attack using a Black Hole tree and then confirms it using its Attack History Database [5]. The Black Hole attack tree had used common symptoms for specific attacks and had observations of what they should fix given the symptoms as shown in Fig. 2 [15].

Jellyfish Attacks. Jellyfish attacks are very similar to Black Hole attacks but instead of taking data packets, it delays the packets. These attacks have three subcategories: recorder attacks, period-dropping attacks, and delay variance attacks. Reorder attacks are caused by using a multi-path routing method. Period Dropping sometimes happens when some nodes drop some packets at a given time. Delay Variance occurs when bad nodes create a random delay in packet transmission because they did not change the data packet order [23].

4 AI Use in Cyber Attack Defense

Artificial intelligence seems like the most efficient defense against network breaches. This is especially due to the rapid evolution of cyber-attacks; machine learning and artificial intelligence can aid us in keeping up with all of the threats that exist today. Due to how large and complex a network can become, as well as the enormous volume of data they can contain, it is simply impossible for humans to secure and detect every single breach. Even software automation is insufficient to prevent network attacks. There are far too many viruses generated each week by many cyber-criminals around the world trying to find the next hole in a network [21]. The field of AI is also projected to increase dramatically within the next 5 years, so the effectiveness of AI in handling and preventing network breaches will increase. AI can not only help with prevention and detection of attacks, but also prediction. A network attack that would normally be invisible to human cyber-technicians can be spotted by AI instantly. This is because AI can examine behavioral patterns with ease, and therefore is able to evaluate the appearance of website traffic as either routine or hazardous and malicious. AI systems can also predict which parts of a network are the most vulnerable before they are breached [20].

5 How AI is Used to Create Cyber Attacks

Although AI can be utilized in the prevention of cyber attacks, it can also be used in cyber attacks. Malicious software has only ever been produced by humans up until this point. Malicious software that can morph on its own, hide on its own, replicate on its own, and think on its own has, however, proved harder to predict. Humans may now create programs that "think" independently and may be able to assault hundreds of targets simultaneously. Future software must be capable of understanding how to evaluate all potential attack vectors, choose the most advantageous course of action, carry it out successfully, and avoid detection. Additionally, these initiatives may be directed at your company. A continuous, round-the-clock, evolutionary, algorithm-driven cyber attack program will be running, "thinking" critically about how to attack. Most crucially, it can change in order to evade detection. These tools, for instance, could be able to identify every single employee who currently works for or has ever worked for your business by searching through Linked In data. After that, it might attack each of their home networks before waiting for one of them to log on to the company network. Since the majority of AI practitioners are excellent at interpreting the information at hand, they are rarely security professionals who can safeguard their systems and data. Adversary AI was created as a result of cybercriminals' ability to infiltrate these systems. The ability of data and AI systems to provide the promised benefit to the business is put at risk by this kind of cyberattack. Cybercriminals can modify the data or add significantly different data sets that are given to the learning model along with the original data once they have gained unauthorized access to the storage network.

Machine learning data poisoning targets only the training data provided to the model, as opposed to the traditional adversarial AI cyberattack, which depends on stealing a pre-trained model. It is easier for hackers to alter the learning of the model itself because fewer highly skewed samples of the input data are required. In order to detect potential problems once an ML model has been trained on the contaminated data, deep AI knowledge will probably be needed, especially in the case of unsupervised learning models.

The hijacking or reverse engineering of AI models is known as AI model theft. Additionally, private AI models are put into use on open networks that may be accessed via API requests. The data being consumed and output from deployed models can also be used to recreate algorithms.

In general, AI-driven hacks will get worse before becoming nearly difficult to find using conventional cybersecurity techniques. It essentially comes down to weighing human effort vs. machine efficiency. Teams working on cybersecurity are being overwhelmed by the complexity and size of this trend. In contrast, it is becoming more expensive and challenging to obtain the sophisticated and skilled cybersecurity personnel that are required to adequately address this danger. These new AI-driven attack methodologies could have fatal and extremely devastating effects. These subtle attacks threaten data security and integrity, which could lead to systemic failures, weakening trust in companies [3].

6   Real World Consequences and Recovery

Network breaches and cyber-crime are becoming more and more of a problem every year. After all, research has show that the average cost of a data breach in 2021 worked out to be around 4.24 million dollars per incident. This was the highest average cost in the history according to the current data. The latest reports also establish that cyber attacks are likely to cost a total of 6 trillion dollars annually by the end of 2022. Part of the reason for this rising cost can be attributed to the COVID-19 pandemic, where cyber attacks rose in severity and frequency. This is due to the fact that dependence on the internet and technology grew as people were confined the their home [12].

One simple way to counter-act cyber attacks is to back up your data. The only way to restore your data without paying a ransom after a malware infection is to have a copy of your valuable data stored elsewhere. With that said, you still must be careful; if you configure your device or computer to back up your data and most valuable files to the cloud and your computer gets attacked by ransomware, it is possible for that ransomware to also spread to your cloud and become infected by the attack as well. It is also a possibility that even if you pay a ransom for your data, you still will never be able to recover it. This is all the more reason to have a back up of your files. Regardless, the best way to deal with an attack is to prevent it from ever happening.

One famous example of a large data breach was against the company Yahoo!. Two hackers named Alexey Belan and Karim Baratov were hired by Russia's secret service to steal information on several high-profile government officials. Belan and Baratov sent Yahoo! employees emails that contained a link to download malware. They only needed one employee to click the download link to gain access to the entire company's server and database. After they successfully tricked an employee, they established a back door to the main Yahoo! server. A backdoor is a hidden entry point in your website or application that offers unrestricted access to it. These can be very hard to detect and can either be set up on purpose or set up maliciously as in the case of the Yahoo! breach. They implemented this to make sure they had easy access to the server in the future. Names, phone numbers, emails, and other sensitive data was leaked in this breach. The company ended up having to setup a settlement fund worth 117,500,000 to pay for the damages it caused to its users. As we can see, even the biggest companies can be brought down with a single click. Due to the costs and dangers of cyber attacks, it is vital to a company's success to have and incident response plan, or IRP. An IRP is a set of instructions designed to mitigate and control the damage of a data breach or network attack [17]. Every single company should have one, as a single attack can destroy a company's reputation and hurt them financially.

7   Results

7.1   IRP Prevention

Even with all of the prevention techniques at our disposal, we can never make our networks completely secure. One thing that is just as important as preventing network attacks is how we can recover from them. As we mentioned previously, one way to recover from a data breach is to have an IRP ready. Since the frequency of these breaches is so high, responding fast and efficiently to these attacks is a must. An IRP typically has four steps. The first step is preparation. Before any incident ever happens, you should prepare and perform a risk assessment analysis and identify where the vulnerable parts in your network are. The next step is identification. In this step, you will detect deviations from typical operations in your system and evaluate the severity of the incident. Next is containment. Once your team finds the breach, their first priority is to contain it and prevent more damage from occurring. After that, there is the eradication of the threat. You must identify the root cause of the attack and remove any other malware and patch the vulnerability, so it cannot be exploited again in the future. The final step is recovery, where you bring the affected systems back to normal operation after you have dealt with all the threats [17].

7.2   Machine Learning Methods to Detect Cyber Attacks

Machine learning approaches in attack detection are used for three main purposes: detection, attack classification, and analysis. Training data goes through a series of pre processes before being used in model training.

Support Vector Machine. A decision boundary between two classes is found using the Support Vector Machine (SVM), a vector space-based machine learning technique farthest from any point in the training data. When an attack has been identified once, SVM can be used with the classification model to perform a secure packet transfer between various sensor nodes [4].

Naive Bayes. A supervised learning technique, the Naive Bayes (NB) classifier, is based on the Bayes theorem and several conditional independence assumptions about the attributes. It integrates prior knowledge and observable data to determine explicit probabilities for the hypothesis.

Extreme Gradient Boosting. A machine learning approach called Extreme Gradient Boosting (XGBoost) is based on gradient-boosted decision trees. By avoiding the issue of overfitting during algorithm training, XGBoost, one of the new-generation community learning algorithms, improves the model's overall accuracy. This method's primary success factor is the purpose function it employs during the learning process [24].

Autoencoders. Autoencoders (AE) are uncontrolled neural networks that attempt to match the output to the same vector by taking a vector as input. An input can be used to represent data in a higher or lower dimension by taking the input, altering its size, and then rebuilding the input. These adaptable neural networks can unsupervised train to encrypt compressed data. A suitable model can be created with fewer computer resources by training one layer per iteration. When hidden layers have smaller dimensions than input and output layers, the network is utilized to encrypt data.

k- Means Clustering. Among unsupervised learning techniques, k- Means clustering is one of the most popular machine learning algorithms. Data samples are sorted into K groups based on how similar they are. Similar characteristics of objects from other groups are shared within each group. K is the user-specified number of clusters. The center of gravity for each cluster is then randomly selected after the number of clusters has been established. The distance between the center of gravity and data points is calculated using the Euclidean equation. The data points that are clustered are those closest to the gravitational center. It is determined that the value obtained serves as the new weight center by calculating the average separation between these data points. Up until no more data points are transferred between them, the process is repeated. The performance of the intrusion detection system can be enhanced by using a variation of the K-means algorithm to generate new, tiny training datasets that accurately replicate the training dataset, minimize the classifiers' training time, and build new, smaller training datasets [9].

Recurrent Neural Network. A directed loop is formed by connections between units in a recurrent neural network (RNN). RNN can display dynamic temporal behavior. It has the ability to process inputs using its own input memory, unlike forward propagation neural networks. RNNs are a good technique for voice and handwriting recognition because of this property. Unlike other deep learning models, RNN features hidden states and a structure that enables prior outputs to be used as input.

8 Conclusion

Security in cyber-physical contexts is increasingly important as our reliance on network devices grows. Machine learning approaches and intrusion detection systems, such as rule- and signature-based intrusion detection systems, have improved cybersecurity. The classification abilities of deep learning-based detection systems were also improved according to the current data [7]. The success of deep learning techniques is quite impressive. Research on unique attack-type applications has increased as a result of more attack diversity. The only area where early intervention tactics may be improved is the detection of attacks. Multivariate statistical metrics for attack detection and gauging the effectiveness of traditional models for AI based machine learning applications in cyber security can both be investigated further. The categorisation of attacks is crucial in this regard. For each kind of attack, there should now be enough information available. As we have discussed, the threat of network attacks is real and the cost is high. It would not be a stretch to say our future is completely reliant on how we are able to defend against the network attacks we have discussed. Those in the past fought with swords and defended with shields, while today we fight with computer viruses and protect ourselves with firewalls.

References

1. Hu, Y.C., Perrig, A., Johnson, D.B.: Wormhole attacks in wireless networks. IEEE J. Sel. Areas Commun. **24**(2), 370–380 (2006)
2. Ahmad, T., Truscan, D., Vain, J., Porres, I.: Early detection of network attacks using deep learning. In: 2022 IEEE International Conference on Software Testing, Verification and Validation Workshops (ICSTW), pp. 30–39. IEEE, April 2022
3. Guembe, B., Azeta, A., Misra, S., Osamor, V.C., Fernandez-Sanz, L., Pospelova, V.: The emerging threat of AI-driven cyber attacks: a Review. Appl. Artif. Intell. **36**(1), 2037254 (2022)
4. Borkar, G.M., Patil, L.H., Dalgade, D., Hutke, A.: A novel clustering approach and adaptive SVM classifier for intrusion detection in WSN: a data mining concept. Sustain. Comput. Inform. Syst. **23**, 120–135 (2019)
5. Tiruvakadu, D.S.K., Pallapa, V.: Confirmation of wormhole attack in MANETs using honeypot. Comput. Secur. **76**, 32–49 (2018)
6. Yan, R., Xiao, X., Hu, G., Peng, S., Jiang, Y.: New deep learning method to detect code injection attacks on hybrid applications. J. Syst. Softw. **137**, 67–77 (2018)
7. Hanif, H., Nasir, M.H.N.M., Ab Razak, M.F., Firdaus, A., Anuar, N.B.: The rise of software vulnerability: taxonomy of software vulnerabilities detection and machine learning approaches. J. Netw. Comput. Appl. **179**, 103009 (2021)

8. Al-Yaseen, W.L., Othman, Z.A., Nazri, M.Z.A.: Multi-level hybrid support vector machine and extreme learning machine based on modified K-means for intrusion detection system. Expert Syst. Appl. **67**, 296–303 (2017)
9. Chen, T., Guestrin, C.: Proceedings of the 22nd ACM SIGKDD International Conference on Knowledge Discovery and Data Mining (2016)
10. Maliha, M.: A supervised learning approach: detection of cyber attacks. In: 2021 IEEE International Conference on Telecommunications and Photonics (ICTP), pp. 1–5. IEEE, December 2021
11. Sivasankari, N., Kamalakkannan, S.: Detection and prevention of man-in-the-middle attack in IoT network using regression modeling. Adv. Eng. Softw. **169**, 103126 (2022)
12. Morse, E.A., Raval, V., Wingender, J.R., Jr.: Market price effects of data security breaches. Inf. Secur. J. Glob. Perspect. **20**(6), 263–273 (2011)
13. Kuppa, K., Dayal, A., Gupta, S., Dua, A., Chaudhary, P., Rathore, S.: ConvXSS: a deep learning-based smart ICT framework against code injection attacks for HTML5 web applications in sustainable smart city infrastructure. Sustain. Cities Soc. **80**, 103765 (2022)
14. Tiruvakadu, D.S.K., Pallapa, V.: Honeypot based black-hole attack confirmation in a MANET: black-hole attack confirmation. Int. J. Wirel. Inf. Netw. **25**, 434–448 (2018)
15. Satheeshkumar, S., Sengottaiyan, N.: Defending against jellyfish attacks using cluster based routing protocol for secured data transmission in MANET. Clust. Comput. **22**, 10849–10860 (2019)
16. Kumar, K., Arora, S.K.: Review of vehicular ad hoc network security. Int. J. Grid Distrib. Comput. **9**(11), 17–34 (2016)
17. Levchenko, K., Paturi, R., Varghese, G.: On the difficulty of scalably detecting network attacks. In: Proceedings of the 11th ACM Conference on Computer and Communications Security, pp. 12–20, October 2004
18. Baba, T., Matsuda, S.: Tracing network attacks to their sources. IEEE Internet Comput. **6**(2), 20–26 (2002)
19. Shrivastava, N., Majumder, A., Rastogi, R.: Mining (social) network graphs to detect random link attacks. In: 2008 IEEE 24th International Conference on Data Engineering, pp. 486–495. IEEE, April 2008
20. Ahmad, T., Truscan, D., Vain, J., Porres, I.: Early detection of network attacks using deep learning. In: 2022 IEEE International Conference on Software Testing, Verification and Validation Workshops (ICSTW), pp. 30–39. IEEE, April 2022
21. Osanaiye, O., Alfa, A.S., Hancke, G.P.: A statistical approach to detect jamming attacks in wireless sensor networks. Sensors **18**(6), 1691 (2018)
22. Suryaprabha, E., Saravana Kumar, N.M.: Enhancement of security using optimized DoS (denial-of-service) detection algorithm for wireless sensor network. Soft. Comput. **24**(14), 10681–10691 (2020)
23. Satheeshkumar, S., Sengottaiyan, N.: Defending against jellyfish attacks using cluster based routing protocol for secured data transmission in MANET. Clust. Comput. **22**, 10849–10860 (2019)
24. Chen, T., Guestrin, C.: Xgboost: a scalable tree boosting system. In: Proceedings of the 22nd ACM SIGKDD International Conference on Knowledge Discovery and Data Mining, pp. 785–794 August 2016

DSS for Business Performance
and Stakeholders

A Literature Review on the Contribution of Industry 4.0 Technologies in OEE Improvement

Emna Masmoudi[✉], Laurent Piétrac, and Séverine Durieux

Université Clermont Auvergne, Clermont Auvergne INP, CNRS, Institut Pascal,
63000 Clermont-Ferrand, France
emna.masmoudi@sigma-clermont.fr

Abstract. Overall Equipment Effectiveness (OEE) has remained a valuable performance indicator over the decades. Yet, methods for improving equipment effectiveness have changed and advanced over time. This paper deals with the contribution of the Industry 4.0 in OEE improvement in the context of production systems monitoring and control through an analysis of the current literature. Industry 4.0 provides innovative technologies to enable new ways of tracking, taking decisions and acting upon production system health data. Internet of Things (IoT) when integrated into production systems, enables tracking of operational parameters remotely in real-time. Big Data and Artificial Intelligence enable analyzing historical and current operational data to using the results for predictive maintenance. Simulation and Digital Twins allow to test various production scenarios to measure their impact on production systems performance… This leads to better insights on production performance, identification and minimization of losses, and enhanced decision making in favor of increasing OEE values consistently. In this work, we give an overview of the Industry 4.0 technologies used in the literature. Then we identify and present different use cases that combine a number of these technologies to assure production monitoring and control.

Keywords: OEE · production system · monitoring · control · Industry 4.0

1 Introduction

The ultimate objective of production system monitoring and control is to optimize the production system's efficiency with its current resources capacity [1]. According to [2], to reach this objective, it is necessary to measure performance achieved by the controlled production system and comparing the results to previously set objectives. Then it is necessary to identify production losses, analyze their causes and develop solutions. The latter consist in applying corrective actions when the previously defined objectives are not reached or improvement actions when a potential source of progress has been detected.

One of the effective means to monitor and control production systems is the implementation of Key Performance Indicators (KPIs) and their follow-up. These indicators

© The Author(s), under exclusive license to Springer Nature Switzerland AG 2023
S. Liu et al. (Eds.): ICDSST 2023, LNBIP 474, pp. 69–79, 2023.
https://doi.org/10.1007/978-3-031-32534-2_6

help provide a synthetic view of the use of production equipment and thus make it possible to identify performance degradation and search for their root causes [3].

OEE is a leading KPI widely used to manage production in the literature to measure and monitor the improvement of operational performance of production systems for decades [4]. OEE is a KPI that considers several types of production losses and encompasses 3 main rates affecting the performance of the production system: availability, quality and performance [5]. The analysis of this indicator and its components reveals sources of performance losses and indicates where improvement efforts are to be made. The methods of monitoring and controlling of production with the OEE vary and are changing with the evolution of new technologies to address the limitations of conventional methods. Over the last decade, the world is experiencing a fourth industrial revolution called Industry 4.0 based on large amounts of data, which offers promising potentials for monitoring and controlling production systems [6].

The main objective of this study is to explore the literature around the impact of Industry 4.0 on the monitoring and controlling of production systems based on OEE. For this purpose, in this article, we intend to provide a global view on the evolution of production systems management based on OEE in the context of Industry 4.0 and based on a review of the existing literature.

Then we will propose different use cases that combines Industry 4.0 technologies for production system monitoring and controlling.

2 Method

The methodology used in the study is a six-step process shown in Fig. 1. The process started by a specification of research purpose and research questions. The purpose of this paper is to discuss the contribution of Industry 4.0 technologies to the improvement of production systems monitoring and controlling using OEE.

According to the research motivations outlined in the purpose, this paper answers the following research questions: "How can industry 4.0 improve OEE for production systems?" and "What are the technologies used for this purpose?". These questions aimed to establish the scope of the review, leading to the search command with the keywords. A search for papers was performed using Science Direct and Google Scholar databases. Due to the target of our study, the keywords defined are "Industry 4.0", "OEE" and "Production systems". The authors have searched all publications that had the defined terms in the title, abstract or keywords. The inclusion and exclusion criteria were defined as follows: The only considered language was English. The publications considered are with an open access and describing applications using one or a combination of Industry 4.0 technologies to improve OEE. 140 papers were identified through databases searching. Once collected and the duplicate papers removed, the papers were filtered using defined inclusion and exclusion criteria, resulting in a corpus of 18 papers that are in the scope of our study.

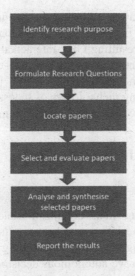

Fig. 1. Research methodology

3 Monitoring and Controlling of Production Systems Based on OEE

3.1 OEE as a KPI

OEE is a KPI that is initially introduced in the contribution of [5], to provide a methodology for estimating the inefficiency of industrial equipment. It has rapidly spread in the industrial and scientific context due to its ease of use and wide applicability. According to a recent study [4], there are more than 850 scientific publications related to OEE between 1996 and 2020. Most of the papers address the problem of improving this indicator using a variety of methods where initial values are compared to final values, thus quantifying the level of improvement achieved. Besides being a KPI to monitor production systems improvement, OEE is used to reveal production losses based on the analysis of its value and the value of its elements since the OEE rate is the result of the product of 3factors: Availability, performance, and quality [7]. Each factor is used to classify the major losses and is therefore used as a basis for defining actions to improve the performance of the equipment.

3.2 Limitations of the Conventional Methods

The accuracy of OEE depends on several aspects such as the data collection accuracy and the measurement frequency. The level of difficulty of data collection is related to the level of the production system complexity and to the data collection method whether it is realized manually or automatically. For manual data collection, some data can be forgotten due to human error such as the difficulty of observing production stoppages in real-time and the time required to gather certain information. It can even lead some manufacturers to abandon the use of this approach considering that the operator will waste time collecting data or that the collected data is unreliable [7]. For the automated data collection, even though it facilitates the acquisition of large amounts of detailed data, the degree to which the resulting OEE rate actually reflects that the production system is performing well depends directly on how well companies are able to interpret and define the underlying factors of OEE [8].

In this context, the promising technologies of Industry 4.0 have enabled favorable conditions to obtain and analyze data in real-time with much less risk of error [9].

4   OEE in the Era of Industry 4.0

4.1   Industry 4.0

Industry 4.0 refers to the new stage in the organization and control of the industrial value chain by the integration and the interaction between the physical and virtual spaces. Its main goal is to enable having flexible manufacturing processes, monitor assets and processes in real time and improve autonomous decision-making processes [10]. The Industry 4.0 concept is proposed to achieve a better level of operational efficiency, productivity, and automation of production systems [11]. This new industrial step has been possible due to the recent evolution and the affordability of a set of technologies. According to [12], these technologies include IoT, Cloud Computing, Cyber-Physical Systems, Big Data and Data Analytics, Additive Manufacturing, Artificial Intelligence, simulation, and Digital Twins. In this paper, we focus on monitoring and controlling production systems related technologies used by the literature to improve OEE.

4.2   Monitoring and Controlling of Production Systems in the Era of Industry 4.0

Combining a powerful indicator as OEE with disruptive technological advances is changing the current production systems monitoring and controlling practice to meet the requirements of a data-driven, real-time, and digitalized context.

Several research works have been conducted to evaluate the impact of Industry 4.0 technologies on the OEE improvement for production systems. The objective of this part is to present, through a representative bibliography, the various technologies used for the measurement and for this purpose.

Simulation is considered as one of the key technologies for implementing Industry 4.0 [13]. It is an important technology for developing planning and exploration models that improve the understanding of how a production system operates under varying conditions and assess the impacts on operational performance. It helps to optimize decision making and operation of complex and intelligent production systems [14]. In [15], authors test different scenarios and evaluate the impact of the implementation of different Industry 4.0 technologies in the production line using OEE. Both [16] and [17] apply gathered data from production system by means of IoT sensors to validate the simulation model that is used later on to test improvement scenarios and make decisions based on the results. Combining IoT wearable sensors and simulation flow model, [18] investigates human working performance. For [19], the study is based on functioning signals as data input to a flow simulation to investigate future system evolution in near time and obtain calculated OEE values. Another study [20] proposes a data-driven approach for increasing OEE by utilizing discrete event simulation with Data Analytics tools (Power BI). While simulation tests different production configurations, Data Analytics tools support data analysis, translating and extracting meaningful information from Big Data stored to improve decision making performance [21].

Other research works adopted integrating Big Data with Artificial Intelligence solutions. This combination is considered in [22] to assure automatic quality prediction and have better quality outcomes. Furthermore, Artificial Intelligence plays an important role in predictive maintenance. Depending on historical production performance data and real time data, [23] investigates using Deep Learning algorithms to predict future values of OEE. Artificial Intelligence is used as well in the detection of future breakdowns like [24] who uses a decision tree model to predict the happening of incoming machine failure. In the works of [25] and [26], classification machine learning algorithms have been utilized in order to automatically detect changeovers in a shopfloor environment impacting to the availability of the assets.

Another technology that we will focus on in this paper is the Internet of Things that consists in extending network connectivity and computing capability to devices to generate, exchange and consume data with minimal human intervention [27]. This allows these objects to have their own existence in the digital world. From a manufacturing perspective, the IoT is a way to digitize production processes. Industrial IoT uses a network of sensors to collect production data and uses various software to transform this data into valuable operational performance information [28]. It is used to solve the problem for complex and heterogeneous plants due to different types of machines and different generations of controllers and communication protocols. For this, [29] proposes a unified OEE data collection method by implementing IoT sensors to detect machine stoppage and capture the stoppage reasons. Besides, production systems like stamping machines necessitates providing a secured data collection for operators. For this reason, [30] focuses on designing and realizing a performance monitoring system for a stamping machine based on IoT to increase the effectiveness of the machine. IoT sensors allow also increasing the frequency of data collection and thus to have an instant and detailed insight of what is actually happening in the production system [31]. [32] underlines that automatic root cause identification in a production system can greatly improve decision-making efficiency. In this study, the authors use IoT and regression algorithms to define the root cause of OEE degradation indicating the measured values that may negatively affect production performance by eliciting historical data. Considered as the next wave in modelling and simulation [33], Digital Twins are used by the literature to monitor and control production systems. A Digital Twin is defined by [34] as "a set of adaptive models that emulate the behavior of a physical system in a virtual system getting real time data to update itself along its life cycle. The Digital Twin replicates the physical system to predict failures and opportunities for changing, to prescribe real time actions for optimizing and/or mitigating unexpected events observing and evaluating the operating profile system". Therefore, Digital Twins are useful for production optimization and operational control [35]. Digital Twins also offer advantages to OEE improvement. [36] provides a decision support system framework based on Digital Twin and IoT to monitor a conventional machine and enable the operator to perceive the machine status, production time, OEE and order scheduling in real-time. [37] focuses on improving production quality by proposing a framework of a Digital Twin that is based on anomaly detection. [38] develops a Digital Twin as a decision support system for a dynamic maintenance task prioritization using simulation-based optimization and genetic programming.

The Table 1 presents a summary of the different Industry 4.0 technologies used in the literature. It also shows that in most cases, several technologies are used together.

Table 1. Industry 4.0 technologies used by the literature to monitor and control production systems

References	Industry 4.0 technologies				
	Simulation	Digital Twin	IoT	Big Data/Data Analytics	Artificial Intelligence
[15, 19]	X				
[20]	X			X	
[16, 18]	X		X		
[17]	X		X	X	
[29, 30, 32]			X		
[31]			X	X	
[22]			X	X	X
[23]			X		X
[24–26]					X
[36]		X	X		
[37, 38]		X			X

4.3   Use Cases of Production Systems Monitoring and Controlling Using OEE

The second aim of this paper is to identify and present different use cases that combine a number of Industry 4.0 technologies to assure production systems monitoring and control. Then we classify the applications into those use cases according to their purpose in relation to the OEE.

We identify three general use cases: evaluation of current state, prediction of future state and decision making.

The first use case concerns the assessment of the current state of the production system and thus the current value of OEE. It includes data collection, identification and classification of performance losses, visualization, and analysis of what happened in the past or what is currently happening in the production. All these elements are complementary and have a common target which is to assess the current state of the production system. The first step to calculate accurate OEE rates is to collect reliable operational data which is not an easy task for certain cases. For instance, [29] focuses on this point by implementing IoT sensors for legacy machines that originally do not provide an interface for data collection. The authors use sensors to detect the machine stoppage in the first place and send an alert to allow operator to define stoppage reason on a Human Machine Interface which provide data for OEE calculations. Also, [30] proposes to set up IoT sensors on stamping machines to overcome security issues and have access to all the data collected displayed on a user interface. Another important point in this use case is the identification and classification of performance degradation causes. In this context, in [25] and in an extended research [26], the same research group is interested in automatically distinguishing the changeover phase operations from the production phase by an Artificial Intelligence trained model. This contributes to cover the aspect of maintaining production system availability and particularly to improve identification of heterogenous changeover processes that depends on different workers who perform different procedures to changeover a machine. They start by implementing different sensors on a CNC milling machine with very low data accessibility to have a big amount of data that they use later to train the classification machine learning algorithm. In terms of anomaly detection related to production quality, [37] implements a production twin that replicates the current pressing process which laid the foundation for an anomaly detection algorithm to detect defective pressing processes. The algorithm uses Gaussian process models for the detection of anomalies in the pressure curves of the system. This puts the light on the quality component of OEE and how Industry 4.0 technologies can be used to gain insight into quality issues causes and thus to adjust before production quality degradation. The developed solution enables to detect faulty products and too-high pressures at the machine. An additional topic covered by the literature that uses Industry 4.0 technologies having an overview of real-time condition of the production system. This aspect is covered by [31] and [36] by providing a dashboard that displays data visually. The first one [31] by developing an OEE SCADA system that provides a comprehensive view of the manufacturing production line regarding performance, quality, and availability, the second one [36] by implementing a data-driven Digital Twin for a conventional machine facilitating an interconnected system that can monitor a machine's conditions in real-time.

The second use case concerns the prediction of the possible evolution of the production system. It involves prediction of the future value of OEE based on historical data or by the prediction of incoming failures. For the part of predicting the possible evolution of production performance, the literature treats the problem in different ways using different Industry 4.0 technologies namely simulation for the case of [19] to investigate preventively or in near-real-time the evolution of production performance when variabilities are considered for some parameters. Another method purely based on historical production performance data is proposed by [23] that lean on Artificial Intelligence algorithms to predict OEE value with a daily frequency. The authors point to the relevance of this approach to apply on fresh product packaging production system where unexpected downtime can easily lead to product waste. Concerning the failure prediction in the context of improving OEE, different authors base their methods on IoT gathered historical production data to explore the happening of incoming failure but in a variety of ways. [24] applies an Artificial Intelligence algorithm to this data to predict failure in near real-time which contributes to reducing the undesired production breakdowns and thus increase equipment availability. On the other hand, [32] develops, for a given KPI, an analysis algorithm that exploits the KPI and follows its dependencies until the root measures for the performance degradation has been identified. Finally, that measure is presented to the user as the source that will negatively affect the performance of production in the near future.

The last use case is about using the current or predicted OEE rate to make decisions and control production systems. This includes testing possible changes in production to evaluate the best improvement scenario, anticipating an action to avoid a failure or acting in real-time to restore a breakdown. In a logic of using OEE as an indicator of enhancing production systems performance and making improvement decisions, many research works depended on simulation. This is whether to test the effect of changing some parameters of the production system [16, 17], or to assess the impact of Industry 4.0 technologies implementation of the production system [15]. The benefit of using simulation in these situations is having a testing space without the need to interrupt the real system. Others [38] combine simulation-based optimization tool and genetic programming in a Digital Twin-based decision support system to conduct short-term corrective maintenance task prioritization. The authors propose this approach to address the problem of pre-defined prioritizations in a dynamically changing production environment. With the proposed use cases, we managed to gather reviewed papers considering their common purpose in relation to OEE which is summarized in Table 2.

Table 2. Reviewed papers according to their common purpose in relation to OEE

Use Case	Element of the Use Case	References
Evaluation of current state	Data collection	[18, 29–31]
	Identification and classification of performance losses	[25, 26]
	Visualization, and analysis of what happened in the past or what is currently happening in the production system	[18, 30, 31, 36, 37]
Estimation of future State	Prediction of the future value of OEE based on historical data	[19, 23]
	Prediction of incoming failures	[22, 24, 32]
Decision making	Testing possible changes in production to evaluate the best improvement scenario	[15–17, 20]
	Anticipating an action to avoid a failure or acting in real-time to restore a breakdown	[38]

5   Conclusion

In this paper, we review the state of the research about the integration of Industry 4.0 by one or multiple technologies into monitoring and controlling production systems through the OEE indicator. This study finds that Industry 4.0 technologies can be applied on different complementary perspectives in relation to improving OEE to over-come traditional methods limitations. Real-time gathering data by IoT replaces periodic and manual data collection and enables better, continuous, and remote monitoring of operational parameters of production systems. These connected devices provide better quality, more detailed, real-time and more accurate data which improves OEE calcu-lations. Besides, the analysis with Data Analytics or Artificial Intelligence algorithms allows predictive maintenance and makes OEE improvement more proactive instead of being reactive. Moreover, these advanced technologies with the provided current state of production systems, allow to take a condition-based approach to maintenance. This approach prolongs the time between planned maintenance when production system is in good condition. This increases productive hours and minimizes unplanned downtimes. In addition, simulations and Digital Twins can offer an insight over quality issues and a better guidance for diagnostics by reproducing production system's behavior as well as testing its possible evolution to predict production future performance.

A second contribution of this work is the classification of the studied literature into three use cases according to their purpose in relation to the OEE indicator. The first use case gathers papers that tend to evaluate the current state of production system. The second use case consists in predicting the evolution of production performance whether through predicting directly future values of OEE or through predicting incoming failures. The last use case concerns papers that use OEE values in decision-making. This classification showed that in every use case, researchers can use the same technologies to treat different OEE related problems and can use different technologies to achieve the same target and this depends on the production system studied.

The research has identified that Industry 4.0 technologies provide a lot of benefits to improving OEE. The exploitation of this potential didn't reach its limits yet and still have a lot more to offer. There are combinations that are able to cover the purpose of all the use cases such as the Digital Twin and Artificial Intelligence. As future work, we intend to explore this duo in all the use cases.

References

1. Stavropoulos, P., Chantzis, D., Doukas, C., Papacharalampopoulos, A., Chryssolouris, G.: Monitoring and control of manufacturing processes: a review. Procedia CIRP **8**, 421–425 (2013). https://doi.org/10.1016/j.procir.2013.06.127
2. Dhaevers, V., Riane, F., Duvivier, D., Meskens, N.: Vers un pilotage souple de la performance des systèmes de production. In: 7e Congrès international de génie industriel. Trois-Rivières, Quebec, Canada (2007)
3. Lorino, P.: La performance et ses indicateurs. Elément de definition. In: Indicateurs de performances. Hermès Sciences, Lavoisier, pp. 23–28 (2001)
4. Ng Corrales, L.C., Lambán, M.P., Hernandez Korner, M.E., Royo, J.: Overall equipment effectiveness: systematic literature review and overview of different approaches. Appl. Sci. **10**(18) (2020). https://doi.org/10.3390/app10186469
5. Nakajima, S.: Introduction to TPM. Productivity Press, Cambridge (1988)
6. Xu, L.D., Xu, E.L., Li, L.: Industry 4.0: state of the art and future trends. Int. J. Prod. Res. **56**(8), 2941–2962 (2018). https://doi.org/10.1080/00207543.2018.1444806

7. Muchiri, P., Pintelon, L.: Performance measurement using overall equipment effectiveness (OEE): literature review and practical application discussion. Int. J. Prod. Res. **46**(13), 3517–3535 (2008). https://doi.org/10.1080/00207540601142645

8. Hedman, R., Subramaniyan, M., Almström, P.: Analysis of critical factors for automatic measurement of OEE. Procedia CIRP **57**, 128–133 (2016). https://doi.org/10.1016/j.procir.2016.11.023

9. Chen, B., Wan, J., Shu, L., Li, P., Mukherjee, M., Yin, B.: Smart factory of Industry 4.0: key technologies, application case, and challenges. IEEE Access **6**, 6505–6519 (2018). https://doi.org/10.1109/ACCESS.2017.2783682

10. Fettermann, D.C., Gobbo Sá Cavalcante, C., Domingues de Almeida, T., Luz Tortorella, G.: How does Industry 4.0 contribute to operations management? J. Ind. Prod. Eng. **35**(4), 255–268 (2018). https://doi.org/10.1080/21681015.2018.1462863

11. Thames, L., Schaefer, D.: Software-defined Cloud manufacturing for Industry 4.0. Procedia CIRP **52**, 12–17 (2016). https://doi.org/10.1016/j.procir.2016.07.041

12. Kamble, S.S., Gunasekaran, A., Gawankar, S.A.: Sustainable Industry 4.0 framework: a systematic literature review identifying the current trends and future perspectives. Process Saf. Environ. Prot. **117**, 408–425 (2018). https://doi.org/10.1016/j.psep.2018.05.009

13. Han, Y., Jeong, J., Ko, M.H., Lee, S., Kim, J.: Analysis of global competitiveness of engineering modeling and simulation technology for next manufacturing innovation: using quantitative analysis of patents and papers. ICIC Express Lett. **9**, 339–346 (2018)

14. de Paula Ferreira, W., Armellini, F., De Santa-Eulalia, L.A.: Simulation in Industry 4.0: a state-of-the-art review. Comput. Ind. Eng. **149**, 106868 (2020). https://doi.org/10.1016/j.cie.2020.106868

15. Tumbajoy, L.M., Muñoz-Añasco, M., Thiede, S.: Enabling Industry 4.0 impact assessment with manufacturing system simulation: an OEE based methodology. Procedia CIRP **107**, 681–686 (2022). https://doi.org/10.1016/j.procir.2022.05.045

16. Abd Rahman, M.S., Mohamad, E., Abdul Rahman, A.A.: Enhancement of overall equipment effectiveness (OEE) data by using simulation as decision making tools for line balancing. Indonesian J. Electr. Eng. Comput. Sci. **18**(2), 1040–1047 (2020). https://doi.org/10.11591/ijeecs.v18.i2.pp1040-1047

17. Abd Rahman, M.S.B., Mohamad, E., Abdul Rahman, A.A.B.: Development of IoT—enabled data analytics enhance decision support system for lean manufacturing process improvement. Concurr. Eng. **29**(3), 208–220 (2021). https://doi.org/10.1177/1063293X20987911

18. Fera, M., et al.: Towards digital twin implementation for assessing production line performance and balancing. Sensors **20**(1), 97–114 (2019). https://doi.org/10.3390/s20010097

19. Caterino, M., et al.: Simulation techniques for production lines performance control. Procedia Manuf. **42**, 91–96 (2020). https://doi.org/10.1016/j.promfg.2020.02.027

20. Lindegren, M., Lunau, M., Pereira, M., Ribeiro da Silva, E.: Combining simulation and data analytics for OEE improvement. Int. J. Simul. Model. **21**, 29-40 (2022). https://doi.org/10.2507/IJSIMM21-1-584

21. Sadiku, M.N.O., Ashaolu, T.J., Ajayi-Majebi, A., Musa, S.M.: Big data in manufacturing. Int. J. Sci. Adv. **2**(1), 63–66 (2021). https://doi.org/10.51542/ijscia.v2i1.11

22. Bonada, F., Echeverria, L., Domingo, X., Anzaldi, G.: AI for improving the overall equipment efficiency in manufacturing industry. In: Romeral Martínez, L., Osornio Rios, R.A., Delgado Prieto, M. (eds.) New Trends in the Use of Artificial Intelligence for the Industry 4.0. IntechOpen (2020). https://doi.org/10.5772/intechopen.89967

23. Brunelli, L., Masiero, C., Tosato, D., Beghi, A., Susto, G.A.: Deep learning-based production forecasting in manufacturing: a packaging equipment case study. Procedia Manuf. **38**, 248–255 (2019). https://doi.org/10.1016/j.promfg.2020.01.033

24. Chee Him, L., Yu, Y.P., Lee, W.P., Abdul Rahman, T.: Improvement of overall equipment effectiveness from predictive maintenance. In: Conference Proceedings: International Conference on Digital Transformation and Applications (ICDXA), pp. 72–75 (2020). https://doi.org/10.56453/icdxa.2020.1005

25. Engelmann, B., Schmitt, S., Miller, E., Bräutigam, V., Schmitt, J.: Advances in machine learning detecting changeover processes in cyber physical production systems. J. Manuf. Mater. Process. 4(4) (2020). https://doi.org/10.3390/jmmp4040108

26. Miller, E., Borysenko, V., Heusinger, M., Niedner, N., Engelmann, B., Schmitt, J.: Enhanced changeover detection in Industry 4.0 environments with machine learning. Sensors 21(17) (2021). https://doi.org/10.3390/s21175896

27. Rose, K., Eldridge, S., Chapin, L.: The internet of things: an overview. In: Marsan, C. (ed.) Understanding the Issues and Challenges of a More Connected World. The Internet Society (ISOC), Geneva, Switzerland (2015)

28. Boyes, H., Hallaq, B., Cunningham, J., Watson, T.: The industrial internet of things (IIoT): an analysis framework. Comput. Ind. 101, 1–12 (2018). https://doi.org/10.1016/j.compind.2018.04.015

29. Zhou, J., Wang, Y., Chua, Y.Q.: Machine OEE monitoring and analysis for a complex manufacturing environment. In: 15th IEEE Conference on Industrial Electronics and Applications (ICIEA), Kristiansand, Norway, pp. 1413–1418 (2020). https://doi.org/10.1109/ICIEA48937.2020.9248351

30. Maulana, G.G.: Production monitoring system using overall equipment effectiveness (OEE) method to improve stamping machine performance. Jurnal Polimesin 20(2) (2022). https://doi.org/10.30811/jpl.v20i2.2560

31. Li, Y.H., Inoue, L.C.G.V., Sinha, R.: Real-time OEE visualisation for downtime detection. In: 20th International Conference on Industrial Informatics (INDIN), Perth, Australia, pp. 729–734 (2022). https://doi.org/10.1109/INDIN51773.2022.9976067

32. Papacharalampopoulos, A., Giannoulis, C., Stavropoulos, P., Mourtzis, D.: A digital twin for automated root-cause search of production alarms based on KPIs aggregated from IoT. Appl. Sci. 10(7), (2020). https://doi.org/10.3390/app10072377

33. Rosen, R., von Wichert, G., Lo, G., Bettenhausen, K.D.: About the importance of autonomy and digital twins for the future of manufacturing. IFAC-PapersOnLine 48(3), 567–572 (2015). https://doi.org/10.1016/j.ifacol.2015.06.141

34. Semeraro, C., Lezoche, M., Panetto, H., Dassisti, M.: Digital twin paradigm: a systematic literature review. Comput. Ind. 130 (2021). https://doi.org/10.1016/j.compind.2021.103469

35. Tao, F., Zhang, H., Liu, A., Nee, A.Y.C.: Digital twin in industry: state-of-the-art. IEEE Trans. Ind. Inf. 15(4), 2405–2415 (2019). https://doi.org/10.1109/TII.2018.2873186

36. Wang, K.J., Lee, Y.H., Angelica, S.: Digital twin design for real-time monitoring – a case study of die cutting machine. Int. J. Prod. Res. 59(21), 6471–6485 (2021). https://doi.org/10.1080/00207543.2020.1817999

37. Trauer, J., Pfingstl, S., Finsterer, M., Zimmermann, M.: Improving production efficiency with a digital twin based on anomaly detection. Sustainability 13(18) (2021). https://doi.org/10.3390/su131810155

38. Frantzén, M., Bandaru, S., Ng, A.H.C.: Digital-twin-based decision support of dynamic maintenance task prioritization using simulation-based optimization and genetic programming. Decis. Anal. J. 3 (2022). https://doi.org/10.1016/j.dajour.2022.100039

MAMCABM: A Data-Driven Stakeholder-Based Decision-Support System that Considers Uncertainties

He Huang[1]([✉])([iD]), Shiqi Sun[1]([iD]), Lina Liu[1,2]([iD]), Koen Mommens[1]([iD]),
and Cathy Macharis[1]([iD])

[1] Vrije Universiteit Brussel, Pleinlaan 2, 1050 Ixelles, Belgium
{He.Huang,Shiqi.Sun,Koen.Mommens,Cathy.Macharis}@vub.be
[2] Nanjing University, Xianlin Road 163, Nanjing 210023, People's Republic of China
liulina@smail.nju.edu.cn

Abstract. In recent years, decision-making in mobility has increasingly relied on data support and consideration of uncertainty. However, conventional decision-making methods such as Multi-Criteria Decision Making (MCDM) and Multi-Criteria Group Decision Making (MCGDM) have limitations in accounting for the complexity and dynamics of real-world mobility situations. This has led to an interest in Agent-Based Modeling (ABM), which can capture the heterogeneity and interactions of individuals in a system. On the other hand, MCDM remains a legitimate method that allows for the consideration of conflicting interests simultaneously. Moreover, it is still valuable to involve stakeholders in the decision-making process, as they can provide important insights and perspectives that may not be captured by purely analytical methods.

This paper presents a novel decision-support system (DSS) that combines Multi-Attribute Multi-Criteria Analysis (MAMCA) and ABM to support mobility decision-making under conditions of uncertainty, called MAMCABM. The DSS provide stakeholders with a comprehensive decision making tool to assess and compare alternative scenarios based on different criteria, where ABM provides rich data support. Furthermore, MAMCABM also accounts for uncertainties that are generated in different steps. MAMCABM is demonstrated on a real-world case study of a road adjacent to a university campus, where different types of vehicles, cyclists and pedestrians interact in complex ways. The results of the MAMCABM analysis highlight the importance of considering multiple criteria and uncertainty in mobility decision-making, and provide valuable insights for improving the road situation by taking into account the preferences of different stakeholders.

Keywords: Group decision-making · MCDM · ABM · uncertainty · data-driven

S. Liu et al. (Eds.): ICDSST 2023, LNBIP 474, pp. 80–96, 2023.
https://doi.org/10.1007/978-3-031-32534-2_7

1   Introduction

In social and public decision-making problems, normally there is a need to consider several conflicting interests and concerns simultaneously, e.g., sustainable factors like economic development, environmental protection and social equity [42]. Therefore, the multi-criteria decision-making (MCDM) methods are considered as one of the suitable decision-making methods, as they provide a systematic approach for considering non-monetary criteria alongside monetary criteria [34]. Especially in the mobility sector, considering multiple factors that are relevant to mobility such as cost, time, safety, etc., can help policymakers evaluate possible solutions comprehensively for specific problems such as transportation mode selection, public transportation planning, and road policy appraisal [46].

Another important factor for successful mobility decision making is the involvement of stakeholders [4]. The stakeholders are the individuals and interest groups that will affect or be affected by the decision taken [12]. By considering the conflicting interests of different stakeholder groups, the analysis of decision-making problems can be more comprehensive. The group decision-making frameworks in MCDM like Multi-Actor Multi-Criteria Analysis (MAMCA) allow the involvement of different stakeholder groups with different criteria, which can help stakeholders appraise the alternatives based on their priorities [17,31]. MAMCA has been served as the decision-support tool in the mobility sector for almost 20 years and successfully supported different complex mobility decision-making problems [30]. Yet, while MAMCA has been widely used, recent developments in the field have highlighted the need for robust data support and the incorporation of uncertainty which MAMCA needs to address in order to enhance its overall decision-making quality and reliability [39].

In recent years, the integration of data support into decision making processes has become increasingly important, particularly in the mobility sector where various factors and stakeholders need to be considered [43]. With the advent of advanced simulation techniques, it is now possible to incorporate large amounts of data into decision making processes, providing a more realistic and informed picture of the problem at hand. One such simulation technique is Agent-Based Modeling (ABM), which allows for the simulation of complex systems by modeling the interactions between individual agents [13,23,45]. By incorporating data support into ABM simulations, the accuracy and realism of the results can be significantly improved, that better support the stakeholders in differentiating the preferences of different alternatives.

Uncertainty is another factor that becomes more and more important in mobility decision making as the mobility system always arises uncertainties including unexpected events, changing conditions, and varying preferences [28]. The uncertain factors in the evaluation may influence the accuracy of the decision making [29]. Considering uncertainty in mobility decision making is important because it can help to ensure that decisions are robust and resilient to changes and unexpected events [21]. It can make stakeholders informed choices that are better able to withstand the impacts of uncertainty and ensure that the outcomes of their decisions are consistent with their goals and objectives. Previously, a range-based MAMCA is developed that considers the uncertainty of the alternative performance. However, more types of uncertainties can be considered [3].

In this study, we present a new data-driven decision-support system (DSS) that combines ABM and MAMCA to evaluate the different road policies, called MAMCABM (MAMCA plus ABM). It consists of two parts that work in synergy. On the one hand, the ABM provides robust data support for the objective criteria evaluation of alternatives in MAMCA. On the other hand, MAMCA involves multiple stakeholder groups in the evaluation which provide the preferences of the subjective criteria evaluation. Furthermore, several types of uncertainties are considered in different steps of the DSS. In the next section, we first review the previous literature. Then, we present our DSS, illustrating the structure and introducing methods used in this system. The MAMCABM then is applied in a didactic case that evaluates road policies surrounding a university campus.

2   Method

2.1   Previous Study of DSS in Mobility and Transportation – The Combination of MCGDM and ABM

Over the past several decades, the mobility and transportation DSS has played an increasingly important role in enhancing the mobility systems in adaptability, effectiveness, resilience, sustainability, etc. [8]. From early transportation planning models to the latest intelligent transport systems, DSS has enabled policymakers to analyze complex transportation data and make informed decisions in real time. Today, DSS is a critical component of mobility management, providing a powerful tool for policymakers, planners, and stakeholders to design, implement, and evaluate mobility solutions [9]. Among them, a combining MCDM and ABM in DSS offers the advantages of incorporating complex decision-making factors and interactions, accounting for decision-maker preferences in dynamic and uncertain environments. However, there is a limited number of studies that extend the MCDM to a group decision making context, i.e., MCGDM [14].

On the other hand, MCGDM has been proven a effective decision-making approach in mobility and transportation sector [22,26,27,35,48]. One of the stakeholder-based MCGDM framework, MAMCA, has successfully supported the decision-making process in mobility and transportation projects in different countries. It emphasizes the importance of stakeholder involvement, where the stakeholders are identified in the early stage of the framework (see Fig. 1). After the stakeholders are identified, it is possible to define different criteria for them based on their priorities. MAMCA allows for a flexible choices of decision-making methods, i.e., for different decision-making context, it is possible to apply different combination of weight elicitation methods and MCDM methods [16,32]. The stakeholders will have their evaluation independently. At the end of the analysis, they will be confronted with the overall preferences evaluated by all stakeholders. Then, they need to discuss and find a compromise solution.

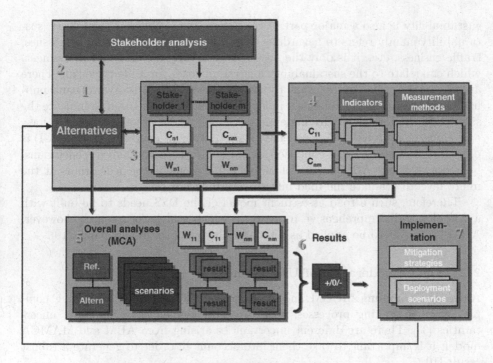

Fig. 1. MAMCA framework [31]

While MAMCA is based on the data input of the stakeholders, there are improvement potentials that ABM can facilitate. ABM defines behavior rules and characteristics at the individual level. Therefore, the heterogeneity can be treated well, which also ensures the validity of the output data. Besides, alternatives can be tested in a costless way in a virtual environment, and each agent in ABM is generating plenty of data every time unit for rich input for MAMCA. In addition, ABM also considers time as a dimension for evaluation. MAMCA only evaluates at the time when data is sampled, while ABM also simulates time-dependent variables in a system. By inputting the data into MAMCA, this method enables assessment of how time-dependent variables in a system influence decisions over time.

A DSS entails a comprehensive model that integrates every group of stakeholders' perspectives into consideration. For road infrastructure engineering, the prerequisite is a proper evaluation of road users' preferences. Research on road assessment has been conducted in various aspects. For road safety and assessment and accident prediction, an important indicator is the crash modification factor (CMF). CMF is a ratio that measures the expected accident after a countermeasure is implemented. The calculation is based on accident prediction models (APMs, [47]). For instance, [40] present a tool as an APM to calculate CMF for highways at a micro level. [1] propose a regression APM at a macro level. Interested readers are referred to [2] and [47] for further information. Besides, sustainability is also a major part of the assessment. While for road users, sustainability mainly refers to hazardous chemicals, noise, fuel consumption issues, traffic easiness, etc., it is only the "use" phase in the sustainability assessment, which can relate to the sustainability analysis of roads for a life cycle [20]. There are also other indicators relevant to the assessment of roads. World bank published the international roughness index (IRI), which can be used to indicate the safety and comfort of the driving experience [36]. There are also models to forecast congestion on roads. For pavements, the pavement condition index (PCI) is used to reflect the general condition. ABM is also used to analyze pedestrians' behavior. [24] use ABM to model individual movements of pedestrians at the micro level to evaluate the road infrastructure design.

Therefore, such a road assessment model of the DSS needs to be built with a complex and comprehensive framework, which still lacks research, however. ABM is also yet to be applied as a tool for the purposes of this paper [19].

2.2   The Consideration of Uncertainty

Although combining MCDM and ABM offers advantages in simulating complex decision-making processes, there are still challenges in handling uncertainties [33]. There are different uncertainties arising from ABM and MAMCA model, it is important to take them into account in order to generate a robust result [10].

Specifically, the accuracy of data used in ABM simulations can be a source of uncertainty, as it relies on assumptions and extrapolations that may not perfectly reflect reality [6,25]. To simulate the features of reality more accurately, input variables such as turning possibility, preferred speed, and vehicle profiles are made stochastic to reflect the random behavior of humans. Additionally, uncertainty is necessary for the ABM to represent long-term changes in a shorter-term simulation. The interactions among agents in ABM generate output data that becomes a suitable input with uncertainty for MAMCA.

On the other hand, the input from the stakeholders during the evaluation in MAMCA can also generate inaccuracies [3]. While objective data is normally used to appraise the performance of alternatives, stakeholders' priorities play a crucial role in determining the importance of different criteria, which make the criteria weights elicited based on subjective information from stakeholders [37]. Furthermore, the criteria weights normally cannot express the exact priority of stakeholders, because of the nature of precision lacking or clarity and may be subject to multiple interpretations [41]. This is particularly the cases where ordinal data is used to elicit criteria weight.

How to take these uncertainties into account when building the DSS by combing ABM and MAMCA is one of the key factor of this study.

2.3   A New Stakeholder-Based DSS Approach

We propose a novel stakeholder-based decision support system called MAMCABM, namely MAMCA plus ABM. It leverages the data support provided by

ABM, incorporates the comprehensive preferences of stakeholders facilitated by MAMCA, and accounts for uncertainties that may arise during various stages of the decision-making process. The process of MAMCABM is illustrated in Fig. 2.

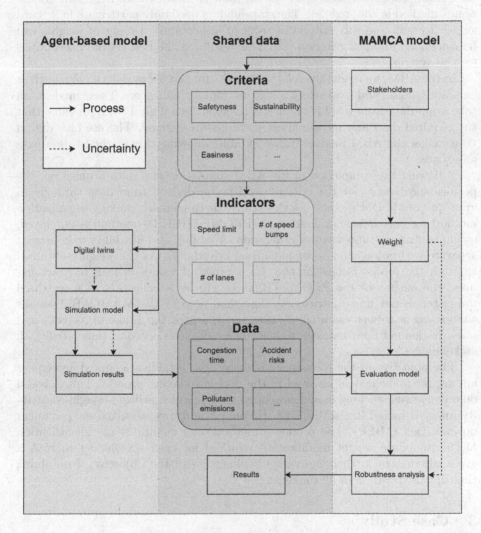

Fig. 2. MAMCABM DSS process

The proposed decision support system, MAMCABM, comprises two evaluation parts, ABM and MAMCA, sharing a common data source. MAMCA commences with problem structuring and alternative definition, which are generalized steps in MCDM and hence not illustrated in Fig. 2. After alternative identification, facilitators of the project must first identify the relevant stakeholders that should be involved in the decision-making process. Subsequently, stakeholders are asked to select the criteria they consider relevant, followed by the structuring of the criteria indicators for alternative evaluation. The next step involves the elicitation of criteria weights by stakeholders. To ease the weight elicitation process for stakeholders with limited MCDM knowledge, the robust Simos method is adopted [38]. The stakeholders need only participate in a "card game" to rank and sort criteria in order of importance, a range of weights can be calculated for each criterion [38]. This results in the first set of uncertainties for the system.

In the ABM, we model the road infrastructure and use various models such as emissions, noise, and road safety to output data for indicators. These models can take input data from real life or, alternatively, from a digital twin, provided that the required data and measurement methods are defined. The use of a digital twin makes the ABM module transplantable, allowing this method to evaluate any roads.

Following the completion of the ABM simulation and data acquisition, the performance scores for the criteria need to be derived from data through an appropriate MCDM method. In this study, the preference ranking organization method for enrichment evaluation II (PROMETHEE II) method is employed, owing to its non-compensatory evaluation capability and flexibility to construct separate evaluation models for individual criteria [7]. As the weights obtained through the robust Simos method are a range of values instead of exact figures, the output of the PROMETHEE II will be a collection of unweighted uni-criterion net flow matrices [5]. The final step of the MAMCABM entails conducting a robustness analysis that incorporates the range of weights and uni-criterion net flow matrices, to identify a consensus outcome that satisfies all stakeholders.

The objective of the robustness analysis is to establish a shared agreement among the stakeholders involved in the decision-making process. This is based on a consensus reaching model developed by [18] which utilize a weight sensitivity analysis model in PRMETHEE II context and inverse mixed-integer linear optimization (MILP). The proposed methodology facilitates the identification of the minimum weight modification required for each stakeholder to rank a given alternative in their individual rankings, with the objective of obtaining the topmost position in all rankings.

3   Case Study

The MAMCABM DSS was tested on an actual roadway that borders the campus of the Flemish Free University of Brussels (Vrije Universiteit Brussel), and is directly linked to a high-capacity boulevard frequented by diverse types of vehicles including private cars, buses, and freight trucks. Furthermore, this road is heavily utilized by pedestrians and cyclists due to its proximity to the university campus. And two research buildings owned by the university are situated on the opposite side of the roadway, which increase the usage of pedestrian crossings. Given these complex conditions and the diverse individuals utilizing the road, it is imperative to improve the situation while taking into consideration the preferences of various stakeholders. Thus, it provides a good testbed to apply the MAMCABM in order to improve the road situations by considering the preferences of different stakeholders while the different factors are taken into account. The tested area of the real-life road and the simulated road is illustrated in Fig. 3.

Fig. 3. Tested area of the road in satellite (Bottom) and the simulated road in ABM (Top)

The primary issue with the tested area is the high volume of vehicular traffic traversing the area at relatively high speeds. Additionally, there exists an insufficient number of signage to alert drivers of the presence of a significant number of pedestrians and bicyclists crossing the road. The aforementioned safety concerns are compounded by other issues such as noise and air pollution. In an effort to address these issues, the installation of speed bumps has been implemented which make cars decelerate in approaching the zebra crossings. It has been further suggested that the installation of radar speed signs to remind drivers to reduce their speed. This study endeavors to evaluate the efficacy of four following potential alternatives for improving the current conditions along this road: (1) SC1, the tested area without speed bumps or radar speed signs, (2) SC2, the tested area with installed speed bumps, (3) SC3, the tested area with installed radar speed signs, and (4) SC4, the tested area with both speed bumps and radar speed signs. The installed speed bumps and radar speed signs affect the driving speed in different ways, as shown in Table 1.

Table 1. Parameter settings

Parameter	SC1	SC2	SC3	SC4
Preferred speed (km/h)	32	32	28	28
Speed bump speed reduction	0	40%	0	40%

Once the alternatives have been defined, the MAMCABM process commences by identifying the stakeholders. We identify four key stakeholders: the local authority (g_1), the drivers (g_2), the cyclists (g_3), and the pedestrians (g_4). The local authority is responsible for implementing the solution, while the drivers, cyclists, and pedestrians are the groups of individuals who frequently utilize the road. Stakeholders may have varying priorities, which lead to different criteria. To create a comprehensive list, we consulted previous literature and sought advice from experts with a formal procedure [15]. The criteria are listed in Table 3. In addition, we also mark the criteria and their indicators that stakeholders selected as relevant to evaluate in the MAMCABM.

Table 2. Data output of ABM

Data and unit	SC1	SC2	SC3	SC4
Average speed of nearby cars of pedestrians (km/h)	7.8395	6.4117	5.7547	5.5129
Average speed of nearby cars of cyclists (km/h)	15.5732	4.6876	3.4196	6.6035
Average speed of cars (km/h)	23.5806	17.0391	19.7261	15.7378
Average times for cars to slow/stop	2.1511	2.5625	2.5000	2.5181
% more time to drive than expected	51.12	112.35	54.22	89.41
Total amount of CO_2 emission (g)	27680.8471	25930.8420	32495.6425	29916.7016
Other exhaust emissions (g)	67468.3103	53164.7391	76045.6679	62274.1123
Total petrol consumed (L)	70.3805	44.6895	53.0422	63.5022
Total diesel consumed (L)	4.1342	4.0831	4.5447	3.7483
Noise (dB)	65.3856	65.6373	65.4314	65.8116

Table 3. Criteria list with attributes

Criteria Group	Criteria	Subcriteria	Description	Indicator	Unit	Promethee II Preference Model	Orientation	Selected by
Environmental	Pollution	Emission of GHGs	Green house gases (GHGs) emissions	Emission of CO2	g	V-shape	Min	91, 92, 93, 94
		Hazardous Exaust Emissions	Emission of NOx, CO, VOC, PM	Emission of NOx, CO, VOC, PM	g	V-shape	Min	91, 92, 93, 94
	Biodiversity	Biodiversity effect	Possible effect to the nearby creatures	/	5-point Likert scale	V-shape	Max	91, 92, 93, 94
Social	Noise	Traffic Noise	Noise level estimation	Road-side noise level	dB	V-shape with indifference	Min	91, 93, 94
	Safety	Ambient Safety of Cyclists	Attributes of the nearby cars of cyclists	Surrounding car time*speed	s*km/h	V-shape	Min	91, 93
		Ambient Safety of Pedestrians	Attributes of the nearby cars of pedestrians	Surrounding car time*speed	s*km/h	V-shape	Min	91, 94
	Easiness of Use	Driving Behaviour	Reactions due to detected pedestrians/cyclists	Times to slow/stop	/	V-shape	Min	91, 92
		Driving Experience	Driving time expectation	Practical time/expected time	%	V-shape	Min	91, 92
Economic	Cost	Building cost	Immediate cost incurred for the countermeasures	Building cost	Euro	V-shape	Min	91
		Maintenance cost	Long-term cost for the countermeasures	Maintenance cost	Euro	V-shape	Min	91
		Fuel consumption	Fuel consumed during the simulation span in Euro	Total fuel consumption	Euro	V-shape	Min	92

The four scenarios are simulated in the ABM. Preliminary data has shown noticeable effects on various stakeholder groups, which is shown in Table 2. In the ABM, drivers actively detect and give way to pedestrians and cyclists. Interesting observations are noted through the interactions among each member of the stakeholder groups. Cyclists have nearby cars driving at a higher average speed than pedestrians because the cycling lane is parallel to one of the driving lanes. The radar speed sign is thus also a more effective measure for cyclists than pedestrians. An unusual rise in *average speed of nearby cars for cyclists* is noticed for SC4 as the strictest scenario. A possible reason is that cars driving slower have smoother experiences while passing a zebra crossing, thus the average speed at the junction is higher. This explanation also applies to the result data of *average times to slow/stop* and *% more driving time than expected*, i.e. the strictest is not necessarily the worst. The data used to calculate the emissions and fuel consumption are simulated according to the data of FEBIAC (Fédèration Belge de l'Automobile & du Cycle) and calculated using the COPERT model. Noise is calculated by CoRTN model [44].

Afterward, a workshop was organized to engage representatives of stakeholders in an interactive decision-making process using MAMCA. The purpose of the event is to gather stakeholder feedback on the selection criteria for evaluating alternatives. After being informed the problem structure, alternatives, and criteria list, the stakeholder representatives first select the criteria they think relative as shown in Table 3. The stakeholders implemented the revised Simos method using a card playing process [11]. They organized the cards sequentially, beginning with the least important criterion and ending with the most important. When certain criteria shared equal importance, they were placed in the same row or stacked. If one criterion was deemed twice as important as another, a white card was placed between them. The stakeholders also determined the z value, which establishes the constant interval between the most and least important criteria. Subsequently, stakeholders were required to assess the alternatives for subjective criteria, such as biodiversity, for which values could not be derived from the ABM. Finally, the performance of the alternatives was aggregated using a weighted sum approach:

$$P(a_m) = \sum_{n=1}^{N} w_n \times p_{m,n}, \tag{1}$$

where the overall performance score of alternative a_m, denoted as $P(a_m)$, is computed by taking the sum of the product of each criterion n's performance for a_m and its corresponding weight w_n which is elicited by revised Simos method. After calculating the alternative performances for all stakeholders, we can obtain an overall view on stakeholders' preferences, which is illustrated in Fig. 4. The colored lines in Fig. 4 represent the alternatives, with individual scores for various stakeholders depicted as markers on these lines. It is evident that stakeholders have differing preferences, making it challenging to reach a consensus based on the original MAMCA approach. Moreover, simply aggregating their scores could lead to compensation issues. Therefore, we address the robustness aspect of the

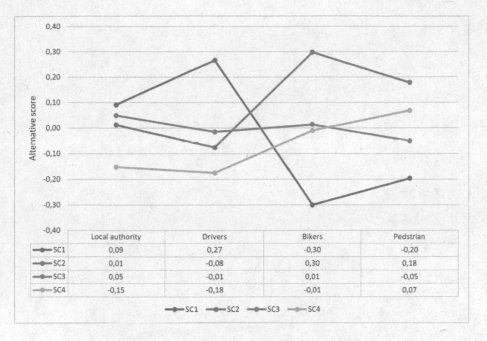

Fig. 4. MAMCA view with the alternative performance data

revised Simos method and employ an inverse optimization approach, as proposed
by Huang et al. [18]. The results from the consensus-reaching model is illustrated
in Fig. 5, which displays the discrete outputs resulting from the optimization
process. In this 2D plot, both ranking distances and weight distances for the
optimized results are represented as $(X, Y) \in \mathbb{R}^2$. Here, X signifies the weight
distance, referring to the minimum total weight modification required for all
stakeholders to rank one alternative at a superior position Y. Meanwhile, Y
represents the ranking distance of a single alternative in relation to the best
possible position and can be denoted as:

$$Y = \sum_{s=1}^{S} y_s = \sum_{s=1}^{S} (p_s - 1), s = 1, 2, \ldots, S, \qquad (2)$$

where p_s represents the current position of the alternative for stakeholder g_s,
in this case $S = 4$. When all stakeholders rank a single alternative as the best
option, $Y = 0$. The outcomes for various alternatives are represented by connected lines. The modified weight are then compared in the robustness analysis
for the revised Simos method to determine whether the weights maintain consistency, as described by [38]. In Fig. 5, inconsistent results are illustrated with
dashed lines.

We can see that no single alternative can be ranked in the best position by
all stakeholders while maintaining the consistency of the robustness analysis in
the Simos method. However, comparing to the traditional MAMCA approach,

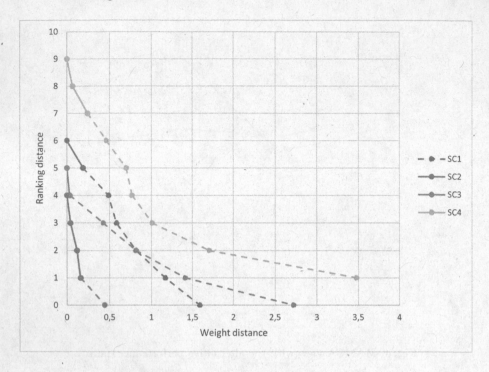

Fig. 5. Consensus reaching model result

the MAMCABM results offer a visually and mathematically driven recommendation for alternative selection, enhancing the decision-making process. Among the alternatives, SC2 demonstrates the most favorable performance. It can be ranked as the top alternative for all stakeholders with minimal weight modification and is only one step away from preserving consistency. The only inconsistency occurs when stakeholder g_2 "Driver" attempts to rank SC2 as the best option. Despite this, SC2 can be considered a compromise solution. Stakeholders may be persuaded to accept SC2 through negotiation or by conducting an iterative evaluation afterward.

4   Conclusion

The combination of MAMCA and ABM, namely MAMCABM DSS provides a promising approach for decision-making in complex systems with uncertain and dynamic environments. The proposed DSS allows for the integration of stakeholder preferences, comprehensive data support and uncertainties to evaluate alternatives. This paper presents a case study regarding the effects of road safety measures on road users using the DSS. Four scenarios are proposed to generate data as the input for the four corresponding alternatives in MAMCA. It turns out that the preferences of different stakeholder groups vary in the tested alternatives, which provides useful managerial implications for decision-makers.

Nevertheless, the benefits of the MAMCABM model are apparent when compared to the conventional MAMCA framework. The MAMCABM model considers various uncertainties at different stages of the evaluation process and tries to identify a consensus solution by implementing a robustness analysis following the application of the optimization model.

There are also a few aspects to be improved in the MAMCABM. First, the data input for the ABM can be extracted from Internet of Things (IoT) devices employed in the tested area. This allows for collecting real-time data in more dimensions, being an essential part of the digital twin. Then for the ABM, more data can be calculated at the individual level to give more insights into the effect than an overall index. For instance, the case study could produce more significant results if the noise and emission were measured per agent rather than in general.

References

1. Ágoston, G., Madlenák, R.: Road safety macro assessment model: case study for Hungary. Period. Polytech. Transp. Eng. **49**(1), 89–92 (2020)
2. Ambros, J., Jurewicz, C., Turner, S., Kieć, M.: An international review of challenges and opportunities in development and use of crash prediction models. Eur. Transp. Res. Rev. **10**(2), 1–10 (2018). https://doi.org/10.1186/s12544-018-0307-7
3. Baudry, G., Macharis, C., Vallée, T.: Range-based multi-actor multi-criteria analysis: a combined method of multi-actor multi-criteria analysis and monte carlo simulation to support participatory decision making under uncertainty. Eur. J. Oper. Res. **264**(1), 257–269 (2018)
4. Bayley, C., French, S.: Designing a participatory process for stakeholder involvement in a societal decision. Group Decis. Negot. **17**(3), 195–210 (2008). https://link.springer.com/article/10.1007/s10726-007-9076-8
5. Behzadian, M., Kazemzadeh, R.B., Albadvi, A., Aghdasi, M.: PROMETHEE: a comprehensive literature review on methodologies and applications. Eur. J. Oper. Res. **200**(1), 198–215 (2010)
6. Bienzeisler, L., Lelke, T., Wage, O., Huck, L.M., Friedrich, B.: Uncertainty and variability analysis of agent-based transport models. Transp. Res. Procedia **62**, 719–726 (2022)
7. Brans, J.P., De Smet, Y.: PROMETHEE methods. Int. Ser. Oper. Res. Manage. Sci. **233**, 187–219 (2016). https://link.springer.com/chapter/10.1007/978-1-4939-3094-4_6
8. Brauer, B., Eisel, M., Kolbe, L.: The state of the art in smart city research - a literature analysis on green IS solutions to foster environmental sustainability. In: PACIS 2015 Proceedings (2015). https://aisel.aisnet.org/pacis2015/74
9. Calderón, F., Miller, E.J.: A literature review of mobility services: definitions, modelling state-of-the-art, and key considerations for a conceptual modelling framework. Transp. Rev. **40**(3), 312–332 (2020). https://www.sciencedirect.com/science/article/pii/S0144164722001003
10. Dewar, J.A., Wachs, M., Corporation, R.: Transportation planning, climate change, and decision making under uncertainty (2008). https://rosap.ntl.bts.gov/view/dot/17367

11. Figueira, J., Roy, B.: Determining the weights of criteria in the electre type methods with a revised Simos' procedure. Eur. J. Oper. Res. **139**(2), 317–326 (2002)
12. Freeman, R.E., Harrison, J.S., Wicks, A.C., Parmar, B., de Colle, S.: Stakeholder theory: the state of the art. In: Stakeholder Theory: The State of the Art, pp. 1–343 (2010). https://www.cambridge.org/core/books/stakeholder-theory/FEA 0B845888E463076284961856724C9
13. Ghadimi, P., Heavey, C.: A review of applications of agent-based modelling and simulation in supplier selection problem. In: Proceedings - 8th EUROSIM Congress on Modelling and Simulation, EUROSIM 2013, pp. 101–107 (2015)
14. Gonzalez-Feliu, J., Pronello, C., Salanova Grau, J.M.: Multi-stakeholder collaboration in urban transport: state-of-the-art and research opportunities. Transport **33**(4), 1079–1094 (2018). https://journals.vilniustech.lt/index.php/Transport/article/view/6810
15. Huang, H., Canoy, R., Brusselaers, N., Te Boveldt, G.: Criteria preprocessing in multi-actor multi-criteria analysis. J. Multi-Criteria Decis. Anal. 1–15 (2023)
16. Huang, H., Lebeau, P., Macharis, C.: The multi-actor multi-criteria analysis (MAMCA): new software and new visualizations. In: Moreno-Jiménez, J.M., Linden, I., Dargam, F., Jayawickrama, U. (eds.) ICDSST 2020. LNBIP, vol. 384, pp. 43–56. Springer, Cham (2020). https://doi.org/10.1007/978-3-030-46224-6_4
17. Huang, H., Mommens, K., Lebeau, P., Macharis, C.: The multi-actor multi-criteria analysis (MAMCA) for mass-participation decision making. In: Jayawickrama, U., Delias, P., Escobar, M.T., Papathanasiou, J. (eds.) ICDSST 2021. LNBIP, vol. 414, pp. 3–17. Springer, Cham (2021). https://doi.org/10.1007/978-3-030-73976-8_1
18. Huang, H., Smet, Y.D., Macharis, C., Doan, N.A.V.: Collaborative decision-making in sustainable mobility: identifying possible consensuses in the multi-actor multi-criteria analysis based on inverse mixed-integer linear optimization. Int. J. Sustain. Dev. World Ecol. **28**(1), 64–74 (2021). https://doi.org/10.1080/13504509.2020.1795005
19. Huang, J., Cui, Y., Zhang, L., Tong, W., Shi, Y., Liu, Z.: An overview of agent-based models for transport simulation and analysis. J. Adv. Transp. **2022** (2022)
20. Inti, S., Tandon, V.: Towards precise sustainable road assessments and agreeable decisions. J. Clean. Prod. **323**, 129167 (2021). https://www.sciencedirect.com/science/article/pii/S0959652621033539
21. Jeon, C.M.: Incorporating uncertainty into transportation decision making: sustainability-oriented approach. Transp. Res. Rec. **2174**, 58–67 (2010)
22. Kannan, G., Murugesan, P., Senthil, P., Haq, A.N.: Multicriteria group decision making for the third party reverse logistics service provider in the supply chain model using fuzzy TOPSIS for transportation services. Int. J. Serv. Technol. Manage. **11**(2), 162–181 (2009)
23. Kedir, N.S., Raoufi, M., Fayek, A.R.: Fuzzy agent-based multicriteria decision-making model for analyzing construction crew performance. J. Manage. Eng. **36**(5), 04020053 (2020)
24. Kerridge, J., Hine, J., Wigan, M.: Agent-based modelling of pedestrian movements: the questions that need to be asked and answered. Environ. Plann. B. Plann. Des. **28**(3), 327–341 (2001)
25. Kieu, L.M., Malleson, N., Heppenstall, A.: Dealing with uncertainty in agent-based models for short-term predictions. Roy. Soc. Open Sci. **7**(1), 191074 (2020). https://royalsocietypublishing.org/doi/10.1098/rsos.191074
26. Kundu, P., Kar, S., Maiti, M.: A fuzzy multi-criteria group decision making based on ranking interval type-2 fuzzy variables and an application to transportation

mode selection problem. Soft Comput. **21**(11), 3051–3062 (2017). https://link.springer.com/article/10.1007/s00500-015-1990-0

27. Liu, S., Song, Z., Zhong, S.: Public transportation hub location with stochastic demand: an improved approach based on multiple attribute group decision-making. Discrete Dyn. Nat. Soc. **2015** (2015)

28. Lyons, G., Davidson, C.: Guidance for transport planning and policymaking in the face of an uncertain future. Transp. Res. Part A: Policy Pract. **88**, 104–116 (2016)

29. Lyons, G., Marsden, G.: Opening out and closing down: the treatment of uncertainty in transport planning's forecasting paradigm. Transportation **48**(2), 595–616 (2021). https://link.springer.com/article/10.1007/s11116-019-10067-x

30. Macharis, C., Bernardini, A.: Reviewing the use of multi-criteria decision analysis for the evaluation of transport projects: time for a multi-actor approach. Transp. Policy **37**, 177–186 (2015)

31. Macharis, C., De Witte, A., Ampe, J.: The multi-actor, multi-criteria analysis methodology (MAMCA) for the evaluation of transport projects: Theory and practice. J. Adv. Transp. **43**(2), 183–202 (2009)

32. Macharis, C., Turcksin, L., Lebeau, K.: Multi actor multi criteria analysis (MAMCA) as a tool to support sustainable decisions: state of use. Decis. Support Syst. **54**(1), 610–620 (2012)

33. Mahmassani, H.S.: Uncertainty in transportation systems evaluation: issues and approaches. **9**(1), 1–12 (2007). https://dx.doi.org/10.1080/03081068408717264, https://www.tandfonline.com/doi/abs/10.1080/03081068408717264

34. Massam, B.H.: Multi-criteria decision making (MCDM) techniques in planning. Progr. Plann. **30**(PART 1), 1–84 (1988)

35. Mousavi, S.M., Antuchevičienė, J., Zavadskas, E.K., Vahdani, B., Hashemi, H.: A new decision model for cross-docking center location in logistics networks under interval-valued intuitionistic fuzzy uncertainty. **34**(1), 30–40 (2019). https://journals.vgtu.lt/index.php/Transport/article/view/7442/6442, https://dspace.vgtu.dev.effective-webwork.de:8080/xmlui/handle/123456789/78294

36. Múčka, P.: International roughness index specifications around the world. Road Mater. Pavement Design **18**(4), 929–965 (2017)

37. Pelissari, R., Oliveira, M.C., Abackerli, A.J., Ben-Amor, S., Assumpção, M.R.P.: Techniques to model uncertain input data of multi-criteria decision-making problems: a literature review. Int. Trans. Oper. Res. **28**(2), 523–559 (2021). https://onlinelibrary.wiley.com/doi/full/10.1111/itor.12598, https://onlinelibrary.wiley.com/doi/abs/10.1111/itor.12598, https://onlinelibrary.wiley.com/doi/10.1111/itor.12598

38. Siskos, E., Tsotsolas, N.: Elicitation of criteria importance weights through the Simos method: a robustness concern. Eur. J. Oper. Res. **246**(2), 543–553 (2015)

39. Šoštarić, M., Vidović, K., Jakovljević, M., Lale, O.: Data-driven methodology for sustainable urban mobility assessment and improvement. Sustainability **13**(13), 7162 (2021). https://www.mdpi.com/2071-1050/13/13/7162/htm, https://www.mdpi.com/2071-1050/13/13/7162

40. Souleyrette, R.R., Tanzen, R., Green, E.R., Staats, W.N., Lause, F.V.I.: Crash modification factor recommendation list. Technical report (2020). https://uknowledge.uky.edu/ktc_researchreports/1703

41. Stewart, T.J.: Dealing with uncertainties in MCDA. Int. Ser. Oper. Res. Manage. Sci. **78**, 445–466 (2005). https://ideas.repec.org/h/spr/isochp/978-0-387-23081-8_11.html

42. Stojčić, M., Zavadskas, E.K., Pamučar, D., Stević, Ž., Mardani, A.: Application of MCDM methods in sustainability engineering: a literature review 2008–2018. Symmetry **11**(3), 350 (2019). https://www.mdpi.com/2073-8994/11/3/350/htm, https://www.mdpi.com/2073-8994/11/3/350

43. Torre-Bastida, A.I., Del Ser, J., Laña, I., Ilardia, M., Bilbao, M.N., Campos-Cordobés, S.: Big Data for transportation and mobility: recent advances, trends and challenges. IET Intell. Transp. Syst. **12**(8), 742–755 (2018). https://onlinelibrary.wiley.com/doi/full/10.1049/iet-its.2018.5188, https://onlinelibrary.wiley.com/doi/abs/10.1049/iet-its.2018.5188, https://ietresearch.onlinelibrary.wiley.com/doi/10.1049/iet-its.2018.5188

44. Department of Transport, U.: Calculation of road traffic noise (1988)

45. Usman, F., Murakami, K., Dwi Wicaksono, A., Setiawan, E.: Application of agent-based model simulation for tsunami evacuation in Pacitan, Indonesia. In: MATEC Web of Conferences, vol. 97, p. 01064 (2017)

46. Yannis, G., Kopsacheili, A., Dragomanovits, A., Petraki, V.: State-of-the-art review on multi-criteria decision-making in the transport sector. J. Traffic Transp. Eng. (Engl. Edn.) **7**(4), 413–431 (2020)

47. Yannis, G., et al.: Road traffic accident prediction modelling: a literature review. Proc. Inst. Civ. Eng. - Transp. **170**(5), 245–254 (2017). https://doi.org/10.1680/jtran.16.00067

48. Żak, J., Fierek, S., Kruszyński, M.: Evaluation of different transportation solutions with the application of macro simulation tools and multiple criteria group decision making/aiding methodology. Procedia - Soc. Behav. Sci. **111**, 340–349 (2014)

BPR Assessment Framework: Staging Business Processes for Redesign Using Cluster Analysis

George Tsakalidis⬥, Nikolaos Nousias⬥, and Kostas Vergidis(✉)⬥

Department of Applied Informatics, University of Macedonia, Thessaloniki, Greece
{g.tsakalidis,nnousias,kvergidis}@uom.edu.gr

Abstract. In response to increasingly competing environments, organizations are examining how their core business processes (BPs) may be redesigned to improve performance and responsiveness. However, there is a lack of approaches for evaluating Business Process Redesign (BPR) at design time and systematically applying BPR in the case of eligible models. The aim of this research is to demonstrate in practice how the BPR Assessment Framework evaluates the redesign capacity of process models prior to implementation. From the two discrete operation modes of the framework, the paper focuses on the Staging Mode that accounts for the classification of sets of organizational processes. The staging is supported with a clearly defined methodology that is based on partitional clustering and is demonstrated by using a process model repository from literature, initially containing 1000 process models. Based on the findings, the models have varying BPR capacity and the results are consistent to the rational claim that a rising structural complexity denotes a low capacity for BPR. The framework proved to be a convenient and straightforward method for classifying the process models of the repository to categories of low, moderate, and high plasticity and external quality. The contribution of the approach lies to the fact that it can be readily used by practitioners in the course of BPR decision making.

Keywords: Business Process Redesign · Business Process Measurement · Cluster Analysis · Business Process Analytics

1 Introduction

The emergence of Business Process Redesign (BPR) stems from the need to be adaptable to the evolving organizational change by applying various techniques and approaches [1], towards modifying the process design depending on the feedback of the process run-time, and/or the performance attributes [2]. The prospect of continuously modifying and improving (i.e. redesigning) the various business operations played a central role in the emergence of business processes (BPs) as a concept and is embodied in most Business Process Management (BPM) lifecycles (e.g. in [3, 4]). As a structural model element, BPR is a first-class citizen in BPM lifecycles, even though it is incorporated into these models in diverse ways.

© The Author(s), under exclusive license to Springer Nature Switzerland AG 2023
S. Liu et al. (Eds.): ICDSST 2023, LNBIP 474, pp. 97–110, 2023.
https://doi.org/10.1007/978-3-031-32534-2_8

Although a detailed analysis of a BP typically sparks assorted ideas and perspectives for redesign, it is usually conducted in a non-systematic way, and is predominantly considered a creative activity [5]. Due to the fact that, in most cases, there are more than one redesign options, these are evaluated against the anticipated benefits and strategic objectives of the organization. The optimal ones are manually selected and further analyzed to identify neglected problems in a procedure that comprises a BPR methodology. To sum up, only a few redesign approaches in literature investigate how the improvement procedure can be methodologically supported, or executed to reduce the uncertainty from the AS-IS to the TO-BE process [6].

What is also overlooked is the evaluation of the BPR impact prior to its implementation since most approaches deal with BPR at runtime. Adesola and Baines [7] propose a Business Process Improvement (BPI) Methodology that bears enhanced feasibility, usability and usefulness, but the evaluation of the redesign criteria is not performed in conjunction with the available redesign method and most importantly it takes place after the execution and analysis of the process. In another approach, Lee [8] introduces BPR as a distinct step of a BP-integrated Information Technology (IT) evaluation methodology. The redesign evaluation incorporates the study of existing BPs and the establishment of redesign objectives to construct the design of new processes. The redesign evaluation step is linked to the performance evaluation that provides feedback and revision-redesign options, which indicates that it is also conducted at runtime. In the majority of existing redesign approaches there is no consideration of the model type, its complexity level, the overall redesign feasibility, or, most importantly, the applicability of particular redesign heuristic(s).

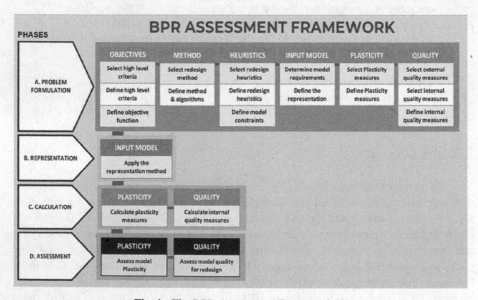

Fig. 1. The BPR Assessment Framework [9]

In previously published work [9] the authors introduced the *BPR Assessment Framework* (Fig. 1), an artefact aiming to evaluate the redesign capacity of process models by assessing their plasticity and external quality, towards facilitating BPR practitioners in decision-making. The main components of the proposed framework are six (Objectives, Method, Heuristics, Input Model, Plasticity and Quality) and are construed in four consecutive phases (Problem Formulation, Representation, Calculation and Assessment).

The aim of this paper is to demonstrate how the *BPR Assessment Framework* is applied in practice and highlight its convenient and straightforward use. The paper presents one of the operation modes of the framework, namely the *Staging Mode*, that accounts for the assessment of sets of organizational BPs. The staging is performed on a BP repository from literature and selected metrics are calculated for a selection of models (Sect. 2). Section 3 presents how input models are categorized to distinct categories of plasticity and external quality through cluster analysis. Section 4 demonstrates the practical evaluation of models in different categories and the paper is finalized with a conclusions section.

2   Operation Modes of the BPR Assessment Framework

The BPR Assessment framework is meant to facilitate process modelers during BPR decision-making. As a tool, it can be operated in two different ways [10]:

– In the case that a set of organizational BPs need to be assessed in terms of BPR capacity, to select the most appropriate candidate process models (*Staging Mode*) (Fig. 2).

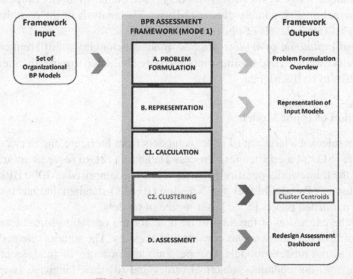

Fig. 2. Staging Operation Mode.

– When a practitioner intends to decide on the application of BPR to a unique process model, based on its redesign capacity (*Measuring Mode*).

Regarding the first *Staging Mode*, the framework is operated for a large set or library of organizational BPs and involves the implementation of a clustering method after the calculation phase to characterize BPs based on their similarity. In this case, the similarity refers to their ability to be redesigned. The method, initially introduced in [11] and further applied in [9], is contributing towards indicating which of the process models should be selected for BPR based on the calculated values of the internal measures. Practitioners may benefit from this method by focusing on the subset of their BPs that are considered best candidates for BPR. The second Measuring Mode requires the previous Staging Mode since the assessment of unique process models is based on measuring the proximity (Euclidean distance) of each model from the previously extracted cluster centroids. Nevertheless, it will not be further examined in this paper. The next subsection presents the adopted methodology in the first framework mode.

2.1 Staging Mode Methodology

The adopted methodology includes the following steps, which are elaborated in the next sections:

1. *Selection of input models:* A set of organizational BPs is selected to be used as framework inputs.
2. *Calculation of internal measures:* The metrics related to plasticity, modifiability and correctness are calculated for each model and the values are aggregated in lists.
3. *Categorization of models through Cluster analysis:* The authors employ a data mining technique for grouping process models based on the similarity of their plasticity and external quality, namely cluster analysis. The analysis of the resulting clusters indicates different levels of plasticity and quality.
4. *Practical evaluation of models:* Process models belonging to different clusters are practically evaluated and business modelers are facilitated towards the identification of the BPs to be redesigned.

2.2 Selection of Input Models

The authors selected a large set of process models from literature, the Service Oriented Architecture (SOA)-based Business Process Database [12], to serve as source of input models for the framework operation. The repository is comprised of 1000 BPs modelled with the Business Process Model and Notation (BPMN) standard and has been used in previously published papers [5, 11] as a source of models.

Before the extraction of the data to be used for the operation of the framework, a pre-processing of the database was considered necessary. The authors selected BPs that: (a) refer to actual process models, (b) are complete in terms of fundamental BPMN elements, (c) do not contain syntactical errors and (d) their language is in English. The methodology adopted for the analysis of the database was also applied in [11] and initially involved opening all 1000 BPMN models using the Camunda Modeler or System Analysis Program (SAP) Signavio Process Manager. Based on the inclusion criteria, many of the models in the repository were excluded. In particular, a large number of BP cases (530) in the database do not represent real process models as they consist initial unfinished conceptual models. Moreover, some of the cases would not open by using the aforementioned modeling tools due to corrupted/non-compatible file (16), while others had obvious syntactical errors (17). Lastly, 3 models were missing and in their place were duplicates of other processes. From the remaining actual cases, 155 of them are not complete, in the sense that they include activity nodes with no descriptive or indicative labels. Regarding the languages of the actual cases in the database, their majority is in English (212), while Spanish, French, German, and Dutch are alternative languages used during the modeling procedure (67 cases). The next pre-processing step involved removing duplicates from the set of 226 cases that included the 212 complete process models in English and 14 more complete cases that were translated into English.

This procedure resulted in eighty-six unique actual BP cases from the initial set of 1000 cases that were further examined and given an appropriate title to convey their context. The final eighty-six unique BPs selected for the demonstration of the Staging Mode of the framework [11, 13] consist of the 8.7% of all processes in the database.

2.3 Calculation of Internal Measures

This step involves the calculation of internal measures - determined in the Problem Formulation phase of the framework - for the eighty-six BP cases. Specifically, the authors selected the Degree of Activity Flexibility (DoAF), Sequentiality (Ξ), Connectivity Level between Activities (CLA), Control Flow Complexity (CFC), Number of Activities (NOA), Number of Sequence Flows between Activities (NSFA), Number of Sequence Flows from Gateways (NSFG), Number of Activities, Joints and Splits (NoAJS), Total Number of Gateways (TNG) and Token Split (TS) internal measures for predicting the plasticity of input models [9, 14] – or else the applicability of the Resequencing (RESEQ) and Parallelism (PAR) heuristics. Similarly, the internal quality measures that predict Modifiability and Correctness are Gateway Mismatch (GM), Gateway Heterogeneity (GH), Average Gateway Degree (AGD), and Maximum Gateway Degree (MGD).

Based on the internal measure values, the models' size varies from 2 to 27 activities and from 0 to 10 gateway nodes. Since process models used in literature are small to moderate in size, the experimental material is considered to have a sufficient variation in size. Their structural complexity also has a sufficient variation since there are models with CFC = 0 to CFC = 16 and they are comprised of 0 to 17 sequence flows from gateways. The values are rounded to three decimal places and their variability was also analyzed by considering the standard deviation (SD) of each metric. The results of DoAF metric showed a SD close to zero (0,165) which indicates that the data points tend to be very close to the mean, which is also considered very low (0,141). This small variability indicates that most of the diagrams have a very low DoAF value ranging between 0,024 and 0,306.

3 Categorization of Models Through Cluster Analysis

Cluster analysis is employed to create model sets of different model plasticity and external quality. These clusters will serve as distinctive categories that characterize the redesign capability of the models they include.

3.1 Cluster Analysis and Parameter Selection

The authors use a partitional clustering method to group the process models in categories called clusters [11], based on the metric values indicating model plasticity and external quality. The selected algorithm is K-means, the most popular partitional centroid-based algorithms for unsupervised learning problems and is found to deliver reliable results [15].

The application of the K-means algorithm requires the definition of several parameters. The first and most important parameter to be established is the number of clusters for the data to be grouped in. Since the number of clusters is meant to partition the process models to categories of model plasticity and quality, essentially representing the number of categories, that number is set to three (Low, Moderate and High). Based on the number of instances in the dataset, more clusters would partition the models into very small groups that would not allow for trustworthy interpretation. Another significant parameter for centroid-based clustering methods is the proximity measure. Towards establishing similarity in a data set, a proximity (or distance) measure needs to be selected and formally defined before clustering. In the clustering process of this research, the selected measure is Euclidean distance [16], which is a very popular method commonly used as the default distance metric for many cluster analysis tools [17]. Lastly, the K-means algorithm requires an initialization method to assign the first three centroid values. Random initialization, during which the initial centroids are randomly placed in the Euclidean space, is chosen, since during the experiments no need for a more sophisticated initialization method was revealed. The cluster analysis was performed separately for plasticity and external quality, by using the IBM SPSS software.

Table 1. Final Cluster Centers & ANOVA Table (Plasticity).

Final Cluster Centers			ANOVA Table					
	Cluster			Cluster		Error		
	1	2	3	Mean Square	df	Mean Square	df	F '	Sig.
Ξ	0,588	0,239	0,377	0,512	2	0,084	83	6,127	0,003
TS	1	3	0	21,891	2	2,609	83	8,390	0,000
NOA	14	20	7	933,845	2	7,282	83	128,248	0,000
NSFA	9	7	3	329,867	2	8,697	83	37,928	0,000
NSFG	4	14	3	367,935	2	6,216	83	59,188	0,000
NOAJS	16	27	8	1431,921	2	9,639	83	148,556	0,000
TNG	2	7	2	88,011	2	2,187	83	40,245	0,000
CLA	2,085	4,213	2,715	12,659	2	4,060	83	3,118	0,049
CFC	3	10	3	177,401	2	6,160	83	28,798	0,000
DOAF	0,108	0,096	0,161	0,031	2	0,027	83	1,156	0,320

3.2 Clustering of Input Models Based on Plasticity

The clustering of the set of eighty-six BPs based on their plasticity revealed three discrete clusters - categories - of models. Convergence achieved due to no change in cluster centers with a maximum absolute coordinate change for any center being zero after 4 iterations. The distribution of the cases to the three formed clusters is the following: cluster 2 contains only 7 cases (8,1%), cluster 1 contains 25 cases (29,1%) and cluster 3 54 cases (62,8%). A next step is a more in-depth analysis of the results and the impact each metric has on the proposed clustering method. Table 1 presents the final cluster centers for each of the selected internal measures and the Analysis of Variance (ANOVA) table, which shows how the sum of squares are distributed according to the source of variation, and hence the mean sum of squares. The F-value in the ANOVA is calculated as the fraction of the variation between sample means to the variation within the samples. As it is evident, the F-values of the DoAF metric are very low (1,156) which entails that this variable contributes the least to the cluster solution. This is also indicated by the large sig. value (0,320), which is not close to the acceptable < 0,05 significance level. On the other hand, NOA and NOAJS are the variables with large F values that provide the greatest separation between the three clusters.

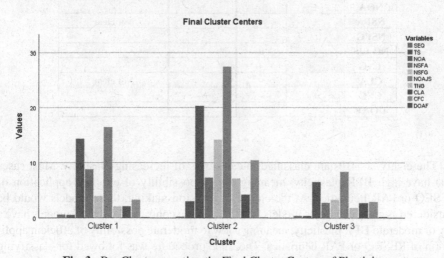

Fig. 3. Bar Chart presenting the Final Cluster Centers of Plasticity.

Figure 3 presents a bar chart showing the three formed clusters. What it is observed is that for almost all measures, cluster 3 refers to low values, cluster 1 to moderate values and cluster 2 to high values. The plasticity of models refers to the applicability of the RESEQ and PAR heuristics and based on the conducted experiments there is a positive or negative correlation according to how each metric evolves between clusters. This correlation indicates that the applicability of RESEQ is more efficient for models with high values of Ξ, NOA, NSFA, CFC and DoAF, and low CLA, while the applicability of PAR is more efficient for low values of TS, NSFG, NOAJS, TNG, CLA and CFC and high NSFA. Since the metrics depicting plasticity are not contradicting in nature – except in the case of CFC - the authors assume that the correlation of the metrics with overall plasticity is the one presented in Table 2. Regarding CFC, a low value denotes a more efficient application of PAR heuristic, while a high value denotes high applicability of RESEQ. By observing how each metric evolves between the three clusters and by considering the correlation of the metrics with the overall plasticity in Table 2, the authors assume that cluster 2 refers to the models with low plasticity, cluster 1 to the ones with moderate plasticity and cluster 3 to the ones with a high plasticity. This cluster sequence is confirmed by the fact that the correlation of all metrics is consistent, except for Ξ, NSFA and CLA metrics.

Table 2. Correlation between Plasticity and the Internal Measures.

Metric	RESEQ	PAR	Overall Plasticity	Cluster Sequence $(2 \rightarrow 1 \rightarrow 3)$
Ξ	+		+	Not clear
TS		-	-	-
NOA	+		+	-
NSFA	+	+	+	Not clear
NSFG		-	-	-
NOAJS		-	-	-
TNG		-	-	-
CLA	-	-	-	Not clear
CFC	+	-	+/-	-
DOAF	+		+	+

The eighty-six BPs are classified to categories of increasing plasticity. Most cases (54) have high BPR plasticity, meaning a high possibility of efficient application of RESEQ or PAR heuristics. At the course of decision making, these models would be considered as good candidate models for BPR. On the contrary, the rest 32 models have a low or moderate BPR plasticity, meaning a low to moderate possibility of efficient application of RESEQ or PAR heuristics. The same procedure was followed for classifying the process models of the repository, based on their external quality.

3.3 Clustering of Input Models Based on External Quality

The clustering of the eighty-six BPs based on their external quality also revealed three discrete model clusters. Convergence achieved due to no change in cluster centers with a maximum absolute coordinate change for any center being zero after only 2 iterations. The distribution of the cases to the three formed clusters is the following: cluster 3 contains 19,8% of the cases, cluster 2 contains the majority of cases (79,1%) and cluster 1 contains only one instance (1,1%).

Table 3. Final Cluster Centers & ANOVA Table (Quality).

| Final Cluster Centers | | | ANOVA Table | | | | | |
| | Cluster | | Cluster | | Error | | | |
	1	2	3	Mean Square	df	Mean Square	df	F	Sig.
AGD	10,000	2,389	3,284	32,750	2	1,543	83	21,230	0,000
MGD	19	2	4	140,427	2	1,673	83	83,932	0,000
GH	0,000	0,180	0,226	0,032	2	0,172	83	0,187	0,830
GM	2	2	7	191,813	2	2,596	83	73,892	0,000

A next step is a more in-depth analysis of the results and the impact each metric has on the proposed clustering method. Table 3 presents the final cluster centers for each of the selected internal measures and the ANOVA table. The F-values in the ANOVA indicate that three out of four metrics contributed to the cluster solution, while GH did not contribute, having an F-value close to zero (0,187) and a very high sig. value (0,830). The biggest contribution to the separation of the clusters was performed by MGD (83,932) and GM (73,892). Their sig. values are under the acceptable $< 0,05$ significance level.

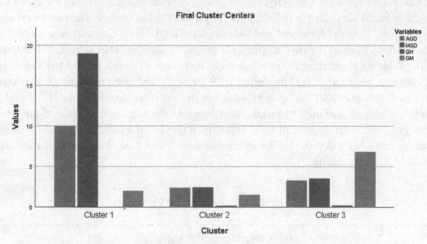

Fig. 4. Bar Chart presenting the Final Cluster Centers of Quality.

Figure 4 presents a bar chart with the three formed clusters. What is observed is that for AGD and MGD, cluster 2 refers to low values, cluster 3 to moderate values and cluster 1 to high values. For the remaining measures GH and GM, their values rise from cluster 1 to cluster 2 and then cluster 3. Nevertheless, GH has proved to have the lowest contribution to the clustering results and GM has the same value for cluster centroids 1 and 2.

As presented in [18] the external quality measures of modifiability and correctness have a negative correlation to all four selected internal measures, namely AGD, MGD, GH and GM. This means that low metric values entail high modifiability and correctness. By observing how each metric evolves between the three clusters in Table 3 and by considering the negative correlation of the metrics with modifiability, correctness and therefore external quality, the authors assume that cluster 1 refers to the models with low quality, cluster 3 to the models with moderate quality and cluster 2 to the models with a high quality. This cluster sequence is consistent to the correlation of AGD and MGD metrics.

In the same sense, the eighty-six BPs are classified to categories of increasing external quality. It is observed that sixty-eight (68) process models are considered to have high external quality for BPR, since they are both easy to modify and have a low probability of containing semantic and syntactical errors. This fact renders them as good candidates for BPR except for 18 models that have a low or moderate external quality.

4 Practical Evaluation of Models

The repository of process models was classified in the previous sections regarding the model plasticity and external quality for BPR. The models were categorized differently in terms of plasticity or quality, nevertheless, both clustering procedures proved to be consistent with each other, leading to similar results. The authors introduced three discrete categories for BPR Capacity, i.e., "Low", "Moderate" and "High" for cases that were categorized accordingly in both plasticity and external quality. The two intermediate categories "Low to Moderate" and "Moderate to High" BPR Capacity account for BP cases that had either of the two scorings for plasticity and the other scoring for external quality (Table 4). Regarding the set of models, forty seven models proved to have a high BPR capacity, ten models had moderate BPR capacity and one model was categorized to have both low plasticity and quality, which is the worst scoring. Models 21, 71 and 80 had a low plasticity and high external quality leading the authors to classify them under the category of moderate overall BPR capacity. Right after, a small presentation of two indicative cases with diverse BPR capacity demonstrates how this categorization may facilitate decision-making.

Table 4. BPR Capacity of the BP Repository.

Final Categories of BPR Capacity													
Low	Low to Moderate	Moderate		Moderate to High				High					
59	22	21	70	7	37	56	86	1	11	19	41	53	69
	78	28	71	10	39	58		2	12	20	45	54	75
	79	34	74	25	40	60		3	13	23	46	57	76
		38	80	29	42	63		4	14	24	47	61	77
		64	82	31	43	67		5	15	26	48	62	81
				33	44	72		6	16	27	49	65	84
				35	51	73		8	17	30	50	66	85
				36	55	83		9	18	32	52	68	
1	3	10		25				47					

4.1 Case Study with Low BPR Capacity

The BP case with a low scoring in both plasticity and external quality is model 59 and serves as a typical example of low BPR capacity from the BP repository. The BP case is numbered 214 in the repository and refers to the "New Employee Procedures" (Fig. 5). A more visible figure is provided in the following URL: t.ly/ug_W.

The process is mostly consisted of parallel activities that are executed by a company's HR, IT, reception, safety team, etc., when a new employee is registered. The process has its activities distributed in different AND branches which entails that most of these activities are bound to implicit constraints as the authors defined them in [19]. In this sense, the model is very constrained for the application of RESEQ heuristic, while the very high degree of parallelism also delimits any further applicability of PAR. In regard to the external quality, the model has very high AGD and MGD values due to the existence of many gateway branches and, thus, sequence flows from or to gateways. This fact denotes that the model has a low modifiability rate and correctness (high probability of errors).

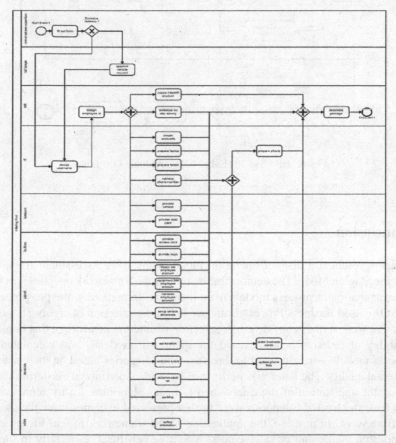

Fig. 5. BP Case 59 (Label 214) - New Employee Procedures.

4.2   Case Study with High BPR Capacity

Many BP cases of the repository had a high scoring in both plasticity and external quality and model numbered 30 is a typical example of high overall BPR capacity. The BP case is labelled 122 and refers to the process of "Account Opening" (Fig. 6). The model is small is size with 9 activities and 4 gateways, all of which are XOR nodes. There is a low control flow complexity (CFC = 2), since only 2 XOR split gateways exist in the model and only 6 sequence flows from gateways. The model is highly structured with a GM equal to zero and more than half of the activities are ordered sequentially ($\Xi = 0,555$), a fact that reduces the possibility of implicitly constrained activities, and conversely increases the applicability of RESEQ or PAR. The external quality of the model is high due to low gateway heterogeneity and mismatch, while the average and maximum gateway degree of the model is also low.

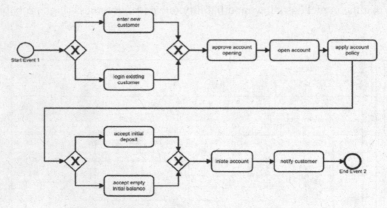

Fig. 6. BP Case 30 (Label 122) - Account Opening.

5   Conclusion

This paper presented a distinct operation mode of the BPR Assessment framework, namely the Staging Mode. The demonstration of how the framework operates was based on the examination of process models from literature. In particular, the pre-processing of the SOA-based Business Process Database led to the selection of eighty-six process models that were further considered. A selection of internal measures - that depict the applicability of redesign heuristics and the quality of models - was calculated, and the process models were clustered to three discrete categories based on their plasticity and external quality. The latter was performed by using a partitional clustering method involving the application of the established k-means algorithm. Lastly representative models from the created categories were further presented to demonstrate the usability of the framework. In practice, the application of the framework to real-life processes from industry, public and private sectors, would be beneficial, especially in the case of updated BP repositories, so that the clustering and selection of the right BP models would be kept up to date with the business evolution. The contribution of the approach lies to the fact that it can be readily used by practitioners in the course of BPR decision making, thus, increasing both the BPR effectiveness and the robustness of the varying methods. As future research to address the limitations of the approach, the authors intend to investigate the applicability of the rest BP behavior heuristics, namely Knockout (KO) and Exception (EXCEP) and incorporate them in the framework. Lastly, further research will be conducted to interrelate other – than modifiability and correctness - external quality measures with the applicability of BPR, such as completeness, consistency and modularity.

References

1. Tsakalidis, G., Vergidis, K.: Towards a comprehensive business process optimization framework. In: Presented at the 19th Conference on Business Informatics (CBI), Thessaloniki, Greece (2017)
2. Mendling, J., Decker, G., Hull, R., Reijers, H.A., Weber, I.: How do machine learning, robotic process automation, and blockchains affect the human factor in business process management? Commun. Assoc. Inf. Syst. **43**, 19 (2018)
3. Mendling, J., et al.: Blockchains for business process management-challenges and opportunities. ACM Trans. Manag. Inf. Syst. (TMIS) **9**, 1–16 (2018)
4. Szelągowski, M.: Evolution of the BPM lifecycle. In: Federated Conference on Computer Science and Information Systems (2018)
5. Tsakalidis, G., Vergidis, K., Kougka, G., Gounaris, A.: Eligibility of BPMN models for business process redesign. Information **10**, 225 (2019). https://doi.org/10.3390/info10070225
6. Zellner, G.: A structured evaluation of business process improvement approaches. Bus. Process Manag. J. (2011)
7. Adesola, S., Baines, T.: Developing and evaluating a methodology for business process improvement. Bus. Process Manag. J. (2005)
8. Lee, I.: Evaluating business process-integrated information technology investment. Bus. Process Manag. J. (2004)
9. Tsakalidis, G., Nousias, N., Madas, M., Vergidis, K.: Systematizing business process redesign initiatives with the BPR: assessment framework. Presented at the 2022 IEEE 24th Conference on Business Informatics (CBI), Amsterdam, The Netherlands 17/06 (2022)
10. Tsakalidis, G.: A framework for systematic evaluation of business process redesign (BPR) initiatives using the notion of model plasticity (2022)
11. Fotoglou, C., Tsakalidis, G., Vergidis, K., Chatzigeorgiou, A.: Complexity clustering of BPMN models: initial experiments with the K-means algorithm. In: Moreno-Jiménez, J.M., Linden, I., Dargam, F., Jayawickrama, U. (eds.) ICDSST 2020. LNBIP, vol. 384, pp. 57–69. Springer, Cham (2020). https://doi.org/10.1007/978-3-030-46224-6_5
12. BPOSCTeam: SOA-Based Business Process DataBase (2017). https://sites.google.com/site/bposcteam2015/ressources
13. Fotoglou, C.: Assessing the complexity of BPMN models for redesign using cluster analysis (2019). http://dspace.lib.uom.gr/handle/2159/24617
14. Kokkinis, V.: Business process model plasticity: inclusion and evaluation of the PAR heuristic (2022). https://dspace.lib.uom.gr/bitstream/2159/27171/1/VasilisKokkinisMsc2022.pdf
15. Jain, A.K.: Data clustering: 50 years beyond K-means. Pattern Recogn. Lett. **31**, 651–666 (2010)
16. Amelio, A., Tagarelli, A.: Data mining: clustering. In: Encyclopedia of Bioinformatics and Computational Biology: ABC of Bioinformatics, p. 437 (2018)

17. Kassambara, A.: Practical guide to cluster analysis in R: Unsupervised machine learning. STHDA (2017)
18. Sánchez-González, L., García, F., Ruiz, F.: BPMIMA: Business Process Model Improvement based on Measurement Activities. University of Castilla-La Mancha, Ciudad Real - Spain (2015)
19. Tsakalidis, G., Vergidis, K., Tambouris, E.: Business process model plasticity: measuring the capacity to redesign prior to implementation. In: 2021 IEEE 23rd Conference on Business Informatics (CBI), pp. 31–41. IEEE (2021)

A Lean Knowledge Management Processes Framework for Improving the Performance of Manufacturing Supply Chain Decisions in an Uncertain World

Jiang Pan[✉] , Shaofeng Liu , Sarah Tuck , and Aira Ong

Plymouth Business School, University of Plymouth, Plymouth, UK
{jiang.pan,shaofeng.liu,s.tuck,aira.ong}@plymouth.ac.uk

Abstract. As a consequence of the COVID-19 pandemic and the ongoing Russian-Ukraine war, global supply chain has been disrupted, causing worldwide shortages and affecting consumer patterns. To combat this circumstance and build more resilient manufacturing supply chains, this paper develops a Lean Knowledge Management Processes framework to improve manufacturing companies' knowledge management performance. Ultimately, it contributes to providing decision makers with sufficient and high-quality information and knowledge to make more accurate decisions in this uncertain world. The framework is empirically tested by partial least squares structural equation modelling approach with survey data using 359 responses from two types of manufacturing industries (i.e., machinery and electronics manufacturing and food and drink industry), two types of business sizes (i.e., SMEs and Large companies), and three countries (i.e., the US, China, and the UK).

Keywords: supply chain uncertainty · lean knowledge management · knowledge flow · decision support system · decision making

1 Introduction

In the past three years, the Brexit, extreme weather conditions, COVID-19 pandemic, Russia-Ukraine war, and energy crises have caused drastic disruption to global supply chains and economy. There is clear evidence of increasing cost of raw materials, and labour and product shortages, reflecting shocks to the supply capacity of businesses and/or the inability to respond as quickly to the changes in demand for goods and services [1]. The mutual interdependence between firms located in different geographical regions requires an uninterrupted supply chain for smooth business operations especially at times of high disruption and uncertainty [2].

Against this backdrop, mitigating supply chain disruptions by improving knowledge management (KM) performance has emerged as critical, and now commands considerable academic attention [3–5]. It has been proved that effective KM practices can help companies to develop new capabilities essential for business model innovations, create flexibility in operations [6], and ultimately build a resilient supply chain model to overcome external shocks and disruptions [7]. In addition, with the help of recent progresses in emerging technologies (e.g., big data, artificial intelligence, cloud computing, and digital twins), the speed of data collection, analysis, sharing and knowledge creation have been significantly increased [8]. To handle and keep up with such rapid and large amounts of knowledge flow generated by supply chain operators and their customers, manufacturing companies need to develop a holistic approach to improving their overall KM performance. Since KM is a multi-dimensional domain. It contains many activities and processes (which are discussed in the literature review), these processes are linked together and could influence each other. Only focusing on improving one aspect of KM may make the effort in vain.

Lean thinking has been successfully implemented in almost all types of manufacturing industries worldwide for more than twenty years. Its purpose is to eliminate wastes (i.e., inefficient activities or processes) in all aspects of a business, such as reducing overproduction and unnecessary inventory, eliminating inappropriate processes and movement, as well as reducing defects and waiting time [9]. It is a comprehensive approach. By clearly outlining all production and logistics operations, companies are able to distinguish all value-adding and non-value-adding processes. Non-value-adding processes should be improved or eliminated so that the overall production process can be improved. Therefore, this paper is concerned with the potential of using lean thinking for improving knowledge management performance in manufacturing supply chains. The focus of the paper is to develop a Lean-Knowledge Management Processes (Lean-KMPs) framework in order to provide decision makers in today's uncertain world with sufficient and quality information/knowledge applied and shared at the right time, in the right place, and at the right cost. This concept echoes the ultimate goal of Lean thinking (i.e., "*right product, right place, right time, right quantity, right quality, and right cost*" [9]).

2 Literature Review

2.1 Knowledge Management and Knowledge Management Processes

Knowledge Management (KM) is understanding the organisation's knowledge flows, and implementing knowledge-related activities such as acquiring, selecting, generating, internalising, and externalising knowledge in order to create value for an organisation. It is concerned with ensuring that the right data, information and knowledge are available in the right form to the right users and processors at the right time for the right cost [10]. The role of effective management of knowledge is evident in producing innovation, reducing lead times, improving quality, and increasing customer satisfaction. KM can improve communications within business partners, and provide more informed knowledge by sharing best practices, lessons learned, and the rationale for strategic decisions [11]. The failure to capture and transfer supply chain knowledge leads to a risk of reinventing the wheel, wasted activity, uncertainty, and impaired supply chain performance. Hence, knowledge management is regarded as an essential cornerstone for a supply chain to develop sustainable competitive advantage in order to remain at the forefront of excellence in a level play-field market [12].

Knowledge Management Processes may also be referred to as the KM lifecycle or knowledge chain. It is a systematic process comprised of multiple phases [10]. Many researchers have developed different sets of phases based on their particular application [10, 13, 14]. Among these diverse KM processes, Holsapple and Singh knowledge chain model is probably one of the most influential knowledge management frameworks [14]. Over the last two decades, many researchers have developed their own KM models by either modifying or adding elements to Holsapple and Singh's model. Hence, it is also adopted in this research for representing the full knowledge management processes. Thus, the knowledge chain model contains five phases: knowledge acquisition, knowledge selection, knowledge generation, knowledge internalisation, and knowledge externalisation. These five phases are not necessarily performed in any strict pattern, but rather there can be various sequences, overlaps, and iterations [10].

Knowledge Acquisition (KA) refers to the way organisations identifying needed knowledge from external environment and transform it into a form that can be used to generate new knowledge.

Knowledge Selection (KS) means that organisations identify needed knowledge within their existing knowledge resources and provide the knowledge in the correct form to an activity that needs it (i.e., to an acquiring, internalising, generating, or externalising activity).

Knowledge Generation (KG) is an activity where organisations create knowledge by discovering it or deriving it from existing knowledge. It reflects the ability of an organisation to create useful and new solutions and ideas for different aspects of the activities within the organisation, such as developing products and services, deriving demand forecasts, making decisions, plans and strategies, recognising or solving problems, inventing managerial practices and technological processes.

Knowledge Internalisation (KI) involves modifying existing knowledge resources by refining or even restructuring them fundamentally. Examples of knowledge internalisation include knowledge sharing, in-house training, populating a data warehouse, posting an idea on an intranet, publishing a policy manual, broadcasting a new regulation, modifying organisational culture or infrastructure, and making experts' knowledge available by developing expert systems.

Knowledge Externalisation (KE) means using existing knowledge to produce organisational output for release into the environment. It transforms raw materials into products and services (i.e., embodiments of knowledge in outward forms) for external consumption [10].

2.2 Lean Thinking and Its Application in KM Processes

The purpose of Lean thinking is to eliminate wastes in all aspects of a business, such as reducing lead time, space, energy, materials, stress and overburden, defects, pollution, and changeover, processing, and work times. Lean thinking is also about value. Every activity or process of business should provide value to their customer. The end-customer should not pay for the cost, time, and quality penalties of wasteful processes [9]. By mapping process throughout the manufacturing and delivery operations, it is possible to sort value adding and non-value-adding activities. Non-value-adding activities are wastes which should be improved or cut out of the process.

[15–17] argued that the concept of Lean thinking (i.e., the removal of waste and pursuit of perfection) can be applied to any system where product flows to meet the demand of the customer, user or consumer. These elements are very similar to information and knowledge management where information flows and work are undertaken to add value to the information and knowledge to meet the demand of the knowledge user. A value flow model as applied to a manufacturing system is presented in Fig. 1 which also depicts the analogous model of value and flow for information and KM systems. This analogous value flow model for knowledge management can be applied to any knowledge processing activity. For example, the processes of explicit data generation for operational decision-making, or the acquisition and management of information records for knowledge repository. In these two examples, there is an intrinsic value in the data itself, and added value is generated by the mechanisms by which the data and information is acquired, organised, selected, generated, exchanged, internalised, and externalised [10]. In addition, these mechanisms and the information itself may generate or contain some type of wastes just as may happen in manufacturing systems [15].

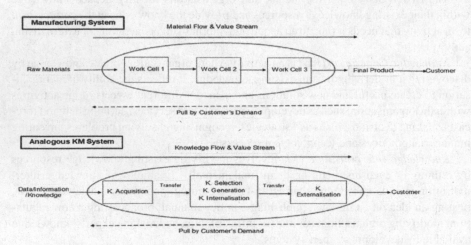

Fig. 1. The value flow model for knowledge management (source: adapted from [15])

2.3 Identifying Lean Wastes and Lean Principles in Knowledge Management Processes

Central to successful Lean implementation is the understanding and characterisation of waste and value from the customer's (or end user's) perspective. [15] defined both *Wastes* and *Value* in the context of Lean KM in order to facilitate their classification. Values of information "*depend upon whether the information supports decisions marking…and also whether it offers current value or potential value in the future*". Waste can be considered as the barriers to prevent information/knowledge flow and reduces information users' ability to access their required information and knowledge. These wastes may include the effort to overcome difficulties in retrieving or accessing critical information and knowledge, or the activities required to validate and correct low-quality information (e.g., to gather required information again and checking) [18].

Based on the above two definitions, [15] and [18] categorised six types of wastes (see Table 1) and five Lean principles with the aim to improve software intensive mechatronics companies' KM performance.

Table 1. Waste Categories in Lean KM

Waste Category	Examples
Over & under stock	• Excessive information • Loss or lack of information • Excessive documentation; unnecessary details
Unnecessary motion & transfer	• Manual intervention due to the lack of integration between systems • Information is handled by several people before arriving at the user, which causes errors, losses, duplication, and redundancy
Waiting	• Waiting for required information and knowledge • Information does not flow (waiting for intervention)
Unnecessary processing	• double handling (inappropriate handling process) • Inaccurate information; necessary corrective actions • Increase in resources to process corrective action
Defect	• Flawed/inaccurate information • Information formats (lack of common/compatible standards) • Information systems (problems in converting information)
Overproduction	• Excessive number of systems • Multiple data sources (several systems with the same information)

Source: Adapted from [18]

The five principles of Lean KM as guidance for conducting KMPs, deeply described by [15], are summarised in the following:

1) *Value:* information and knowledge must supply value to knowledge users.
2) *Value stream:* a series of processes and activities that deliver knowledge must be mapped. This includes processes that support the acquisition, selection, generation, internalisation, and externalisation of information.
3) *Flow:* knowledge should be made to flow efficiently, particularly the most valuable knowledge.
4) *Pull:* knowledge should be delivered as it is requested or needed by knowledge users.
5) *Continuous improvement:* perfection should be pursued by continually removing wastes and regularly reviewing the knowledge management system, that is creating a culture of continuous improvement.

3 Conceptual Framework Development

3.1 Latent Variables Development

After reviewing the previous studies from the Sect. 2.3, the researcher identified four features of wastes that may exist in KMPs of a manufacturing supply chain, which are: 1) excessive information and documentation; 2) failure of information and knowledge demand; 3) inappropriate data and information processing system; and 4) inaccurate data and information. In accordance with these four features, four Lean-KM Wastes have been developed in this research, which includes: 1) *Information Overload*; 2) *Low Quality Information*; 3) *Inappropriate IT System*; 4) *Insufficient Knowledge Inventory*. For the sake of avoiding repetition in the concepts presented in Table 1, there is no correspondence for *Waiting, Transport* and *Motion*, since waste from *Waiting* is related to or caused by the 4 Lean-KM Wastes (i.e., time is wasted in searching, locating, correcting, or re-inventing necessary knowledge). In addition, the concept of improving the effectiveness of knowledge flow (i.e., *Transport & Motion*) is merged with Lean-KM Principles which is discussed later in this section. Moreover, the reason why *Inappropriate IT System* is corresponding to *Inappropriate Processing* is because nowadays most transactional data, technological processes, and documents are managed and processed by IT system. Hence, ill-designed IT system could have a negative impact on the knowledge management performance of a company, which also corresponds to the concepts of *Unnecessary Processing* and *Overproduction* in Table 1. Furthermore, the concept of *Inventory* in the classic seven wastes has been evolved into *Over & Under Stock* presented in Table 1, it is further divided into two categories in this research: *Information Overload* and *Insufficient Knowledge* Inventory, in order to make the concept of Lean-KMPs more concise and precise.

Inspired by concepts from [15] and [19] about the Lean Principles, this research developed two Lean-KM Principles in the context of manufacturing supply chain, as shown in Table 2. It can be noticed that the concepts of *Specifying Value* and *Identifying the Value Stream* have been combined into *Identification & Usage of Valuable Information and Knowledge*. Since the knowledge chain model (i.e., KMPs) is a knowledge value stream, the Lean-KMPs model is built upon it, so there is no need to re-identify the value stream. Moreover, the KMP is a spiral of continuous process, if the Lean-KM Wastes and Lean-KM Principles can be integrated into KMPs, it will become a continuous improvement process. Thus, *Continuous Improvement* is not included in the Lean-KM Principles as well for avoiding repetition. Lastly, *Pull* is also not included in the Lean-KM Principles, because pure pull principle is not feasible in supply chain KM. In supply chain operation, information, and knowledge delivery systems (e.g., MRP and ERP systems) are task oriented. They usually would apply mixed information delivery methods (i.e., push and pull). The whole operation processes, each task in the process, and the necessary knowledge for each task is clearly defined in these systems. With the help of such IT systems, task related information and knowledge can be *"pushed"* automatically to users. Users, however, can also access previous business operation records at their own discretion from the system's database [17]. Therefore, manufacturing practitioners would choose systems which not only allow users to have additional flexibility of pulling content based on their needs, but also push the content to them at a predefined frequency [18].

Table 2. The Five Lean Principles in Manufacturing and Two Lean-KM Principles

Manufacturing Systems	Knowledge Management
Specifying Value	Identification & Usage of Valuable Information and Knowledge
Identifying the Value Stream	
Making Flow	Encouraging Information and Knowledge Flow
Pull	N/A
Continuous Improvement	N/A

3.2 Lean-KMPs Framework

Figure 2 depicts the conceptual research model of Lean-KMPs in this study. This model contains two main hypotheses, which are: H1: Lean-KM Wastes have negative impacts on KMPs, H2: Lean-KM Principles have positive impact on KMPs. Each hypothesis is comprised of several sub-hypotheses which will be discussed in the following in detail.

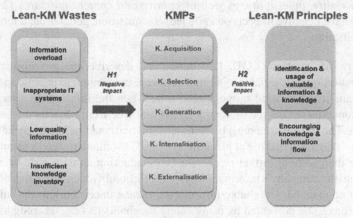

Fig. 2. Lean-KMPs

Information Overload (IO). Too much information can be as much of a burden as too little. Too much information could cause information overload. Because human's information absorbing and processing ability (the quantity of information one can uses for making decision or solving problem within a certain period of time) is limited [20]. Information overload can be defined as a state in which a decision maker faces a set of information (i.e., an information load with informational characteristics such as an amount, a complexity, and a level of redundancy, contradiction and inconsistency) comprising the accumulation of individual informational cues of differing size and complexity that inhibit the decision maker's ability to optimally determine the best possible decision. Information overload affects decision making in two ways: First, the affected decision maker may be unable to locate the most critical information or knowledge due to sheer volume. Second, information overload may cause decision makers to fail to use the relevant information at hand leading to the inefficient use of decision-making time [21].

Inappropriate IT System (IIS). It is impossible to achieve an effective supply chain without support from a well-designed information technology (IT) system. In the past two decades, enterprise resource planning (ERP) systems have become the most important development in enterprises' use of IT systems [22]. ERP's main purpose is to integrate all aspects of a business, such as order processing, production planning, purchasing, manufacturing, sales, distribution, financial management, and customer management, and so on, so as to support the strategy, operations and decision-making functions in a supply chain. The data and information generated from above aspects is stored, processed, and delivered in real-time to the relevant members including suppliers, managers, staff, and customers. Although ERP systems can help information flow seamlessly across diverse business functions, business units and geographic boundaries, however, using a badly developed one may in fact damage all these benefits expected to the organisation [23]. Researchers have identified several key factors that may negatively affect the successful implementation of ERP system, which include *incompatibility, lack of extended enterprise functionality, inflexibility*, as well as *culture and content mismatch* [24]. These factors may have negative impacts on knowledge acquisition, generation, internalisation and externalisation.

Low Quality Information (LQI). [25] define and describe quality information with four information quality variables: in time, accurate, convenient to access, and reliable. In time means it is delivered in the agreed time when the information user wants it. Accuracy concerns the degree of completeness and free from obvious mistakes in the information. The information must be complete and corrected before being entered into the company's decision making or planning system. Convenient to access means the ease of using the data without further processing (e.g., adapting an item code or entering it manually into the company's information system). Reliability means that the information will remain unchanged. Unreliable information means uncertainty to the information user, which has to be prevented by using safety mechanisms (e.g., keeping high safety stock and maintaining excessive production capacity). In this research, the authors will adopt the definition provided by [25] for the waste of low quality information as follows: the negative effects caused or the effort wasted by using low quality information which is inaccurate, not easy to access, unreliable, and untimely. There are two reasons that cause low quality information or information distortion when data and information are shared among supply chain partners. The first reason is the partner's attitudes, such as lack of trust and commitment, opportunistic behaviour, too much enthusiasm, inter alia, that change the content of knowledge by adding or subtracting erroneous information. The second reason is time-related problems which occur due to lack of information sharing technologies, irregularities and late responses [25]. In a supply chain, sharing and using low quality information could cause serious damage to collaboration and knowledge generation processes among supply chain members.

Insufficient Knowledge Inventory (IKI). The waste of insufficient knowledge inventory includes the resources and activities that are necessary to overcome the lack of information or knowledge. It also means the effort to reinvent wheels or re-discovering knowledge all over again, knowledge and experience that the company has already used but simply allowed to disappear. A company should encourage employees to think, create, and use the thought of all employees, not just managers [15]. This type of waste also refers to knowledge users wasting time in waiting for necessary information and knowledge to make critical decisions. Great business opportunities never last long. An opportunity could easily be lost while decision makers wait for information and knowledge. This type of waste could be caused by poorly managed knowledge acquisition, selection, generation and internalisation [15].

Identification and Usage of Valuable Information and Knowledge (IUVI). In the knowledge chain context, the value stream can be considered to represent the series of processes and activities that ultimately result in the presentation of the information to the information consumer [15]. *"The series of processes"* includes the acquisition, selection, generation, internalisation, and externalisation of information (knowledge), which are the processes of a knowledge chain. Hence a knowledge chain can be regarded as a value stream. One of the most important functions of KM is to identify and recognise value-adding processes and knowledge resources in order to make sure that every member in the knowledge chain provide specific knowledge resources which meet the knowledge user's requirements in the right form, at the right time and the right cost [10]. This is consistent with the Lean Principle. Therefore, the information or knowledge provider should facilitate the acquisition, creation, storage, processing, and supplying of information or knowledge that generates value (other knowledge) for supporting organisations to make sound decisions and strategies so as to achieve all their goals and objectives [10].

Encouraging Information & Knowledge Flow (EIKF). The Flow Principle of Lean suggests that the value stream should be made to flow. In the case of supply chain knowledge and information, its aim is to ensure that knowledge flows efficiently and only the most valuable (i.e., relevant, timely and accurate, scarce, and accessible information) knowledge flows [15]. In order to achieve this, there are four elements that have been developed, they are *shared language, expanding the communication channel, trustful environment within organisation,* and *trustful relationship with business partners* [26]. These elements have positive impacts on knowledge acquisition, generation, and internalisation [26, 27].

3.3 Contributions and Managerial Implications

The study contributes to the supply chain knowledge management literature in several ways. First, most Lean-KM related studies were conducted in service and high-tech companies, such as health care, engineering and IT development, since these companies are knowledge-intensive industries comparing to the manufacturing sector and their KM issues usually are spotted relatively early and easily [17]. This research brought the Lean thinking back to its origin place—the manufacturing industries to improve their KM performance. Second, due to lack of common definition of Lean-KM for the manufacturing supply chain context in the extant literature, there are no tailored Lean-KM practices for this context. In order to fill this gap, the author of this research has developed 4 Lean-KM Wastes and 2 Lean-KM principles through rigorous review and analysis of the literature. Third, the literature review highlighted the relative lack of a holistic approach for improving the whole knowledge management processes. Instead, previous research efforts mainly focused on using Lean thinking to improve companies' knowledge sharing or knowledge generation related activities. A holistic approach was adopted in this research where the 5 knowledge management processes (i.e., KA, KS, KG, KI, and KE) were identified. Hence, this approach has the potential to deliver considerably greater benefit for manufacturing supply chain. Lastly, to answer the call from [17] for more rigorous industry specific empirical studies and evidence on Lean-KM, the researcher collected 359 usable quantitative datasets which come from three different countries: China, the US and the UK; two types of manufacturing industries: Machinery and electronics manufacturing, and food and drink industry; two different business sizes: SMEs and large enterprises. In addition, three pairs of multi-group analyses were conducted between countries, industries, and different sized companies to identify the differences when the Lean-KMPs model was applied in these different contexts. This research expanded the application of Lean-KM theory and would have greater implications for manufacturing practitioners to improve the KM performance with their supply chain partners.

4   Methodology for Evaluating the Lean-KMPs Framework

Quantitative methods have been applied to evaluate the Lean-KMPs model. Observed variables derived from latent constructs are explored and selected based on rigorous literature review, in-depth discussions, item review, and pilot study with experts to avoid ambiguity or misunderstandings in the instruments (i.e., questionnaire) and to suggest modifications.

Survey based quantitative data has been obtained from the top, senior and middle managers from SMEs and large manufacturing companies engaged in machinery and electronics manufacturing industry, and food and drink industry in the USA, China and the UK. The hyperlink of the online questionnaires was emailed and texted to potential respondents. To increase response rates, respondents were promised to be offered anonymity and an executive summary of findings. The responses were measured on a 5-points Likert scale that consists of a scaling procedure enabling the respondents to express their views and opinions on a scale ranging from low and negative answers to high and positive ones [28]. By the end of the data collection, 359 usable sample were collected, 182 from China, 139 from the USA, and 38 from the UK.

In the stage of data analysis, SPSS software (version 24) was used to identify outliers to make sure the data were reliable and valid. Subsequently, a partial least squares structural equation modelling (PLS-SEM) approach was employed to examine the relationships between the Lean-KMPs variables using SmartPLS statistical packages (version 3.0), since this software is very strong at analysing multiple relationships simultaneously. It is also very easy to use so that researchers can be more focused on their research without taking too much time on learning the software.

5   Conclusions

As a consequence of the COVID-19 pandemic and the ongoing Russian-Ukraine war, global supply chain has been disrupted, causing worldwide shortages and affecting consumer patterns. To combat this circumstance and build more resilient manufacturing supply chains, this paper presented a Lean-KMPs framework to improve manufacturing companies' knowledge management performance. Ultimately, this contributes to providing decision makers with sufficient and high-quality information and knowledge to make accurate decisions in this uncertain world.

This paper presents two new contributions. First, most Lean-KM related studies were conducted in service and high-tech companies, such as health care, engineering and IT development, since these companies are knowledge-intensive industries comparing to the manufacturing sector and their KM issues usually are spotted relatively early and easily. This research brought the Lean thinking back to its origin place—the manufacturing industries to improve their KM performance. Second, due to lack of common definition of Lean-KM for the manufacturing supply chain context in the extant literature, there are no tailored Lean-KM practices for this context. In order to fill this gap, the author of this research has developed four Lean-KM Wastes and two Lean-KM Principles through rigorous review and analysis of the literature.

The limitation of this research is that the present study employed a post-positivistic approach using quantitative questionnaires as a method of data collection between different contexts (China vs. the USA; SMEs vs. large Business; machinery and electronics manufacturing vs. food and drink industry). However, the post-positivistic approach could neither empirically provide an in-depth explanation on how these five KMPs are enhanced or constrained by the Lean-KM Wastes and Lean-KM Principles, nor uncover the factors leading to differences between different groups. Such in-depth explanations can only be achieved by an interpretive approach. Hence, future studies could adopt a qualitative methodology using in-depth interviews with business managers to increase understanding about how the identified KMPs can be improved by the Lean thinking, and the variations in different contexts.

References

1. Office for National Statistics. https://www.ons.gov.uk/businessindustryandtrade/internationaltrade/articles/earlyinsightsintotheimpactsofthecoronaviruspandemicandeuexitonbusinesssupplychainsintheuk/february2021tofebruary2022. Accessed 03 Jan 2023

2. Irfan, I., Sumal, M.S.U.K., Khurshid, F., Chan, F.T.S.: Toward a resilient supply chain model: critical role of knowledge management and dynamic capabilities. Ind. Manag. Data Syst. **122**(5), 1153–1182 (2022)
3. Schippers, M., Rus, D.: Optimising decision-making processes in times of COVID-19: using reflexivity to counteract information processing failures. Front. Psychol. **12**, 650525 (2021)
4. Yang, J., Xie, H., Yu, G., Liu, M.: Antecedents and consequences of supply chain risk management capabilities: an investigation in the post-coronavirus crisis. Int. J. Prod. Res. **59**(5), 1573–1585 (2021)
5. Wang, Y., Yan., F., Jia, F., Chen, L.: Building supply chain resilience through ambidexterity: an information processing perspective. Int. J. Logist. Res. Appl. Res. Appl. 1–18 (2021)
6. Ramdani, B., Binsaif, A., Boukrami, E.: Business model innovation: a review and research agenda. New Engl. J. Entrep. **22**(2), 89–108 (2019)
7. Umar, M., Wilson, M., Heyl, J.: The structure of knowledge management in inter-organisational exchanges for resilient supply chains. J. Knowl. Manag. **25**(4), 826–846 (2021)
8. Ju, Y., Hou, H., Yang, J.: Integration quality, value co-creation and resilience in logistics service supply chains: moderating role of digital technology. Ind. Manag. Data Syst. **121**(2), 364–380 (2021)
9. Hines, P.: The principles of the lean business system. S A Partners (2010)
10. Holsapple, C.W., Singh, M.: The knowledge chain model—activities for competitiveness. Expert Syst. Appl. **20**, 77–98 (2001)
11. Batista, L., Dora, M., Toth, J., Molnar, A., Malekpoor, H., Kumari, S.: Knowledge management for food supply chain synergies—a maturity level analysis of SME companies. Prod. Plan. Control **30**(10–12), 995–1004 (2019)
12. Dhaigude, A.S., Kapoor, R., Gupta, N., Padhi, S.S.: Linking supply chain integration to supply chain orientation and performance—a knowledge integration perspective from Indian manufacturing industries. J. Knowl. Manag. **25**(9), 2293–2315 (2021)
13. Mahdi, O.R., Nassar, I.A., Almsafir, M.K.: Knowledge management process and sustainable competitive advantage: an empirical examination in private universities. J. Bus. Res. **94**, 320–334 (2019)
14. Liu, S.: Knowledge Management: An Interdisciplinary Approach for Business Decisions. Kogan Page Limited, London (2020)
15. Hicks, B.J.: Lean information management: understanding and eliminating waste. Int. J. Inf. Manag. **27**, 233–249 (2007)
16. Iuga, M.V., Kifor, C.V., Rosca, L.I.: Lean information management: criteria for selecting key performance indicators at shop floor. Acad. J. Manuf. Eng. **13**(2), 72–77 (2015)
17. Redeker, G.A., Kessler, G.Z., Kipper, L.M.: Lean information for lean communication: analysis of concepts, tools, references, and terms. Int. J. Inf. Manag. **47**, 31–43 (2019)
18. Santhiapillai, F.P., Chandima Ratnayake, R.M.: Identifying and defining knowledge-work waste in product development: a case study on lean maturity assessment. IEEE Xplore, pp. 834–838 (2018)
19. Womack, J.P., Jones, D.T.: Lean Thinking: Banish Waste and Create Wealth in Your Corporation. Simon and Schuster, London (1996)
20. Stanton, J.V., Paolo, D.M.: Information overload in the context of apparel: effect on confidence, shopper orientation and leadership. J. Fashion Mark. Manag. **16**(4), 454–476 (2012)
21. Roetzel, P.G.: Information overload in the information age: a review of the literature from business administration, business psychology, and related discipline with a bibliometric approach and framework development. Bus. Res. **12**, 479–522 (2019)
22. Ruivo, P., Oliveria, T., Neto, M.: ERP use and value: Portuguese and Spanish SMEs. Ind. Manag. Data Syst. **112**(7), 1008–1025 (2012)

23. Kulikov, I., Semin, A., Skvortsov, E., Ziablitchaia, N., Skvortsova, E.: Challenges of enterprise resource planning (ERP) implementation in agriculture. Entrep. Sustain. Issues **7**(3), 1847–1857 (2020)
24. Saade, R.G., Nijher, H.: Critical success factors in enterprise resource planning implementation. J. Enterp. Inf. Manag. **29**(1), 72–96 (2016)
25. Forslund, H., Jonsson, P.: The impact of forecast information quality on supply chain performance. Int. J. Oper. Prod. Manag. **27**(1), 90–107 (2007)
26. Wah, N.C., Zawawi, D., Yusof, R.N.R., Sambasivan, M., Karim, J.: The mediating effect of tacit knowledge sharing in predicting innovative behaviour from trust. Int. J. Bus. Soc. **19**(3), 937–954 (2018)
27. Panahifar, F., Byrne, P.J., Salam, M.A., Heavey, C.: Supply chain collaboration and firm's performance: the critical role of information sharing and trust. J. Enterp. Inf. Manag. **31**(3), 358–379 (2018)
28. Hair, J.F., Hult, G.T.M., Ringle, C.M., Sarstedt, M.: A Primer on Partial Least Squares Structural Equation Modelling (PLS-SEM), 3rd edn. SAGE Publication, London (2022)

Integrating Existing Knowledge to Accelerate Buildings Renovation Rates in Europe

Charikleia Karakosta[1]([✉]) [iD], Zoi Mylona[2] [iD], Jason Papathanasiou[3], and John Psarras[1]

[1] Decision Support Systems Laboratory, School of Electrical and Computer Engineering, National Technical University of Athens, 9, Iroon Polytechniou str., 15780 Zografou, Athens, Greece
{chkara,john}@epu.ntua.gr
[2] HOLISTIC IKE, 507, Mesogion Av.Ag. Paraskevi, 15343 Athens, Greece
zmylona@holisticsa.gr
[3] Department of Business Administration, University of Macedonia, 156, Egnatia Street, 54636 Thessaloniki, Greece
jasonp@uom.edu.gr

Abstract. Nowadays, boosting the implementation of energy efficiency measures in buildings and subsequently, mainstreaming energy efficiency financing is of paramount importance for the European Union towards achieving its goal of carbon-neutrality by 2050. Unfortunately, statistics have shown that a lot of effort is needed to achieve the Europe's targets, since energy efficiency is not yet considered as an attractive investment by the financial sector. The lack of expertise and knowledge, as well as the different perspective of project developers and financing institutions are some indicative challenges that have to be overcome. Specific to energy efficiency in buildings this is reflected by the current insufficient trends observed in the renovation rates of buildings, which reveal the urgent need for action since this is the largest consumer of energy in Europe. Furthermore, a combination of public and private funding through innovative financing instruments is required to overcome current barriers that prevent mobilization of necessary investments. The aim of this paper is to set up a role-based methodological approach for the deployment of an integrated matchmaking mechanism on an ICT platform to boost energy efficiency investments in an easy-access and trust-worthy way. The methodology envisages to follow a multidisciplinary perspective which takes into account the interactions between various key factors, such as stakeholders and barriers, so as to facilitate the complex set of decision-making actions for building renovation. The core of concept centres around the definition of the roles of the potential users of a big data for buildings platform, their interdependency and requirements with the ultimate purpose of accelerating renovation rates.

Keywords: Decision Support · Energy Efficiency · Sustainable Finance · Private Finance · Big Data Platform · Building Sector

1 Introduction

A better performing and smarter building stock is considered the foundation stone of the European Union's (EU) energy strategy towards decarbonisation. Indeed, energy

S. Liu et al. (Eds.): ICDSST 2023, LNBIP 474, pp. 124–136, 2023.
https://doi.org/10.1007/978-3-031-32534-2_10

Efficiency investments in buildings have a direct effect on reducing energy consumption towards achieving the EU energy and climate objectives for 2030 and 2050, while also driving economic growth [1].

In order to achieve efficient energy use, updates in industry processes, building stock and other sectors are needed, and, thus, capital should be oriented to energy efficiency investments. With regards to the building sector, it uses 23% of the global primary energy and approximately 30% of global electricity [2]. Most of those existing buildings are not energy efficient. Many rely on fossil fuels for heating and cooling and use old technologies and wasteful appliances. Energy poverty remains a major challenge for millions of Europeans. More specifically, in Europe, the percentage of energy consumption by the building sector is 40%, while buildings are responsible for 36% of its greenhouse gas emissions from energy [3].

The Covid-19 crisis has also brought into sharper focus our buildings, their importance for our lives and their fragilities. As Europe seeks to overcome the Covid-19 crisis, renovation offers a unique opportunity to rethink, redesign and modernise our buildings to make them fit for a greener and digital society and sustain economic recovery [4]. Since today's renovation rate of around 1% of buildings per year, a timely transition of the EU building sector towards climate-neutral levels by 2050 cannot be ensured [3].

The building sector is expected to undergo a substantial transformation over the next few decades to meet the goals set out by the European Union in relation to the transition towards a clean energy economy [5]. It is estimated that the majority of buildings in which EU citizens currently live, work and use for recreational, educational or other purposes are in need of an energy efficiency upgrade. Energy renovations —which entail various intervention measures on the envelope of a building and its technical systems resulting into significant energy efficiency improvements— are an important pillar for achieving the EU energy efficiency target for 2030 and the transition towards climate-neutral Europe by 2050 [6]. Despite this, actual energy renovations taking place today neither meet the rate, scale nor the depth aligned with their energy efficiency potential [7].

In this respect, nowadays, more than ever, boosting the implementation of energy efficiency measures in buildings and subsequently, mainstreaming energy efficiency financing is of paramount importance [8, 9]. Unfortunately, statistics have shown that a lot of effort is needed to achieve the European Union targets. Investments should be realized, and energy efficiency measures are considered necessary to update building stock and manufacturing processes. New elements should include the reinforcement of existing financial instruments, establishment of new financial models or supporting mechanisms and a more active participation of financial institutions [10].

Energy Efficiency is not yet considered as an attractive investment by the financial sector [11]. The lack of expertise and knowledge, as well as the different perspective of project developers and financing institutions are some indicative challenges that have to be overcome, already from the first stages of investments generation and conceptualisation [12]. There is a significant lack of information which include also gaps created by asymmetric information that are not well monitored or documented. The energy efficiency in general is difficult to be observed commonly, given also its multi-disciplinary nature, thus requires standardisation approaches. Consequently, this further intensifies the lack of information. Stakeholders advocates energy efficiency in a different way (i.e., project developers concern more about initial investment cost while engineers look for annual savings) [13].

In order to fill this gap, stakeholder engagement is considered important to get an alternative perspective, and perhaps shift the focus from related activities to intended results. The purpose of this paper is two-fold: (i) to analyse and understand the market needs towards the increase of the energy efficiency investments and (ii) to leverage this analysis and translate into a user-friendly ICT-enabled marketplace for the key players of these investments. To this end, the multidisciplinary problem of understanding and bringing together the key players of the energy efficiency investments will be taken into account and key barriers and bottlenecks could be faced or eliminated in the most optimised way. The core of concept centres around the definition of the roles, their relationships and requirements of the potential users of a big data for buildings platform offering aggregated energy efficiency projects and packaged solutions with the ultimate purpose of accelerating renovation rates.

2   Effective Engagement of Key Actors

The first principal when think to develop a holistic methodological approach to build packaged energy efficiency solutions is to effectively engage key actors. According to literature, to identify the current situation and main barriers for the building sector's energy efficiency increase and promotion of related investments, relevant targeted stakeholders should be engaged [14]. Experts' and energy efficiency stakeholders' opinion becomes crucial for addressing the issues and finding the best practices in the energy efficiency sector. Stakeholder engagement is considered important, since involvement of key stakeholders is very useful to get an alternative perspective, and perhaps shift the focus from related activities to intended results at an early stage [15]. Stakeholders have experience, advice, information and valuable insights to be considered. Addressing their concerns early in the process can lead to obstacles avoidance and same valuable time and money.

In this approach is envisaged that the required knowledge for the development of an ICT platform is provided by several stakeholder groups that are active along the entire energy efficiency investment value chain (Fig. 1). It is vital for the whole process to effectively engage key actors; thus, a participatory approach should take place with the utilisation of various actions, from training workshops and events to bilateral consultations and dedicated surveys [16].

To ensure the effectiveness of energy financing in the building sector, it is important not only to identify all the relevant target groups, but also to understand what type of effort and messages should be used for reaching each one of them [17]. In that regard, on the one hand key actors should be identified, while on the other well-defined consultation activities should be proposed, including specific and concrete actions, in order to ensure the active participation of the identified stakeholders [18]. The scope is to identify all the relevant groups, organisations and experts of the building sector's energy efficiency financing value chain and compile a list in view of a balanced professional, institutional and geographic representation of stakeholders (Fig. 1).

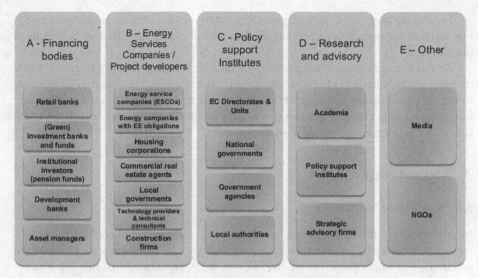

Fig. 1. Stakeholder Groups in Energy Efficiency Financing

The involvement of key stakeholders is very useful to get an alternative perspective, which often stimulates a shift of the focus from an activity to intended outcomes in the early stage and to clearly communicate main ideas about the project in terms of objectives, milestones and outputs. However, the involvement of stakeholders with different, and sometimes opposite, views, backgrounds, aims and expectations might increase confusion. Furthermore, dealing with a large number of stakeholders might be an overwhelming exercise and an extra challenge.

Smart energy services are gradually developing beyond the margins of energy savings, and they are growingly aiming at taking advantage of additional revenue streams and satisfying a range of different consumer needs (e.g., indoor quality, security, etc.). However, high upfront costs of project evaluation and risk assessment lowers the ability of institutional investors and private ones to invest in energy efficiency projects. Projects, therefore, must be developed in a manner, which allows them to be aggregated, traded in bundles and create a platform where projects can easily be bundled, assessed and where a matchmaking process is provided to accelerate deal flow.

Of course, not all stakeholder groups are equal, and some are more important when focusing on solving the problem of promoting energy efficiency financing in building sector than others. Financing bodies and companies/project developers are the major recipient of all actions and can therefore be marked as key beneficiaries. Additional target groups which enable the development, implementation, testing and exploitation of the ICT platform are policy makers and policy support institutes, researchers, and academics in business and techno economic fields, and other groups.

From a different angle this very purpose may be considered as an effort of bringing together energy services and sustainable finance within an efficient ICT-enabled marketplace.

To this end, a role-based methodology should be followed in order to ensure transparency, independency and clarity about each role scope and potential. The dynamic nature of a role also provides flexibility in the very unstable field of energy efficiency investments while ensuring autonomy and easy access to information and data to each role to act independently and achieve its purpose.

3 Methodology

3.1 Role-Based Methodology

More particularly, this study focuses on building up a role-based methodology for designing an ICT-enabled platform that aggregates energy efficiency projects to packaged solutions, it is important to define the roles of the potential users of this big data for buildings platform (Fig. 2). Relationships and requirements of potential users should also be defined. The methodology identifies as the "commodity" to be traded in this big data platform are the energy savings cash flows stemming from the energy efficiency projects, while the following key categories of market actors are identified:

- Supply side: Actors interested to develop energy efficiency projects for which they seek (additional) funds, hence "supplying" energy savings i.e., the "commodity". The supply side should be able to supply energy savings by developing project pipelines that appear attractive for the financing partners to invest. These can be public or private parties with different projects and different financing access and credibility profiles (public authorities, private asset managers, private owners, social housing administrators, communities/cooperatives, etc.).
- Demand side: Actors interested to invest in sustainable projects for which they offer funds, hence "demanding" cash flows derived from energy savings i.e., the "commodity". The demand side adopts a standardized approach on how potential projects are assessed in terms of their expected return and associated risks. They may comprise energy companies with EEOs, financing partners and even public or private funds.
- The intermediaries/service providers – comprise several other actors including e.g., the aggregator, the technical consultant/validator, the ESCO, the data services provider (big data platform provider).

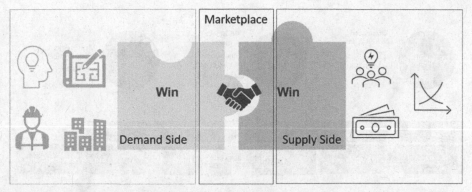

Fig. 2. Role-based Methodology to Unlock the Potential of Big Data in Buildings and Energy Efficiency Projects under an ICT Platform

In order to facilitate the deployment and implementation of an ICT solution to act as a facilitator, key stakeholders of both "demand" and "supply" side actors should play important role (Fig. 2). In fact, the ICT-platform in order to work as a marketplace and act as the facilitator of these two sides, it has to be built up in such a way for the "commodity" which is the energy efficiency project to be traded in the market by the "demand" and "supply" side actors, the project managers and financiers respectively.

Co-creation of the platform should be based on and mirror with the needs and demands evaluation of "demand" and "supply" side in order all discrete options and diversity to be present in the marketplace for an efficient and trust-worthy aggregation and match-making process.

3.2   Integrated Solution for Matchmaking of the Interested Parties

An integrated solution for matchmaking of the interested parties is proposed to be deployed on an ICT Platform to boost energy efficient investments in an easy-access and trust-worthy way. In particular, the matchmaking mechanism acting as a facilitator on making the energy efficiency in buildings a marketplace, considers the market needs and key actors' requirements, creating an environment that market actors can interact by closing deals in a comfortable, predictable, and risk-free environment. The proposed methodology is based on three (3) major platform stages Fetch-Process-Deliver (Fig. 3).

On the Fetch stage, all important information on building renovation projects will be gathered in a structured way, while the Process stage as the core of the marketplace, will proceed with the matchmaking and aggregation process. In other words, all the packaging of building renovations for appropriate financing is taking place here, taking also into account opportunities for capturing revenue streams beyond energy savings. Finally, the Deliver stage enhances the flow of real, project-based monitored information on energy efficiency projects and energy savings results. This information is used to deliver appropriate feedback that act as an input information in the Fetch stage.

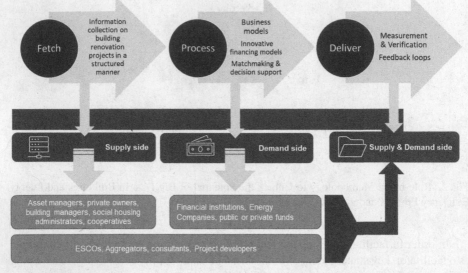

Fig. 3. Flow Chart for Matchmaking and Aggregating Energy Efficiency Projects

As already mentioned, stakeholder engagement is considered important to get an alternative perspective. All key stakeholders in the building sector that participate in the entire energy efficiency investments' value chain, are the ones that provide the required knowledge, information and key insights for the development and validation of the ICT platform. They also expect to receive specific contribution for the energy efficiency marketplace established (Table 1).

Table 1. Platform's Input and Output to Each Stakeholder Group

Stakeholder	Side	Input	Output
Financing bodies	Demand	✓ Building renovation projects analysis ✓ Market regulations ✓ Financing schemes ✓ Standardisation procedures ✓ Energy efficiency policy impact ✓ Market indicators	✓ Standardisation procedures on energy efficiency investments ✓ Trustworthy energy efficiency portfolios ✓ Reduction of implementation risks ✓ Credibility profiles

(continued)

Table 1. (*continued*)

Stakeholder	Side	Input	Output
ESCOs	Supply/Demand	✓ Monitoring and M&V procedures ✓ Contracting and management indicators ✓ Marker indicators ✓ Aggregation mechanisms ✓ IoT-enabled energy services information ✓ Energy services solutions ✓ Energy efficiency measured impact	✓ Appealing energy efficiency projects portfolio preparation ✓ Increased the probability of financing energy efficiency projects ✓ M&V data access ✓ Energy services validation ✓ Credibility profiles ✓ Standardisation procedures on energy efficiency investments ✓ Trustworthy energy efficiency portfolios ✓ Reduction of implementation risks
Project developers	Supply/Demand	✓ KPIs establishment and assessment ✓ Benchmarking of assets ✓ Techno-economic assessment ✓ Market indicators ✓ Energy efficiency measured impact	✓ Appealing energy efficiency projects portfolio preparation ✓ Increased the probability of financing energy efficiency projects ✓ M&V data access ✓ Energy services validation ✓ Credibility profiles ✓ Standardisation procedures on energy efficiency investments ✓ Trustworthy energy efficiency portfolios ✓ Reduction of implementation risks
Building Owners/Users	Supply	✓ Building monitoring data ✓ Energy savings monitoring ✓ Market needs assessment	✓ Appealing energy efficiency projects portfolios ✓ M&V data access ✓ Increased the probability of financing energy efficiency projects ✓ Trustworthy energy efficiency portfolios ✓ Energy services validation ✓ Credibility profiles ✓ Energy demand reduction

The two sides of stakeholders' position in the methodology are showcased in Fig. 3 and they have been strategically selected for a practice-proven support and active engagement for the validation of trustworthy opportunities ready for uptake. Their active participation includes relevant indicators and cost-optimal aggregates that are derived in the form of optimised large, standardised, financeable project packages of energy efficiency measures. In that way, further customisation and readjustment of prototype inputs and outputs are enabled.

3.3   User Requirements of the ICT-Enabled Platform

In order to depict the full canvas of the market needs and to provide the necessary framework for key actors this section provides the user requirements per stage of the ICT-enabled platform (Fig. 4).

At the 1st stage Fetch the aim is to collect information on building renovation projects in a structured manner ensuring that key information related to the technical, commercial and risk-related aspects are properly declared by each project at the state of entering into the platform. There are various building uses by various types of ownership and administration models, so through a standardised online form buildings projects are classified by their typology and other similarities or energy and environmental KPIs (Key Performance Indicators). Building typologies classify buildings into distinct categories in accordance to their physical characteristics, functional use and historical context and are based on several criteria such as a) ownership and use information (occupancy, location, functional use etc.), b) technical data (floor area, energy consuming equipment, benchmarks, level of automation, construction method, year of construction/renovation), c) renovation measures (envelop, equipment, automation).

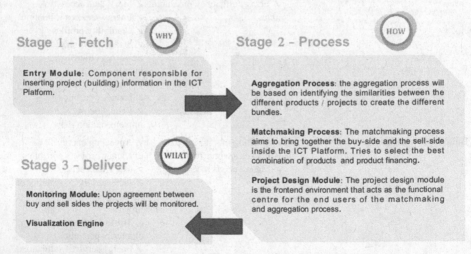

Fig. 4. User Requirements and Key Modules of the ICT-enabled Platform

On the Process stage, the focus is on packaging of building renovations for appropriate financing taking also into account opportunities for capturing revenue streams beyond energy savings. Data collected through the previous Fetch stage are fed into analytics services (Machine Learning, Artificial Intelligence, digital twins, etc.) for the aggregation process and use visualisation tools for the purposes of proposing optimal solution packages that serve both demand and supply side needs and preferences (matchmaking process).

Finally, the Deliver stage enhances the flow of "real" information on energy efficiency and energy services results and use it for delivering appropriate feedback. The more the databases are populated by data deriving from real-life renovation projects, the more its analytical functions become more robust and fine-tuned. Information requirements here are energy, productivity and financial data deriving from the implemented projects.

Therefore, and after analysing the key players needs for an energy efficiency projects marketplace, the user requirements that is being taken into account for the development of and effective and reliable ICT-enabled platform are as follows:

- Comprehensive access to information: the marketplace should provide access to detailed information about energy efficiency projects, including technical specifications, costs, and estimated energy savings.
- Matchmaking capabilities: the marketplace should have a matching algorithm that connects supply and demand side effectively, i.e. the right energy efficiency projects to the most appropriate and sustainable financing instruments and bodies based on their needs and preferences and other investment criteria.
- Ease of use: the marketplace should be user friendly and easy to navigate, with clear interactive interface.
- Transparency: the marketplace should be transparent about critical information, such as costs, funding instruments etc. using trustworthy ranking techniques and other relevant information in order to enable informative decision support.
- Trustworthiness: the marketplace should be trustworthy and credible to ensure quality and minimize risks.
- Feedback mechanism: the marketplace should have a feedback mechanism to allow users monitor, review and rate the implementation of the proposed solutions so as to benefit other users from their experience and to provide a continuous integration of data flow back in the methodology which eventually increases the marketplace's reliability.
- Integration with other platforms: the marketplace should be able to integrate with other energy efficiency platforms (energy management systems, energy auditing systems etc.) to provide functionalities for a more integrated experience.
- Security: the marketplace should ensure robust security to protect data (buildings and financial once) from fraud and other ethical issues.

It should be highlighted that the proposed work is part of the European project ENERGATE funded by the LIFE – Programme for Environment and Climate Action (GA No. 101076349) with full title is "Energy Efficiency Aggregation Platform for Sustainable Investments" initiated in January 2023 and scheduled for completion in June 2025. ENERGATE aims to present a robust decision-making process leading to the creation of an effective energy efficiency marketplace, bringing together energy services and sustainable finance techniques to accelerate the renovation rate of buildings by increasing the chances for projects to be financed. Thus, it is envisaged that the methodology introduced in this study is co-created, materialised, tested and validated through pilot applications and participatory approach of stakeholders within the frame of the particular European project aiming not only to the marketplace launch but the publication of key insights and best practices as well.

4 Conclusions

Nowadays, energy efficiency is considered one of the most important instruments towards achieving Europe's environmental targets, while preserving the business as usual in most economic sectors.

Energy efficiency projects represent an attractive investment opportunity; however, many technical obstacles and controversial perspectives and needs should be overcome.

The present study proposes a methodology to increase transparency and efficiency of decision-making processing towards the promotion of energy efficiency investments in buildings and thus increase the renovation rates. With the ultimate purpose to be the acceleration of building renovation rates by effective financing, the energy efficiency ICT-enabled platform proposed brings together energy services and sustainable finance, increasing the chances for energy efficiency projects for buildings to be financed, since it supports the development, implementation, monitoring and enforcement for increased energy efficiency. ICT-enabled solution relies greatly on its target groups and brings to the table the co-creation of a marketplace which leads to a win-win situation for the key players of energy efficiency investments in buildings. The presented role-based methodology analyses the market needs, the user requirements and the solution potential for each key stakeholder customizing the contribution in a view of the target groups' needs. The user requirements of the energy efficiency marketplace are based on the market needs and key stakeholders' preferences and include user friendly access, comprehensive project information, effective matchmaking algorithms, trustworthiness and security and feedback and monitoring mechanisms.

To this end, the single-entry ICT solution that is proposed may contribute to the specific needs of each target group as follows:

Companies and project developers:

- Increase the probability of financing their EE projects.
- Assist them in the process design, by the replicability of project ideas and the information contained in the building typology.

Banks and Financing Institutes:

- Reach ready-made, de-risked projects and build portfolios.
- Structuring and financial closure of demonstrated financeable packages.

Policy makers and local authorities

- Synthetic set of targeted recommendations on policy framework, market architecture and risk mitigation strategies in the country context.

Research and advisory

- Create energy efficiency building renovation financing typologies, case studies and pilots, supporting the research and literature in energy efficiency in buildings.

Other

- Create awareness, communication and marketing to create and support the demand for energy efficiency investments.

References

1. Chen, Z., Freihaut, J., Lin, B., Wang, C.D.: Inverse energy model development via high-dimensional data analysis and sub-metering priority in building data monitoring. Energy Build. **172**, 116–124 (2018). ISSN 0378-7788, https://doi.org/10.1016/j.enbuild.2018.04.061
2. Lin, B., Chen, Z.: Net zero energy building evaluation, validation and reflection – a successful project application. Energy Build. **261**, 111946 (2022). ISSN 0378-7788, https://doi.org/10.1016/j.enbuild.2022.111946
3. EU - European Union: EU Energy in Figures: Statistical Pocketbook 2022. Directorate-General for Energy, Publications Office of the European Union (2022). https://data.europa.eu/doi/10.2833/334050
4. Karakosta, C., Mylona, Z., Karásek, J., Papapostolou, A., Geiseler, E.: Tackling COVID-19 crisis through energy efficiency investments: decision support tools for economic recovery. Energy Strateg. Rev. **38**, 100764 (2021). ISSN 2211-467X, https://doi.org/10.1016/j.esr.2021.100764
5. Geske, J.: The value of energy efficiency in residential buildings – a matter of heterogeneity?!. Energy Econ. **113**, 106173 (2022). ISSN 0140-9883. https://doi.org/10.1016/j.eneco.2022.106173
6. Yen, Z.: Group, Long Finance, WWF: Financing the transition: Sustainable infrastructure in cities (2015). Accessed 04 Jan 2023. http://www.longfinance.net/lf-research/80-uncategorised/915-financing-the-transition-sustainable-infrastructure-in-cities.html
7. Agrawal, R., De Tommasi, L., Lyons, P., et al.: Challenges and opportunities for improving energy efficiency in SMEs: learnings from seven European projects. Energy Effic. **16**, 17 (2023). https://doi.org/10.1007/s12053-023-10090-z
8. Loureiro, T., Gil, M., Desmaris, R., Andaloro, A., Karakosta, C., Plesser, S.: De-risking energy efficiency investments through innovation. Proceedings **65**(1), 3 (2020). https://doi.org/10.3390/proceedings2020065003
9. Triple-A: Enhancing at an Early Stage the Investment Value Chain of Energy Efficiency Projects. European Union Horizon 2020 Research and Innovation Programme, Grant Agreement No 846569 (2022). https://www.aaa-h2020.eu/
10. Karakosta, C., Papapostolou, A., Vasileiou, G., Psarras, J.: 3 - Financial schemes for energy efficiency projects: lessons learnt from in-country demonstrations. In: David, B.-D., Rosales-Asensio, E. (eds.), Energy Services and Management, Energy Services Fundamentals and Financing, pp. 55–78. Academic Press (2021). ISBN 9780128205921, https://doi.org/10.1016/B978-0-12-820592-1.00003-8
11. Mexis, F.D., Papapostolou, A., Karakosta, C., Psarras, J.: Financing sustainable energy efficiency projects: the triple-a case. Environ. Sci. Proc. **11**, 22 (2021). https://doi.org/10.3390/environsciproc2021011022

12. Papapostolou, A., Mexis, F.D., Karakosta, C., Psarras, J.: A multicriteria tool to support decision-making in the early stages of energy efficiency investments. In: Cabral Seixas Costa, A.P., Papathanasiou, J., Jayawickrama, U., Kamissoko, D. (eds.) Decision Support Systems XII: Decision Support Addressing Modern Industry, Business, and Societal Needs. ICDSST 2022. LNBIP, vol. 447, pp. 190–220. Springer, Cham (2022). https://doi.org/10.1007/978-3-031-06530-9_15

13. Papantonis D., Tzani D., Burbidge M., Stavrakas V., Bouzarovski S., Flamos A.: How to improve energy efficiency policies to address energy poverty? Literature and stakeholder insights for private rented housing in Europe. Energy Res. Soc. Sci. **93**, 102832 (2022). ISSN 2214–6296, https://doi.org/10.1016/j.erss.2022.102832

14. Kleanthis, K., Koutsandreas, D., Karakosta C., Doukas H., Flamos, A.: Bridging the transparency gap in energy efficiency financing by co-designing an integrated assessment framework with involved actors. Energy Rep. **8**, 9686–9699 (2022). ISSN 2352-4847, https://doi.org/10.1016/j.egyr.2022.07.066

15. Karakosta, C., Fujiwara, N.: Scaling up and intensifying stakeholders engagement for evidence-based policymaking: lessons learned. In: Hashmi, I.A., Choudhury, S. (eds.), Encyclopedia of Renewable and Sustainable Materials, pp. 773–782 (2020)

16. Höfer, T., Madlener, R.: A participatory stakeholder process for evaluating sustainable energy transition scenarios. Energy Policy **139**, 111277 (2020). https://doi.org/10.1016/j.enpol.2020.111277

17. Karakosta, C., Papapostolou, A.: Energy efficiency trends in the Greek building sector: a participatory approach. Euro-Mediterr. J. Environ. Integr. (2023). https://doi.org/10.1007/s41207-022-00342-2

18. Mexis, F.D., Papapostolou, A., Karakosta, C., Sarmas, E., Koutsandreas, D., Doukas, H.: Leveraging energy efficiency investments: an innovative web-based benchmarking tool. Adv. Sci. Technol. Eng. Syst. J. ASTESJ **6**(5), 237–248 (2021). ISSN: 2415-6698, https://doi.org/10.25046/aj060526

Equity-Based Allocation Criteria for Water Deficit Periods: A Case Study in South Africa

Sinetemba Xoxo[1]([✉]) [iD], Jane Tanner[1] [iD], Sukhmani Mantel[1] [iD], David Gwapedza[1] [iD], Bruce Paxton[2] [iD], Denis Hughes[1] [iD], and Olivier Barreteau[3] [iD]

[1] Institute for Water Research, Rhodes University, Makhanda, Eastern Cape, South Africa
g13x2945@campus.ru.ac.za
[2] Freshwater Research Centre, Cape Town, Western Cape, South Africa
[3] G-EAU, INRAE, AgroParisTech, Cirad, IRD, Montpellier SupAgro, Univ Montpellier, Montpellier, France

Abstract. Managing water resources and preventing water-related disasters requires investing in tools that aid knowledge-based group decision-making at local levels. We contribute to this toolbox by demonstrating the utility of the Analytic Hierarchical Process (AHP) for establishing an expressed equity-based allocation criteria (called community weighting index) for deficit conditions. Preference for water supply during low-flow conditions in the Twee area supports the principle of proportionality and for multipurpose use. High endemism of fish species in the rivers draining the Twee sub-catchment, the socio-economic importance of farmers, the constitutional protection of the domestic water user, and the tourism sector's importance ranking all justify the established index and revealed acceptance of proportionality. Using the AHP for community weighting can facilitate cooperative and inclusive water management decision-making while mitigating ongoing conflicts and ensuring community understanding. In the future, the results will be combined with hydrological and environmental flow estimates to determine the risk of water deficits.

Keywords: AHP Application · Decentralisation · Decision-Support Systems · Equitable water allocation · Koue Bokkeveld · Water User Association

1 Introduction

Water supply restrictions (including operating rules) that are designed to match hydrological variability are necessary to mitigate the impacts of uneven water availability, climate change and increased competition for water [1, 2]. If water restrictions are to be accepted as optimal solutions to ensure a sustainable supply of water, a comparative understanding of assigned water values/objectives for the different users/sectors remains a crucial goal [3, 4]. Conflicting reactions to the implementation of environmental water requirements (EWR) that may suggest further reductions in supply for current socio-economic beneficial use is another reason why it is becoming more urgent to comprehend values attributed to different water users and how they relate to both water and environmental sustainability [5–7]. This is despite the EWR having its own restrictions due

S. Liu et al. (Eds.): ICDSST 2023, LNBIP 474, pp. 137–155, 2023.
https://doi.org/10.1007/978-3-031-32534-2_11

to natural variability [7]. Advancing this thinking in local water policy planning holds the potential for cultivating cooperative and efficient management of water resources, which is envisaged by the National Water Act (NWA) 36 of 1998 in the South African case [8, 9].

Inherited attitudes and slow institutional reforms propagating from colonial water laws in the country are some of the reported barriers against inclusive and sustainable water management [10]. Drawing attention to changes in water entitlements, which shape the behaviour of water users and water governance, whose full outline has been provided elsewhere [11, 12], can help better grasp the attitudes mentioned by interviewees in Knüppe and Meissner [10]. For over 340 years, the South African water law provided at least two clusters of water rights: public, private, and common rights, all pivoted around the agricultural sector [12]. Perverse actions of agricultural users are unsurprising given the historical prioritisation of agriculture in the beneficial use of water, biased towards irrigation, mining and industrial use [10].

Under the Dutch East India Company (Dutch Rule), water rights were based on approval from the state as the owner of all water resources (except small streams and rising water on private property) (Figure 1). The Cape Colony water act (Act 32 of 1906) was later adopted by four provinces of the Transvaal (northern parts of South Africa).

British rule took over a colony with scarcer land than water; hence, the Irrigation and Conservation Act of 1912 introduced a dual water rights system where running water was public, and groundwater or rainfall captured by one's property was private [11]. This way, Anglican law eroded the state ownership of rivers. It adopted land tenure-based proportional water use water through the *riparian doctrine*, with a minor provision for non-riparian owners to use the remaining supply. Entitlements to public water were prioritised for animal support, irrigation, and the promotion of mechanical appliances on a first-come-first-served basis (Fig. 1). Riparian owners were also entitled to Flood flashes that follow irregular rains— classified as surplus water. Per the Millennium Ecosystem Assessment [13, 14], a narrow concentration on agricultural development and economic growth aided by the lack of scientific guidance [15, 16] enable the neglection of environmental costs of depriving major streams and estuaries of critical silt delivered by "flash floods—surplus water" on which they rely

Appreciating the scarce nature of water resources, the need to protect the agricultural sector and a rapidly growing industrial sector up north, the Apartheid regime resuscitated the state ownership of rivers alongside the *riparian doctrine* through the Water Act of 1956 [17]. In order to maintain normal flows for the benefit of bottom-stream users, restrictions on riparian owners required that some water be returned to the channel [18]. This was the closest representation of environmental flows in modern language. Non-riparian owners received allocations with the water courts' approval or by willing riparian users exchanging water (the latter was uncommon) [12].

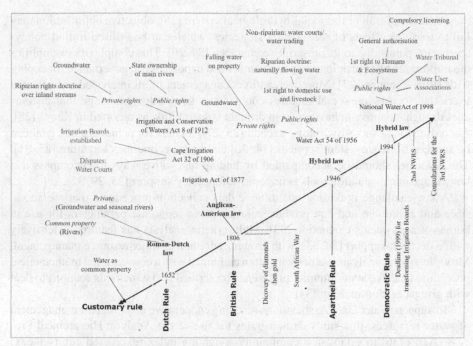

Fig. 1. General phylogeny of South African water law (not to scale) depicting lines of descent of different entitlements and different forms of water, reproduced based on Tewari [11] and Thompson [12]. Water rights categories are shown in blue. (Color figure online)

Although fairness, redress and decentralised governance are manifested as constitutional imperatives by the South African water legislature [8], the successful implementation of all the reforms introduced by the NWA remains a challenge for effective management [10]. Fairness entails a fair distribution beyond basic human requirements [19]. Redress speaks to equal opportunity (in access and decision-making), favouring previously dis-advantaged individuals that were previously oppressed based on race or sex [20]. To ensure the NWA reaches its objectives at the grassroots level, Water User Associations are proposed as inclusive and democratic institutions for fair access and sound water management [8]. However, progress in institutional reforms remains overdue, with only 39 out of 111 irrigation boards being transformed into Water User Associations nationwide [21]. Part of the problem could be attributed to the flawed introduction of the NWA without adequate institutional capacity support as endorsed by the United Nations [22]. Despite their importance, these institutions remain underrepresented in literature [21].

Given the water scarcity and the slow progress of the NWA transformative agenda, calls for exploratory procedures that enable comprehensive assessments of water restriction implications for various users/sectors [1, 2] are particularly relevant for Water User Associations. Producer-driven technical approaches, including those aiming to maximise profitability while minimising environmental degradation or natural capital valuation procedures, are the standard methods for optimal water allocation [23, 24]. Because of the evolutionary trait of the social-hydrological system [25], objective optimisation may fail to trace the effects of reallocation strategies, which can be utilised to find policy-leveraging points due to its prescriptive character [24, 26]. This complexity exemplifies the importance of a participatory nature embedded in polycentric governance for coping with climate change [27]. Moreover, a direct engagement of all interested and affected users that focuses on social realities could foster knowledge exchange that encourages drought-adaptive behaviour from drought vulnerability, as reported in Kenya [28]. According to the socio-hydrology agenda [25, 29], lessons for achieving this goal can be sourced from ecosystem services [14, 30] and hydro-economics literature [23, 31]. The outcomes should be accompanied by finding innovative ways to encompass this knowledge into evaluation tools is imperative for policy support [25, 29, 32].

A key challenge is finding quantitative data collection procedures that are accessible and affordable and can produce relevant socio-economic parameters for use in human-water systems evaluation [33]. Multi-criteria analysis has featured extensively within decision-support [34, 35], with growing adoption in water resource management. Multiple-criteria analysis methods are often combined with a conventional mathematical procedure to arrive at community preference (described in the methods section) to deal with group decision-making [34].

To support Water User Associations reaching cooperative and efficient management of water resources, this study demonstrates the use of the Analytic Hierarchical Process (AHP) [36] to establish a community weighting index (expressed equity index) for perceived implications of water restrictions. This index indicates socio-economic preferences among water users. Given the trade-offs between human and environmental welfare [37], its interpretation can be broadened to reflect the community mentality towards environmental sustainability as a consequence of satisfying EWRs [38].

2   Methods

2.1   Study Area

Just over 200 km north of Cape Town lies an attractive pristine-commercial agricultural landscape, the Twee *wyk* [E21H quaternary catchment of the Koue Bokkeveld region (Fig. 2)], that is ideal for investigating the socio-hydrology of commercial farming catchments in South Africa. The primary catchment hosting the Twee *wyk* is known as the least inhabited in the country, with only 0.25% of the national population [39]. The existence and survival of the semi-arid Twee *wyk* socio-hydrological system are due to the cool Mediterranean climate, the erratic winter rainfall, and the synclinal valleys of the groundwater-rich Cape Supergroup system that gives rise to a complex topography shown in Fig. 2. The hydroclimatic nature of the area and global trade have driven the move towards growing deciduous, citrus, and stone fruit (covering 530 ha) for the export market. Maintaining the needed 40% contribution in environmental flows to support downstream socio-economic activities and the requisite 33% (1 073 Mm^3/a) yearly flow contributions to the Doring estuary is one of the primary issues for water users in the area [40, 41]. Meeting these environmental water requirements (EWR) for river flow is particularly challenging given that the Koue Bokkeveld is within the Cape Winelands District's authority, a significant agricultural employer in the Western Cape

[42]. Projected estimates for year 2040–2070 by Tanner *et al*. [43] indicate a 1.4 to 5.4% reduction in natural flows from the Twee, highlighting negative ecohydrological impacts of climate change in the sub-catchment. This predicament is worsened by the largely unregulated water use in the area, despite the resource overallocation [10, 44].

The three physical factors mentioned above gave rise to the Groot Winterhoek Strategic Water Source Area (of which the Twee *wyk* is a part)—high water yielding areas (N = 22) that collectively contribute 50% of South Africa's surface water with only 5% of the country's total surface area [45]. The older Winterhoek Subgroup shales (deposited during the Ordovician period) decompose to generate moderate to steep clay-rich and productive soils along the valley floor. On the other hand, the Silurian-Devonian Nardouw Subgroup Sandstones weather to generate nutrient-poor and shallow sandy soils favoured by the indigenous Cape Floristic Region Fynbos vegetation [46]. The landowners in the Koue Bokkeveld have contributed to biodiversity protection since 1971 [47] chiefly because the Cape Floristic Region is one of South Africa's eight UNESCO World Heritage Sites[1], and more have been urged to contribute to conserving the natural landscape [48]. Biodiversity protection is demonstrated by 85% of the catchment area being protected (Fig. 2C), resulting in complete protection of the Groot Winterhoek as a national strategic resource [45, 47]. Forest Wilderness Areas and Nature Reserves also contribute to biodiversity protection in the catchment (Fig. 2C). Acknowledgements to *nature conservation authorities* (i.e., World Wildlife Fund, Freshwater Research Centre, and the Western Cape Department of Agriculture through LandCare[2]) that collaborate with land owners in the area, resulting in 10–40% biodiversity tax incentives [49].

Current Context and Framing a Desirable Future (2050 vision)

In a workshop held in May 2022, the landowners in the Twee shared their concerns over current conditions and a 2050 vision for the catchment. During the workshop, water users in the catchment raised concerns that link to demand management, supply management and land/climate issues. While the water user's concerns and aspirational goals overlap, such overlaps are not interrogated here; the raw stakeholder contributions are communicated. The 2050 vision of the sub-catchment was presented in a subsequent workshop as three vision statements that were confirmed for accuracy by the water users.

- To achieve sustainable catchment management.
- Fair water usage, ensuring dry season flows and riverine health.
- Effective cooperation between all stakeholders for water use on the basis that benefits all landowners and the environment.

The water users indicated that executing the aspirational goals can adequately address the current concerns and meet the 2050 sub-catchment vision. This vision tightly overlaps the third National Water Resource Strategy (2020–2030) [50], indicating that the stakeholders in Twee who attended the workshop intend to contribute to national development objectives.

---

[1] https://www.gov.za/faq/travel-tourism/which-heritage-sites-are-south-africa.

[2] https://www.elsenburg.com/programmes/landcare/.

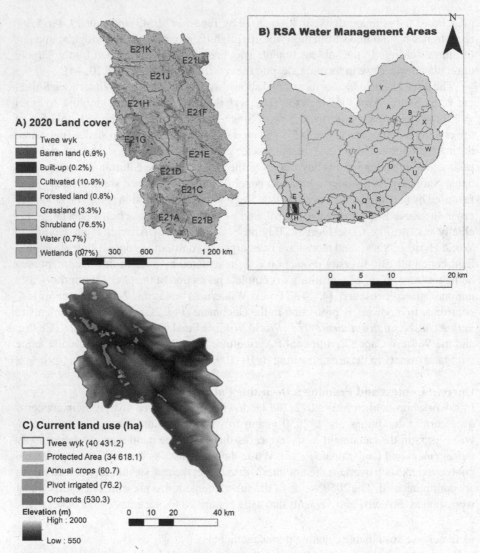

Fig. 2. Context map of the Twee wyk (E21H). All data was sourced from freely available national datasets provided by (WR 2012, DFFE 2021, DFFE 2023); available at 1:1,000,000 and 20 m pixel sizes with an overall accuracy of 85% or more.

2.2 Ranking Water Users for Supply Priority: Community Weighting

The main goal of this study was pre-defined, with the various water users and the environment considered as criteria and decision-makers (Fig. 3). The catchment's four main water user groups emerged from a previous ARDI (Actors, Resources, Dynamics, and Interactions) [51] workshop held on May 4th, 2022 in Kunje Guest Farm. The workshop had 14 attendees, which belonged to one of the four water user groups: farmers (commercial and smallholders), residents, recreation operators (weekend farmers) and interest group representatives. The ARDI workshop aimed to establish a baseline understanding of the sub-catchment regarding water use. Consistent with the NWA [8], the water user groups can be classified based on volumetric use, economic circumstances, and return flow contribution. All but one farmer (the largest commercial farmer) participated in the AHP exercise. Only three out of six weekend farmers could be part of the process. Since the EWR cannot speak for itself, proxies in the form of interest group stakeholders who know the tributaries were used. Each tributary within the catchment was allocated a single representative. Inputs were based on water users' subjective judgments (e.g., operation costs, sentiments, and preferences) originating from knowledge, experience, and expertise and are standardised to one standard measurement scale.

Each water user (n = 13, representing the four main water user groups locally) completed the judgement matrix with the help of a research team member and an Afrikaans-English translator in less than 30 min. Following an explanation of the AHP procedure, six pairwise comparisons were provided by each user to complete the decision matrix using a pre-set spreadsheet (step 3-Fig. 3). The comparisons were done following the prompt: *"for water assurance, which water user group is more important, and how much more on a scale of 1 to 9?"* A justification was also requested for each comparison. The spreadsheet normalised the matrix and provided the user with their hierarchy and consistency index (step 4 in Fig. 3). Given the subjective nature of the procedure (decision uncertainty) [36], consistency was improved by slightly adjusting the judgments by plus

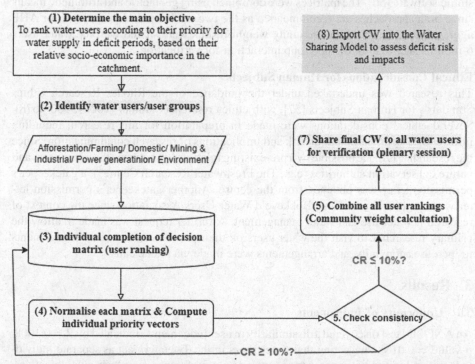

Fig. 3. Workflow followed in this research. CR denotes consistency ratio and CW, the community weight.

144   S. Xoxo et al.

or minus one or two points in the scale to achieve a consistency index of ≤ 0.1 [52], while adhering to the original hierarchy.

Combining the Multiple Matrices to get the Community Weight Index
The decision-support systems based on the AHP method typically generate group preference from individual judgments using individual priorities or lumping individual judgments [53]. The choice between these two depends on the assumption of whether the decision-makers act jointly or unilaterally. Individual judgement-based aggregation is adopted when diverse water users with a special interest in water management are freely willing to abandon their individual preferences for the good of the socio-hydrological system, in which case the individuals become a group [53, 54]. Merging individual preferences using aggregation of individual priorities is suitable when community members act as separate individuals with a limited willingness to forfeit their values/objectives for the greater good [53]. In this case, geometric or arithmetic means can be used as mathematical procedures to compute the group's hierarchical preference. However, the merged weights must be of acceptable consistency, which can be derived from valid original AHP matrices [55].

The completed decision matrices were used to build a database of individual judgements, which were later used to compute the community weight index. To better understand stakeholder motives, we assess for uniformity using the Analysis of Similarity (ANOSIM) statistic, which interprets individual judgements as distances, via the R-studio software [56]. The matrices were combined using geometric and arithmetic means since both approaches are recommended as the two mathematical procedures for AHP aggregation [53, 54]. The community weight results were shared with the water users 6-months later in a follow-up group interaction for verification.

Ethical Considerations for Human Subjects
This research was undertaken under the guidance of the Rhodes Research Ethics Standards for Human Subjects [57], with ethics reference number (2022–5386-6678). Several ethical considerations were made in preparation for this research, including informed consent, participation risk and implications of research communication. Since the research was made possible by a pre-existing relationship between the water users and nature conservation authorities (e.g., The Freshwater Research Centre[3]), a gatekeeper's permission letter was obtained from the centre. Another gatekeeper's permission letter was sought from the Koue Bokkeveld Water Users Association since the context of research is water use and water management. A further request was made to allow the primary researcher to visit the water users on their properties for further engagements to increase anonymity, and arrangements were made via phone calls.

3 Results

3.1 Uniformity of Judgements

An ANOSIM test discovered a dissimilarity in user judgements (indicated by $R = 0.1008$, p-value $= 0.018$), suggesting that water users in the Twee *wyk* act as separate individuals with a limited willingness to accept a group preference over their own objectives.

---

[3] https://www.frcsa.org.za/resource-protection-and-conservation/sustainable-water-use/.

Driven by some of the reasons listed in Table 1, eight of the thirteen water users preferred economic productivity above environmental protection, whereas six preferred the reverse (Fig. 4). This mismatch in the user preference hierarchy led to the adoption of priority-based integration, which accepts the arithmetic and geometric means for group aggregation. The dissimilarity is better visualised in Fig. 4, showing the most preference placed on environmental protection (EWR priority) and water productivity (farmer priority). All consistency ratios were within acceptable limits (CR $\leq$ 0.1).

Table 1. Summary table of water user justifications (preference statements) for community weights.

Preference of the EWR	Preference of farmers
Protection of endemic fish species (e.g., Twee Red fin and Clanwillan yellow fish); Delivery of environmental benefits; Managing the environment for the benefit of larger society and the natural ecosystems	Food security consideration at different scales; Primary livelihood & survival; Employment creation; Technological investments; Need to repay bank loans/dividends to equity holders; Inadequate storage facilities leading up to reliance of run-of-river abstraction
Preference of the Resident	**Preference of the weekender**
Mostly uses spring water; Generates income elsewhere; Not an active player in catchment economics; Do not abstract surface water; Local Resident and enjoys constitutional guarantee of water rights	No significant impact on surface water availability; Option to move away to avoid water shortages

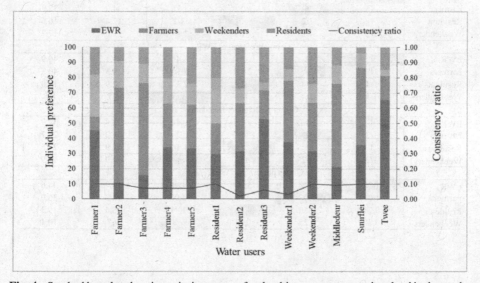

Fig. 4. Stacked bar plot showing priority vectors for the thirteen water users involved in the study, labelled based on their water user classification/group. Consistency ratios for each water user is also shown on the graph, with all Consistency ratios $\leq$ 0.1.

3.2 Group Objectives

Table 2 depicts the individual and aggregated preferences of Twee *wyk* water user groups, adhering to the AHP aggregation rules of agreement and uniformity with slight differences in priority vectors. During periods of reduced assurance in water supply, farmers preferred economic efficiency, shown by the following hierarchy farmers > EWR > weekenders > residents. The EWR group established preferential prioritisation of environmental preservation and productive use (as shown by the following preference: EWR ≥ farmers > residents > weekenders). Residents favoured environmental preservation, shown by the following hierarchy EWR > farmers ≥ residents > weekenders. Weekenders (tourism operators) slightly preferred economic efficiency (36% to farmers) over environmental protection (34/35% to EWR), ending up with the following hierarchy for supply: farmers > EWR > residents > weekenders. All the group weights were below the fairness threshold (Gini < 0.4), suggesting overall equity.

Table 2. Supply preference/objectives for the four user groups using the aggregation of individual judgements (geomean and arithmetic mean) given the mismatch in individual water user priorities. Since all judgement matrices were consistent (CR ≤ 0.1), it was assumed that all aggregated matrices were also within consistency limits.

Water users	EWR	Farmers	Residents	Weekenders	Group preference (geomean)	Group preference (mean)
Group preference: Farmers						
EWR	1	1	1 1/2	1 1/2	28.1	27.9
Farmer	1	1	2	2	34.9	37.9
Resident	1	1/2	1	1/2	17.4	16.6
Weekender	1/2	1/2	1 1/2	1	19.6	17.7
Group preference: EWR						
EWR	1	1	5	4	41.1	40.9
Farmers	1	1	2 3/4	7 1/4	39.3	40.3
Residents	1/4	1/4	1	2 3/4	12.9	10.0
Weekenders	1/4	1/4	1/4	1	6.7	8.8
Group preference: Residents						
EWR	1	1 1/2	1 1/2	4	38.9	37.9
Farmers	1/2	1	1	2	24.2	23.7
Residents	1	1	1	1 1/2	24.9	23.5
Weekenders	1/2	1/2	1/2	1	11.9	14.9
Group preference: Weekenders						
EWR	1.00	1.00	1.41	4.90	35.4	34.6
Farmers	1.00	1.00	2.00	4.00	36.3	36.0
Residents	0.71	0.50	1.00	1.41	18.6	19.3
Weekenders	0.20	0.25	0.71	1.00	9.7	10.1

3.3 Community Weights Using the AHP Method

Community weighting by the Twee *wyk* community and water user groups is illustrated in Fig. 5, highlighting the community's objective productive use and environmental protection. Per Fig. 5, the geometric and arithmetic mean aggregation derived a uniform hierarchy for supply in dry periods (community weight) [farmer (34 or 35%) = EWR (35 or 34%) > residents (18%) > weekenders (13%)]. The water users accepted the aggregated weights following a request to consider rearrangements in water user groups:

As you present it, the weights make sense and can be accepted. But in retrospect, weekenders and residents can almost be one user, resulting in an even weighting for the three user groups.

This comment was similar to those received during farm visits. Some water users questioned the possibility of decomposing the farmers' group based on economic circumstances or the nature of operations. In this regard, one user said:

It might be interesting to decompose the farmers based on their size or economic activity, as this would reveal interesting trends of water use impact and adaptive capacity. Two commercial farmers may fare differently (due to a secondary source of income) if one is also active in ecotourism, which will generate water quality impacts during peak tourism seasons.

4 Discussion

This paper presents the AHP procedure [58] as a quick and robust participative method for understanding water user contribution to community well-being based on subjective socio-economic and environmental preferences. As expected, individual water user ranking of the four main user groups in the sub-catchment allowed water users to contribute equally and consistently to establishing priority vectors (community weights), demonstrating AHP's recorded strength for eliciting socio-economic data [34]. Platforms that permit equal contribution regarding water resource governance are important for facilitating effective governance [21]. By using the AHP technique, other similar situations can assure inclusive involvement and perhaps plant the seeds of efficient local water governance. Once processed, such data will provide regulators with user-expressed evidence to support a supply preference to one user group over another, which can also reconcile conflicts due to competing interests [59].

Methodically, adopting the AHP method as a tool of stakeholder engagement at a Water User Association level allowed equal participation and inclusion of perceived fairness from all. Including all affected water users that start with classifying water users in the Twee through the ARDI process can be seen as an expression of procedural fairness, one of the essential equity dimensions [60]. This procedural advantage can also help reduce potential participant-induced bias, often confronting group interactions better outlined elsewhere [23]. The AHP's sensitivity to qualitative and quantitative inputs to arrive at trade-off calculations (subjective nature of AHP) [36] allowed us to leverage water users' memory in creating a foundation for a fair distribution of water risks and benefits among the Water User Association members. Computational requirements of the AHP method were overcome by using interactive AHP spreadsheets that allowed water users to focus only on the pairwise comparison and consistency thereof [61].

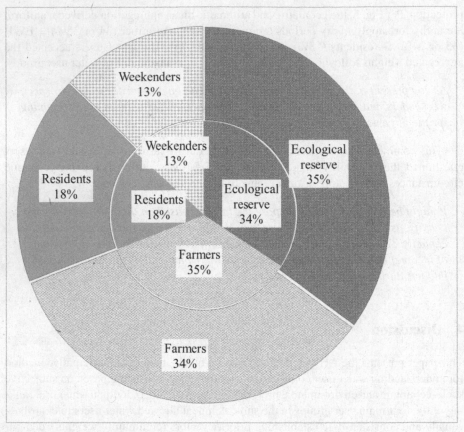

Fig. 5. Community weights derived using the geomean (outer donut) and arithmetic means (inside donut).

When the water user decision matrices and preferences are combined, they give a community weighting index indicating a social equity index for deficit periods [1, 38]. The AHP survey results show that the Twee *wyk* community recognises proportional sharing and is becoming strongly environmentally aware while valuing water's productive benefit. The identified proportionality view of fairness in the Twee indicates that water users in the area acknowledge social differences [24]. This is despite the Koue Bokkeveld being the most farmed area in the entire Olifants-Doring drainage area [40]. Such a discovery would not be possible if the economic index was derived based on pure economic terms such as productivity or profit losses.

The importance of the EWR and farmers in the Koue Bokkeveld community was mainly due to the biodiversity of the Middledeur and Twee rivers [40] and the socio-economic importance of farmers [42]. Currently, 85% (Fig. 2C) of terrestrial ecosystems in the Twee wyk are formally protected, demonstrating landowners' enthusiasm for environmental conservation. With respect to instream ecosystems, the alarming findings by Tanner *et al.* [43] and unsatisfied low-flow EWR [40] raise serious concerns about the need to regulate upstream human activities better. Achieving the catchment vision for 2050 supported by a local government [48] sustainability imperative could be the right step in this direction. Drought adaptation behaviours such as soil development, conservation agriculture, and investment in precision irrigation systems indicate a step towards the instream ecosystem protection. Increments in alien invasive species removal that may increase also be hydrologically beneficial for the catchment [62]. Meanwhile, as stated by water users, overcoming legal and economic constraints that lead to low investments in water storage facilities, which, if successful, could balance demand management and increased supply, remains a challenge. The downstream effects of reservoir construction, as assessed by van Loon *et al.* [63], will require attention from regulators.

Despite the community's stated environmental value for water use, greater attention should be paid to farmers, particularly for complying with low flow releases towards unaltered flow conditions (B-level) [41]. Farmers accept the local role of water releases socio-economically and towards the environment (e.g., protecting endemic fish communities). These provisions can be traced from the motivations of prioritising the EWR provided by farmers over themselves in some instances. One concern expressed by the water users during the feedback session (see paraphrased comment below) is the inconsistent application of EWR across catchments, which may constrain farmers from complying with water releases.

The EWR for the Doring River integrity will not be successfully provided upstream users alone; complying with the B-level water discharge is becoming increasingly difficult and an impediment to growth because someone right downstream from us will use up all the water we discharge. In a way, we are essentially benefitting someone else at our expense ~ Commercial Farmer

The previous comment corroborates interview statements collected by Knüppe and Meissner [10] in the Olifants-Doring catchment, whereby legacy water use patterns remain a barrier to sustainable water management (including EWR compliance). Farmers behaving as if water entitlement is still linked to land ownership, as previously permitted by the Water Act 54 of 1956 through the *riparian doctrine,* is a defining feature of the stated barrier [10, 18]. In this context, a recommendation would be to boost assistance for interest organisations already operating in catchment areas. Interest organisations in the catchment have demonstrated their educational impact in sensitising water users to the benefits of biodiversity protection resulting in considerabe terrestrial protection, and may have played a role in shaping the community weight evaluated here [10].

A decline in farming activities in the catchment could result in job losses in a region heavily dependent on the agricultural sector and could raise the already high unemployment rate in the nation [39, 42]. This would be contrary to the catchment vision for the catchment. Socio-hydrology research in Australia suggests that agricultural growth is eventually followed by environmental consciousness, which results in the restoration of degraded ecosystems [64]. Within the socio-hydrology context, the Twee community's growing choice for ecological sustainability alongside financial benefit could signal a pendulum swing [64] that may eventually result in increased instream environmental protection alongside terrestrial protection (Fig. 2C). Regarding the catchment vision and water consumption, it is still unclear how the water users in the sub-catchment would respond to a scenario of expanding tourism and diminishing farming. This scenario will be explored from the perspective of water consumption in subsequent activities by assessing the sensitivity of impacts to various community weight combinations, as suggested by stakeholders to look at water use sector overlaps.

4.1 Implications of Community Weights

Researchers and water regulators can use the index to explore water users' sensitivity to water supply shortages and tolerance after investing in technical solutions [1, 38]. Moreover, establishing the index may encourage the inclusion of the often disregarded socio-cultural, environmental, and political values and objectives for water use [24, 65]. Understanding the multiple viewpoints in water resource decision-making can lead to more sustainable solutions while raising awareness of the water user impacts on local communities and ecosystems [37].

One of the key take-home messages from the procedure followed here is that, similar to water management, equity is context-specific. Although the water users engaged here fall into various water user classes (emerging farmers, commercial farmers, rural domestic users, recreation, and the often excluded EWR), motivations for their judgement matrices were based on spatially-explicit experiences shaped by historical, social norms and future catchment vision [24]. Therefore, outcomes from one area may not be generalisable to similar contexts. Instead, investments should be made in multiple case study applications and comparative evaluations of community weights (fairness) as envisioned in the socio-hydrology arena [66].

One limitation that can be highlighted relates to the priority aggregation procedure. In the Twee case, water users were found to not act in harmony, thus resulting in AHP aggregation based on individual priorities (using geomean and arithmetic mean aggregation). An assumption of the equal importance of water users may be incorrect, as power imbalance exists at all levels of decision-making [67]. This limitation can be addressed by adopting a weighted geometric or arithmetic mean approach to reflect the relative importance of users [53, 55], which could not be done here given the limited access resources to interact with water users. Voting systems are alternative options for supporting group decision-making in areas with limited data availability or linguistic data. Unlike the AHP aggregation options described above, voting systems do not assume group homogeneity, making them ideal for use in areas where the group is large (e.g., regional scale) and there is no clear preference [68].

In a water-scarce country like South Africa, one critical question of demand management is the consequence of deficit and vulnerability to those impacts [1, 69]. The approach of deriving community weights discussed in this paper and the utility of community support in the socio-hydrology toolbox is still short of modelling approaches that centralise human agency instead of integrating it as a boundary condition, as seen in other hydrological modelling tools [66]. In the final model [38] currently being tested with the water users of the Twee *wyk*, the community weights presented here will answer the larger question, "how do supply shortfall and absence/access of technical solutions impact water user groups?" This question will be answered by combining community weighting with a deficit-impact index and desktop-based EWR estimates to elicit water user vulnerability to supply reduction to evaluate the cross-sectorial impacts of the derived equity index [38].

Until now, the CW index has been discussed in terms of socially perceived equity. The equal weighting of the EWR to the farmer, out of the value of multidimensional use or proportionality, reflects the motivation of water users to reduce socioeconomic vulnerability due to deficits. However, successfully delivering on the NWA redress principle necessitates first satisfying the human right and the EWR before considering allocation [8]. Unlike previous legal systems, the current water legislation gives the state the final say on the costs and benefits (environmental and otherwise) of water use under compulsory permitting. With the state's discretion in mind, the slightly contradictory allocation values demonstrated by the results presented here with the current water legislation pose a risk of continued human-environmental conflict. The equity outcomes determined using the above-mentioned procedure will provide a clearer picture of this potential conflict.

References

1. Hughes, D.A., Mallory, S.J.L.: The importance of operating rules and assessments of beneficial use in water resource allocation policy and management. Water Policy 11, 731–741 (2009). https://doi.org/10.2166/wp.2009.035
2. Seppälä, O.T.: Effective water and sanitation policy reform implementation: need for systemic approach and stakeholder participation. Water Policy 4, 367–388 (2002). https://doi.org/10.1016/S1366-7017(02)00036-3
3. Adom, R.K., Simatele, M.D.: The role of stakeholder engagement in sustainable water resource management in South Africa. Nat. Resour. Forum 46, 410–427 (2022). https://doi.org/10.1111/1477-8947.12264
4. Biggs, R., Rhode, C., Archibald, S., et al.: Strategies for managing complex social-ecological systems in the face of uncertainty: examples from South Africa and beyond. Ecol. Soc. 20, 52 (2015)
5. Pastor, A.V., Palazzo, A., Havlik, P., et al.: The global nexus of food–trade–water sustaining environmental flows by 2050. Nat. Sustain. 2, 499–507 (2019). https://doi.org/10.1038/s41893-019-0287-1
6. Mekonnen, M.M., Hoekstra, A.Y.: Four billion people facing severe water scarcity. Sci. Adv. 2, e1500323 (2016). https://doi.org/10.1126/sciadv.1500323
7. Overton, I.C., Smith, D.M., Dalton, J., et al.: Implementing environmental flows in integrated water resources management and the ecosystem approach. Hydrol. Sci. J. 59, 860–877 (2014). https://doi.org/10.1080/02626667.2014.897408
8. RSA: The National Water Act (No. 36 of 1998). Gov. Commun. Inf. Syst. 398, 101 (1998)
9. Colvin, J., Ballim, F., Chimbuya, S., et al.: Building capacity for co-operative governance as a basis for integrated water resource managing in the Inkomati and Mvoti catchments, South Africa. Water SA 34, 681–690 (2008). https://doi.org/10.4314/WSA.V34I6.183669
10. Knüppe, K., Meissner, R.: Drivers and barriers towards sustainable water and land management in the Olifants-Doorn water management area, South Africa. Environ. Dev. 20, 3–14 (2016). https://doi.org/10.1016/J.ENVDEV.2016.09.002
11. Tewari, D.D.: A detailed analysis of evolution of water rights in South Africa: an account of three and a half centuries from 1652 AD to present. Water SA 35, 693–710 (2009). https://doi.org/10.4314/wsa.v35i5.49196

12. Thompson, H.: Water Law: A Practical Approach to Resource Management and The Provision of Services. Juta & Co LTD., Cape Town (2006)

13. Millennium Ecosystem Assessment (2005) Ecosystems and human well-being: Wetlands and water synthesis. Washington DC

14. Brauman, K.A., Daily, G.C., Duarte, T.K., Mooney, H.A.: The nature and value of ecosystem services: an overview highlighting hydrologic services. Annu. Rev. Environ. Resour. **32**, 67–98 (2007). https://doi.org/10.1146/annurev.energy.32.031306.102758

15. King, J., Louw, D.: Instream flow assessments for regulated rivers in South Africa using the building block methodology. Aquat. Ecosyst. Health Manag. **1**, 109–124 (1998). https://doi.org/10.1080/14634989808656909

16. Hughes, D.A., Hannart, P.: A desktop model used to provide an initial estimate of the ecological instream flow requirements of rivers in South Africa. J. Hydrol. **270**, 167–181 (2003). https://doi.org/10.1016/S0022-1694(02)00290-1

17. Tempelhoff, J.: The Water Act, No. 54 of 1956 and the first phase of apartheid in South Africa (1948–1960). Water Hist. **9**, 189–213 (2017).https://doi.org/10.1007/s12685-016-0181-y

18. Union of South Africa (1956) The Water Act. https://leap.unep.org/countries/za/national-legislation/water-act-no-54-1956

19. Movik, S.: A fair share? Perceptions of justice in South Africa's water allocation reform policy. Geoforum **54**, 187–195 (2014). https://doi.org/10.1016/J.GEOFORUM.2013.03.003

20. Stein, R.: Water law in a democratic South Africa: a country case study examinisng the introduction of a public rights system. S. Afr. J. Environ. Law Policy **13**, 181–195 (2006). https://doi.org/10.10520/AJA10231765_181

21. Meissner, R., Funke, N., Nienaber, S., Ntombela, C.: The status quo of research on South Africa's water resource management institutions. Water SA **39**, 721–732 (2013). https://doi.org/10.4314/wsa.v39i5.17

22. UN. ESCAP (2000) Principles and practices of water allocation among water-use sectors (ST/ESCAP/SER.F/80). In: Water resources series (UN. ESCAP), 80th ed. United Nations, New York, pp 146–154

23. Booker, J.F., Howitt, R.E., Michelsen, A.M., Young, R.A.: Economics and the modelling of water resources and policies. Nat. Resour. Model. **25**, 168–218 (2012). https://doi.org/10.1111/J.1939-7445.2011.00105.X

24. Keeler, B.L., Derickson, K.D., Waters, H., Walker, R.: Advancing water equity demands new approaches to sustainability science. One Earth **2**, 211–213 (2020). https://doi.org/10.1016/j.oneear.2020.03.003

25. Sivapalan, M., Savenije, H.H.G., Blöschl, G.: Socio-hydrology: a new science of people and water. Hydrol. Process. **26**, 1270–1276 (2012). https://doi.org/10.1002/hyp.8426

26. Thompson, S.E., Sivapalan, M., Harman, C.J., et al.: Developing predictive insight into changing water systems: use-inspired hydrologic science for the anthropocene. Hydrol. Earth Syst. Sci. **17**, 5013–5039 (2013). https://doi.org/10.5194/HESS-17-5013-2013

27. Ostrom, E.: Polycentric systems for coping with collective action and global environmental change. Glob. Environ. Chang. **20**, 550–557 (2010). https://doi.org/10.1016/J.GLOENVCHA.2010.07.004

28. Wens, M., Veldkamp, T.I.E., Mwangi, M., et al.: Simulating small-scale agricultural adaptation decisions in response to drought risk: an empirical agent-based model for semi-arid Kenya. Front. Water **2**, 15 (2020). https://doi.org/10.3389/FRWA.2020.00015/BIBTEX

29. Blair, P., Buytaert, W.: Socio-hydrological modelling: a review asking "why, what and how?" Hydrol. Earth Syst. Sci. **20**, 443–478 (2016). https://doi.org/10.5194/hess-20-443-2016

30. Chan, K.M.A., Satterfield, T., Goldstein, J.: Rethinking ecosystem services to better address and navigate cultural values. Ecol. Econ. **74**, 8–18 (2012). https://doi.org/10.1016/J.ECO LECON.2011.11.011

31. Yoon, J., Klassert, C., Selby, P., et al.: A coupled human-natural system analysis of freshwater security under climate and population change. Proc. Natl. Acad. Sci. U. S. A. **118**, e2020431118 (2021). https://doi.org/10.1073/pnas.2020431118

32. Di Baldassarre, G., Sivapalan, M., Rusca, M., et al.: Socio-hydrology: scientific challenges in addressing a societal grand challenge. Water Resour. Res. 2018WR023901 (2019). https://doi.org/10.1029/2018WR023901

33. Troy, T.J., Pavao-Zuckerman, M., Evans, T.P.: Debates—perspectives on socio-hydrology: socio-hydrologic modeling: tradeoffs, hypothesis testing, and validation. Water Resour. Res. **51**, 4806–4814 (2015). https://doi.org/10.1002/2015WR017046Key

34. Mendoza, G.A., Martins, H.: Multi-criteria decision analysis in natural resource management: a critical review of methods and new modelling paradigms. For. Ecol. Manag. **230**, 1–22 (2006). https://doi.org/10.1016/J.FORECO.2006.03.023

35. Huang, I.B., Keisler, J., Linkov, I.: Multi-criteria decision analysis in environmental sciences: Ten years of applications and trends. Sci. Total Environ. **409**, 3578–3594 (2011). https://doi.org/10.1016/J.SCITOTENV.2011.06.022

36. Saaty, T.: Fundamentals of Decision Making and Priority Theory with the Analytic Hierarchy Process: Analytic Hierarchy Process Series, vol. 6. RWS Publications, Pittsburgh (2000)

37. Cook, B.R., Spray, C.J.: Ecosystem services and integrated water resource management: different paths to the same end? J. Environ. Manag. **109**, 93–100 (2012). https://doi.org/10.1016/J.JENVMAN.2012.05.016

38. Pienaar, G.W., Hughes, D.A.: Linking hydrological uncertainty with equitable allocation for water resources decision-making. Water Resour. Manag. **31**(1), 269–282 (2016). https://doi.org/10.1007/s11269-016-1523-3

39. StatsSA (2011) Geography metadata (Report no. 03-01-47). In: Census 2011 Metadata. Statistics South Africa, South African Environmental Observation Network, Pretoria, South Africa, p 144

40. Paxton, B., Dobison, L., Kleynhans, M., Howard, G.: Developing an elementary tool for Ecological Reserve monitoring in South Africa's Freshwater Ecosystem Priority Areas (FEPAs): A Pilot study in the Koue Bokkeveld (WRC Report No. 2340/1/16). Water Research Commission, Pretoria (2017)

41. DWS (2016) National Water Act (36 of 1998). Classes and resource quality objectives of water resources for the olifants-doorn catchments. South Africa

42. STATS SA (2020) Census of commercial agriculture – Western Cape, Report No. 11–02–02 (2017). Pretoria, South Africa

43. Tanner, J., Mantel, S., Paxton, B., et al.: Impacts of climate change on rivers and biodiversity in a water-scarce semi-arid region of the Western Cape South Africa. Front. Water **4**, 143 (2022). https://doi.org/10.3389/FRWA.2022.949901/BIBTEX

44. DWS (2016) Department of Water and Sanitation schedule classes of water resources and resource quality objectives for catchments of the Lower Vaal in Terms of Section 13 (1)(a) and (B) of the National Water Act (Act No . 36 of 1998). Pretoria, South Africa

45. Nel, J.L., Le Maître, D.C., Roux, D.J., et al.: Strategic water source areas for urban water security: making the connection between protecting ecosystems and benefiting from their services. Ecosyst. Serv. **28**, 251–259 (2017). https://doi.org/10.1016/J.ECOSER.2017.07.013

46. Rebelo, A.G., Boucher, C., Helme, N., et al.: Fynbos Biome. In: Mucina, L., Rutherford, M.C. (eds.) Vegetation of South Africa, Swaziland and Lesotho. Strelitzia 19, pp. 52–167 (2006)

47. DFFE (2023) South Africa Protected Areas Database (SAPAD_IR_2022_Q3_01). Pretoria, South Africa
48. Witzenberg Municipality (2019) Annual Report 2019/20. Ceres
49. van Wyk, E.: Tax incentives for biodiversity conservation in the Western Cape. Meditari Account. Res. **18**, 58–75 (2010). https://doi.org/10.1108/10222529201000005
50. DWS (2021) Draft National Water Resources Strategy 3 version 2.6. Pretoria, South Africa
51. Etienne, M., Du Toit, D.R., Pollard, S.: ARDI: a co-construction method for participatory modeling in natural resources. Ecol. Soc. **16**, 44 (2011)
52. Saaty, T.L.: The modern science of multicriteria decision making and its practical applications: the AHP/ANP approach. Oper. Res. **61**, 1101–1118 (2013). https://doi.org/10.1287/opre.2013.1197
53. Forman, E., Peniwati, K.: Aggregating individual judgments and priorities with the analytic hierarchy process. Eur. J. Oper. Res. **108**, 165–169 (1998). https://doi.org/10.1016/S0377-2217(97)00244-0
54. Aczél, J., Saaty, T.L.: Procedures for synthesizing ratio judgements. J. Math. Psychol. **27**, 93–102 (1983). https://doi.org/10.1016/0022-2496(83)90028-7
55. Grošelj, P., Zadnik Stirn, L.: Acceptable consistency of aggregated comparison matrices in analytic hierarchy process. Eur. J. Oper. Res. **223**, 417–420 (2012). https://doi.org/10.1016/J.EJOR.2012.06.016
56. R Core Team (2020) R: The R Project for Statistical Computing. https://www.r-project.org/. https://www.r-project.org/. Accessed 6 Dec 2022
57. Rhodes Universtiy (2014) Research ethics policy: Research Involving Human Participants. Makhanda
58. Saaty, R.W.: The analytic hierachy process- what it is and how it is used. Math. Model. **9**, 161–176 (1987)
59. Pahl-Wostl, C., Lebel, L., Knieper, C., Nikitina, E.: From applying panaceas to mastering complexity: toward adaptive water governance in river basins. Environ. Sci. Policy **23**, 23–34 (2012). https://doi.org/10.1016/j.envsci.2012.07.014
60. Seigerman, C.K., McKay, S.K., Basilio, R., et al.: Operationalizing equity for integrated water resources management. J. Am. Water Resour. Assoc. **00**, 1–18 (2022). https://doi.org/10.1111/1752-1688.13086
61. Munier, N., Hontoria, E.: Shortcomings of the AHP method. In: Uses and Limitations of the AHP Method. Management for Professionals, pp. 41–90. Springer, Cham. (2021). https://doi.org/10.1007/978-3-030-60392-2_5
62. Le Maître, D.C., Forsyth, G.G., Dzikiti, S., Gush, M.B.: Estimates of the impacts of invasive alien plants on water flows in South Africa. Water SA **42**, 659–672 (2016). https://doi.org/10.4314/wsa.v42i4.17
63. Van Loon, A.F., Rangecroft, S., Coxon, G., et al.: Streamflow droughts aggravated by human activities despite management. Environ. Res. Lett. **17**, 044059 (2022). https://doi.org/10.1088/1748-9326/AC5DEF
64. Kandasamy, J., Sounthararajah, D., Sivabalan, P., et al.: Socio-hydrologic drivers of the pendulum swing between agricultural development and environmental health: a case study from Murrumbidgee River basin, Australia. Hydrol. Earth Syst. Sci. **18**, 1027–1041 (2014). https://doi.org/10.5194/HESS-18-1027-2014
65. Palmer, C., Munnik, V., du Toit, D., et al.: Practising Adaptive IWRM (Integrated Water Resources Management) in South Africa. Pretoria, South Africa (2018)
66. Pande, S., Sivapalan, M.: Progress in socio-hydrology: a meta-analysis of challenges and opportunities. WIREs Water **4**, 1–18 (2017). https://doi.org/10.1002/wat2.1193
67. Denby, K., Movik, S., Mehta, L., Van Koppen, B.: The trickle down of IWRM: a case study of local-level realities in the inkomati water management area, South Africa. Water Altern **9**, 473–492 (2016)

68. Zahir, S.: Clusters in a group: decision making in the vector space formulation of the analytic hierarchy process. Eur. J. Oper. Res. **112**, 620–634 (1999). https://doi.org/10.1016/S0377-2217(98)00021-6
69. Lerat, J., Tomkins, K., Shao, Q., et al.: How to quantify uncertainty in water allocation models? An exploratory analysis based on hypothetical case studies. IAHS-AISH Publ. **347**, 146–152 (2011)

DSS Applications for Sustainability - Health, Energy and Transportation

Attracting Financing for Green Energy Projects: A City Readiness Index

Aikaterini Papapostolou$^{(\boxtimes)}$, Charikleia Karakosta, Filippos Dimitrios Mexis, and John Psarras

Decision Support Systems Laboratory, School of Electrical and Computer Engineering, National Technical University of Athens, Ir. Politechniou 9, Zografou, 157 80 Athens, Greece
{kpapap,chkara,pmexis,john}@epu.ntua.gr

Abstract. Standard population projections show that virtually all global growth will be in urban areas over the next thirty years. At the same time, the last decades of constant economic and population growth, the modern lifestyle of developed countries and the creation of new needs have led to an increase in energy use per capita and at an overall level resulting in environmental pollution and strengthening of the greenhouse effect. It is essential, therefore, not only at a county level but also at a city level to boost investments in green energy projects. However, important barriers hinder local authorities from investing in this kind of projects. Among others, these barriers include the lack of internal capacity to identify and implement innovative financing schemes, high cost of financing or lack of private financing. This paper presents a software tool for assessing cities' readiness to receive the necessary financial assistance in order to implement green energy projects. The cities' performance is evaluated along three axes (i) Investment Attractiveness, (ii) Utilisation of Financial Resources and (iii) Project Implementation, while the methodology is based on multicriteria analysis. A pilot application in ten European cities has been conducted, and fruitful outcomes have been derived from the comparative analysis.

Keywords: Energy Transition · Sustainable Energy · Green Projects · Green Financing · City Readiness · Assessment Tool · Pilot Application · Europe

1 Introduction

Cities play a powerful role in driving investment that can shape the transition to a greener economy and more equitable society [1]. Cities are essential actors in stimulating projects with green potential in sectors such as buildings, transport, water and waste; and urban finance is one of the promising ways in which this can be achieved [2]. The transition to green cities is an essential process that will require overcoming many challenges, particularly with regard to technology, governance and financing [3]. Regarding technology, smart cities have to overcome issues related to electric energy supply, digitalisation and interconnection so as to electrify transport while also enhancing the grid and enabling it to support the production from renewables [4]. All the above imply actions from local administrations, which brings to the forefront another challenge: the decisiveness and availability of local governance to support and advance towards the sustainability direction. Central governments, and provincial and municipal bodies, are unlikely to fund the required infrastructure developments by themselves, given budgetary deficits and levels of debt [5]. Investors, whether banks, institutional investors, specialist funds and investment firms, need a return on investment and are unlikely to commit funds to infrastructure unless tangible opportunities meet their risk-reward criteria [6].

The attraction and engagement of investors to finance and implement projects that will contribute to the green development and smart readiness of a city are of crucial importance. This implies the involvement of companies, market actors and municipalities to create a clear investing framework to create appealing opportunities for investors [7].

In literature, a City Capability Assessment Framework exists, established by Spyridaki et al. [8] focusing on the capacities of cities to finance and implement sustainable energy-related projects. Gibberd et al. [9] propose a City Capability Framework that strengthens the relationship between city sustainability strategy, targets and indicators and city planning and implementation process and shows how this may work through practical examples.

The present paper introduces a methodological framework based on multicriteria analysis that evaluates cities' performance under the scope of their readiness to receive and exploit investments that will pave the way towards the transition to a green, sustainable future. The methodological framework is materialised through the development of a software tool that evaluates the cities along three main axes while implementing the application of the proposed tool in ten European cities. Through the pilot testing, outcomes have been derived and presented, performing a comparative analysis.

Apart from the introductory Section, the following manuscript includes the sections Materials and Methods, the Application and Results, and the Conclusions.

2 Materials and Methods

The assessment framework was created on the basis of a process defined in the United Nations Development Programme (UNDP) Capacity Assessment Methodology [10], which involves defining the capabilities to be measured, the desired future capability levels and, finally, the assessment of existing capabilities by appropriately defined means (Fig. 1).

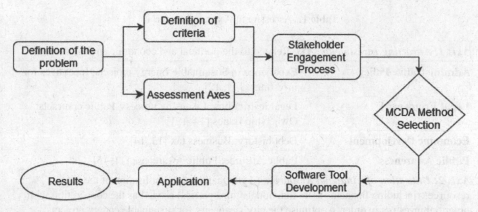

Fig. 1. Flowchart of the Methodological Approach and Application

Problem Definition

The problem that the proposed methodology and the respective tool are aiming to tackle is the lack of a common framework that could potentially be used to estimate a city's readiness to implement green projects and become a "smart city". The estimation and the respective assessment are based on the evaluation of non-homogeneous variables, which have to properly be identified and defined. Another issue that has to be solved when it comes to the realisation of the assessment is the proper quantification of the criteria, which in the specific methodology is being addressed by the utilisation of a 5-grade linguistic scale.

Assessment Axes and Definition of Criteria

The assessment framework structure and the criteria that measure the city capacities have been developed along three axes based on the study of Spyridaki et al. [8].

Stakeholder Engagement Process

A participatory approach is considered necessary to outline the stakeholders' opinions and needs and to re-form and evaluate the proposed methodology [22]. Several studies implement various stakeholder engagement and clustering techniques, such as the k-means clustering technique [23], while other studies focus on and prioritise the mainstreaming of stakeholder research [24].

In order to apply the proposed methodology, stakeholders were engaged through the participation in a survey in order to externalise the performance of 10 cities from 9 different EU countries (i.e. Greece, Slovenia, Austria, Portugal, Romania, Ireland, Croatia, France, and Bulgaria). The stakeholders involved in the survey were staff from the cities' municipalities that were involved in the procedure of identifying financing for green energy projects (Table 1).

Table 1. Assessment Axes and Criteria

Axis 1: Attracting Investments (A₁): Related to the political and economic environment	
Administrative Policy	Experience in Sustainable Energy projects; Incentives for investment [11, 12]
Legal Framework	Legal restrictions; Licensing process; Public contracts; Ownership issues [14–19]
Economic Development	Debt history; Business tax [13, 14]
Public Awareness	Public Attitude; Public Awareness [11, 15]
Axis 2: Utilisation of Financial Resources (A₂): Quantifies the utilisation of the city's resources (including financing from individuals/third parties) as well as the cooperation with potential investors in order to optimise the city's capacity for sustainable energy projects	
Capital Management	Budget for green projects; Approved budget; Cooperation with other cities [11, 16–19]
Finding Funds	Staff to find financing; Personnel for undertaking projects; Evaluation process [20, 21]
Axis 3: Project Implementation (A₃): The management possibilities and monitoring systems in practice are explored. Having dedicated staff supporting project management and supervision processes ensures qualified project results and improves investment efficiency	
Organisation and Management	Project control staff, Personnel training, Educational programs available [17, 21]
Check and Monitoring	Measurement & Verification processes; Quality & Assurance methods [18, 21]

Assessment Method

After externalising the value of each indicator based on the input data from the survey and determining their scale, a multi-step evaluation process is applied to evaluate the City Readiness Index (CRI). The evaluation method followed is a Multicriteria Decision Analysis (MCDA). First of all, the survey input is used to normalise the indicators so as to express them on a common numerical basis, regardless of their measurement scale. From this point of view, the indicators in each axis and pillar can be easily summed up using a value-added system to conclude the performance per axis and/or pillar. The quantification of the qualitative criteria has been realised by using a 5-grade scale based on the methodology of Doukas et al. [25] and the 2-tuple model by Herrera et al. [26]. All criteria are of strict increasing preference. Moreover, for the sake of simplicity, it is assumed that there is no strong evidence for the significance between the degree of each pillar and the individual values of the corresponding indicators. Therefore, all criteria contribute equally to the value-added system so that the higher their values, the better the quality of the pillar.

Based on the above, the CRI can be evaluated as the weighted sum of the city's performance in each of the three axes (A₁, A₂, A₃) as follows:

$$CRI(A1, A2, A3) = w_{A1} * A1 + w_{A2} * A2 + w_{A3} * A3 \tag{1}$$

The weights should sum to one and are determined by the decision-makers involved, according to their preferences. Similarly, the city's performance on each of the three axes is a function of the indicators involved and is evaluated as follows:

$$A1 = w_{P1} * P_1 + w_{P2} * P_2 + w_{P_3} * P_3 + w_{P_4} * P_4 \qquad (2)$$

$$A2 = w_{P_5} * P_5 + w_{P_6} * P_6 \qquad (3)$$

$$A3 = w_{P_7} * P_7 + w_{P_8} * P_8 \qquad (4)$$

In the above equations, the P_i symbols represent the city's performance on each pillar based on the criteria of the indicators. The weights for Eqs. (2)–(4) are determined by the final decision-makers and users of the tool, according to their preferences.

According to the described evaluation framework, an "Excellent" city benchmark is an ideal city that achieves the highest scores in all three axes of the evaluation and, therefore, during the operation of the aggregation evaluation. The "Excellent" city can be used as a reference point for each city to monitor its performance, focusing either on specific performance axes or on the overall performance of the City. In addition, the proposed framework can be used to compare cities with each other.

Heterogeneous information from indicators is converted into qualitative information, expressed with the help of 2-tuple, an expression model consisting of a qualitative term and a numerical value evaluated on a scale [−0.5,0.5), as defined by Herrera [26] and appropriately adapted for energy-related applications by the Doukas [25] et al..

Development of Assessment Tool

The application of the methodological framework has been conducted through the development of an integrated assessment tool. The assessment tool was designed and implemented in Microsoft Office Excel, utilising the integrated Visual Basic for Applications (VBA) programming language. Although the software developed is not yet open access, the authors may provide the software, upon request, to researchers and stakeholders for further testing and deployment. The model of the tool is based on the 2-tuple presentation model by F. Herrera [26], enriched with multiple visual and user input interfaces.

The structure of the software consists of **four basic modules** that perform the main functions and a final report interface that presents the output of the tool.

Data: It enables the user to enter the cities and the indicators with their data.

5-grade scale: It transforms the input data on a scale from 1 to 5 based on the 2-tuple model. The quantitative scale from 1 to 5 corresponds to the qualitative scale Insignificant, Low, Medium, High, Excellent.

Settings: The user can adjust the preferences and the criteria weights.

Results: The outputs of the methodology application are presented. The user receives a comprehensive knowledge of the city's performance with data visualisations and graphs, making the analysis more interactive, user friendly and understandable.

Dashboard: The control panel summarises the results of the assessment. It enables users to make direct comparisons of city performance and quickly see the basic data from the other modules.

3   Comparison with Indices from the Respective Literature

Several studies exist that aim to produce a city readiness index. Each approach incorporates distinct principles and focuses on different city sustainability aspects. Neder et. Al [27] performs an application of the Urban Adaptation Index (UAI) to assess the potential capacity of cities to deal with climate change impacts. The index combines a set of structural (generic capacity) and climate-specific (specific capacity) elements covered in the scientific literature on urban adaptive capacity, and integrates insights provided by Brazilian municipal practitioners. In comparison to the index proposed by the present manuscript, the index of Neder et. Al focuses mainly on public policies and climate risk management, leaving aside the potential for development, investments, and strategy to achieve funding.

In addition, several city readiness indices exist, which are focused on specific sustainability aspects. For example, Torres et. Al has developed the Socio-Climatic Vulnerability Index (SCVI)—which aggregates information on the intensity of climate change with social factors that may influence the vulnerability of the population in a given region [28]. Zayed has developed a city readiness index, specifically for cycling friendliness in cities, identifying a set of five primary indicators of city readiness to adopt cycling from a statistical analysis of the urban and environmental attributes of bicycle-friendly city (BFC) notion [29]. Lynn et Al. Proposes a framework for the Assessment of a City's Digital Readiness, that can be used by local stakeholder sand regional and national policymakers to understand digital town readiness and digital competitiveness; compare a town against selected national and international benchmarks; and stimulate stakeholder engagement on digital strategies for town development [29].

The evaluation of cities and regions for sustainability aspects does not only concerns adademic researchers. Institutes, think tanks and consulting companies are also explore and develop indices, in order to quantify and compare cities and regions. Ernst and Young (EY) has developed the Climate Change Readiness Index (CCRI) for the Middle East and North Africa (MENA) region, to track responses to climate change in Egypt, Jordan and the six members of the Gulf Cooperation Council (GCC). This index is mainly focusing on the vulnerability, measuring how well governments are tackling the factors in their control, in particular how they are adapting their economies and societies to climate change and how well they are mitigating the phenomenon by reducing emissions [30]. Besides, Deloitte has introduced a City Mobility Index that measures urban mobility performance three broad thematic areas: performance, policy-making and practicality and providing a holistic perspective on city mobility [31].

As observed from the literature review and the relevant indices developed, the majority focus on environmental, climate change and government policy level, while several are calculated on a country level, rather than city level. The index proposed from the methodology developed and introduced in the present manuscript focuses on a city level, while also takes into account a holistic approach of assessing city's readiness sustainable investments, including investment attraction, utilisation of resources and proper project implementation. Although the literature review have came across various indices that aim to assess the city's readiness in a variety of subjects (mobility, climate change adaptation), there is a scarcity on indices that focus entirely on the city's readiness of selecting and adopting sustainable project. The proposed index assesses these aspects in terms of readiness in investment undertake, which provides useful instrument to policy makers, local authorities and city's stakeholders to pave the way to make cities greener, overall.

4 Application and Results

This section summarises the results of the assessment of 10 European cities and the calculation of the City Readiness Index through the City Assessment Tool. The results are shown in the graphs of Fig. 2 and 3.

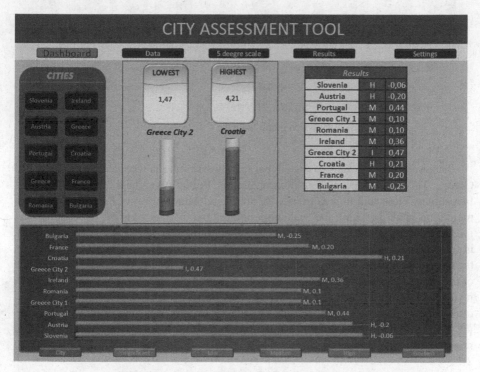

Fig. 2. City Readiness Assessment Tool – Dashboard

The highest score/rating is observed for the city located in Croatia, followed by the cities in Slovenia and Austria. The city in Croatia scores excellently in the implementation of projects, while the city's rating in the utilisation of financial resources is also high. Especially, in the "Organization and Management" criterion the Croatian city has received a score of 5, that corresponds to an excellent rating on the qualitative scale of the evaluation framework. At the same time, the "Control and Monitoring" criterion (in the same axis) receives the second highest score of all the other indicator categories. Even the lowest rating for the city of Croatia falls within the High scale and corresponds to the "Legal Framework" criterion.

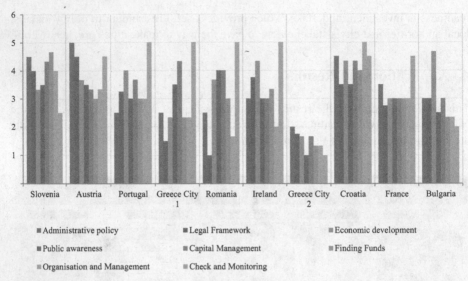

Fig. 3. Evaluation graph from the City Assessment Tool

The evaluation has demonstrated that the lowest rating is received by the City 2 of Greece. This city has poor score in the criterion "Public Awareness" of the "Attracting Investments" axis and in the criterion "Control and Monitoring" of the "Project Implementation" axis. In detail, the evaluation in these two indicators is the lowest possible, judged as "Insignificant". The very poor evaluation that City 2 of Greece demonstrates, is perfectly explained, considering that the highest score it performs is only two points on the quantitative scale of five. Overall, it receives a "Low" rating on the qualitative scale of the framework. At the same time, the rest of the indicators receive a low rating, which justifies the overall "Insignificant" rating. It is imperative for that city to correct and improve the performance in the criteria related to the axis of project implementation, as the evaluation is very low. The measures that could be taken to improve the qualification require internal restructuring without the influence of any other external factor (Table 2). .

Despite the difference observed in the evaluation outcomes between the ten cities, the majority receives a "Medium" rating. Specifically, six out of ten cities receive the "Medium" rating, three receive "High" rating, one the "Insignificant" rating. Therefore, we observe that more than half of the cities are in the middle value of the qualitative rating scale defined by the framework. This shows a general tendency for Europe's cities to make a good effort to improve in various areas, to attract investment and to be able to chase subsidies. Regarding the poor performance of Greece in the CRI, it has to be noted that the country has been in a general crisis in recent years and municipalities should take measures to improve cities in various sectors. This will enable them to attract investments and /high expectations in order to contribute to the general recovery of the Greek economy. Of course, the second city that participated in the evaluation and is located in Greece was rated with an "Average" value, which indicates that efforts are being made at the level of cities and regions. Specifically, the Greek cities performed a

Table 2. Evaluation of cities per criterion

Indicator	Slovenia	Austria	Portugal	Greece City 1	Romania	Ireland	Greece City 2	Croatia	France	Bulgaria
Administrative policy	4,50	5,00	2,50	2,50	2,50	3,00	2,00	4,50	3,50	3,00
Legal Framework	4,00	4,50	3,25	1,50	1,00	3,75	1,75	3,50	2,75	3,00
Economic development	3,33	3,67	4,00	2,33	3,67	4,33	1,67	4,33	3,00	4,67
Public awareness	3,50	3,50	3,00	3,50	4,00	3,00	1,00	3,50	3,00	2,50
Capital Management	4,33	3,33	3,67	4,33	4,00	3,00	1,67	4,33	3,00	3,00
Finding Funds	4,67	3,00	3,00	2,33	3,00	3,33	1,33	4,00	3,00	2,33
Organisation and Management	4,00	3,33	3,00	2,33	1,67	2,00	1,33	5,00	3,00	2,33
Check and Monitoring	2,50	4,50	5,00	5,00	5,00	5,00	1,00	4,50	4,50	2,00

"High" to "Moderate" evaluation both in the axis of "Implementation of projects" and in the axis of "Utilisation of financial resources".

5 Conclusions

The evaluation process using the City Assessment Tool has highlighted the barriers and issues that are preventing cities from achieving remarkable results. In particular, the lack of local strategy forms an obstacle, as potential investors perceive a vague political environment regarding sustainable energy policy, where risk mitigation mechanisms are absent. Moreover, such an environment can create a situation where the legal framework related to green investments is incomplete and therefore public procurement, acquisition and ownership permits create barriers in implementing such investments. Each community should be able to employ or train permanent/temporary staff in order to ensure that programmes are carried out in accordance with specific requirements, to maintain and integrate draft programmes, to oversee and report on overall progress.

Regarding the challenges for the CRI calculation process, a main barrier has been the data scarcity, which emerges from the lack of organised and in-depth data recording from the city local authorities. Also, the dispersion of the available data is limited, both at local and regional level, making the calculations more difficult. In detail, the data scarcity is identified in the lack of comparative data from various years from the energy consumption of cities and regions, and the respective GHG emissions. The possession of aforementioned type of data would lead to a more detailed and accurate depiction of the energy baseline and consumption of the cities. Future knowledge of these quantities will lead to safer conclusions about the performance of the regions, as well as the level of commitment to the implementation of actions aimed at achieving the desired objectives.

The process of evaluation and comparative analysis of cities has highlighted the inherent problems in achieving high results. In summary, the lack of technologies for forecasting and monitoring projects and related infrastructure, the bureaucracy and the strict legal framework, the lack of information of citizens on green development issues, the poor financial management made by cities and the general economic recession led to the moderate evaluation of the majority of cities.

The methodology presented in the previous chapters consists of a useful basis for assessing the performance of cities and regions. On top of this evaluation there are several additional elements and functions that can be developed, expanded and form an even more complete system.

A first extension that would give a better picture of the progress and performance of a set of European and not only cities, in relation to the other entries in the system, is the more detailed comparison of their sizes and results. For example, it would be quite interesting for the user to see if for each rating indicator it is above or below the average of the rest. Also, the comparison could be limited to cities belonging to the same geographical area or country, those that are similar in size both in area and population, or to cities that are energy at about the same level. All this should be combined with adaptive, dynamic graphs, in order to achieve a better visual presentation.

Another useful element would be for administrators to have a plethora of statistics regarding system entries. For example, how many cities per country or per geographical area use the system, which are the cities that show the best results per year and the averages of the evaluation indicators overall or per country and region.

An extension concerning the indicators would be the entry of data for purely energy purposes in order to obtain a more detailed picture of consumption and other energy aggregates. At the same time, the possibility of choosing action plans at the level of different buildings, can lead to the improvement of the accuracy of the results due to the avoidance of generalised assumptions. Then, on the basis of these elements, further groupings could be carried out, perhaps dynamically defined by the user of the system.

Finally, the tool implemented, along with the necessary modifications and improvements, could in the future be an auxiliary tool and an extension of a decision support system (DSS), with which to cooperate and enable users to evaluate at the end of a period the results they have brought and whether they have improved over time.

The modern economic crisis has stripped away some of the inherent flaws of the current system. At the same time, however, it created an opening for significant changes to be made to this system to help create a better, more sustainable, and desirable future. This opportunity must not be missed. We should defend a more integrated model that takes account of the human factor so that the economy, society and the environment are compatible with each other.

References

1. Hammer, S., Kamal-Chaoui, L., Robert, A., Plouin, M.: Cities and Green Growth: A Conceptual Framework (2011)
2. Merk, O., Saussier, S., Staropoli, C., Slack, E., Kim, J.-H.: Financing Green Urban Infrastructure (2012). https://www.oecd.org/cfe/regionaldevelopment/WP_Financing_Green_Urban_Infrastructure.pdf

3. Marinakis, V., Karakosta, C., Papadopoulou, A.G., Psarras, J.: Sustainable energy action plan for the covenant signatories: the choice of emission factors. In: Reyes, D. (ed.) Sustainable Development: Processes, Challenges and Prospects, pp. 129–142. Nova Science Publishers, Inc (2015)
4. Karakosta, C., Doukas, H., Psarras, J.: Technology transfer through climate change: setting a sustainable energy pattern. Renew. Sustain. Energy Rev. **14**, 1546–1557 (2010). https://doi.org/10.1016/j.rser.2010.02.001
5. Karakosta, C.: A holistic approach for addressing the issue of effective technology transfer in the frame of climate change. Energies (Basel) **9**, 503 (2016). https://doi.org/10.3390/en9070503
6. Yen, Z.: Long Finance: Financing the Transition: Sustainable Infrastructure in Cities (2015)
7. Papapostolou, A., Mexis, F.D., Karakosta, C., Psarras, J.: A multicriteria tool to support decision-making in the early stages of energy efficiency investments. In: Cabral Seixas Costa, A.P., Papathanasiou, J., Jayawickrama, U., Kamissoko, D. (eds.) Decision Support Systems XII: Decision Support Addressing Modern Industry, Business, and Societal Needs. ICDSST 2022. Lecture Notes in Business Information Processing, vol. 447, 190–202. Springer, Cham (2022). https://doi.org/10.1007/978-3-031-06530-9_15
8. Spyridaki, N.-A., Kleanthis, N., Tzani, D., Matosović, M.D., Flamos, A.: A City capability assessment framework focusing on planning, financing, and implementing sustainable energy projects. Sustainability **12**, 8447 (2020). https://doi.org/10.3390/su12208447
9. Gibberd, J.: Strengthening sustainability planning: the city capability framework. Procedia Eng. **198**, 200–211 (2017). https://doi.org/10.1016/j.proeng.2017.07.084
10. United Nations Development Programme: UNDP capacity assessment methodology (2008). https://www.undp.org/publications/undp-capacity-assessment-methodology
11. Mosannenzadeh, F., di Nucci, M.R., Vettorato, D.: Identifying and prioritizing barriers to implementation of smart energy city projects in Europe: an empirical approach. Energy Policy **105**, 191–201 (2017). https://doi.org/10.1016/J.ENPOL.2017.02.007
12. G20 Energy Efficiency Finance Task Group (EEFTG): G20 Energy Efficiency Investment Toolkit, Paris, France (2017)
13. The Economist Intelligence Unit: Benchmarking the Future Competitiveness of Cities, London, UK (2013)
14. International Renewable Energy Agency (IRENA): Financial Mechanisms and Investment Frameworks for Renewables in Developing Countries, Abu Dhabi, UAE (2012)
15. Commission, E.: Smart Cities Stakeholder Platform: Financing Models for Smart Cities. Belgium, Brussels (2013)
16. UN-Habitat: Financing Sustainable Urban Development: Challenges and Opportunities, Nairobi, Kenya (2013)
17. European Federation of Agencies and Regions for Energy and the Enviroment (FEDARENE): Innovative Financing Schemes in Local and Regional Energy Efficiency Policies, Brussels, Belgium (2015)
18. Institute, W.: EUROCITIES: Benchmark of Renewable Energy Sources and Distributed Energy Generation. Belgium, Brussels (2013)
19. CityInvest: A Guide for the Launch of a One Stop Shop on Energy Retrofitting: RenoWatt's Experience in Liège, Brussels, Belgium (2017)
20. Guillermo, A., de Cunto, A., Kontinakis, N., Saraceno, P.P.: Peer Powered Cities and Regions: Report on Needs Assessment. Belgium, Brussels (2017)
21. Commission, E.: Guidance Document on Indicators of Public Administration Capacity Building. Belgium, Brussels (2014)
22. Karakosta, C., Fujiwara, N.: Scaling up and intensifying stakeholders engagement for evidence-based policymaking: lessons learned. In: Hashmi, S., Choudhury, I.A. (eds.) Encyclopedia of Renewable and Sustainable Materials, pp. 773–782 (2020)

23. Höfer, T., Madlener, R.: A participatory stakeholder process for evaluating sustainable energy transition scenarios. Energy Policy **139**, 111277 (2020). https://doi.org/10.1016/j.enpol.2020.111277

24. Lehtinen, J., Aaltonen, K.: Organizing external stakeholder engagement in inter-organizational projects: opening the black box. Int. J. Project Manage. **38**, 85–98 (2020). https://doi.org/10.1016/j.ijproman.2019.12.001

25. Doukas, H., Tsiousi, A., Marinakis, V., Psarras, J.: Linguistic multi-criteria decision making for energy and environmental corporate policy. Inf. Sci. (NY). **258**, 328–338 (2014). https://doi.org/10.1016/j.ins.2013.08.027

26. Martinez, L., Herrera, F.: A 2-tuple fuzzy linguistic representation model for computing with words. IEEE Trans. Fuzzy Syst. **8**, 746–752 (2000). https://doi.org/10.1109/91.890332

27. Neder, E.A., et al.: Urban adaptation index: assessing cities readiness to deal with climate change. Clim. Change **166**, 1–20 (2021). https://doi.org/10.1007/S10584-021-03113-0/FIGURES/3

28. Torres, R.R., Lapola, D.M., Marengo, J.A., Lombardo, M.A.: Socio-climatic hotspots in Brazil. Clim. Change. **115**, 597–609 (2012). https://doi.org/10.1007/S10584-012-0461-1/TABLES/3

29. Zayed, M.A.: Towards an index of city readiness for cycling. Int. J. Transp. Sci. Technol. **5**, 210–225 (2016). https://doi.org/10.1016/J.IJTST.2017.01.002

30. Ernst and Young: The EY MENA Climate Change Readiness Index (2023)

31. The Deloitte City Mobility Index | Deloitte Insights Middle East. https://www2.deloitte.com/xe/en/insights/focus/future-of-mobility/deloitte-urban-mobility-index-for-cities.html

Building Risk Prediction Models for Diabetes Decision Support System

Sarra Samet[✉] and Ridda Mohamed Laouar

Laboratory of Mathematics, Informatics and Systems (LAMIS), University of Larbi Tebessi,
12004 Tebessa, Algeria
{sarra.samet,ridda.laouar}@univ-tebessa.dz

Abstract. Diabetes mellitus early detection is one of the most important issues in the literature nowadays. It contributes to the development of many deadly conditions, including heart disease, coronary disease, eye disease, kidney disease, and even nerve damage. As a result, its prediction is critical. Over the years, several academics have attempted to build an accurate diabetes prediction model. However, due to a lack of relevant data sets and prediction methodologies, this area still has substantial outstanding research concerns. The study attempts to solve the challenges by investigating healthcare predictive analytics. This project employs supervised learning through the application of 3 classification algorithms to early anticipate diabetes with high performance. To train and evaluate the prediction models, we used a sizable diabetes dataset based on actual health data gathered from the Centers for Disease Control and Prevention, which was properly pre-processed in this study, such as how the imbalance was handled utilizing resampling technique. We went with the Logistic Regression Algorithm, Decision Tree Algorithm, and Random Forest Algorithm to analyze the dataset. Based on several evaluation matrices, the results reveal that the RF algorithm outperformed other machine learning algorithms with an F1score of 93.01%. The results of the trial indicate that our suggested model outperforms cutting-edge alternatives. This study's findings may be useful to health professionals, organizations, students, and researchers working in diabetes prediction research and development.

Keywords: Machine Learning · Artificial Intelligence · Decision Support System · Health Care · Data Mining · Diabetes

1 Introduction

Diabetes is a condition that occurs when the pancreas fails to create enough insulin or when the insulin produced is ineffective, and it can lead to significant problems. It is one of the most common diseases in the world today [1, 2].

© The Author(s), under exclusive license to Springer Nature Switzerland AG 2023
S. Liu et al. (Eds.): ICDSST 2023, LNBIP 474, pp. 171–181, 2023.
https://doi.org/10.1007/978-3-031-32534-2_13

Since the outbreak of the COVID-19 epidemic, health has become a priority for many people. Diabetes is one of those diseases that has increased in the last 12–15 years. People with diabetes have also been found to be particularly vulnerable during the COVID-19 pandemic. Because of its ease of onset and difficulties of complete eradication, diabetes is frequently addressed [3, 4]. Therefore, because it incorporates several aspects, it is still difficult to anticipate. Numerous predictive, quantitative, and statistical models are used to predict and identify illness. As data mining approaches, strategies, and tools become increasingly promising for predicting diabetes and later reducing treatment costs for multiple people, its position in medical health care is apparent [5–7].

The most recent advancement in ML has improved the computer system's ability to detect and categorize pictures, forecast illnesses, and enhance decision-making through data analysis. Applications for machine learning (ML) aim to educate the computer system to perform better than a person. The model is trained using the supervised learning technique, and it is then evaluated using test data [8, 9].

We aim to use three machine learning algorithms which at the time of writing, are the methods most frequently utilized in the literatura to construct a binary classification that can predict whether or not a person has diabetes. Finally, the outcomes are evaluated in terms of performance and scalability.

There is a vast amount of patient information available at hospitals. These data may offer much more insights if they are successfully recovered, allowing for the prediction of diseases months or even years in advance. In machine learning, models are created based on the collected and processed data [10, 11].

There are several diabetes prediction models available. However, due to the complexities of diabetes's causation, the prediction performance of models based on survey data must be improved. Furthermore, while many diabetes risk factors have been discovered, such as obesity and age, others have yet to be found. That's why the Behavioral Risk Factor Surveillance System dataset is used. The existing diabetic disease prediction methods use a tiny dataset. Our system's goal is to operate on a larger dataset in order to improve overall system efficiency. In this work, a machine learning approach for predicting early-onset diabetes was presented. We discovered that the Random_forest performs exceptionally well on the test dataset and is also quite resilient to volatility. They properly anticipated all of the test set examples, demonstrating its validity in a real-life setting.

2   Methodology and Materials

In Fig. 1 we can see the whole proposed methodology to follow in this paper:

Fig. 1. Proposed methodology

The chosen dataset is first loaded, and in order to do the proper analytics on it, pre-processing and exploratory data analysis are required. The next phase involves applying machine learning algorithms to create prediction models that must be assessed using various performance measures. All of this is done to help in choosing the model that is most appropriate for the task and to help in making intelligent decisions.

2.1 Dataset Utilized

The dataset is from an annual health-related telephone survey (https://www.kaggle.com/datasets/cdc/behavioral-risk-factor-surveillance-system) done by the Centers for Disease Control and Prevention (CDC) to discover various risk factors that collects state data on U.S. citizens regarding their health-related risk behaviors, chronic health issues, and usage of preventive services.

From Fig. 2 the dataset has 253680 entries, and data columns is of 22 columns total the attribute diabetes_binary is the target which means being diabetic or not.

```
Data columns (total 22 columns):
 #   Column                Non-Null Count   Dtype
---  ------                --------------   -----
 0   Diabetes_binary       253680 non-null  float64
 1   HighBP                253680 non-null  float64
 2   HighChol              253680 non-null  float64
 3   CholCheck             253680 non-null  float64
 4   BMI                   253680 non-null  float64
 5   Smoker                253680 non-null  float64
 6   Stroke                253680 non-null  float64
 7   HeartDiseaseorAttack  253680 non-null  float64
 8   PhysActivity          253680 non-null  float64
 9   Fruits                253680 non-null  float64
 10  Veggies               253680 non-null  float64
 11  HvyAlcoholConsump     253680 non-null  float64
 12  AnyHealthcare         253680 non-null  float64
 13  NoDocbcCost           253680 non-null  float64
 14  GenHlth               253680 non-null  float64
 15  MentHlth              253680 non-null  float64
 16  PhysHlth              253680 non-null  float64
 17  DiffWalk              253680 non-null  float64
 18  Sex                   253680 non-null  float64
 19  Age                   253680 non-null  float64
 20  Education             253680 non-null  float64
 21  Income                253680 non-null  float64
```

Fig. 2. Dataset information

2.2 Pre-processing and EDA of the Dataset

To begin, we established data preprocessing that contains the following: Cleaning of data (removing nulls if they exist, removing duplicates), Data is divided into Features (x) and Target (y), Preprocessed datasets are saved in files to make it easier to remember data and run code. As the data was not balanced, over-sampling was used to balance it. And to facilitate processing, standard scaling is used to X-features.

After duplications deletion we get a dataset of (229474,22) (Fig. 3):

```
dataset.duplicated().sum()
```

24206

```
dataset = dataset.drop_duplicates()
```

```
dataset.shape
```

(229474, 22)

Fig. 3. Dataset after dropping duplicates.

Handling imbalanced datasets with oversampling which is a data mining and data analytics approach for modifying uneven data classes to generate balanced datasets (Fig. 4 and Fig. 5):

```
from imblearn.over_sampling import RandomOverSampler
sm = RandomOverSampler()
X_over_sampled , y_over_sampled = sm.fit_resample(X , y )
print("X_balanced shape is " , X_over_sampled.shape )
print("y_balanced shape is " , y_over_sampled.shape )
```

X_balanced shape is (388754, 21)
y_balanced shape is (388754,)

Fig. 4. Overcoming imbalanced data.

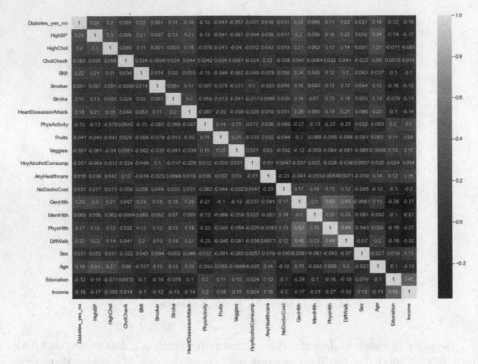

Fig. 5. Correlation Graph Plot.

3   Modeling

Machine learning approaches were applied in this work to predict the prognosis of early diabetes, and the anticipated conclusions were obtained. We divided the dataset into 70% for training and 30% for testing, resulting in 272127 and 116627 records, respectively.

Because of its high classification capacity, the decision tree is a prominent machine learning approach in the medical profession. Random forests are also extensively utilized since they may generate a large number of decision trees.

3.1   Logistic Regression (LR)

LR is a ML technique using parameters. The decision boundary is defined by the parameters and the activation function. The activation is Sigmoid, and the parameters are learned by inspecting the dataset [12].

3.2   Decision Tree (DT)

DT is a classification problem-solving supervised machine learning algorithm. The primary goal of employing DT in this study effort is to forecast the target class using a decision rule derived from past data. It predicts and classifies using nodes and internodes. Root nodes categorize instances based on various characteristics. The root node may contain two or more branches, whereas the leaf node represents categorization. DT selects each node at each step by assessing the maximum information gain across all characteristics [13].

3.3   Random Forest (RF)

The name "forest" indicates that it will be densely forested. The RF Classifier is a collection of decision trees drawn from a randomly chosen training subset. To create predictions, the model consists of many decision trees that use bootstrapping, random selections of functions, and average voting [14].

4   Results and Discussion

The most common disease that affects people is diabetes. It is brought on by high blood sugar levels and insufficient insulin production. There are several symptoms and indicators of diabetes that need to be looked for before doing a clinical evaluation. Although the newly identified indicators are simple to spot in a manual, accurately predicting diabetes remains a significant difficulty [15, 16]. To tackle this axe we performed 3 supervised machine learning algorithms on the CDC data set to investigate the prediction of diabetes.

The dataset was split across 70% training and 30% validation. The same training and validation data were provided to all algorithms. The following figures show each classifier's confusion matrix (Fig. 6, Fig. 7 and Fig. 8):

		Truth data			
		Class 1	Class 2	Classification overall	User's accuracy (Precision)
Classifier results	Class 1	41463	16886	58349	71.06%
	Class 2	14439	43839	58278	75.224%
	Truth overall	55902	60725	116627	
	Producer's accuracy (Recall)	74.171%	72.193%		

Overall accuracy (OA): 73.141%

Fig. 6. LR's binary classification confusion matrix.

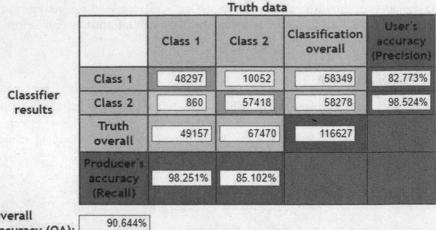

Truth data

		Class 1	Class 2	Classification overall	User's accuracy (Precision)
Classifier results	Class 1	48297	10052	58349	82.773%
	Class 2	860	57418	58278	98.524%
	Truth overall	49157	67470	116627	
	Producer's accuracy (Recall)	98.251%	85.102%		

Overall accuracy (OA): 90.644%

Fig. 7. DT's binary classification confusion matrix.

Truth data

		Class 1	Class 2	Classification overall	User's accuracy (Precision)
Classifier results	Class 1	51352	6997	58349	88.008%
	Class 2	719	57559	58278	98.766%
	Truth overall	52071	64556	116627	
	Producer's accuracy (Recall)	98.619%	89.161%		

Overall accuracy (OA): 93.384%

Fig. 8. RF's binary classification confusion matrix.

The next figure shows our model's performance comparison in term of accuracy, sensitivity, precision and F1 Score. As can be noticed, the best results were obtained with the RF classifier, followed by the DT classifier. LR turned out the worst in this situation (Fig. 9).

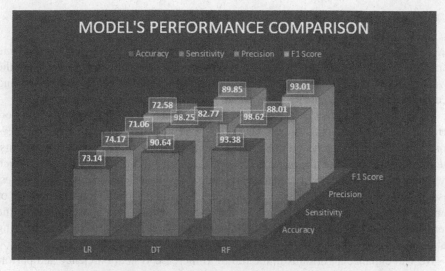

Fig. 9. Model's performance comparison graphic.

Table 1 displays new ML techniques in the literature for diabetes prediction applying distinctive Diabetes Databases. Only the accuracy performance metric was constant across the studied literature, while sensitivity, specificity, and other related measures were not consistently given.

Table 1. Recent works achievement comparison.

work	Collection	Algo	Accuracy
Our work	**dataset has 253680 entries, and data columns is of 22 columns**	**LR** **DT** **RF**	**73.14%** **90.64%** **93.38%**
Eric Adua et al. [17]	dataset contained 438 instances (participants) with eleven (11) different features (attributes)	DT	81%
Sasmita Padhy et al. [18]	offline questionnaire with 15 questions about health, family history, and lifestyle were used to recruit a total of 10221 people for the study	LR	87.2%
Raja Krishnamoorthi et al. [19]	data set consists of 768 rows and 9 columns	LR	83%
Zaigham Mushtaq et al. [20]		RF (SMOTE)	80.7%
Adel Al-Zebari et al. [21]		LR	77.9%

5   Conclusions

Due to the digital age, the large amount of clinical data available has enabled machine learning techniques to perform well in medical diagnosis and prognosis. With the advancement of machine learning techniques and artificial intelligence, researchers and medical practitioners have begun to embrace and apply illness risk estimate [22].

Three supervised machine learning algorithms were developed, with the best performing one. This was discovered to be the RF, which attained an accuracy of 93.38%, sensitivity of 98.62%, precision of 88.01%, and an F1 score of 93.01% in experiments. The main contribution of this paper is the strategies used to preprocess the data, which is why we can validate how crucial data preprocessing is. Because errors, redundancies, missing values, and inconsistencies all affect the set's integrity, we must address all of them for a more accurate result. In addition, a huge dataset was chosen to boost the overall efficiency of the system and the algorithms used resulted in high-performing diabetes predictive models.

We will enhance algorithms in the future to increase system efficiency and performance. We will also try to work on certain features to help fight diabetes even more effectively. Make it a full diagnostic system for use in hospitals as well. The automated diagnosis of the condition will enable medical professionals to complete tests in a shorter amount of time while also enabling patients to take early safeguards in the event that a person has the disorder.

References

1. Syed, A.H., Khan, T.: Machine learning-based application for predicting risk of type 2 diabetes mellitus (t2dm) in saudi arabia: a retrospective cross-sectional study. IEEE Access **8**, 199539–199561 (2020). https://doi.org/10.1109/ACCESS.2020.3035026
2. Woldemichael, F.G., Menaria, S.: Prediction of diabetes using data mining techniques. In: Proceedings of the 2nd International Conference on Trends Electron. Informatics, ICOEI 2018, pp. 414–418 (2018). https://doi.org/10.1109/ICOEI.2018.8553959
3. Chaves, L., Marques, G.: Data mining techniques for early diagnosis of diabetes: a comparative study. Appl. Sci. **11**, 1–12 (2021). https://doi.org/10.3390/app11052218
4. Muhammad, L.J., Algehyne, E.A., Usman, S.S.: Predictive supervised machine learning models for diabetes mellitus. SN Comput. Sci. **1**(5), 1 (2020). https://doi.org/10.1007/s42979-020-00250-8
5. Samet, S., Laouar, M.R., Bendib, I., Eom, S.: Analysis and prediction of diabetes disease using machine learning methods. Int. J. Decis. Support Syst. Technol. **14**, 1–19 (2022). https://doi.org/10.4018/IJDSST.303943
6. Reddy, S.S., Sethi, N., Rajender, R.: Safe prediction of diabetes mellitus using weighted conglomeration of mining schemes. In: Proceedings of the 4th International Conference on Electronics, Communication and Aerospace Technology. ICECA 2020, pp. 1213–1220 (2020). https://doi.org/10.1109/ICECA49313.2020.9297390
7. Ladha, G.G., Pippal, R.K.S.: A computation analysis to predict diabetes based on data mining: detail study. SAMRIDDHI: J. Phys. Sci. Eng. Technol. **14**, 103–107 (2022). https://doi.org/10.18090/samriddhi.v14i01.16
8. Samet, S., Laouar, M.R., Bendib, I.: Use of machine learning techniques to predict diabetes at an early stage, pp. 1–6 (2021). https://doi.org/10.1109/icnas53565.2021.9628903

9. Samet, S., Laouar, M.R., Bendib, I.: Diabetes mellitus early stage risk prediction using machine learning algorithms, pp. 1–6 (2021). https://doi.org/10.1109/icnas53565.2021.962 8955

10. Jacob, S.M., Raimond, K., Kanmani, D.: Associated machine learning techniques based on diabetes based predictions. In: 2019 International Conference on Intelligent Computing and Control System. ICCS 2019, pp. 1445–1450 (2019). https://doi.org/10.1109/ICCS45141. 2019.9065411

11. Mujumdar, A., Vaidehi, V.: Diabetes prediction using machine learning algorithms. Procedia Comput. Sci. **165**, 292–299 (2019). https://doi.org/10.1016/j.procs.2020.01.047

12. Makino, M., et al.: Artificial intelligence predicts the progression of diabetic kidney disease using big data machine learning. Sci. Rep. **9**, 1–9 (2019). https://doi.org/10.1038/s41598-019-48263-5

13. Faruque, M.F., Asaduzzaman, Sarker, I.H.: Performance analysis of machine learning techniques to predict diabetes mellitus. In: 2nd International Conference on Electrical, Computer and Communication Engineering. ECCE 2019, pp. 7–9 (2019). https://doi.org/10.1109/ECACE.2019.8679365

14. Samet, S., Laouar, M.R., Bendib, I.: Predicting and staging chronic kidney disease using optimized random forest algorithm. In: Proceedings of the 2021 International Conference on Information System and Advanced Technologies, ICISAT 2021 (2021). https://doi.org/10. 1109/ICISAT54145.2021.9678441

15. Perveen, S., Shahbaz, M., Keshavjee, K., Guergachi, A.: Prognostic modeling and prevention of diabetes using machine learning technique. Sci. Rep. **9**, 1–9 (2019). https://doi.org/10. 1038/s41598-019-49563-6

16. Abhari, S., Kalhori, S.R.N., Ebrahimi, M., Hasannejadasl, H., Garavand, A.: Artificial intelligence applications in type 2 diabetes mellitus care: focus on machine learning methods. Healthc. Inform. Res. **25**, 248–261 (2019). https://doi.org/10.4258/hir.2019.25.4.248

17. Adua, E., et al.: Predictive model and feature importance for early detection of type II diabetes mellitus. Transl. Med. Commun. **6**, 1–15 (2021). https://doi.org/10.1186/s41231-021-00096-z

18. Padhy, S., Dash, S., Routray, S., Ahmad, S., Nazeer, J., Alam, A.: IoT-Based hybrid ensemble machine learning model for efficient diabetes mellitus prediction. Comput. Intell. Neurosci. **2022**, 1–11 (2022). https://doi.org/10.1155/2022/2389636

19. Krishnamoorthi, R., et al.: A novel diabetes healthcare disease prediction framework using machine learning techniques. J. Healthc. Eng. **2022** (2022). https://doi.org/10.1155/2022/168 4017

20. Mushtaq, Z., Ramzan, M.F., Ali, S., Baseer, S., Samad, A., Husnain, M.: Voting classification-based diabetes mellitus prediction using hypertuned machine-learning techniques. Mob. Inf. Syst. **2022**, 1–16 (2022). https://doi.org/10.1155/2022/6521532

21. Al-Zebari, A., Sengur, A.: Performance comparison of machine learning techniques on diabetes disease detection. In: 1st International Informatics Software Engineering Conference on Innovation Technologies and Digital Transformation. IISEC 2019 – Proceedings, pp. 2–5 (2019). https://doi.org/10.1109/UBMYK48245.2019.8965542

22. Samet, S., Laouar, M.R., Bendib, I.: Comparative analysis of diabetes mellitus predictive machine learning classifiers. In: Laouar, M.R., Balas, V.E., Lejdel, B., Eom, S., Boudia, M.A. (eds.) 12th International Conference on Information Systems and Advanced Technologies ICISAT 2022. ICISAT 2022. Lecture Notes in Networks and Systems, vol. 624, pp. 302–317. Springer, Cham (2023). https://doi.org/10.1007/978-3-031-25344-7_27

AHP Method Applied to the Evaluation of Costs and Pollution Emitted by Combined Means of Transport, Case of SMMC Port Toamasina

Jean Baptiste Rakotoarivelo[✉]

IUGM, University of Mahajanga, Georges V Street, Building Kakal Mahajanga be, 652 401 Mahajanga, Madagascar
rjbravelo@yahoo.fr

Abstract. This article is based on the application of multicriteria support methods to decision-making. Within the Conventional Goods Handling Company, we encourage decision-makers in society to adopt assessment methods and available techniques based on strong assumptions in line with today's reality, to take sufficient account of the objectives of integrated development. Indeed, this aimed at all aspects of development, and to integrate into the analysis of many projects different aspects and their impact on the national economy. The problems presented call for the development of new instruments more appropriate to the particular context of combined transport in the case of the SMMC (SMMC: Conventional Goods Handling Company). The purpose of this work is to model a transport system within society. Modelling could be seen as a generalization of the system so that it is standard and applicable to similar systems, taking into account three criteria: ecological, economic and traffic We have estimated the performance of the following five alternatives: pollution, energy, noise, time and damage in which we can estimate the costs of expenditure and the amount of pollution emitted during the transport journey from the port to the final destination of the goods. This makes it possible to consider collective points of view and plan integral resources in a decision support system concerning port activities through the Hierarchical Analytical Decision-Making Process (AHP (AHP: Analytical Hierarchy Process)) method.

Keywords: Pollution · energy · noise · time and damage

1 Introduction

The company further emphasizes activities on recognized skills and whose consolidation would allow them to remain viable and competitive. The study focused on the tools and AHP method for designing a model of the combined transport system. This method considers a set of evaluation criteria, and a set of alternatives whose best decision must be made. In our research, the objective is, among the existing alternatives for the transport of goods between origin and final destination, to see the transport routes that give a good compromise between ecological, economic and traffic factors. To this end, the

S. Liu et al. (Eds.): ICDSST 2023, LNBIP 474, pp. 182–202, 2023.
https://doi.org/10.1007/978-3-031-32534-2_14

overall objective is to evaluate the cost of transport and its related pollution, in which the decision-maker can see the reality and to define the decision to be taken with the aim of minimising expenditure. We studied three identification cases: Ecological; composed of environmental and economic criteria; composed of cost, time, accident, and traffic criteria composed of transhipment criteria. The performance of possible alternatives for choosing an operating system will be deployed in five factors: pollution, energy, noise, damage and transhipment time. We presented the overall approach of an overview of our treatment based on the information on the different criteria and alternatives illustrated in Fig. 1. This figure is characterized by its solid presentation, foundation of information processing processes to combine different sources based on modeling of multicriteria support method to the AHP decision.

We have chosen this theme to demonstrate that transport occupies a prominent place in the internal and external environment of society if we talk about the different quantities of pollution, and the material and human damage caused by the different means of transport. To this end, we have included in the study the cost of preserving the ozone layer, according to the Rio[1] Convention, environmental costs, such as pollution, dust, energy consumption, and noise pollution. It is essential to integrate these parameters into the management of the farm. To this end, we ask the question: How to evaluate the costs and pollution emitted by the different means of transport to preserve the environment? On the other hand, the negative aspects that prevent us, because the major problem in our territory is the difficulty of predicting future events because of the scarcity of data on the ground (lack of measuring instruments relating to events), national economic and political change, technological development and its value, ecological change and other unpredictable changes.

Combined transport is the key point that links the different road of the operating system with the management of port logistics. Indeed, these are the activities necessary to obtain raw materials, intermediates and finished products in the right place, in a better time and in optimal quantity.

The operation of the material handling sector uses different means of transport: boat, conveyor belt, crane, tractor, elevator, truck, and train. We considered the pick-up points of the goods, their destinations and the quantities to be transported. As a result, we choose 14 transport roads, including the movement made by wheelbarrow handling equipment inside the departure and/or arrival of the Port of Toamasina. The estimate made in our research is approximate, but adequately illustrates the varying order of measurable indicators.

---

[1] Adopted on 9 May 1992 in New York and signed on 4 June 1992 within the framework of the United Nations Convention on Development in Rio de Janeiro, the Framework Convention on Climate Change entered into force on 21 March 1994. It was signed by 178 states, plus the European Union. Its main objective is defined in Article 2: "to stabilize greenhouse gas concentrations at a level that prevents dangerous anthropogenic interference with the climate system".

2 Methodology

The AHP method applied consists first of all in representing a decision problem by a hierarchical structure reflecting the interactions between the various elements of the problem, and then in making pairwise comparisons of the elements of the hierarchy and finally in determining the priorities of the actions. The realization of comparison by pair or binary is carried out by the determination of importance expressed by the Saaty scale from 1 to 9 [1] which allows the comparison and the choice between pre-established options. We carried out three phases of treatment:

- **The first step represents** the different cost formulas relating to the valuation caused by means of transport, the value is expressed in euros.
- **The second step (a, b, c)** consists of the pairwise comparison which leads to a matrix of the corresponding judgment for each case of criteria and sub-criteria and the evaluation of pollution alternative.
- **The third step:** results.

   The realization of this research is reflected on the 14 roads for the transport of goods to or from the port of Toamasina.

   The roads are coded by the letter K, distribute as follows K01 to K06 outside, and K07 to K014 displacement inside the port Toamasina [2].

K01 : Antananarivo	K02 : Fianarantsoa /Tuléar	K03 : Mahajanga / Antsiranana
K04 : Fort Dauphin/Antsirabe	K05 : Manakara/ Morondava	K06 : Morarano chrome / Antalaha

K07 : Mole A Est	K08 : Mole A Ouest	K09 : Mole B
K010 : Mole C1	K011 : Mole C2	K012 : Mole C3
K013 : Magasin mole A	K014 : Magasin mole B	

3 Objective and Expected Results

In order to measure the interest of the use of each of the various modes of transport, it seems relevant to refer to the externalities provided by each of the modes, and this through the study of the impact of transport on the environment. Our objective is on the criteria for all combined transport activities with a potential impact on air pollution and climatic conditions. To this end, to evaluate them, we determined using a treatment and calculation: the quantity of gas emitted on each route, the relative expenses and its costs related to the various trips inside and outside the Port of Toamasina. The ultimate objective is the minimization of costs and the reduction of pollution effects in order to preserve the environment so that the decision-maker can see the reality and define the decision to be taken in order to minimize the expense.

4 Treatment

The alternatives will be evaluated from the different equations that have been modelled.
   Starting from the priorities of these found for each criterion, we will make calculations to explain which measure of judgments is to be considered.

In each criterion, our objective is to minimize the criteria and sub-criteria illustrated in the following Table 1.

Table 1. Evaluation Criteria and Sub-Criteria

Criteria	Objective	Sub-criteria	Objective
Environment	Minimize environmental impacts	Pollution	Minimize emission of gaseous pollutants
		Energy	Minimize energy consumption
		Noise	Minimize noise pollution
Transshipment	Minimizing the impacts of transshipments	Time	Minimize transshipment times
		Damage	Minimize product losses due to transshipments
Cost	Minimizing the economic costs of transport		
Time	Minimize transport times		
Accident	Minimize accident-related impacts		

Source: Author

We presented the structure of the decision problem by choosing a combined transport system by breaking down the problem into a hierarchy of interrelated elements.

At the top of the hierarchy is the overall objective, the second level is the elements contributing to achieving this objective, the third level is the criteria and the last level that of the alternatives.

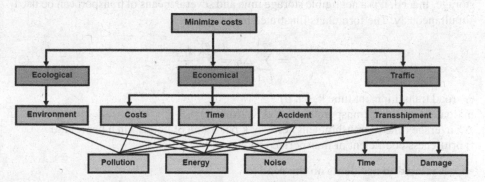

Fig. 1. Understanding the AHP Treatment Package

This approach consists in carefully expressing the structure of the hierarchy that will reflect on the problem to be solved.

This hierarchical structure clarifies the problem and makes it possible to identify the contribution of each element to the final decision.

The purpose of each analysis is to target the best criterion and the best alternative in relation to the higher hierarchical level.

Step - 1: For this purpose, we considered the different calculations to evaluate certain costs related to our research

• **Cost of transport and number of means of freight transport**

The transport of goods mobilizes specialized stakeholders, freight forwarders, whose role is to implement carriers, freight forwarders or agents responsible for carrying out customs clearance or clearance operations. The cost expression for each road K is illustrated by Eq. 1 [3].

$$C_k = \sum_{i=1}^{n}(C_{1t} + \Delta t_i . C_{2t} + d_i . C_{3t}) . \mu_{it} \tag{1}$$

C_k: Cost of freight transport on road K
C_{1t}: cost of fixed costs due to the use of transport t,
Δ_{ti}: transport time of a branch I of the k road,
C_{2t}: cost of hourly charges due to the use of transport t,
d_i: Distance from branch I of road K, (in km)
C_{3t}: Cost of tonne/kilometre charges due to the use of transport t, (in €.km)

$$\mu_{it} = \frac{m}{Capacité_t} \tag{1a}$$

$\mu_{it:}$: Number of means of transport t used in branch i of road k
m = load of products transported on road K, (in tonnes)
Capacity t: Transport capacity of the means of transport t, (in tonnes).

• **Transport time**

To calculate the transport time, we use the average speed of each means of transport and the distance travelled. We assume that the transport is without long-term intermediate storage. Indeed, it is a negligible storage time and several means of transport can be used simultaneously. The formula is illustrated below [3].

$$T_k = \sum_{i=1}^{n=1} \Delta t_i = \sum_{i=1}^{n} \frac{d_i}{t} \tag{2}$$

θ_k: road transshipment time k, (en h)
m: load of products transported on road K, (tonnes)
Δ_i: average time of transhipment i of way k per tonne of goods, (in h per tonne)
f: brittleness coefficient of transported products

• **Cost related to accidents on the road k**

Accidents involving means of transport have both financial and human impacts. We use a calculation model to determine the economic cost of transport accidents, taking into account social costs (without taking into account product losses), accident costs expressed in Eq. 3 [4]

$$A_k = \sum_{i=1}^{n} a_i = \sum_{i=1}^{n} \frac{m . d_i . \alpha_i}{1000} \tag{3}$$

A_k: cost related to accidents on the road k, (en €)

a_i: cost related to accidents on a branch I of the road k, (en €)
d_i: distance from branch I of the road k, (en km)
α_i: average cost of accidents per tonne kilometre of transport t, in (€.(t .km)$^{-1}$)

• **Transhipment time of the k road**
Time due to transhipments refers to the time taken to transfer the goods between two means of transport. A road k, with n branches, has n + 1 transshipments. The model in Eq. 4 [4] estimates this time taking into account the load of the transsshipped products and its fragility.

$$\theta_k = \sum_{i=1}^{n} m \cdot \Delta_i \cdot f \qquad (4)$$

θ_k: transhipment time of road k, (in h)
m: load of products transported on road K, (tonnes)
Δ_i: average time of transhipment i of way k per tonne of goods, (in h per tonne)
f: brittleness coefficient of transported products

• **Estimated amount of damage due to transhipment**
Damage due to transhipments refers to the loss, destruction of products during the transhipment stage. A road k, with n branches, has n + 1 transhipments. The model in Eq. 5 [4] provides an estimate of the amount of damage taking into account the load of the transsshipped products and its fragility.

$$D_k = \sum_{i=1}^{n} m \cdot \delta_i \cdot f \qquad (5)$$

D_k: estimated amount of damage due to load transfers from road k, (kg)
m: load of products transhipped on road K, (tonnes)
δ_i: transhipment damage quality i per tonne of product transhipped, (kg per tonne)
f: brittleness coefficient of transported products

• **Pollution and dust emitted by gas on the road k**
Most air pollutants are emitted by modes of transport. The main pollutants are sulphur dioxide (SO2), nitrogen oxide (NOX), carbon dioxide (CO2), non-methane hydrocarbons (NMHC) and volatile organic compounds (VOCs).
    The combination of these chemicals causes additional effects. The quantity emitted by each pollutant gas j on the road k inside the port is expressed by Eq. 6 [4]:

$$P_{kj} = \sum_{i=1}^{n} P_{ij} = \sum_{i=1}^{n} m \cdot d_i \cdot \rho_{ij} \qquad (6)$$

P_{kj}: pollution emitted by gas j on road K, (kg)
ρ_{ij}: pollution emitted by gas J on a branch I of road K, (kg)
m: load of products transported on road K, (in tonnes)
d_i: distance from branch I of road K, (in km)

ρ_{ij}: quantity of pollution j emitted by the means of transport T, per tonne kilometre, in (kg/t.km)

• **Power consumption on the k road**
Primary energy consumption is also an environmental factor and was considered in the calculation. Indeed, it is a main indicator of natural resource consumption. We consider not only the final consumption of energy by means of transport but also the energy consumed for the final energy generation. This formula is presented by Eq. 7 [4]:

$$E_k = \sum_{i=1}^{n} e_i = \sum_{i=1}^{n} \frac{m \cdot d_i \cdot \varepsilon_i}{1000} \tag{7}$$

E_k: energy consumption on road k, (in kJ)
e_i: consommation d'énergie sur une branche i du chemin k, (en kg)
m: load of products transported on road K, (tonnes)
d_i: distance from branch I of road K, (in km)
ε_t: energy consumption factor of the means of transport t, (in kJ.(t.km)$^{-1}$

• **Noise: Cost related to noise impacts on the K road**
How to economically assess the cost of noise pollution?

Noise causes nuisances and impacts on human health, we accept a study conducted by [5] which proposes a method to quantify the cost of noise generated by means of transport expressed by Eq. 8 [4] the calculation of the cost of noise along a road k

$$B_k = \sum_{i=1}^{n} b_i = \sum_{i=1}^{n} \frac{m \cdot d_i \cdot \beta_i}{1000} \tag{8}$$

B_k: cost related to noise impacts on road k, (in €)
b_i: cost related to noise impacts on a branch i of the k road, (in €)
m: load of products transported on road K, (in tonnes)
d_i: distance from branch I of road K, (in km)
β_t: average noise cost per tonne kilometric of transport t, in €.(t.km)$^{-1}$

Step-2 (a, b, c) consists of the pairwise comparison which leads to a matrix of the corresponding judgment for each case of criteria and sub-criteria and the evaluation of pollution alternative
Step 2a: Pairwise comparison of criteria:
The pairwise comparison of the active elements to achieve this objective: ecological, environmental and traffic, is carried out between the respective criteria: environment, cost, time, accident and transhipment.

For example at the Economic case level: The cost and time criterion are important, and we assign a corresponding weight according to the Saaty scale and the other criteria are less important having the relative weight to the scale.

We have an overall comparison summary of the criteria illustrated in Table 2. We performed the same approach for the other criteria and have a judgment matrix with the full priority vector value, the maximum mean, the consistency index and the consistency ratio.

The treatment outcome results in a full outcome matrix of criteria illustrated in Table 3, 4 and Table 5. This treatment imperatively requires that the consistency ratio must ≤10% for an acceptable level of consistency, otherwise the calculation procedures may require certain revisions.

Table 2. Summary of Comparison Between Criteria

Comparison	Most Criterion Important	Scale	Evaluation
Cost-Time	Cost-Time	Also important	1
Cost-Environment	Cost	Major	9
Cost-Transshipment	Cost	Much more important	5
Cost-Accident	Cost	Major	9
Temps-Environnement	Time	Major	9
Time-Environment	Time	Slightly larger	3
Accident Time	Time	Major	9
Environment-Transshipment	Transshipment	Much more important	5
Transshipment-accident	Accident	Slightly larger	3

Source: Author

Table 3. Full Criterion Judgment Matrix: Economic Case

Economic	Cost	Time	Environment	Transshipment	Accident	Priority
Cost	1	1	9	5	9	0,4160
Time	1	1	9	3	9	0,3740
Environment	1/9	1/9	1	1/5	1	0,0388
Transshipment	1/5	1/3	5	1	3	0,1297
Accident	1/9	1/9	1	1/3	1	0,0416
$\lambda_{max} = 5,09$			IC = 0,0215	RC = 1,92%		

Source: Author

Table 4. Full Criterion Judgment Matrix: Ecological Case

Ecological	Cost	Time	Environment	Transshipment	Accident	**Priority**
Cost	1	1	1/9	5	2	**0,1284**
Time	1	1	1/9	3	2	**0,1068**
Environment	9	9	1	9	9	**0,6542**
Transshipment	1/5	1/3	1/9	1	2	**0,0602**
Accident	1/2	1/2	1/9	1/2	1	**0,0503**
$\lambda_{max} = 5,41$			IC = 0,1038	RC = 9,27%		

Source: Author

Table 5. Full Criterion Judgemnt Matrix: Traffic Case

Traffic	Cost	Time	Environment	Transshipment	Accident	**Priority**
Cost	1	1	1	3	4	**0,2708**
Time	1	1	1	4	3	**0,2761**
Environment	1	1	1	3	4	**0,2708**
Transshipment	1/3	1/4	1/3	1	4	**0,1189**
Accident	1/4	1/3	1/4	1/4	1	**0,0635**
$\lambda_{max} = 5,24$			IC = 0,0604	RC = 5,39%		

Source: Author

Step 2b: Pairwise comparison of sub-criteria

It is the binary comparison of sub-criterion pollution, energy, noise for each case of criterion environment, cost, time, accident, transhipment and the sub-criteria time, damage of criterion transhipment.

In carrying out this treatment, we do the same approach of processing the criteria of step 2a, and we have results of a complete judgment matrix of sub-criteria for the three criteria economic, ecological, traffic and the transshipment sub-criterion represented by Table 6, 7, 8 and Table 9.

Table 6. Full Economic Case Sub-Criterion Judgement Matrix

Economic	Pollution	Energy	Noise	**Priority**
Pollution	1	1/3	5	**0,2674**
Energy	3	1	9	**0,6689**
Noise	1/5	1/9	1	**0,0637**
$\lambda_{max} = 3,03$	IC = 0,0146		RC = 2,51%	

Source: Author

Table 7. Full Judgment Matrix of Ecological Case Sub-Criterion

Ecological	Pollution	Energy	Noise	Priority
Pollution	1	3	7	0,6434
Energy	1/3	1	5	0,2828
Noise	1/7	1/5	1	0,0738
$\lambda_{max} = 3,07$	IC = 0,0328		RC = 5,65%	

Source: Author

Table 8. Full judgment matrix of traffic case sub-criteria

Traffic	Pollution	Energy	Noise	Priority
Pollution	1	1	5	0,4796
Energy	1	1	3	0,4055
Noise	1/5	1/3	1	0,1150
$\lambda_{max} = 3,03$	IC = 0,0146		RC = 2,51%	

Source: Author

Table 9. Transshipment sub-criterion full judgement matrix

Transshipment	Time	Damage	Priority
Time	1	1,5	0,6000
Damage	1/1,5	1	0,4000
$\lambda_{max} = 2,00$	IC = 0,00 RC = 0,00%		

Source: Author

We have summarized in Fig. 2 the calculation processing results for each AHP hierarchy level, it is the final phase of the treatment of the global priorities of the criteria and sub-criteria obtained by the weighting of the local priorities of a level by the overall priority of the next higher level surrounded by the colored frame in red color.

Table 10 summarizes the prioritization results for each criterion. The results of calculations contribute to the determination of costs and pollution.

Step 2c: Evaluation of alternatives
The priorities of the alternatives with respect to each criterion and sub-criterion (factor immediately above) are, in general, the normalized inverse values of the results of the equations in the model. This is necessary because the overall goal is to minimize the cost.

Indeed, it is a question of optimizing the road of least the least impact, and we evaluated the criteria/sub-criteria in order of importance. In this case, we realized Eq. 9 which gives us the priority of the road k for the factor: Cost = C, Time = T, Energy =

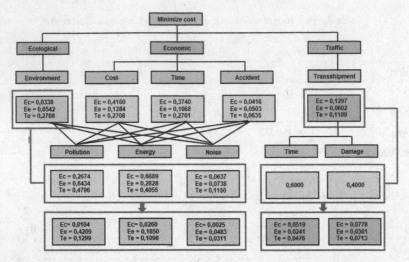

Fig. 2. Hierarchical Level Processing Overview. Source: Author

Table 10. Weights of criteria and sub-criteria "global priority"

Criteria		Scénario		
		Economic	Ecological	Traffic
Cost (C)		0,4160	0,1284	0,2708
Time (T)		0,3740	0,1068	0,2761
Accident (A)		0,0416	0,0503	0,0635
Transshipment	Time (TT)	0,0778	0,0361	0,0713
	Damage (D)	0,0519	0,0241	0,0476
Environnement	Pollution (P)	0,0104	0,4209	0,1299
	Energy (E)	0,0260	0,1850	0,1098
	Noise (B)	0,0025	0,0483	0,0311

Source: Author

E, Noise = B, Transhipment Time = TT, Damage = D, and Accidents = A [8].

$$FX_k^n = \frac{\frac{1}{X_k}}{\sum_{i=1}^k \frac{1}{X_K}} \; for \; X \in \{C, T, E, B, TT, D, A\} \tag{9}$$

X_k: Criterion/sub-criterion X of the road k

FX_k^n: Normalized (priority) factor of the (alternative) road k relative to the criterion X

The approach used is to calculate separately the quantity of each gas emitted and then to normalize the value found for this gas between the alternatives illustrated by an equation below by the priority of the road k corresponding to the pollution factor [8].

$$FP_k^N = \frac{1/\sum_j w_j \cdot P_{ji}^N}{\sum^k (1/\sum_j w_j \cdot P_{ji}^N)} \tag{10}$$

P_{ji}^N: Normalized value of the quantity emitted of gas j from all K road
w_j: Importance (weight) of pollutant j
FP_k^N: normalized (priority) factor of the (alternative) road relation to the pollution criterion

An aggregation between the different gases is then carried out taking into account the importance given for each pollutant (weighted average).

For the alternative "Pollution" we have a different approach compared to other types of alternative because there are different polluting gases emitted along a road k. It makes no sense to add up a varied amount of gases emitted because they have a different order of magnitude.

Table 11. Summary of comparison between criteria

Comparison	Most Important Criterion	Scale	Evaluation
CO_2 - NO_x	CO_2	Slightly larger	3
CO_2 – SO_2	CO_2	Much more important	5
CO_2- NMHC	CO_2	Very much more important	7
CO_2 – Poussière	CO_2	Very much more important	7
NO_x – SO_2	NO_x	Slightly larger	3
NO_x - NMHC	NO_x	Much more important	5
NO_x – Poussière	NO_x	Much more important	5
SO_2 - NMHC	SO_2	Slightly larger	3
SO_2 - Poussière	SO_2	Slightly larger	3

Source: Author

Table 11 and 12 representing the pairwise comparison and the results obtained are used to determine the amount of gas emitted on each of the 14 trips.

We used an approach to simplify the order of ranking of intensity judgments (Excellent, Good, Bad, and Worst) valid for all criteria and the sub-criterion and we perform the pairwise comparison in order to obtain the intensity importance judgment matrix, this result is illustrated by Table 13.

The procedure for ranking an alternative k in relation to an intensity of a criterion/sub-criterion is defined as follows. We assume:

A: set of alternatives from the road from K01 to K14.

X: refers to the criteria/sub-criteria of (cost (C), time (T), pollution (P), energy (E), noise (B), transhipment time (TT), damage (D) and accident (A)).

Table 12. Matrix of judgement of pollution criteria "full priority"

Pollution	CO_2	NO_x	SO_2	NMHC	Dust	Priority
CO_2	1	3	5	7	7	**0,5049**
NO_x	1/3	1	3	5	5	**0,2586**
SO_2	1/5	1/3	1	3	3	**0,1274**
NMHC	1/7	1/5	1/3	1	1	**0,0546**
Dust	1/7	1/5	1/3	1	1	**0,0546**
$\lambda_{max} = 5,14$			IC = 0,0342	RC = 3,05%		

Source: Author

Table 13. Matrix of Importance Judgments of Intensities with Priorities

Intensities	Excellent	Good	Bad	Worse	Priority
Excellent	1	2	3	5	**0,4709**
Bon	1/2	1	2	4	**0,2840**
Mauvais	1/3	1/2	1	3	**0,1715**
Pire	1/5	1/4	1/3	1	**0,0736**
$\lambda_{max} = 4,05$		IC = 0,0171		RC = 1,9%	

Source: Author

For X ∈ (C, T, P, E, B, TT, D, A), the ranking is illustrated by Eq. (11) below.

$$
\left.
\begin{array}{l}
I_{x1} = 0{,}75 \times \text{Max} (A_x) \\
I_{x2} = 0{,}50 \times \text{Max} (A_x) \\
I_{x3} = 0{,}25 \times \text{Max} (A_x) \\
I_{xn} : \text{interval}
\end{array}
\right\}
\begin{array}{ll}
\text{Si } (X_k \leq I_{x3}) & \Rightarrow k \in \{\text{Excellent}\}/ X \\
\text{Si } (I_{x3} < X_k \leq I_{x2}) & \Rightarrow k \in \{\text{Good}\}/ X \\
\text{Si } (I_{x3} < X_k \leq I_{x1}) & \Rightarrow k \in \{\text{Bad}\}/ X \\
\text{Si } (X_k > I_{x3}) & \Rightarrow k \in \{\text{Worse}\}/ X
\end{array}
$$

Aggregation is obtained by multiplying the priority of each criterion/sub-criterion with the priority of the intensity where the alternative was assigned (Eq. (11)). Then, we have added up the values found, we can order in descending order, the values thus obtained provide the ranking of the roads [8].

$$
W(k) = \sum_X W_X^g x I X_K^I \tag{11}
$$

W(k): Full priority of the alternative

$W(k)$: Overall priority of the criterion/sub-criterion (C, T, P, E, B, TT, D, A)

W_X^g : Ideal priority of the intensity where road k has been ranked against the criterion/sub-criterion X

IX_K^I : Ideal priority of the intensity where road k has been ranked against the criterion/sub-criterion X

5 Results

The parameters used for calculations are presented in Table 14. The parameters of speed, gas emission, energy consumption, noise and accident are well established, while the other parameters, transhipment time and damage due to transhipments are considered variable and specific for each problem.

We consider a maximum possible value for the capacity in tonnes of goods used in the calculations.

Table 14. Theoretical Model Parameter

Means of transport		Cost			Time	Environment								Transshipment		Accident
						Pollution					Energy	Noise		Time	Damage	
type	Capacity	Number	fixed	Timely	Km	Speed	CO2	NOx	SO2	NMHC	poussière	energie	bruit	Temps	Dégat	Accident
	tonne	Unit	€	€/h	€/Km	km/h	g/t km	mg/tkm	mg/tkm	mg/tkm	mg/tkm	kj/tkm	€/1000 tkm	h/tonne	Kg/tonne	€/1000tkm
Truck	30	34	200	20,00	0,40	80	71	542	41	38	13	966	7,40	0,10	0,03	7,60
Tractor	25	2	100	38,00	0,20	25	71	542	41	38	13	966	1,50	0,02	0,01	1,00
Elevator	16	2	100	40,00	0,10	5	71	542	41	38	13	966	2,00	0,02	0	0,00
Train	1800	1	300	26,00	0,30	100	35	544	20	54	15	473	6,00	0,20	0,02	2,00

Emission factor [6], noise factor [7]

• Evaluation of the matrix of judgments of alternatives

The application of the formula of Eqs. (1, 2, 3, 4, 5, 6, 7, 8) makes it possible to arrive at the results of the values of the performance matrix of the alternatives represented in Table 15. The application of Eq. (9, 10) yields the results of the weights (normalized values P^N) of the pollution factor for each alternative shown in Table 16.

The application of Eq. (12) makes it possible to calculate the amount of emission of gaseous pollutants and dust. Table 17 shows the result of the quantity of gas emitted and the normalized value, used on the calculation of the overall performance of the pollution criterion in relation to each alternative considered [8].

$$E = \frac{P_j^N}{W_j} \times 1000 \tag{12}$$

E: emission of gaseous pollutants
P_j^N: Normalized value of the quantity emitted of gas j among all roads k
W_j: Importance (weight) of pollutant j

Table 15. Performance matrix of alternatives against criteria

Matrix of performance	Cost	Times	Accident	Pollution	Energy	Noise	Time of transshipment	Damage
	€	h	€	%	KJ	€	h	Kg/tonne
K01	30,38	9,27	3,55	5,48	532,43	4,96	340,00	0,05
K02	60,37	26,23	15,94	17,03	2026,69	15,53	240,00	0,06
K03	69,07	31,15	18,94	20,23	2407,29	18,44	240,00	0,06
K04	58,84	25,37	15,42	16,47	1960,03	15,01	240,00	0,06
K05	58,84	25,37	15,42	16,47	1960,03	15,01	240,00	0,06
K06	74,90	33,32	17,27	23,49	2355,54	19,78	340,00	0,05
K07	1,24	0,43	0,01	0,09	10,20	0,02	120,00	0,03
K08	1,23	0,35	0,01	0,06	8,38	0,01	120,00	0,03
K09	1,23	0,37	0,01	0,07	8,75	0,01	120,00	0,03
K10	1,26	0,65	0,02	0,13	15,63	0,02	120,00	0,03
K11	1,26	0,65	0,02	0,13	15,63	0,02	120,00	0,03
K12	1,28	0,91	0,02	0,18	21,78	0,02	120,00	0,03
K13	1,24	0,41	0,01	0,08	9,83	0,02	120,00	0,03
K14	1,23	0,34	0,01	0,07	8,02	0,01	120,00	0,03

Source: Author

Table 17 was used to determine the values of the classification intervals of Eqs. (10) and (11). The absolute measurement synthesis yields the results of the verbal evaluations shown in Table 18 and the numerical evaluations shown in Table 19 below.

We obtained the ranking intervals by multiplying the percentage (0.25%, 0.50%, 0.75%) of Eq. (10) and (11) by the numerical values of the alternatives of each criterion/sub-criterion (Table 19). We took the maximum values of each alternative shown in Table 20.

• **Graphical representation of numerical evaluation of alternatives:**
The evaluation criteria in Tables 18 and 19 make it possible to graphically represent each criterion/sub-criterion evolution according to the situation of the alternatives (good, bad, excellent, worse). The analysis of the different figures leads to the final result of the situation of the corresponding roads.

- **Analysis of criteria: "costs", "time", "accidents", "energy", "noise"**
Analysis of Fig. 3 of the criteria: "costs", "time", "accidents", "energy", "noise", makes it possible to note this:
From road **K01 to K07**, the curves take the form of a letter V. This means that achieving the final goal of "minimizing expenditure" is impossible, because the intensities of the ranking intervals of verbal alternatives (Table 18) vary between **good and worse.**
As for the **K07 to K14,** the curves become constant, this means that the situation makes it possible to reach the final decision of the objective, that is, the minimization of

Table 16. Weight of the pollution factor for each alternative

Roads	CO2		NOX		SO2		NMHC		Dust	
	Tonnes	p^N	Kg	p^N	Kg	p^N	Kg	p^N	Kg	p^N
ko1	2,34	0,00118	1,90	0,00049	2,55	0,00033	1,57	0,00009	1,90	0,00010
k02	0,62	0,00031	0,67	0,00017	0,67	0,00009	0,67	0,00004	0,67	0,00004
k03	0,52	0,00026	0,56	0,00015	0,56	0,00007	0,56	0,00003	0,56	0,00003
k04	0,64	0,00032	0,69	0,00018	0,69	0,00009	0,69	0,00004	0,69	0,00004
k05	0,64	0,00032	0,69	0,00018	0,69	0,00009	0,69	0,00004	0,69	0,00004
k06	0,46	0,00023	0,50	0,00013	0,50	0,00006	0,45	0,00002	0,48	0,00003
k07	122,70	0,06195	133,31	0,03447	133,22	0,01697	133,36	0,00728	133,31	0,00728
k08	228,22	0,11523	162,20	0,04194	162,09	0,02065	162,26	0,00886	162,20	0,00886
k09	143,03	0,07222	155,39	0,04018	155,29	0,01978	155,45	0,00849	155,39	0,00848
k10	80,07	0,04043	86,99	0,02250	86,93	0,01108	87,02	0,00475	86,99	0,00475
k11	80,07	0,04043	86,99	0,02250	86,93	0,01108	87,02	0,00475	86,99	0,00475
k12	57,45	0,02901	62,41	0,01614	62,37	0,00795	62,43	0,00341	62,41	0,00341
k13	127,29	0,06427	138,28	0,03576	138,19	0,01761	138,34	0,00755	138,29	0,00755
k14	155,95	0,07874	169,42	0,04381	169,31	0,02157	169,48	0,00925	169,42	0,00925

Source: Author

Table 17. Emission of gaseous pollutants and associated priorities

Roads	0,5049		0,2586		0,1274		0,0546		0,0546		Agrégation %
	CO2		NOX		SO2		NMHC		Dust		
	Tonnes	p^N	Kg	p^N	Kg	p^N	Kg	p^N	Kg	p^N	
k01	2,34	0,00118	1,90	0,00049	2,55	0,00033	1,57	0,00009	1,90	0,00010	5,48
k02	0,62	0,00031	0,67	0,00017	0,67	0,00009	0,67	0,00004	0,67	0,00004	17,03
k03	0,52	0,00026	0,56	0,00015	0,56	0,00007	0,56	0,00003	0,56	0,00003	20,23
k04	0,64	0,00032	0,69	0,00018	0,69	0,00009	0,69	0,00004	0,69	0,00004	16,47
k05	0,64	0,00032	0,69	0,00018	0,69	0,00009	0,69	0,00004	0,69	0,00004	16,47
k06	0,46	0,00023	0,50	0,00013	0,50	0,00006	0,45	0,00002	0,48	0,00003	23,49
k07	122,70	0,06195	133,31	0,03447	133,22	0,01697	133,36	0,00728	133,31	0,00728	0,09
k08	228,22	0,11523	162,20	0,04194	162,09	0,02065	162,26	0,00886	162,20	0,00886	0,06
k09	143,03	0,07222	155,39	0,04018	155,29	0,01978	155,45	0,00849	155,39	0,00848	0,07
k10	80,07	0,04043	86,99	0,02250	86,93	0,01108	87,02	0,00475	86,99	0,00475	0,13
k11	80,07	0,04043	86,99	0,02250	86,93	0,01108	87,02	0,00475	86,99	0,00475	0,13
k12	57,45	0,02901	62,41	0,01614	62,37	0,00795	62,43	0,00341	62,41	0,00341	0,18
k13	127,29	0,06427	138,28	0,03576	138,19	0,01761	138,34	0,00755	138,29	0,00755	0,08
k14	155,95	0,07874	169,42	0,04381	169,31	0,02157	169,48	0,00925	169,42	0,00925	0,07

Source: Author

the expenditure is possible, because the situation in the ranking of verbal alternatives is **excellent**.

Table 18. Verbal evaluation of alternative: absolute synthesis

Evaluation criteria			Distance	Cost	Time	Accident	Environment			Transshipment	
							Pollution	Energy	Noise	Time	Damage
Verbal Evaluation	K01	Truck - Train	741,02	Good	Good	Excellent	Excellent	Excellent	Good	Worse	Worse
	K02	Truck	2098,02	Worse	Worse	Worse	Bad	Worse	Worse	Bad	Worse
	K03	Truck	2492,02	Worse	Worse	Worse	Worse	Worse	Worse	Bad	Worse
	K04	Truck	2029,02	Worse	Worse	Worse	Bad	Worse	Worse	Bad	Worse
	K05	Truck	2029,02	Worse	Worse	Worse	Bad	Worse	Worse	Bad	Worse
	K06	Truck - Train	2812,02	Worse	Worse	Worse	Worse	Worse	Worse	Worse	Worse
	K07	Tractor - Elevator	10,555	Excellent	Excellent	Excellent	Excellent	Excellent	Excellent	Good	Good
	K08	Tractor - Elevator	8,675	Excellent	Excellent	Excellent	Excellent	Excellent	Excellent	Good	Good
	K09	Tractor - Elevator	9,055	Excellent	Excellent	Excellent	Excellent	Excellent	Excellent	Good	Good
	K10	Tractor - Elevator	16,175	Excellent	Excellent	Excellent	Excellent	Excellent	Excellent	Good	Good
	K11	Tractor - Elevator	16,175	Excellent	Excellent	Excellent	Excellent	Excellent	Excellent	Good	Good
	K12	Tractor - Elevator	22,545	Excellent	Excellent	Excellent	Excellent	Excellent	Excellent	Good	Good
	K13	Tractor - Elevator	10,175	Excellent	Excellent	Excellent	Excellent	Excellent	Excellent	Good	Good
	K14	Tractor - Elevator	8,305	Excellent	Excellent	Excellent	Excellent	Excellent	Excellent	Good	Good

Source: Author

- Analysis of criteria: "damage", "time"
The analysis in Fig. 4 shows that the damage criterion curve is in an "S" shape. In roads **K01 to K06**, the curves are constant, but the achievement of the final goal is impossible, because the situation in the ranking of verbal alternatives of the damage criterion is **worse. K06 to K07**, the slope is relatively high, in this case there is a change from the situation Worse to the situation Excellent.

K07 to K14: the curves become constant, the situation leads to the final decision of the objective. Indeed, the minimization of expenditure is possible, since the situation in the ranking of verbal alternatives is **excellent.**

However the curve of the time criterion is composed of the two areas: **K01 to K02**, the slope is high, the situation in the ranking of the verbal alternatives of the time criterion is **good**, the achievement of the final objective is easy.

Table 19. Numerical evaluation of alternatives: absolute synthesis

Evaluation criteria			Distance	Cost	Time	Accident	Environment			Transshipment	
							Pollution	Energy	Noise	Time	Damage
Numerical Evaluation	K01	Truck - Train	741,02	0,6032	0,6032	1,0000	1,0000	1,0000	0,6032	0,1564	0,1564
	K02	Truck	2098,02	0,1564	0,1564	0,1564	0,3642	0,1564	0,1564	0,3642	0,1564
	K03	Truck	2492,02	0,1564	0,1564	0,1564	0,1564	0,1564	0,1564	0,3642	0,1564
	K04	Truck	2029,02	0,1564	0,1564	0,1564	0,3642	0,1564	0,1564	0,3642	0,1564
	K05	Truck	2029,02	0,1564	0,1564	0,1564	0,3642	0,1564	0,1564	0,3642	0,1564
	K06	Truck - Train	2812,02	0,1564	0,1564	0,1564	0,1564	0,1564	0,1564	0,1564	0,1564
	K07	Tractor - Elevator	10,555	1,0000	1,0000	1,0000	1,0000	1,0000	1,0000	0,6032	0,6032
	K08	Tractor - Elevator	8,675	1,0000	1,0000	1,0000	1,0000	1,0000	1,0000	0,6032	0,6032
	K09	Tractor - Elevator	9,055	1,0000	1,0000	1,0000	1,0000	1,0000	1,0000	0,6032	0,6032
	K10	Tractor - Elevator	16,175	1,0000	1,0000	1,0000	1,0000	1,0000	1,0000	0,6032	0,6032
	K11	Tractor - Elevator	16,175	1,0000	1,0000	1,0000	1,0000	1,0000	1,0000	0,6032	0,6032
	K12	Tractor - Elevator	22,545	1,0000	1,0000	1,0000	1,0000	1,0000	1,0000	0,6032	0,6032
	K13	Tractor - Elevator	10,175	1,0000	1,0000	1,0000	1,0000	1,0000	1,0000	0,6032	0,6032
	K14	Tractor - Elevator	8,305	1,0000	1,0000	1,0000	1,0000	1,0000	1,0000	0,6032	0,6032

Source: Author

K02 to K07, the curves take different forms, in this interval, the situation in the ranking of verbal alternatives of the time criterion is **worse**, the achievement of the final objective is complicated. **K07 to K14**, in this interval, the situation allows to realize the final decision of the objective; Indeed, the minimization of expenditure is achievable, because the situation in the ranking of verbal alternatives is **Excellent**.

- Criterion analysis: "Pollution"
Figure 5 is characterized by different shapes of curves, so it indicates that the situation varies in each course from **K01 to K14**, and we thus divide into two zones.

K01 to K07, the curves take the form of a letter "W", in this interval, the decision varies between **excellent** and **worse**, it does not allow to obtain the final decision of the objective, the classification of verbal alternatives is impossible.

Table 20. Interval for defining each intensity

Criteria			Ranking and limit	Cost	Time	Accident	Environment			Transshipment	
							Pollution	Energy	Noise	Time	Damage
Intensities	I4	Excellent	Ranking	1,0000	1,0000	1,0000	1,0000	1,0000	1,0000	1,0000	1,0000
	I3	Good		0,6032	0,6032	0,6032	0,6032	0,6032	0,6032	0,6032	0,6032
	I2	Bad		0,3642	0,3642	0,3642	0,3642	0,3642	0,3642	0,3642	0,3642
	I1	Worse		0,1564	0,1564	0,1564	0,1564	0,1564	0,1564	0,1564	0,1564
Reference	Ix3	Limit between I3 and I4	Limit	18,73	8,33	4,73	5,87	601,82	4,95	85,00	0,02
	Ix2	Limit between I2 and I3		37,45	16,66	9,47	11,75	1203,65	9,89	170,00	0,03
	Ix1	Limit between I1 and I2		56,18	24,99	14,20	17,62	1805,47	14,84	255,00	0,05

Source : Author

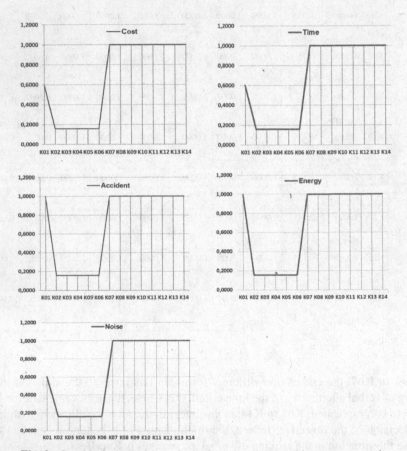

Fig. 3. Graphical presentation of criteria: costs, time, accidents, energy, noise

K07 to K014, the situation allows to reach the final decision of the objective. Indeed, the minimization of expenditure is possible, because the situation in the ranking of verbal alternatives is **excellent**.

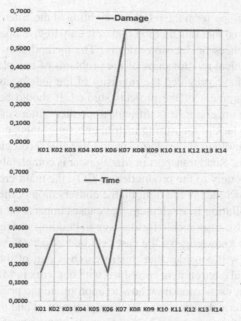

Fig. 4. Graphical presentation of the criteria: damage, time

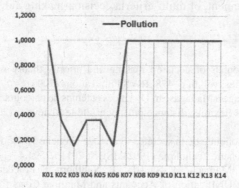

Fig. 5. Graphical presentation of criteria: Pollution

6 Conclusion and Perspectives

Within a port logistics, we have included environmental concerns for the choice of the freight transport system. The performance of the alternatives was modelled taking into account the economic cost, transport time, time and damage related to transhipments, pollutant gas emissions, energy consumption, noise pollution and social costs related to accidents. Pollution is mainly caused by emissions of the greenhouse gases CO_2, NOx, SO_2, $NMHC$. As far as the criteria are concerned, we can define a measurable index for each road envisaged. The estimate is approximate, but adequately illustrates the varying order of measurable indicators. Therefore, the air pollution criterion includes quantitative criteria. To perform the relative weighting of the criteria, we chose the AHP method, and we showed that this method makes it easy to give operative forms to models of criteria preferences or decision-makers. The method also makes it possible to formalize the hierarchical relationships of the problems of complex decisions. Thanks to this approach we have provided the intensity of the judgments of the criteria considered for the development of the projects studied. It should be noted that the data used in this work are uncertain. It is difficult to predict "future events" because of the scarcity of field data (lack of measuring instruments for events), national economic and political change, technological development and its value, ecological change and other unpredictable changes. Road transport in Madagascar is completely dependent on fossil fuels contributing strongly to the production of CO_2, the main greenhouse gas. This is why Madagascar is included in the fight on the conservation of the ozone layer. We are convinced that air pollution is an element that causes impacts on human health, on the environment and is also responsible for damage to building structures. To this end, our work is used to allow knowledge of the cases studied associated with the prevention of the ozone layer. We will consider that this research is part of the idea of valuing the world of the ecological environment combined with our work in Madagascar, or even on a global scale, so that users can know how to appropriate the principle of the different methods of multi-criteria decision support through the event and the situation related to it. Therefore, this work suggests the basis of a multi-criteria application for the choice of a transport system, and we see the richness and potentialities, quite applicable in environmental management, of multi-criteria decision-making aid.

References

1. Saaty, T.L.: Fundamentals of decision making and priority theory with analytic hierarchy process. In: AHP Series, vol. 6, p. 478. RWS Publications (2000)
2. DILAG-TOURS voyage à Madagascar. Distances et temps de parcours. Dernière mise à jour le 01/07/2008, 10 pages (lexique_distance.pdf), consulté le 01 février (2010). http//www.dilag-tours.ch/
3. Cailllat, À., et al.: Économie de la société. 43 quai de Grenelle 75905 Paris Cedex 15, p. 117, 136, 141: édition Hachette Technique (1998). ISBN: 20116.7594.4
4. Link, H., Stewart, L., Maibach, M., Sansom, T., Nellthorp, J.: Procedures of cost estimation are based in UNITE: UNIfication of Accounts and Marginal Costs for Transport Efficiency (2000)
5. INFRAS/IWW: External costs of transport: accident, environmental and congestion costs in Western Europe, 333 p. (2000)
6. IFEU Heidelberg: Ecological Transport Information Tool for Worldwide Transports. Methodology and Data 2nd Draft Report Öko-Institut IVE/RMCON Commissioned by DB Schenker Germany UIC (International Union of Railways) Berlin – Hannover - Heidelberg, May 21th 2010 (2008)
7. Aguezzoul, A., Ladet, P.: Prise en compte du transport dans le choix des fournisseurs. 5ème congrès de la Société Française de Recherche Opérationnelle et d'Aide à la Décision (ROADEF), 26–28 février 2003, Avignon – France (2003)
8. Sawagado, M.: Intégration de l'impact environnemental, sociétal et économique du transport intermodal au sein des chaines logistiques vertes: optimisation multiobjectif par les colonies de fourmis. Thèse de docteur de l'université Paul Verlaine de Metz; 23 nov 2011, vol. 160, p. 56 (2011)

Evaluate the Potential of the Physical Internet for Last Mile Delivery in Developing Countries

Eva Petitdemange[1]([✉]), Sam Ban[1,2], Matthieu Lauras[1], and Sarot Srang[2]

[1] Industrial Engineering Center, University of Toulouse - IMT Mines Albi, Campus Jarlard, 81013 Albi CT Cedex 09, France
{eva.petitdemange,sam.ban,matthieu.lauras}@mines-albi.fr
[2] Industrial and Mechanical Engineering Department, Institute of Technology of Cambodia, Russian Federation Blvd, P.O. Box 86, Tuol Kouk, Phnom Penh, Cambodia
srangsarot@itc.edu.kh

Abstract. Last mile delivery is a crucial component of the supply chain process, particularly in developing countries. However, traditional delivery methods are often characterized by inefficiencies, such as high costs, long delivery times, and poor delivery accuracy. The rise of e-commerce and the growth of online retail have added further pressure to last mile delivery in these countries. To address these challenges, Physical Internet (PI) has emerged as a promising solution. PI is a new paradigm for logistics and supply chain management that aims to increase the efficiency, sustainability, and resilience of the supply chain. This study aims to assess the impact of PI on last mile delivery in developing countries, using a digital model-based approach. By analyzing the potential benefits and limitations of PI, this study will contribute to the literature and provide insights and recommandations into the implementation of PI-based scenarios in last mile delivery in developing countries.

Keywords: Physical Internet · Last Mile Delivery · Developing Countries · Digital Model

1 Introduction

Last mile delivery refers to the final leg of the delivery process, from the transportation hub to the customer's doorstep. In developing countries, last mile delivery is critical for ensuring access to goods and services for the population, particularly for remote and rural areas. The success of last mile delivery can greatly impact the economy, social welfare, and overall quality of life for the people in these regions [5]. It is also crucial for the growth and expansion of e-commerce, as last mile delivery directly affects customer satisfaction and loyalty. Additionally, last mile delivery in developing countries faces unique challenges, such as infrastructure constraints, security issues, and limited access to technology and resources, making it even more important to address and improve [2,6].

© The Author(s), under exclusive license to Springer Nature Switzerland AG 2023
S. Liu et al. (Eds.): ICDSST 2023, LNBIP 474, pp. 203–215, 2023.
https://doi.org/10.1007/978-3-031-32534-2_15

In big cities of developing countries, logistics faces several challenges that can negatively impact the delivery process [8,11]. The measurement of logistics performance in developing countries is hindered by the absence of data, but estimates made by the World Bank (WB) show that these countries consistently fall below the average of the global logistics performance index [10]. On average, the logistics performance index for a developing country is about half that of a developed country. Reda et al. [19], conducted a study on the logistics and supply chain features of developed, emerging, and developing countries. After conducting an extensive literature analysis of over 300 articles, they found that the main logistics issues for developing countries are related to city logistics. They noted that these countries face significant challenges such as high traffic congestion, unsafe roads, rapid population growth, inadequate infrastructure, and expensive, unreliable vehicles. They also mentioned that developing countries are currently exploring various topics related to city logistics such as crowd-shipping, urban consolidation centers, e-commerce delivery, and alternative transportation modes. Despite efforts to improve city logistics in developing countries, the problem remains persistent and has a significant impact on their economy. Developing countries face numerous structural problems [18], including low income, dependence on specific sectors, low productivity, limited employment opportunities, poor health and education, and corruption, as well as specific city logistics issues such as poor road infrastructure, old vehicles, and lack of parking spaces. This is particularly true for Southeast Asian countries like Cambodia [17], whose economy is centered around large cities experiencing rapid population growth. As a result, the main research question for this project is how to improve the performance of freight transport activities in the cities of developing countries through the use of existing means and infrastructure.

These challenges can lead to increased costs, decreased customer satisfaction, and reduced efficiency for businesses. Addressing them is critical for improving last mile delivery in developing countries. We made the assumption that Physical Internet (PI) has the potential to solve these challenges by leveraging its key principles and feature. [3]. The PI aims to optimize the flow of goods, people, and information across the supply chain, with the goal of reducing delivery times and increasing the efficiency of last mile delivery. Additionally, PI provides a platform for sharing resources, such as delivery vehicles, delivery hubs, and sorting centers, reducing the need for businesses to invest in their own infrastructure. The use of PI can also lead to increased security during last mile delivery, with enhanced security measures such as real-time tracking and predictive delivery models reducing theft and security issues. Furthermore, PI leverages digital technologies and geolocation systems to provide more accurate and efficient addressing systems, reducing the difficulties in locating customers in big cities. Lastly, PI is designed to minimize waste and optimize the use of resources, leading to increased sustainability and reduced environmental impact in last mile delivery.

By addressing these challenges, PI has the potential to change last mile delivery, leading to improved efficiency, cost savings, and customer satisfaction. This leads us to formulate the following research Question: "What are the potential benefits of Physical Internet in last mile delivery in developing countries?". In this paper, we aim to assess this potentiel using experiments based on a digital model. Section 2 proposes an overview of the PI paradigm and its potentiality to improve last mile delivery. Section 3 highlights the Research Methodology applied to obtain the results. Section 4 analyses the results and discusses them.

2   Literature Review

2.1   Overview of the Physical Internet

The PI is a concept aimed at revolutionizing the way physical goods are managed, transported, stored, and used for a more efficient and sustainable global logistics system [16]. The PI draws from the principles of the Digital Internet (DI), such as openness, encapsulation, and universal interconnection, to transport physical goods in standardized containers, similar to data packages in the digital world [12]. The PI is defined as "a global logistics system built from the interconnection of logistics networks through a standardized set of collaboration protocols, modular containers, and intelligent interfaces for increased efficiency and sustainability [3]. The PI aims to interconnect logistics networks, share assets, use intermodal transportation, and employ digital technologies for improved efficiency and sustainability. It is based on the principles of standardization, interoperability, collaboration, and modularity [3]. These principles work together to streamline the delivery process and enhance the overall efficiency of the supply chain.

Standardization in PI refers to the standardization of transportation processes, systems, and modes, ensuring greater compatibility and interoperability across the supply chain [16]. Interoperability, on the other hand, enables seamless and efficient flow of goods and information between all participants in the supply chain, allowing for greater connectivity and collaboration [14]. Collaboration, as a principle, fosters cooperation and information sharing among businesses, governments, and customers, contributing to a more efficient and effective supply chain. Lastly, modularity in PI leverages flexible and adaptable transportation modes, providing greater flexibility in the delivery process and increasing the overall efficiency of the supply chain.

By incorporating these principles, PI offers numerous benefits for businesses and customers alike, including improved efficiency, better utilization of resources, increased security, better addressing systems, and improved sustainability. Ultimately, the implementation of PI has the potential to revolutionize the logistics and delivery process, leading to increased customer satisfaction, cost savings, and more efficient, sustainable delivery processes.

The theoretical benefits of PI have been extensively researched and demonstrated in various applications, primarily in developed countries [22]. According to Matusiewicz [13], the PI is an innovative logistics network built on technology and collaboration that deserves the attention of both academics and practitioners However, there is a gap in understanding its potential impact in the rest of the world, particularly in developing countries [7]. This remains an area that requires further exploration.

2.2   State of the Art of the PI in Developing Countries

However, the implementation of the PI in developing countries faces challenges such as the need for coordination and collaboration between transportation providers, regulatory and legal barriers, and a lack of willingness to adopt the new mode of operation. The PI has the potential to revolutionize transportation and logistics, improving efficiency, sustainability, and resilience [19]. It could create a more connected and efficient global supply chain, benefiting consumers, businesses, and the environment [2].

One major challenge is the need for greater coordination and collaboration between different transportation providers and logistics companies. This requires the development of new standards and protocols for intermodal transportation and the sharing of data and infrastructure [15]. In addition, there are regulatory and legal barriers to the development of the PI, including differing safety and environmental regulations across different countries and regions. Basically, such a paradigm shift in logistics requires significant transformations at various levels [9], leading to the need for an adapted information system using advanced technologies to enable the hyperconnection of actors, allowing for increased and standardized information sharing and massive data storage. It is necessary for the actors to evolve towards this new mode of operation and to engage in the effort [7]. The ALICE (Alliance for Logistics Innovation through Collaboration in Europe) grouping has recently published a roadmap formulating the important steps and associated prerequisites for the implementation of the PI by 2050 in developed countries [1] (ALICE-ETP, 2020). Despite these challenges, the PI seems to have the potential to revolutionize transportation and logistics in developing countries, by improving efficiency, sustainability, and resilience. By optimizing the movement of goods and people across different modes of transport and leveraging digital technologies, the PI could create a more connected and efficient global supply chain, benefiting consumers, businesses, and the environment.

In conclusion, while the PI is slowly being implemented globally, it needs to be more widely known and adopted, especially in developing countries. This project aims to determine whether or not the PI is of interest in solving the issue of improving the performance of freight transport activities in cities of developing countries through the use of existing means and infrastructures. The implementation of the PI in developing countries may face challenges, but its potential to revolutionize transportation and logistics makes it worth considering as a solution.

3   Research Methodology

3.1   A Digital Model to Conduct the Experiment

The popularity of hybrid simulation (multi-method simulation modeling), which combines two or more modeling methods such as Discrete-Event Simulation (DES), System Dynamics (SD), and Agent Based Simulation (ABM), has rapidly increased in the last two decades [4, 20, 21]. In this study, we will use a mix of DES and ABM to evaluate different scenarios of city logistics in developing countries with the goal of improving the PI paradigm.

To accurately model city logistics in developing countries, a multi-method simulation model architecture is proposed. (see Fig. 1) This model takes into consideration the unique characteristics of each stakeholder by modeling them as autonomous agents (see Fig. 2) using ABM and DES. The uncertain interactions between stakeholders are also captured using DES.

The environment of these agents is defined using a geographic information system (GIS), which considers factors such as geographical location and access to resources. The last-mile delivery of goods is modeled through interactions between various stakeholders in the network, simulating the order lifecycle process for each scenario.

The simulation results will be evaluated against key performance indicators (KPIs) such as economic, environmental, and technical performance for better decision-making. The proposed method will be tested in real-case scenarios in developing countries.

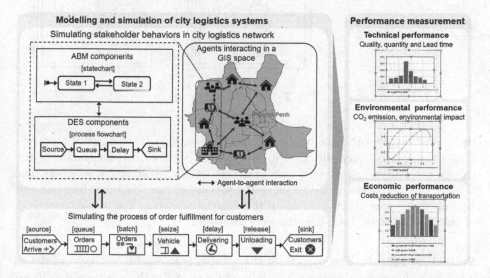

Fig. 1. Simulation modeling of city logistics using multiple methods in developing countries

Digital Model Assumptions. The company operates 24/7 and processes orders on a first-in, first-out basis during the center's operating hours (7:00 am to 8:00 pm). The study assumes unlimited storage capacity and constant order preparation times, and only considers variability related to transport vehicle availability and vehicle speed related to trafic jam. The transport aspect of

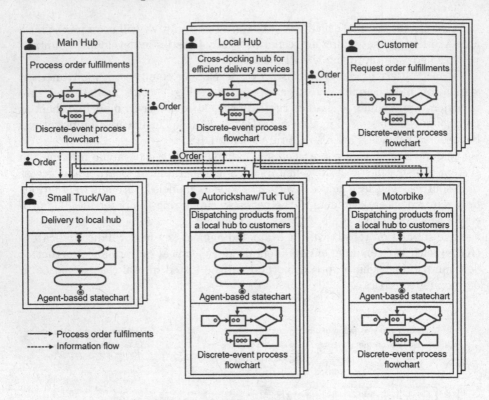

Fig. 2. Agent Description

the model involves the use of the company's own vehicles, primarily motorcycles, to ensure delivery throughout the day, depending on the capacity of the chosen vehicle type (motorcycle, van, tuk, etc.) and a prearranged schedule. The vehicle routing is based on the shortest path algorithm and takes into account the inherent speed characteristics of the vehicle, as well as the traffic conditions of the relevant area, including congestion issues.

Scenarios Tested. The purpose of this section is to establish a basic model as a reference for evaluating the potential usefulness of PI (PI) solutions developed in this research.

The scenario 0 is depicted in the accompanying Fig. 3. The scenario involves a business with one fulfillment center, known as Main, that serves as the storage and preparation center for customer orders in the designated region.

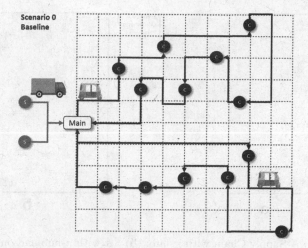

Fig. 3. S0 : the baseline

The scenario 1 (illustrated in Fig. 4a) proposes the addition π-hubs to support last-mile delivery in the city. The city is divided into zones affected to each π-hub. Each π-hub has its own fleet of vehicles to ensure delivery. The hubs are responsible for the preparation, shipment and delivery of orders in their territory, with restocking between the distribution center and hubs done through daily shuttles. The main stock remains at the distribution center with unlimited capacity. In this scenario, the PI hubs act as cross-docking platforms where incoming goods are unloaded, sorted and consolidated, and then loaded onto outgoing vehicles without storage, allowing for faster and more efficient delivery. The main process flows of order fulfillment take place at the π-hubs.

The idea behind scenario 2 (illustrated in Fig. 4b) is to bring the PI concept closer to reality by creating a shared, modular, standard, and interoperable transportation network that connects different transport networks, similar to how the digital internet operates. The use of modular components and standardized materials is crucial for the success of a network as it enables easy connectivity and seamless interaction with other networks.

In this scenario, the priority is on accessibility and a collaborative solution. To achieve this, the proposal is to make use of the numerous means of transport already available in developing cities, such as TukTuks and motorcycle cabs, instead of having each hub having its own fleet of vehicles. The transportation of goods is entrusted to third-party resources that are available on-demand, based on customer expectations and transportation opportunities around the π-hub.

The process in this scenario involves the π-hub receiving incoming goods from the main warehouse and sorting them according to their destination. The π-hub can then use on-demand vehicles from a transportation provider to pick up the sorted goods and deliver them to the customer's location, with the help of the PI Network and information sharing.

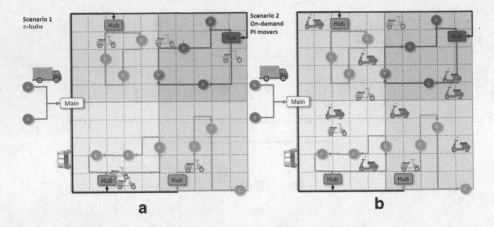

Fig. 4. (a) S1 : A Supply Chain with π-hub, (b) S2: with π-hub and on demand fleet

Key Performance Indicator Used to Assess the Simulation. The results of the simulation are analyzed using Key Performance Indicators (KPIs) to assess the effectiveness of the PI paradigm and the different scenarios. Lead Time is used to measure the transportation time, excluding the preparation time. The Lead Time KPI is used to evaluate the time dimension of the PI paradigm and the delivery of goods in the last-mile (See Eq. 1). LeadTime provides a clear measurement of the time taken from the preparation of goods at the main warehouse to their final delivery at the customer's location, and helps to assess the effectiveness of the delivery process.

$$LeadTime = TimeOrderDelivered - TimeOrderPlaced \tag{1}$$

The cost function KPI is used to assess the financial aspects of the PI paradigm. It provides a measure of the costs incurred in delivering goods from the main warehouse to the customer's location. It takes into account the type of vehicles used, the distance traveled, the fuel consumption, the spare parts replacements and the oil to calculate the overall cost of delivery. This KPI is important for evaluating the efficiency of the PI paradigm in a developing country context. To evaluate the financial aspect, a cost function is used, with the cost function for Scenario 0 and 1 being the same with the price being calculated based on a combination of a fixed initial fee per day and a mileage fare (see Eq. 2). But slightly different for Scenario 2 due to the use of an on-demand vehicle service, we consider a fixed fare for order pickup cost of 5$ per pickup. The differents values used to build the cost function can be found in Table 1.

$$Cost = \sum_{nvehicles} CostPerDay * NbDay + \frac{TotalDistance * VOC}{1000} \tag{2}$$

Additionally, a carbon footprint function is calculated to assess sustainability, which takes into account the type of vehicle used and the mileage traveled by each vehicle. The carbon footprint function KPI is used to assess the sustainability of the PI paradigm. It calculates the amount of carbon dioxide emissions produced during the delivery of goods from the main warehouse to the customer's location (see Eq. 3). This KPI is important for evaluating the environmental impact of the PI paradigm and its alignment with sustainable development goals.

$$CarbonFootPrint = \sum_{nvehicules} f(TotalDistance, Consumption, Type) \qquad (3)$$

Table 1. Data used for KPIs

	Motorbike	TukTuk
Purchase Cost ($)	3000	6000
LifeTime (year)	5	5
Cost per day Depreciation ($/day)	2	4
Vehicle Operating Cost (VOC) ($/1000km) (Maintenance)	76,4	131,6
Consumption (L/100km)	1,84	5,2
On-Demand fare	5$ per course	–

In conclusion, these three KPIs provide a comprehensive evaluation of the PI paradigm in terms of effectiveness, efficiency and sustainability, which are key aspects of the last mile delivery performance in a developing country context.

3.2 Case Study Selection

The Little Fashion Company. The model is based on by the case of "Little Fashion Company," a Cambodian e-commerce company located in Phnom Penh with which the researchers had a partnership throughout the research process.

An Experiment on One Week Data. The simulation has been runned on a one week sample of orders between the 02-08-2021 and the 10-08-2021. This correspond to 9100 orders placed by 8290 differents customers. The type of vehicle and their specifities are detailed in Table 2.

Table 2. Parameters of vehicles in each scenario

	Scenario 0	Scenario 1	Scenario 2
Vehicle Main to Customer	Motorbike	–	–
Vehicle Main to Hub	–	TukTuk	TukTuk
Vehicle Hub to Customer	–	Motorbike	Motorbike
Nb of Motorbike	57	57	100
Capacity of Motorbike	18	18	18
Nb of TukTuk	–	15	15
Capacity of TukTuk	–	50	50

4   Results and Discussion

After Running the simulation for one week for the three scenarios we observe that we were able to deliver respectively 8742, 8854 and 8856 for scenario 0, 1 and 2. As a reminder, there where 9100 orders placed during this week. So the use of PI Scenarios let us reduce the non-served order rate from 4% to 3% so it is 100 extra orders which can be delivered.

Considering the Leadtime, Table 3 summarizes the results obtained. The Median LeadTime is 8.19, 5.11 and 3.72 h for scenario 0, 1 and 2. Adding Local-Hub with motorbike fleet can improve the leadtime by 37% compared to the baseline. However, using LocalHub and on-demand fleet improve the median leadtime by 54% and let us gain one additional hour on the delivery which is quite interesting for a Last Mile Delivery on e-commerce. Meanwhile, the maximum leadtime could seems quite high, however it can be explained by the orders overlapping between two days and which are not delivered the same day it is received. This maximum Leadtime is reduce from 25 h to 19 h. It is an improvement of 24% compared to the baseline.

The Carbon Footprint for each Scenario is detailed in the Table 4. The Scenario 0 considers only TukTuks, Scenario 1 and 2 consider a mix of TukTuks and Motorbikes. The results show that the use of TukTuks as a mode of transportation results in a higher fuel consumption compared to motorcycles, leading

Table 3. Descriptive Statistics(in hour) on LeadTime for Each Scenario.

	LeadTime in hour				
	STD Dev	Min	Median	Mean	Max
Scenario 0	4,84	0,19	8,19	8,36	25,47
Scenario 1	4,46	1,17	5,11	6,61	20,38
Comparaison to Scenario 0	8%	-515%	38%	21%	20%
Scenario 2	4,37	1,18	3,72	5,61	18,99
Comparaison to Scenario 0	10%	-520%	54%	33%	25%

to a higher carbon footprint in Scenario 0. However, by utilizing a hub system and utilizing lighter means of transportation such as motorcycles for last mile delivery, the company was able to achieve a significant reduction in their carbon footprint. In fact, there was a 60% decrease in carbon emissions from the baseline, going from 17.8 tonnes of CO_2 produced per week to only 7 tonnes of CO_2 produced. The implementation of an on-demand vehicle system leads in a decrease in the total distance covered by the vehicles, leading to a slight reduction in the company's carbon footprint from 7.10 tons of CO_2 to 6.90. However, this decrease should be considered with caution as the transportation still occurs and emissions are still produced, only the responsibility is transferred to the on-demand vehicles. Thus, it can be seen as a shift in responsibility rather than a genuine reduction of carbon emissions between Scenarios 1 and 2.

Table 4. Carbon Footprint for each scenario

	Carbon Foot Print			
	Main to Hub	Hub to Customer	Total (ton of C02)	Comparaison to Scenario 0
Scenario 0	17,8		17,8	–
Scenario 1	0,602	6,5	7,10	60,7%
Scenario 2	0,602	6,3	6,90	61,2%

The Table 5 summarizes the cost of each scenario. The cost calculation takes into consideration factors such as depreciation, maintenance, and fuel expenses for the vehicles. For the on-demand fleet scenario, the cost is calculated based on a fixed initial fee and a mileage fee. The scenario with its own fleet of TukTuk (Scenario 0) incurs the highest weekly cost of 10,000$. By switching to a fleet of motorcycles in Scenario 1, the cost is reduced by 30% to 6,986$. The implementation of an on-demand fleet (Scenario 2) results in an even greater reduction of 73% to 2,705$, with a fixed pickup cost of 5$ (which is an estimated value).

Table 5. Vehicle Operating Cost for each Scenario

	Vehicle Operating Cost (USD)			
	Main to Hub	Hub to Customer	Total (USD)	Comparaison to Scenario 0
Scenario 0	10000		10000	–
Scenario 1	382	6604	6986	30%
Scenario 2	382	2460	2705	48%

5 Conclusion

The digital model based study of PI implementation for last mile delivery in a developing country reveals that it can lead to significant improved delivery performance, reduced carbon footprint, and decreased costs for the company. The results of the simulation for a one-week period show that the implementation of PI leads to a 1% orders increase in the number of orders delivered, a reduction in the median lead time by 54%, and a decrease in the carbon footprint by 60%. Additionally, the cost reduction from $10,000$ to $2,705$ demonstrates the potential financial benefits of implementing PI in such a context. These results suggest that PI can play a crucial role in improving last mile delivery in developing countries and can lead to a more sustainable, efficient and effective supply chain system.

In conclusion, the results of this digital model based study highlight the potential of PI in enhancing last mile delivery in developing countries. However, it is important to acknowledge the limitations of this study such as the one-week sample, limited stock information in the digital model, and lack of collaboration and shared transportation in the model. Moreover, it would have been interesting to compare our results to existing studies in the litterature, however we have not found any relevant article to be compared with. The study is currently focused on a single company, therefore, it would be interesting to include other companies to examine the potential of coordination and collaboration between them. Another interesting aspect to consider is the scenario of the growth of electric vehicles in developing countries and how this can be analyzed through the digital model. Additionally, the model could be used as a decision support tool to determine the optimal placement of π-hubs. Further research is needed to expand the simulation and address these limitations to provide a more accurate evaluation of the impact of PI on last mile delivery.

References

1. ALICE: ALICE roadmap to physical internet - ALICE alliance for logistics innovation through collaboration in Europe (2020). https://www.etp-logistics.eu/alice-physical-internet-roadmap-released/
2. Arvianto, A., Sopha, B.M., Asih, A.M.S., Imron, M.A.: City logistics challenges and innovative solutions in developed and developing economies: a systematic literature review. Int. J. Eng. Bus. Manag. 13, 18479790211039723 (2021)
3. Ballot, E., Montreuil, B., Meller, R.D.: The Physical Internet. La Documentation Française (2014)
4. Brailsford, S.C., Eldabi, T., Kunc, M., Mustafee, N., Osorio, A.F.: Hybrid simulation modelling in operational research: a state-of-the-art review. Eur. J. Oper. Res. 278(3), 721–737 (2019)
5. Crainic, T.G., Montreuil, B.: Physical internet enabled hyperconnected city logistics. Transp. Res. Procedia 12, 383–398 (2016)
6. De Guimarães, J.C.F., Severo, E.A., Júnior, L.A.F., Da Costa, W.P.L.B., Salmoria, F.T.: Governance and quality of life in smart cities: towards sustainable development goals. J. Clean. Prod. 253, 119926 (2020)

7. Grest, M., Lauras, M., Montreuil, B.: Assessing physical internet potential for humanitarian supply chains. In: HICSS 2021–54th Hawaii International Conference on System Sciences, pp. 2048–2056 (2021)

8. Hu, W., Dong, J.; Hwang, B.G., Ren, R., Chen, Z.: A scientometrics review on city logistics literature: research trends, advanced theory and practice. Sustainability 11(10), 2724 (2019)

9. Kim, J.: Smart city trends: a focus on 5 countries and 15 companies. Cities 123, 103551 (2022)

10. Kraay, A.: Methodology for a world bank human capital index. World Bank Policy Research Working Paper (8593) (2018)

11. Lagorio, A., Pinto, R., Golini, R.: Research in urban logistics: a systematic literature review. Int. J. Phys. Distrib. Logistics Manag. (2016)

12. Maslarić, M., Nikoličić, S., Mirčetić, D.: Logistics response to the industry 4.0: the physical internet. Open engineering 6(1) (2016)

13. Matusiewicz, M.: Logistics of the future-physical internet and its practicality. Transp. J. 59(2), 200–214 (2020)

14. Montreuil, B.: Toward a physical internet: meeting the global logistics sustainability grand challenge. Logistics Res. 3, 71–87 (2011)

15. Montreuil, B., Meller, R.D., Ballot, E.: Towards a physical internet: the impact on logistics facilities and material handling systems design and innovation (2010)

16. Montreuil, B., Meller, R.D., Ballot, E.: Physical internet foundations. In: Borangiu, T., Thomas, A., Trentesaux, D. (eds) Service Orientation in Holonic and Multi Agent Manufacturing and Robotics, pp. 151–166 (2013). https://doi.org/10.1007/978-3-642-35852-4_10

17. Phun, V.K., Kato, H., Yai, T.: Traffic risk perception and behavioral intentions of paratransit users in Phnom Penh. Trans. Res. Part F: Traffic Psychol. Behav. 55, 175–187 (2018)

18. Phun, V.K., Yai, T.: State of the art of paratransit literatures in Asian developing countries. Asian Transp. Stud. 4(1), 57–77 (2016)

19. Reda, A.K., Gebresenbet, G., Tavasszy, L., Ljungberg, D.: Identification of the regional and economic contexts of sustainable urban logistics policies. Sustainability 12(20), 8322 (2020)

20. Roci, M., Salehi, N., Amir, S., Asif, F.M., Shoaib-ul Hasan, S., Rashid, A.: Multimethod simulation modelling of circular manufacturing systems for enhanced decision-making. MethodsX 9, 101709 (2022)

21. Roci, M., et al.: Towards circular manufacturing systems implementation: a complex adaptive systems perspective using modelling and simulation as a quantitative analysis tool. Sustain. Prod. Consumption 31, 97–112 (2022)

22. Sallez, Y., Pan, S., Montreuil, B., Berger, T., Ballot, E.: On the activeness of intelligent physical internet containers. Comput. Ind. 81, 96–104 (2016)

Towards an Integrative Assessment Model for Port Sustainability Decisions: A Systematic Review

Xiaofang Wu[1]([✉]), Shaofeng Liu[2], Shaoqing Hong[3], and Huilan Chen[2]

[1] Jimei University, Xiamen 361021, China
xiaofang.wu@jmu.edu.cn
[2] University of Plymouth, Plymouth PL4 8AA, UK
[3] Xiamen Suixiang Space Culture Communication Co., Ltd., Xiamen 361027, China

Abstract. The slow pace of sustainability poses questions about what sustainability purposes are served and how to assess the status quo of sustainability for effective decision support. Having recognized the fuzzy concept of sustainability and the lack of sustainability assessments for ports that play key nodes of global logistic networks, this study applies a systematic review method to broadly collect theoretical and practical data from literature databases and relevant organizations, to identify sustainability requirements, port sustainability perceptions, and existing sustainability assessment approaches and methods. Results show that the sustainability concept is moving to eco-centric and context-specific thinking while the port sustainability still lies in traditional triple lines and the elements of the concept lack recognition of the business-environment nexus. Although dozens of specific methods have been available from the existing sustainability assessments, previous assessment approaches rely much on subjective expert judgments or quantitative data, which may affect the reliability and validity of assessments. As such, this study provides a new integrative assessment model for port sustainability decisions to meet ecological needs. The proposed model integrates the interactions between port activities and the environment. It is a data-driven, evidence-based approach to reducing subjectivity and saving time. The proposed assessment model contributes to the understanding the port sustainability situations and finding preferable options in terms of interaction mechanisms.

Keywords: Sustainability purpose · sustainability assessment · approach and methods · systematic review

1 Introduction

Sustainability that aims to perpetuate and enhance the natural environment and resources and to assure social equality and economic vitality [1] has received increasing awareness from governments, non-profit organizations, communities, and the public. Sustainability assessment exercises, which contribute to understanding the sustainability elements, identifying adverse and long-term positive effects of activities, or exploring alternative solutions, have been widely used [2]. Decision makers would like to assess the

© The Author(s), under exclusive license to Springer Nature Switzerland AG 2023
S. Liu et al. (Eds.): ICDSST 2023, LNBIP 474, pp. 216–231, 2023.
https://doi.org/10.1007/978-3-031-32534-2_16

progress towards sustainability; managers also love to assess whether they have managed sustainability programmes successfully or not.

While even so, sustainability assessments still face questions in a specific context, as indicators relevant to its achievement remain uncertain and there is a need to explore appropriate methods [3]. Taking ports which are key nodes in the global transport networks as an example, although sustainability there constantly evolves business ethics and social responsibilities under the initiatives of sustainable ports, eco-port, and green ports [4], the current efforts expressed differential emphases, either environmental management, trade-offs between environmental protection and economic benefits, or ecological conservation over the recent two decades [4]. These indefinite and fragmented purposes would probably affect the consequent approach and method of the effectiveness of decision-making.

For another, a literature search using a keyword combination of "sustainability assessment AND port" only shows 10 port-targeted publications from Scopus and Web of Science databases on 15 November 2022, beginning with the published year of 2016. According to the existing literature, we can find that most of the existing studies merely identified or ranked the sustainability criteria for ports based on literature review or empirical investigation [5, 6]. Although some studies tried to use multi-criteria decision-making (MCDM) or multi-dimensional decision-making (MDDM) approaches to frame the sustainability assessment, they were restricted to port-city plans [7], relocation of container terminals [8], and cruise industry [3].

Sustainability covers broad issues that matter to people, the planet, and prosperity, so the intended assessment might be multidimensional and multimethod. The research question is not to decide what decision criteria are but explores what a set of key insights the sustainability ambition serves, and then how to understand the status quo. To be specific, it is to make a clear goal and a rich methodological knowledge of sustainability assessment for port decisions. This study would not like to get bogged down in conceptual debates of sustainable ports, eco-ports, and green ports, but instead to put sustainability as an umbrella concept, covering all these terms [4]. Overall, this study aims to identify the core requirements of sustainability, explore the port sustainability indicators, and suggest how to assess the sustainability performance, for assisting in port sustainability decisions.

The remainder of the paper is structured as follows: Sect. 2 explains the data collection and analysis methods as well as the sources for material. Findings from the systematic review are presented in Sect. 3. A new integrative sustainability assessment model is proposed in Sect. 5. Finally, Sect. 5 draws conclusions.

2 Methods and Materials

A systematic review that relies on focused and predetermined questions to identify, critiques and analyse the multiple primary studies enables extensively, structurally, and transparently map and manage the existing knowledge [9]. As opposed to depending on the results of observation, interview, and questionnaire, a systematic review provides a further analysis of raw data or published documentaries, to recognize the current situation, generate academic inquiries, and support further solutions for a certain purpose

[10]. It has grown rapidly to integrate theoretical and practical perspectives and findings alongside the increasing numbers of data sources, and the ease of access [10]. This study adopts it to systematically collect and analyse the existing knowledge and puts the judgement of port sustainability status on the "shoulders of giants". The review process follows the data collection, initial data results, refinement, and initial data analysis [11]. All materials are in quest for answering three research questions: (1) What sustainability purposes will be served? (2) How should port sustainability indicators be selected? and (3) How could sustainability assessment be conducted?

2.1 Data Collection

Literature comes from two databases of Web of Science and Scopus for their wide coverage and high quality of peer-reviewed articles in this study. In responding to the first and third questions, broad keyword combinations of "sustainability AND concept OR definition" and "'sustainability assessment' AND approach OR methods" are given to respectively identify relevant papers and a search time frame is set as "from the year of 2020 to 16 December 2022" building on our previous reviews of [3] and [12]. This contributes to focusing on the review of effectiveness of United Nations Sustainable Development Goals (SDGs) after five years. On the other hand, a keyword combination of "port sustainability OR green port OR eco-port OR sustainable port" AND "indicator OR factor OR criteria OR criterion OR index OR indices OR element OR component OR essential OR parameter OR variable" is selected for the two databases searching [4], aiming to answer the second question.

Except for peer-reviewed literature from databases, the port sustainability issues are usually specific and practical which can be accessed from relevant organizational websites. Our previous study of [4] provides over ten international and national organisations that are highly regarded in tackling port sustainability issues for information on this study.

2.2 Initial Search Results and Refinement

Probably due to the vagueness and broadness of the sustainability notion, the first two broad sustainability searching strings still result in thousands of papers over the last three years. This study decides to adopt a "snowballing" approach, which starts with a tentative search and combines backwards and forward snowballing to include the relevant papers [13]. We hereby sort the literature by relevance, read the top 1000 in each search, keep the related papers, and then throw the "snowballs" by tracking their citations and references. In this study, after excluding those without direct discussion of the sustainability concept and sustainability assessment methodology based on a title and abstract screening in the top 1000, a respective of 49 and 44 unduplicated publications remained for the two protocols' searching.

During the port sustainability search, main irrelevant research categories such as Fisheries, Agronomy, and Optics are excluded; as of the Scopus search, unrelated subject areas including Medicine, Biochemistry, and Genetics are removed. In addition, those publications which are not pertinent to port topics based on their titles and abstracts are also ruled out. After refining the duplicated publications and those without author information, a total of 634 articles remained. Moreover, we excluded those only focusing on river or inland ports, dry ports, fishing ports, and cruise ports, because we would like to focus on the commercial seaports for cargo. As an initial result, 571 publications were obtained on 18 November 2022.

To search for port-related organizations, after broadly browsing their websites, we decided to refine the UNCTAD (United Nations Conference on Trade and Development) and IAPH (International Association of Ports and Harbours)'s search to the SDGs in ports. The publications were grouped to environmental commission from the PIANC (World Association for Waterborne Infrastructure), the Green Guides from the ESPO (European Sea Ports Organization), the national initiatives from the USEPA (United States Environmental Protection Agency) and the MPAS (Maritime and Port Authority of Singapore), the evaluation standards from China, and the sustainability plans or corporate social responsibility report from companies, due to their spotlights.

2.3 Initial Data Analysis

In terms of literature search and refinement results for the general sustainability perceptions and sustainability assessment methodology, we find that the recent literature does not pay attention to discussing what sustainability is and how to conduct the generic sustainability assessment, instead it puts sustainability as a goal and applies the assessment methodology into various fields.

It is the same situation that prevailed in respect of ports in the industry. Although the number of literatures from databases shows a rapidly rising trend in the last twenty years (see Fig. 1), by a closer looking into the content of the literature we find that the majority just puts sustainability as a goal of port development, rather than defines it, based on their titles and abstracts. Currently, there are only a few studies targeting assessing the sustainability status of ports. This would affect the effectiveness and efficiency of port sustainability decisions, especially for the organizations' decisions, because they are committed to providing specific objectives, guidelines, and actions towards sustainability based on current research.

3   Results from the Systematic Review

This section presents the main findings from the systematic review in three key themes: sustainability dimensions, sustainability indicators in ports, and sustainability assessment approaches and methods.

3.1 Sustainability Dimensions

Sustainability emerged as an ideal matter of economic, social, and environmental issues in the late 1970s [14]. The first well-developed concept was presented by the report of the World Commission on Environment and Development (WCED) in 1987 to initiate social equity, economic benefits, and environmental protection [15]. Many organizations subsequently adopted the "triple bottom lines" from economic, social, and environmental perspectives, committing to meet the present and future generations' needs. While

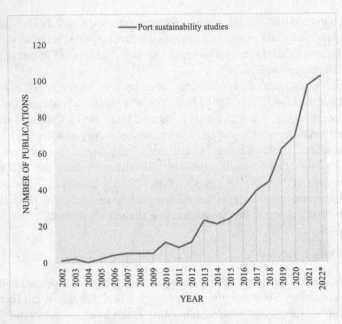

Fig. 1. Distribution of port sustainability studies from databases over the recent 20 years. *Note: publications retrieved up to 18 November 2022

beyond this, eco-centric views that theoretically acknowledge the intrinsic value of nature and target to conserve the natural ecosystems for the facts that the earth is end-in-itself and human existence and development depend on the health of natural ecosystems [12, 16]. Recent cognitions of sustainability from experts, stakeholders, and the public show context-specific thinking such as social justice for business [17] and there is no elite-level definition matching ideas from the public [18].

3.2 Sustainability Indicators in Ports

There are a series of sustainable ports, eco-ports, and green ports under the umbrella of port sustainability. As the previous study by Wu, Zhang [12], the sustainable port initiatives mostly followed the concept of sustainable development from the WECD's report, even though the PIANC emphasized the "nature philosophy" in 2013. The concept of eco-port has emerged to protect the environment and presently keeps a watchful eye on environment management. The term of green port not only aimed to balance the environmental issues and economic needs, but also initiated to integrate the natural or eco-centric viewpoints. Despite different focuses among the concepts, we can summarise the existing indicators for port sustainability in Table 1 based on the analysis of our collected materials.

It can be noted that port sustainability often follows three dimensions and integrates the ecological elements into the environmental concerns for ports. Besides, the economic factors not only concern the economic benefits from port activities by improving the operational capacity, efficiency, and competitiveness, but also matter about the investment in

Table 1. The existing sustainability indicators for ports

Categories	Indicators	Sources
Economy	• Port resources: Geographical location, natural conditions, facility, and equipment; • Port operational capacity and efficiency: Volume of freight handled, cost-effectiveness, service quality, productivity, port calls and turnaround times, cargo handling performance, energy efficiency, function diversity; • Port competitiveness: Effective port operations, service quality, terminal utilization costs, effective resources utilization, automation, intelligent transport system, regional corporation performance, hinterland connection, supply chain performance, maritime connectivity, reliability and customer satisfaction, safety, flexibility; • Investment: Foreign direct investment, special investment	[19–26]
Society	• Human living conditions: Port-city relationships, exposure to hazards, human health, cultural resources, knowledge development, social accidents, human rights, housing and income, regional development, traffic congestion, violence, relationship with local communities, sanitation, equity in employment relations; • Working environment: Fire and explosion prevention, accidents, regular security check on equipment, occupational disease, toxicity; • Human resources: Employment, seafarers crisis resulting from a pandemic, career development, employee welfare, training and education, employee turnover rate; • Communication and collaboration: Privileges, sustainability goals sharing, sustainability responsibilities sharing, parties' relationship, stakeholder collaboration, public awareness; • Regulations and plans: Strategic plans, legal and regulatory developments for automated systems and greenhouse gas emissions reduction, environmental management system (EMS), sustainability policy framework, and the role of port authorities	[5, 19, 21, 22, 24–27]

(continued)

Table 1. (*continued*)

Categories	Indicators	Sources
Environment	• Air quality and climate: Carbon oxides (COX), Methane (CH4), Hydrocarbons (HC), Particular Matters (PM), Sulphur oxides (SOX), nitrogen oxides (NOX), Ozone, volatile organic compound (VOC), Nonmethane Hydrocarbon (NMHC), Aldehyde, water vapor, Chlorofluorocarbons (CFC); • Water consumption and quality: Water consumption, suspended solids (SS), biochemical oxygen demand (BOD), chemical oxygen demand (COD), oil content, chemical spills, ballast water discharge; • Waste: Amount of solid waste, waste treatment rate, waste utilization rate; • Soil and sediment: NOX and heavy metal in soil, hydrocarbons in sediment, and dredging operations; • Noise and vibration: Intensity of noise and vibration; • Thermal pollution: Amount of heat released; • Visual pollution: Area occupied by infrastructure, facilities, or transport system; • Energy: Energy consumption, renewable energy, energy saving; • Resource consumption: disposal of vehicle parts, consumption or disposal of steel, plastic, wood, and paper in operation or unloaded, consumption of office supplies, material recycling; • Land use: Area occupied by infrastructure, facilities, or transport system, nature reserve areas; • Ecosystem: Biological preservation, biodiversity, habitat conservation and species health, distance from ecologically sensitive areas, vegetation coverage and landscape	[6, 19–23, 26–28]

ports, while the social and environmental considerations more focus on the impacts of ports on the environment, such as the effects on living conditions, social employment, regional plans, and environmental quality. The indicative recognition of the interaction between the ports and the environment is weak.

3.3 Current Sustainability Assessment Approaches and Methods

3.3.1 Current Approaches for Sustainability Assessment

Based on the collected data, the current sustainability assessment used MCDM, LCA (Life Cycle Assessment) and MDDM-based approaches to construct the assessment processes (see Fig. 2). The MCDM and MDDM-based assessments intend to select alternatives while the LCA-based assessments tend to observe the impacts of ports. We can also find both MCDM and MDDM-based approaches depend on expert judgement although the latter emphasizes on recognizing the interaction between activity and environment [29, 30]. The LCA-based processes can assist in quantitatively recognizing the impacts with life-cycle views, but it relies much on the amount and quality of data and are often used for products.

MCDM-based:

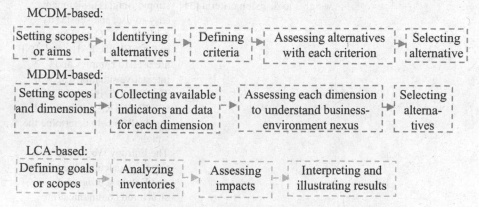

Fig. 2. The general sustainability assessment approaches [3]

3.3.2 Specific Methods for Sustainability Assessment

As sustainability assessment is inherently a decision-making task, current literature used a series of specific decision-making tools to select the alternatives (see Table 2). However, they mostly rely on weighting indices and ignore the actual measurement of sustainability actions impacts. On the other hand, Table 3 summarises the existing methods of sustainability impact assessment. Specifically, the assessment methods based on human preferences are highly subjective and the results are easily influenced by limited knowledge and experience; those methods based on physical and environmental economic perspectives focus on the valuation or monetization of impact gains and losses; in addition to this, "causality-based" or "data-driven" methods stand out by the assessment rationales for sustainability assessment. However, the causality-based methods including Material Flow Analysis (MFA), DPSIR (Drivers, Pressures, State, Impact, and Response) model, and System Dynamics (SD) are easily restricted by the complexities of systems. Although the ICR (Impact, Confidence, and Relationship) model contributes to data-driven decision-making, it still relies on subjective expert scores.

Table 2. The existing sustainability decision-making methods

Methods	What the method does	Comparisons
Analytic Hierarchy Process (AHP)	It is a structured outranking technique by quantifying the weights to decision criteria [31]	The AHP is a well-known tool as its dynamic re-evaluation, simple weights assignment, easy-to-use, and sensitivity analysis [31]. Complementary to the AHP, the FAHP and ANP are used to complex and interactive situations[32, 33] The TOPSIS, PROMETHEE and ELECTRE are used with the AHP, to help determine the weights The Entropy Weight Method targets to calculate the weights and Delphi scoring as a structured communication method can be used in conjunction with other methods
Fuzzy Analytic Hierarchy Process (FAHP)	It applies fuzzy numbers to assign the weights [32]	
Analytic Network Process (ANP)	It is a ranking tool through building a network of elements [33]	
Technique for Order of Preference by Similarity to Ideal Solution (TOPSIS)	It is a technique to select the alternative by using the shortest Euclidean distance from an ideal solution and the greatest distance from a negative ideal one [34]	
Preference Ranking Organization Method for Enrichment Evaluations (PROMETHEE)	It is an outranking tool based on a pairwise comparison between different alternatives [35]	
Elimination and Choice Expressing the Reality (ELECTRE)	It is an outranking method to discard the unacceptable alternatives and select the best one [36]	
Entropy Weight Method	It is a weighting method to measure the dispersion of values [34]	

(continued)

Table 2. (*continued*)

Methods	What the method does	Comparisons
Delphi	It is a structured decision method based on a panel of experts	

Table 3. The existing sustainability impact assessment methods

Methods	What the method does	Comparisons
Stakeholder Engagement	It is a process to capture the stakeholders' opinions for assessment [37]	Stakeholder Engagement and Public Participation use human cognition to indicate the effects, while the Emergy Analysis and Exergy Analysis use physical views
Public Participation	It is a process to capture the publics' opinion for assessment [38]	The Cost-benefit Analysis, Environment Accounting, and Environmental Footprints aim to use costs and benefits, profit and investment, and natural capital to connect the environment to the economy
Emergy analysis	It uses equivalent solar energy to measure the environmental and ecological costs [39]	
Exergy Analysis	It is used to measure the environmental and ecological impacts based on thermodynamic analysis [40]	
Cost-benefit Analyses	It uses costs and benefits to estimate and compare the economic effects [41]	
Environmental Accounting	It is used to calculate the profit of environmental financial investment [42]	
Environmental Footprint	It uses environmental burden caused by activities to indicate the impacts [43]	

(*continued*)

Table 3. (*continued*)

Methods	What the method does	Comparisons
MFA	It uses flows or stocks of materials or substances to analyse the physical impacts of human activities [44]	The MFA is limited to be used in a well-defined system and pays attention to a single material [44] and the DPSIR model and SD are challenged by the recognition of causality [45]. Although the ICR model does not matter causality, it is subjective for impacts scoring [3]
DPSIR model	It is a causal framework to help understand complex systems [45]	
SD	It uses stocks, flows, feedback loops, and relevant factors to analyse the dynamic behaviour of systems [45]	
ICR model	It is a model to assess the interactions based on existing knowledge and expert experience [3]	
Data Envelopment Analysis	It is a tool to measure productive efficiency by comparing the inputs and outputs [46]	Both are often used to process data and have high demands on data [46, 47]
Monte Carlo Simulation	It is used to get numerical results based on repeated random sampling [47]	

4   A New Sustainability Assessment Model for Ports

Based on the systematic review, the concept of sustainability seems to be a slippery word in the last decades but moving to ecocentrism and context-specific thinking. Although the common qualities of sustainability which have been shared in the catchphrases are social, economic, and environmental, eco-centric views have already been observed for the basis of human survival. Similarly, the port sustainability remains under question about what decisions to be served and what situations to stay in. There is a lack of sustainability assessment studies for ports although many MCDM, LCA, and MDDM-based sustainability assessment approaches and specific methods are available to serve the processes.

The pursuit of sustainability in a messy must not be a good way of moving ahead in the port industry, so this study suggests a new conceptual model for assessing the sustainability status quo by tracking the practical interactions between port activities and the regional environment, as shown in Fig. 3. Considering the sustainability movements and the advantages and disadvantages of the existing sustainability assessment approaches and methods, the novelties of the new proposed model include:

- It includes an ecological dimension set to highlight the eco-centric views;

- specific elements are identified for each dimension;
- port operations are clearly defined in relation to the four dimensions;
- it uses an input-output model-based index system built on the recognition of the business-environment nexus.

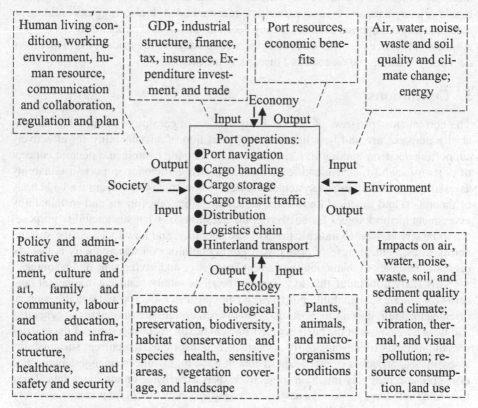

Fig. 3. A sustainability assessment model for ports based on the business-environment nexus

This systematic thinking can contribute to comprehensively perceiving the port sustainability factors and dynamically serving specific circumstances. It must be noted that the achievement of port sustainability is not to reduce port activities or prevent system change, but to make the port activities preserve or conserve the ecosystem as well as the environmental conditions that fit the port's sustainable development.

In addition, instead of the current subjective MCDM or MDDM-based or data-relied LCA-based sustainability assessment approaches, a more transparent, widely-available, integrated, and reliable sustainability assessment approach is still demanding, as well as consequent suitable and supportive tools. Considering the real characteristics of sustainability, that is, complex and uncertain, systematic and dynamic, and short-term and far-sighted, a data-driven evidence-based approach which relies on practical case experience and tries to make trade-offs to adjust to particular situations may be an option to be aligned with a growing body of evidence. In this case, we can use a systematic review to collect the data for developing and enhancing the role of knowledge, reduce the probability of poor decision-making due to insufficient understanding of causality, and provide some evidence to fit specific decision-making.

Nonetheless, this study focuses only on materials that have been issued from literature databases and organizations' official websites. In the future, more investigations to add primary data and evidence would be recommended. It also suggests building an evidence-based database, available to any decision-makers and public to follow the port sustainability processes. It is also recommended to integrate the evidence into their own decisions by taking the essence and discarding the dregs.

5   Conclusions

The current slow progress of sustainability asks us to care more about what sustainability purposes are and how to assess the status quo of sustainability for effectively supporting decision-making in a specific context. Having examined a generic concept of port sustainability and identified a methodological deficiency in port sustainability assessment, this study uses a systematic review to constructively integrate a large body of theoretical and practical knowledge on sustainability perceptions and sustainability assessment methodologies for answering the questions of what sustainability purposes are to be served, how to indicate the port sustainability, and how to assess the sustainability assessment. Instead of primarily acquiring opinions on sustainability issues, the review contributes to managing the current knowledge and saving time and resources.

This study concludes that as common social, economic, and environmental concerns for general sustainability purposes and moving to eco-centric and specific context-oriented thinking, the current port sustainability perceptions are limited to the generality and have a weakness in the business-environment nexus. Although some of the existing specific methods for sustainability assessment can inspire us, the current sustainability assessment approaches cannot adapt to complex and highly uncertain assessment situations, because they rely much on subjective expert experience or sufficient data. These motivated us to have proposed a new integrative assessment model for port sustainability, which sets an ecological dimension to emphasise the ecological issues and designs an index system for considering the business-environment interactions.

Nevertheless, this study is constrained by the existing literature and documents from selected organisations and the data extraction process need a double check. More investigations and the proposed integrative assessment model-based case studies are also needed to enrich the sustainability knowledge and evidence. An evidence-based approach is also suggested to integrate as many cases experience to support decisions making. It contributes to comparing reasonable alternatives and selecting the preferred one by combing specific circumstances and trade-offs.

Acknowledgments. This study is supported by the Jimei University Scientific Research Starting Foundation [ZQ2019037] and the China Scholarship Fund [202108350040].

Informed Consent.   This article does not contain any studies with human participants performed by any of the authors.

Data Availability Statement. Data supporting the results reported can be found in the citations.

Conflict of Interest. The author declares no conflicts of interest.

References

1. United Nations, Transforming our World: The 2030 Agenda for Sustainable Development. 2015, United Nations: New York, USA (2015)
2. Choudhary, A., et al.: An integrated fuzzy intuitionistic sustainability assessment framework for manufacturing supply chain: a study of UK based firms. Ann. Oper. Res. 1–44 (2021)
3. Wu, X.F., Chen, H.L., Min, J.: Sustainability assessment of cruise-industry development: a case study of Xiamen. China. Marit. Policy Manage. **48**(2), 213–224 (2021)
4. Wu, X., Zhang, L., Yang, H.-C.: Integration of eco-centric views of sustainability in port planning. Sustainability **12**(7), 2971 (2020)
5. Lu, C.S., Shang, K.C., Lin, C.C.: Identifying crucial sustainability assessment criteria for container seaports. Marit. Bus. Rev. **1**(2), 90–106 (2016)
6. Rodrigues, V., et al.: Harmonizing sustainability assessment in seaports: a common framework for reporting environmental performance indicators. Ocean Coast. Manage. **202**, 105514 (2021)
7. Schipper, C.A., Vreugdenhil, H., de Jong, M.P.C.: A sustainability assessment of ports and port-city plans: Comparing ambitions with achievements. Transp. Res. Part D: Transp. Environ. **57**, 84–111 (2017)
8. Dushenko, M., Bjorbaek, C.T., Steger-Jensen, K.: Application of a sustainability model for assessing the relocation of a container terminal: a case study of Kristiansand port. Sustainability **11**(1), 87 (2019)
9. Snyder, H.: Literature review as a research methodology: an overview and guidelines. J. Bus. Res. **104**, 333–339 (2019)
10. Saunders, M., Lewis, P., Thornhill, A.: Research Methods for Business Students. Pearson education, London (2019)
11. Wu, X., Zhang, L., Luo, M.: Current strategic planning for sustainability in international shipping. Environ. Dev. Sustain. **22**(3), 1729–1747 (2018). https://doi.org/10.1007/s10668-018-00303-2
12. Wu, X., Zhang, L., Luo, M.: Discerning sustainability approaches in shipping. Environ. Dev. Sustain. **22**(6), 5169–5184 (2019). https://doi.org/10.1007/s10668-019-00419-z
13. Wohlin, C.: Guidelines for snowballing in systematic literature studies and a replication in software engineering. In: ACM International Conference Proceeding Series (2014)
14. Caradonna, J.L.: Sustainability: A history. Oxford University Press, New York (2014)
15. WCED, Report of the World Commission on Environment and Development: Our Common Future. 1987, United Nations: Geneva, Switzerland (1987)
16. Washington, H.: Demystifying Sustainability: Towards Real Solutions, vol. 242. Routledge, London (2015)
17. Whyte, P., Lamberton, G.: Conceptualising sustainability using a cognitive mapping method. Sustainability **12**(5), 1977 (2020)
18. Mosier, S.L., Ruxton, M.M., Park, B.: A moving target concept? the challenge of defining sustainability. Sustain. Climate Change **15**(2), 112–125 (2022)
19. PIANC. WG150 Sustainable Ports-A Guidance for Port Authorities (2013). http://www1.iaphworldports.org/pdf/PIANC_WG150.pdf. Accessed 12 Oct 2018
20. Wang, D., Zhao, Y.: Research on quantitative evaluation indicator system of seaport sustainable development. In: OCEANS 2016 - Shanghai (2016)

21. Wang, X.M.G., et al.: A holistic sustainability framework for oil terminals: the case of China. Int. J. Shipping Transp. Logistics **12**(6), 521–542 (2020)
22. China Waterborne Transport Research Institute. Guidance for Green Port Evaluation (2020). https://xxgk.mot.gov.cn/2020/jigou/syj/202006/t20200623_3314948.html. Accessed 18 Nov 2022
23. Zhao, D., et al.: Green port performance evaluation under uncertainty: a multiple attribute group decision analysis. Int. J. Shipping Transp. Logistics **13**(1–2), 130–155 (2021)
24. UNCTAD. Review of Maritime Transport 2021 (2021)
25. Othman, A., El-Gazzar, S., Knez, M.: A framework for adopting a sustainable smart sea port index. Sustainability (Switzerland) **14**(8), 4551 (2022)
26. Junior, I.C.L., et al.: Probabilistic analysis of the sustainable performance of container terminals. Res. Transp. Bus. Manage. **43**, 100725 (2022)
27. ESPO. Green Guide (2021). https://www.espo.be/media/ESPO%20Green%20Guide%2021%20-%20FINAL.pdf
28. UNCTAD: Sustainable development for ports (1993). http://unctad.org/en/Docs/sddport1_en.pdf. Accessed 2 Jan 2020
29. Wu, X., Zhang, L., Feng, H.: Green strategic planning approach for international shipping activities. Sustainability **12**(1), 41 (2019)
30. Wu, X., Yang, H.-C.: An ecological sustainability assessment approach for strategic decision making in international shipping. Sustainability **13**(20), 11471 (2021)
31. Sakhardande, M.J., Gaonkar, R.S.P.: On solving large data matrix problems in Fuzzy AHP. Expert Syst. Appl. **194**, 116488 (2022)
32. Chan, H.K., Sun, X., Chung, S.-H.: When should fuzzy analytic hierarchy process be used instead of analytic hierarchy process? Decis. Support Syst. **125**, 113114 (2019)
33. Saaty, T.L., Vargas, L.G.: The analytic network process. In: Decision Making with the Analytic Network Process. International Series in Operations Research & Management Science, vol. 195, pp 1–40. Springer, Boston (2013). https://doi.org/10.1007/978-1-4614-7279-7_1
34. Chen, Z.Y.: Port logistics function evaluation model based on entropy weight TOPSIS method. Discret. Dyn. Nat. Soc. **2022**, 1–10 (2022)
35. Wulf, C., et al.: Setting thresholds to define indifferences and preferences in PROMETHEE for life cycle sustainability assessment of European hydrogen production. Sustainability **13**(13), 7009 (2021)
36. Lin, T.Y., et al.: Improved ELECTRE II sustainability assessment framework in power generation technological evaluation. J. Intell. Fuzzy Syst. **43**(5), 6405–6418 (2022)
37. Röös, E., et al.: How well is farmers' social situation captured by sustainability assessment tools? A Swedish case study. Int. J. Sust. Dev. World **26**(3), 268–281 (2019)
38. Lusby, C., Ackermann, L.: Consumer perceptions of cruise line sustainability. Int. J. Sustain. Econ. Soc. Cult. Context **13**(2), 25–37 (2017)
39. Zhan, C., Zhao, R., Hu, S.: Emergy-based sustainability assessment of forest ecosystem with the aid of mountain eco-hydrological model in Huanjiang County. Chin. J. Cleaner Prod. **251**, 119638 (2020)
40. Wang, Q., et al.: Expanding exergy analysis for the sustainability assessment of SJ-type oil shale retorting process. Energy Convers. Manage. **187**, 29–40 (2019)
41. Sjöstrand, K., et al.: Sustainability assessments of regional water supply interventions-combining cost-benefit and multi-criteria decision analyses. J. Environ. Manage. **225**, 313–324 (2018)
42. Murad, S.M.A., et al.: Sustainability assessment framework: a mini review of assessment concept. Chem. Eng. Trans. **72**, 379–384 (2019)
43. Herceg, S., Bautista, S.P., Weiß, K.A.: Sustainability assessment methods. In: Photovoltaic Modules: Reliability and Sustainability, pp. 149–154 (2021)

44. Myllyviita, T., Antikainen, R., Leskinen, P.: Sustainability assessment tools-their comprehensiveness and utilisation in company-level sustainability assessments in Finland. Int. J. Sust. Dev. World **24**(3), 236–247 (2017)
45. Wang, F., et al.: Integrated sustainability assessment of chemical production chains. J. Clean. Prod. **219**, 894–905 (2019)
46. Keshavarz, E., Toloo, M.: A hybrid data envelopment analysis and multi-attribute decision making approach to sustainability assessment. Expert Syst. **37**(4), e12347 (2020)
47. Konstantinos, K., et al.: A multi-criteria decision support framework for assessing seaport sustainability planning: the case of Piraeus. Marit. Policy Manag. 1–27 (2022)

DSS Users and Successful Adoption

An Investigation on Cloud ERP Adoption Using Technology-Organisation-Environment (TOE) and Diffusion of Innovation (DOI) Theories: A Systematic Review

Sin Ting Cheung[1] , Uchitha Jayawickrama[2]([⊠]) , Femi Olan[3] ,
and Maduka Subasinghage[4]

[1] Saïd Business School, University of Oxford, Oxford, UK
[2] Loughborough Business School, Loughborough University, Loughborough, UK
u.jayawickrama@lboro.ac.uk
[3] Essex Business School, University of Essex, Essex, UK
[4] Faculty of Business, Economics and Law, Auckland University of Technology, Auckland,
New Zealand

Abstract. The purpose of this study was to explore the important factors for the adoption of Cloud ERP systems. When organisations make decision on implementation of innovative technology such as Cloud ERP, there is a range of factors to be considered. This paper aims to identify the most significant 9 TOE and DOI factors which have positive influence towards Cloud ERP adoption by conducting a systematic literature review (SLR). A conceptual framework was proposed which is useful reference for potential Cloud ERP adopters who are making decisions on Cloud ERP adoption. The conceptual framework includes the identified 9 factors as independent variables; adoption of Cloud ERP as dependent variable; firm sizes and countries as the two moderating variables.

Keywords: Cloud ERP adoption · Diffusion of Innovation ·
Technology-Organisation-Environment framework · SLR · SMEs · LEs ·
Developed countries · Developing countries

1 Introduction

Cloud Enterprise Resource Planning (ERP) systems offer the same functions as traditional ERPs, but do not require an upfront investment cost for trial period as a traditional ERP [1]. Cloud ERP systems are becoming popular among various company sizes and different economic settings of various countries i.e., developing and developed countries [2–4]. One of the recent industrial reports [5] stated that ERP evolution can help firms achieve competitive advantages and align with the best company practices regardless of company sizes, economic settings and industry sectors.

Diffusion of Innovation (DOI) is a technology adoption theory which investigates how innovative technology is adopted at company and individual levels from the aspects of relative advantage, complexity, compatibility, observability and trialability [6]. On the other hand, Technology-Organisation- Environment (TOE) framework has influential criteria within the technological, organisational and environmental context [7]. This framework covers both internal and external technological aspects of an organisation, including the relative advantage of the technology and its compatibility with the current practices of the organisation [7]. While the internal aspects refer to the availability of resources including the size of firms, volume of slack, communication channel and structure of management [5], the external aspects refer to the competitors in markets, the readiness of technology support and governmental regulations. Both TOE and DOI frameworks can be utilised to explain diffusion of innovation [8]. Through a systematic literature review (SLR), this paper demonstrates how the factors within the DOI and TOE frameworks influence the adoption of cloud ERP across various firm sizes and countries.

2 Systematic Literature Review

We followed the criteria mentioned below when selecting literature for the SLR:

A) Academic journals, conference papers and industrial reports published in scientific databases must be considered - Following this criterion, the data has been systematically retrieved from online libraries including Google Scholar, ScienceDirect, ResearchGate, IEEE Xplore, ACM Digital Library, and Emerald Insight. Duplicated literature and the literature without specifications on geographical regions and company sizes were filtered out in each stage of the data pulling process. A range of specific key search terms (i.e., Cloud ERP adoption, Cloud computing, SMEs, LEs, developing countries, developed countries, DOI and TOE) were used to ensure the literature were aligned with aim of the study.
B) All literature which was published in most popular period of cloud ERP research is analysed - The most popular period of cloud ERP research is between 2015 and 2020, hence the conference papers, industrial reports, academic journal articles published within the period of 2015 to 2020 were considered during SLR.
C) Qualitative research papers, quantitative research papers as well as conceptual papers were analysed.
D) Only research published in English language was selected.

The SLR was conducted in four stages - identification, collection, analysis and processing of existing literature. These steps were taken to ensure that we include all relevant literature and eliminate the irrelevant literature from the results. Identification stage was split into 2 phases: phase 1 – background search and research gap identification, and phase 2 – comparison between developed and developing countries (see Fig. 1). In phase 1, 111 existing literature was used for background search and the identification of research gap. Thereafter, 86 duplications, irrelevant literature and outdated literature was eliminated, which resulted in 25 remaining literature in the sample. In phase 2, 100 literature which was found using Mendeley were used for comparisons between developing and developed countries. 52 irrelevant literature which hindered the comparisons between countries were eliminated, which resulted in 48 remaining in the comparison sample. During the collection process, screening procedure was used to organise the remaining literature. This process has filtered out extra 3 duplications out of the sample. During the analysis process, further screening was carried out to ensure all literature in the sample covered both DOI and TOE factors, and therefore 42 out of the remaining 70 were taken out as they were not considered as valid literature for the analysis. This resulted in 28 valid literature, which was used in SLR to validate the key factors of adopting cloud ERP. Table 1 include the results of the SLR process.

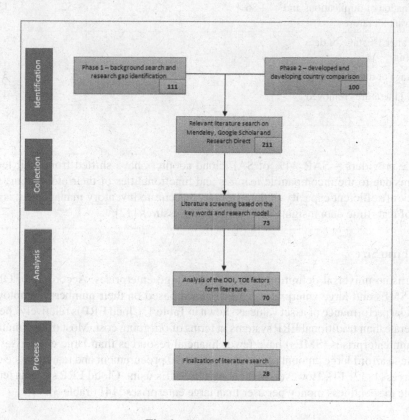

Fig. 1. SLR Framework

2.1 Findings of Systematic Literature Review

Cloud ERP has high scalability, short implementation time and low switching cost compared to traditional ERP systems [9, 10]. More than 76% of financial industries have the intention to shift to Cloud ERP systems because of five main reasons including elimination of infrastructure costs and the total cost of ownership, on-premises upgrade costs and implementing most up-to-date technology [11]. 181 respondents to a survey conducted by Panarama [12] have implemented Cloud ERP from one of the largest cloud

Table 1. Results of SLR

Online Source	Google Scholar, ScienceDirect, ResearchGate, IEEE Xplore, ACM Digital Library & Emerald Insight	Mendeley	Total
Phase 1	111		
Phase 2		100	
Total			211
Elimination of duplications and irrelevant literature	−86	−52	−138
Total after 1st stage of data cleaning			73
2nd stage of duplication removal			−3
Invalid literatures removed			−42
Total			28

service providers – SAP. 44% of SAP cloud adopters have shifted from their legacy systems due to the incompatible features and functionalities of their old systems such as lack of sufficient capacity of data storage, inaccurate inventory management issues, lack of real- time data insights and competitor pressures [12].

2.2 Firm Size

There is no universal definition for SMEs and large enterprises. According to OECD [15], SMEs and large enterprises can be defined based on their number of employees, financial performance or asset value as shown in Table 1. Cloud ERP is relatively cheaper to operate than traditional ERP systems in terms of on-going cost. Most of the small and medium enterprises (SMEs) have fewer financial resources than large enterprises and unable to afford large amount of investments on the procurement and maintenance of IT resources [1, 13, 14]. However, in the long run SMEs using Cloud ERP systems tend to be able to spend less money per user than large enterprises [14] (Table 3).

Table 2. Definition of SME and LE in the EU standard.

Company Type	Number of employees	Annual turnover	Balance Sheet
Small-medium enterprise	< 250	≤ €50 million	≤ €43 million
Large	≥ 250	≥ €50 million	≥ €4350 million

Table 3. Definitions of DOI and TOE Factors

	Factors	Definition	Reference
DOI	Relative Advantage(RA)	Competitive advantage that the adopters of the technology can gain as opposed to another alternative technology	Rogers, 1983
	Compatibility (CO)	Degree of consistency of a technology innovation with past established experiences, existing values and the current needs of potential adopters	Rogers, 1983
	Complexity (CX)	Degree of difficulty for a Cloud ERP to be adopted by an organisation	Rogers, 1983
TOE (T)	Infrastucture(INS)	IT resource alignments with its' business strategies, network and business software system	AlBar and Hoque, 2019
	Security(SR)	Capability to pressure the confidentiality of client's information and protect their data privacy during data convergence	Wilson, 2017; Ali et al. 2020
TOE (O)	Top Management Support (TMS)	Provision of support by the senior staffs who usually are the final decision makers on cloud ERP adoption	Gupta and Misra, 2016
TOE (E)	Competitive Pressure(CP)	Degree of pressure experienced by an organisation from external competitiors within the same industry	Gangwar et al. 2015; AL-Shboul, 2019; Wilson, 2017; Chang, 2020
	Government Regulation	Government support which consists of rules, legislation, policies and laws for protecting the matket of cloud computing	AL-Shboul, 2019; Shahzad et al. 2020

(continued)

Table 3. (*continued*)

Factors	Definition	Reference
Vendor Readiness(VR)	Ability of vendors to provide technical support and customers services including training, 24/7 data srchiving, on-premise back up storages, extra cloud back up, data protection, disaster recovery and business continuity	Gamage, 2019; Zamzeer et al. 2020; Gangwar et al. 2015

2.3 Developed and Developing Countries

There are several indicators to distinguish how different countries support their IT developments. According to United Nations Development Programme [16], HDI is a measurement index of average human development, which includes 'a long and healthy life, being knowledgeable and having a decent standard of living'. In 2018, examples of developed countries with relatively high HDI are Norway, Australia, Germany and United Kingdom which are 0.954, 0.938, 0.939 and 0.92 out of 1 respectively [17]. On the other hand, countries with low HDI scores would be classified as developing countries. Central African Republic, Democratic Republic of the Congo, Liberia and Pakistan are some examples with low HDI scores: 0.381, 0.459, 0.465 and 0.56 respectively [18]. Developing countries own a relatively high HDI scores: Saudi Arabia, Malaysia, Brazil and India are some of the developing countries with high HDI scores which are 0.857, 0.804, 0.761, 0.647 and 0.614. These developing countries with high HDI scores indicate that their governments are willing to invest more resources on infrastructures and support to enhance the development of the country. This reflects the capability of the countries' governments to provide financial support on the development of Cloud ERP within their countries.

Internet speed and the internet penetration are the common factors which determine the internet reliability of the developed and developing countries. The internet speed in developed and developing countries have been recorded as 189kbit/s and 91kbit/s representatively [17]. According to a report [19], 76% and 73% of Chile and Russia's population have access to the internet respectively, while the countries which are less economically developed such as Sub-Saharan Africa has much lower access rate [20]. Emerging economies including Indonesia, India, Bangladesh, and Pakistan have only below an average of 16% of their population having access to the internet. The data above suggests that there is a large difference in terms of the network speed and coverage in developing and developed countries. One of the examples of developing country, Saudi Arabia has infrastructure at the development stage, which has a slower bandwidth and speed than the developed countries [21]. Internet connectivity has been recognised as the main concern of adopting Cloud ERP in both developed and developing countries.

Developing countries like Saudi Arabia and India have relatively high cost of internet connectivity and are still in the infancy stage in terms of IT infrastructures [1, 21–23]. On the other hand, developed countries like Norway has high internet penetration rate and usages of 97.2% [24]. As having a reliable and high-quality internet deems to be the basic requirement of implementing and the operation of Cloud ERP, this is considered as one of the key factors which influences companies' decisions on Cloud ERP adoption.

2.4 Diffusion of Innovation (DOI) Theory

DOI is a technology adoption theory which investigates how innovative technologies are adopted at company and individual levels [9]. It measures the rate at which a technology diffuses into the operations of an enterprise by measuring the number of people who have adopted a technology within a specific period. DOI theory utilizes attributes which act as a measurement which includes relative advantage, complexity, compatibility, observability and trialability.

2.5 Technology-Organisation-Environment (TOE) Framework

TOE framework examines the adoption of innovations [25] using technological, organisational and environmental factors [26]. It evaluates the suitability and feasibility of a technology implementation for an organisation such as Cloud ERP adoption. This framework covers both internal and external technological aspects of an organisation, including the relative advantage of the technology and its compatibility with the current practices of the organisation [10]. Organisational context covers the internal organisational aspects including top management support, size, and management style. Environmental context covers drawbacks and opportunities brought by the innovation. Both TOE and DOI frameworks can be utilised to explain innovation diffusion [8]. This paper will focus on 9 factors within these frameworks as shown in Table 2, which deemed to have relatively more influence on the adoption of Cloud ERP.

2.5.1 DOI Factor - Relative Advantage (RA)

Relative advantage is considered as a crucial indicator for technology adoption [24]. Cloud ERP adopters generally have a higher perception in terms of the benefits of adopting the technology than non-Cloud ERP adopters [25]. It brings adopters relative advantages in terms of economy, scalability, mobility, accessibility and productivity. Cloud service providers charge users on a pay-per-use basis which does not only save the large up-front cost for setting up infrastructure upon adopting an on-premise ERP; it also offers a high degree of flexibility as Cloud ERP users only have to pay for the service that their organisations require [26].

2.5.2 DOI Factor - Compatibility (CO)

Compatibility was used as one of the crucial factors in the studies assessing the diffusion process of innovation [6, 27, 28]. Generally, when the Cloud ERP system is in line with the existing working culture and working practices of the adopting organisations, it is highly likely that the adopters can utilise the benefits offered by the system and the system users' uncertainties towards the new system can be minimized [5]. Despite the high proportion of the existing literature proved that the Cloud ERP adoption is positively related to compatibility, the fact that the possibility of this not being true in some cases cannot be eliminated. There is an argument against positive influence of compatibility in Namibia, which is caused by the existence of uncertainty about the quality of products and the requirement of extra training costs [20].

2.5.3   DOI Factor – Complexity (CX)

A lot of organisations have been reluctant when making decisions on Cloud ERP implementation due to the lack of motivation to analyse the system and train the employees. This especially applies to SMEs more than large enterprises as they do not have much financial resources [28]. This can be minimized by employing cloud service providers who provide quality and reliable services [29]. Zameer et al. [13] stated that SMEs prefer to adopt Cloud ERPs rather than on-premises ERPs as Cloud ERPs are lot easier to work with [13]. Previous research explains that when the technologies are high in complexity, organisations are not willing to integrate complex technologies into their work practices [18, 30–32].

2.5.4   Technological Factor – Infrastructure (INS)

Infrastructure in terms of adoption of Cloud ERP includes network connectivity, security and data integration related aspects. Cloud ERP is becoming the trend and the replacement for on-premises ERP. Although the overall infrastructure requirements for Cloud ERP is less than on-premise ERPs, Cloud ERP has much more reliance on the internet compared to on-premise ERPs [33, 34]. The lack of need for infrastructure investments is beneficial for SMEs than the large enterprises [35]. An industrial report [35] visualised readiness to Cloud computing technologies in 2020 with the Cloud Readiness Index (CRI) of Asian Pacific countries mainly with mature economies in the other regions of the world. The report includes an index which measures three parameters for cloud infrastructure (i.e., international connectivity, broadband quality and power grid, green policy and sustainability) [36]. In the report, developed countries and cities including Hong Kong (23.2 out 30), Taiwan (18.4 out of 30) and United Kingdom (18.8 out of 30) have higher than average score of 13.9 out of 30 in terms of cloud infrastructure. Developing countries have relatively lower scores; India (8.5 out of 30) and Malaysia (13.1 out of 30) both have lower than average scores of the sampled countries in the report. This shows that there is a significant difference between developing and developed countries in terms of the development of infrastructure which explains the different degrees of influence on Cloud ERP adoption in various economies.

2.5.5   Technological Factor – Security (SR)

Security is recognised as one of the main concerns for organisations deciding whether to adopt Cloud ERP [1, 13, 34, 37, 38]. Organisations are concerned about the data sensitivity leakage and data privacy due to the uncertainties in data security [1, 13].

Developing countries as well as developed countries evidence that security have an impact on Cloud ERP adoption [1, 2, 28, 37]. If an organisation transferred the control of data to the cloud service provider, organisations would be concerned whether the data is securely protected by the cloud service provider [39]. A security operation system with proper authentication mechanism ensures the managers or employees can be held accountable when faced with security related issues within an organisation [1, 39]. In the event of a security breach, employees log-in credentials and access time can leave audit trails, which makes it easier to spot the cracks for the data leakage [39].

2.5.6 Organisational Factor - Top Management Support (TMS)

Most of the existing literature suggests that TMS is one of the main factors affecting the success of Cloud ERP adoption in developing countries [13, 18, 31, 40–42] as well as in developed countries [28, 43–45]. This is due to TMS being one of the main sources of motivation for employees to be proactive in process of implementation as they allocate resources efficiently [40–42]. Having TMS confirms high degree of commitment and ongoing support [40]. Compliance, network, security and the people related factors in cloud ERP implementation [13, 40] can improve the work environment, reinforcing communication bridge and enhancing collaboration between employees across departments in organisations [31]. Due to the complexity of Cloud ERP, TMS is required to provide continuous training for employees, which will minimize uncertainties by helping the employees to get the right set of skills [46]. If top management is able to promote inspirational leadership by showing strong commitment towards the adoption of Cloud ERP, the employees will be more likely to work towards the same shared values and goals as held by their organisations [39]. Achieving this will greatly reduce the process turnaround time [39].

2.5.7 Environmental Factor - Competitive Pressure (CP)

According to Fan et al. [26], CP is further digested and categorised into three main types of pressures, including mimetic, coercive and normative pressures. Mimetic pressures are experienced by organisations which blindly follow the behaviour of their competitors in the same industry when they witness the success of the competitors [47]. Organisation with mimetic pressures respond to uncertainties when they implement technologies such as Cloud ERP by 'mimicking' its rivals [47]. In terms of Cloud ERP, competitors that have already adopted Cloud ERP are great examples for non-adopters to learn from before making adoption decisions. Competitors who have adopted cloud ERP initiate CP which encourage non-adopters to adopt the technology [18]. Coercive pressure refers to those originated as a result of pressures imposed by the government, industry associations and the competitive environment of the organization's industry [26]. Normative pressures are formed by the shared values and common norms within an industry [47]. CP helps increase market visibility and enables more accurate data to be obtained from organisations within the same industry [40]. Previous literature has recognised CP as one of the main effective motivators for Cloud ERP adoption [18, 41].

2.5.8   Environmental Factor - Government Regulation (GR)

Government regulations vary between developed and developing countries. European Union consists of 27 countries which is mostly developed countries [48] and data is protected by the European Network and Information Security Agency (ENISA). ENISA has always been used to improve the security in cloud services, especially for SMEs [39]. In contrast with developed countries, developing countries might have less government protection over the businesses and customer data privacy. A lot of developed countries have implemented sufficient data protection over data leakages, which provide safe regulatory environment and government policies for business activities. Developed countries including Taiwan, USA, Germany, France and Norway have full government legislations towards data protection for electronic transactions, and cybercrime [49]. In contrast to developed countries, developing countries might have less government protection over the businesses and customer data privacy. In terms of firm size, no significant differentiation could be found for SMEs and large enterprises in terms of the influence of government regulations (GR) has on Cloud ERP adoption.

2.5.9   Environmental Factor - Vendor Readiness (VR)

Uncertainty is least favourable to the presence of VR. Connectivity loss and data latency are the two major issues faced by cloud ERP users [18]. If the cloud ERP vendors could not support their trading partners with the above-mentioned services, the trust between cloud users and cloud service providers is damaged, which ultimately increases the uncertainty between cloud users and cloud service providers [13, 18]. Previous literature has recognised VR as an important influential factor of the intention to adopt cloud ERP in developed countries [43, 44] as well as in developing countries [1, 13, 17, 37, 39, 41]. Due to the fact that SMEs have limited financial resources, they are less willing to hire in-house IT expertise [39]. If cloud service providers can provide sufficient support, it eliminates the cost and the necessity of an organisation to maintain an internal IT department [1]. Therefore, SMEs are more and flexible and responsive to changes than large enterprises [37]. Technical support on Cloud ERP service is provided by cloud service provider, which eliminates the need for IT infrastructure to be maintained by the SMEs, hence SMEs are heavily reliant on the service quality of their cloud service providers [37]. This is in line with Bhatti [43] which indicated SMEs' reliance on their vendors' support is higher than large enterprises.

2.6   The Identification of the Research Gap

Through the SLR we have categorized the literature which only focuses on SMEs, large enterprises or both and identified the importance of different factors within DOI and TOE frameworks. 21 out of 28 papers identified through the SLR covered both TOE and DOI factors but were limited to either one country or one firm size without comparison. Only one paper covered multiple developing countries in the same analysis. For the firm size, 17 out of 28 papers covered only SMEs, while 5 covered large enterprises and 6 covered both SMEs and large enterprises (see Table 4). The majority of them had findings confirming that technology environment and organisational factors are all contributing factors towards adoption of new technologies in both developing [31, 34, 40, 42], and developed countries [35, 43]. Overall, from the SLR, we identified that there is lack of literature related to developed countries and large enterprises, but none of the literature also provided an overview of comparisons between different firm sizes in developed and developing countries. This was identified as the research gap for this study, which led to the establishment of the proposed conceptual framework (Table 5).

Table 4.   Statistics of SLR in terms of firm sizes and countries

Country / Firm Size	SMEs	Large Enterprises	Both
Developing	9	4	3
Developed	8	1	3
Total	17	5	6

3   Formulation of Conceptual Framework

As a result of the SLR, 9 key adopting factors were identified based on the importance of the potential impacts on the adoption of Cloud ERP technology. Based on the 28 papers found through SLR, this paper illustrates the number of factors that positively influence the adoption of Cloud ERP systems. When a particular factor positively influences the adoption decisions greater than 10 times, that factor was identified as a good indicator and was classified as an important factor. 9 important factors were identified, including relative advantage (RA), compatibility (CO), complexity (CX), infrastructure (INS), security (SR), top management support (TMS), government regulation (GR), competitive pressure (CP), vendor readiness (VR), which also provided us with a reasonable size of papers for further analysis.

Based on the identified 9 factors, a conceptual framework was proposed (see Fig. 2) to indicate the relationships between the 9 key factors and Cloud ERP adoption. As mentioned before, there is lack of research which explains the differences between cloud ERP adoption based on the firm sizes and the type of the countries (i.e., developed or developing). While some of the literature discussed the cloud ERP adoption based on the country type (developed/developing), some explained the cloud ERP adoption based

Table 5. Result of Systematic Literature Review

	Diffusion of innovation					Technology Organisation Environment Framework									
	Relative advantage	Compatibility	Complexity	Trialability	Observability	Infrastructure	Security	Size	Structure	Communication	Top Management Support	Cost	Government /Regulation	Competitive Pressure	Vendor Readiness
*Developing Country	14	11	11	6	4	8	9	8	2	3	17	6	9	10	7
*Developed Country	6	7	3	2	0	2	5	8	0	1	6	3	4	7	4
Total	20	18	14	8	4	10	14	16	2	4	23	9	13	17	11

*Developing Country (AlBar & Hoque, 2019; Al-Ma'Aitah, 2017; AL-Shhoul, 2019; Awa et al. 2016; Ayoubkhan & Airvatham, 2019; Das & Dayal, 2016; Dincă et al. 2019; Gangwar et al. 2015; Gamage, 2019; Gupta & Misra,2016; Gupta et al. 2018; Haberli et al. 2017; Hasheela Miss et al. 2016; Mohammed et al. 2017 Shahzad et al. 2020; Wilson, 2017; Yang et al. 2015; Zamzeer et al. 2020)

*Developed Country (Achabou et al. 2017; Ali et al. 2020; Alsharari et al. 2020; Bhatti, 2017; Chang 2020; Fan et al. 2015; Kimuthia, 2015; Rauleder, 2016; Senarathna et al. 2018; Vasudavan et al. 2018) on the firm sizes, however, there is lack of research which discussed both elements. 'Firm sizes' and 'countries' have been identified as the moderating variables for the relationship between TOE & DOI factors and Cloud ERP adoption (see Fig. 2).

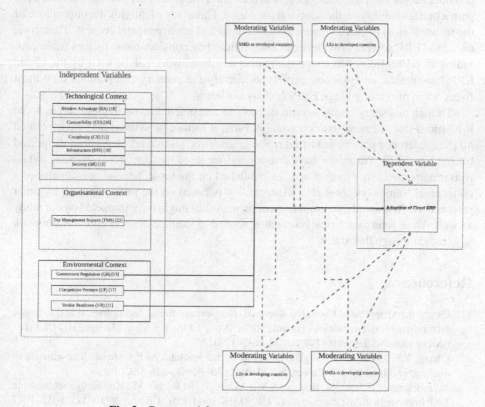

Fig. 2. Conceptual framework on cloud ERP adoption

4 Conclusions

Organisations adopt Cloud ERP to align their existing business strategies with the industry standards and gain competitive advantages [8]. The aim of this paper was to identify the relationships between DOI & TOE factors and Cloud ERP adoption. Based on the SLR, it had been concluded that Cloud ERP provides various advantages over traditional ERP such as having low switching costs, high scalability, and short implementation time. A conceptual framework was developed to indicate the relationships between the identified 9 factors, firm sizes and type of the countries (i.e., developed or developing) and cloud ERP adoption. Although cloud ERP has gained popularity and market growth [51], there are many organizations using traditional ERP systems rather than cloud ERP systems. This research contributes to a better understanding of the factors considered during cloud ERP adoption, so that the adoption of cloud ERP systems can be improved.

The conceptual framework developed by this study can be used by the potential cloud ERP adopters when making cloud ERP adoption decisions. Using this framework cloud ERP service providers can understand the factors which cloud ERP adopters might consider during their adoption decisions, therefore, the cloud ERP service providers can gain a better visibility on the adoption decisions. This study highlights the importance of the technological context, organizational context and environmental context. Therefore, the cloud ERP service providers can ensure that they consider those factors when providing cloud services. Moreover, the conceptual framework can be used by the Cloud ERP consultants, analysts and experts to identify the primary components they must focus when promoting cloud ERP services to clients.

Though this study makes several theoretical and practical contributions, it has some limitations that we need to acknowledge. First, it cannot be assured that we identified all the conference papers, industrial reports, academic journal articles within the period of 2015 to 2020. We might have overlooked some of the conference papers, industrial reports, academic journal articles published on the topic. Second, we developed a conceptual framework through a SLR, thus, it is based on the previous work by other researchers. As a result, the limitations of their studies might have impacted on our study as well. Thus, future empirical research is needed to validate the conceptual framework suggested through this study.

References

1. Gupta, S., Misra, S.C., Kock, N., Roubaud, D.: Organizational, technological and extrinsic factors in the implementation of cloud ERP in SMEs. J. Organ. Chang. Manage. 31(1), 83–102 (2018). https://doi.org/10.1108/JOCM-06-2017-0230
2. Chang, Y.W.: What drives organizations to switch to cloud ERP systems? The impacts of enablers and inhibitors. J. Enterp. Inf. Manage. 33(3), 600–626 (2020)
3. Jayawickrama, U., Liu, S., Hudson, S.M., Akhtar, P., Al Bashir, M.: Knowledge retention in ERP implementations: the context of UK SMEs. Prod. Plan. Control 30(10–12), 1032–1047 (2019)
4. Malik, M.O., Khan, N.: Analysis of ERP implementation to develop a strategy for its success in developing countries. Prod. Plan. Control 32(12), 1020–1035 (2021)
5. Accenture, "2019 ERP Trends," Accent. White Papers (2019). https://www.accenture.com/_acnmedia/pdf-90/accenture-unleashing-exponential-evolution-pdf.pdf
6. Rogers, E.M.: Diffusion of Innovation Third Edition (1983)
7. Tornatzky, L.G., Fleischer, M., Chakrabarti, A.K.: The processes of technological innovation. Lexington Books, Massachusetts (1990)
8. Oliveira, T., Martins, M.F.: Information technology adoption models at firm level: review of literature. In: 4th European Conference on Information Management and Evaluation, ECIME 2010, pp. 312–322 (2010)
9. Bouguettaya, A., Hauswirth, M., Liu, L.: Web information systems engineering - WISR 2011.In: 12th International Conference, Sydney, Australia, October 13-14, 2011 : proceedings / monograph. Springer, Heidelberg (2011). https://doi.org/10.1007/978-3-642-24434-6
10. Seethamraju, R.: Adoption of software as a service (SaaS) enterprise resource planning (ERP) systems in small and medium sized enterprises (SMEs). Inf. Syst. Front. 17(3), 475–492 (2014). https://doi.org/10.1007/s10796-014-9506-5

11. Oracle, The End of Technology Obsolescence ERP Trends in 2018 (2018). https://www.ora
cle.com/a/ocom/docs/erp-trends-report-2018.pdf?source=:em:eo:lpty:pt:RC_NAMK18061
4P00088:FY19TYE&elq_mid=117990&sh=&cmid=NAMK180614P00088
12. Panorama, "The 2020 ERP Report," Int. J. Cult. Prop. vol. 27, no. 1, pp. 1–2 (2020). https://
doi.org/10.1017/s0940739120000090
13. Zamzeer, M., et al.: Determinants of cloud ERP adoption in Jordan: an exploratory study. Int.
J. Bus. Inf. Syst. **34**(2), 204 (2020). https://doi.org/10.1504/IJBIS.2020.10030318
14. Usman, U.M.Z., Ahmad, M.N., Zakariya, N.H.: Factors influencing cloud enterprise resource
planning adoption in SMEs. In: Kim, K., Joukov, N. (eds.) Information Science and Applications, vol. 376, pp. 235–245. Springer, Singapore (2016). https://doi.org/10.1007/978-981-
10-0557-2_24
15. OECD, OECD SME and Entrepreneurship Outlook 2019," OECD SME Entrep. Outlook 2019
(2019). https://doi.org/10.1787/9789264009257-en
16. United Nations Developement Programme, Human Development Index (HDI). http://hdr.
undp.org/en/content/human-development-index-hdi
17. "Bandwidth growing fast but with regional differences," ITU. https://itu.foleon.com/itu/mea
suring-digital-development/bandwidth/
18. Gangwar, H., Date, H., Ramaswamy, R.: Understanding determinants of cloud computing
adoption using an integrated TAM-TOE model. J. Enterp. Inf. Manag. **28**(1), 107–130 (2015).
https://doi.org/10.1108/JEIM-08-2013-0065
19. "Communications Technology in Emerging and Developing Nations," Pew Research Center (2015) https://www.pewresearch.org/global/2015/03/19/1-communications-technology-
in-emerging-and-developing-nations/
20. Sørheller, V.U., Høvik, E.J., Hustad, E., Vassilakopoulou, P.: Implementing cloud ERP solutions: a review of sociotechnical concerns. Proc. Comput. Sci. **138**, 470–477 (2018). https://
doi.org/10.1016/j.procs.2018.10.065
21. Ruangvanich, S., Piriyasurawong, P.: Structural equation model of acceptance cloud learning
for sustainability usage in higher education institutes. Int. J. Emerg. Technol. Learn. **14**, 18–33
(2019). https://doi.org/10.3991/ijet.v14i10.10045
22. Abd Elmonem, M.A., Nasr, E.S., Geith, M.H.: Benefits and challenges of cloud ERP systems –
A systematic literature review. Futur. Comput. Inform. J. **1**, 1–9 (2016). https://doi.org/10.
1016/j.fcij.2017.03.003
23. Hasheela, V., Smolander, K., Mufeti, T.: An investigation of factors leading to the reluctance
of SaaS ERP adoption in Namibian SMEs. Afr. J. Inf. Syst. **8**, 1 (2016)
24. Mahyar, A.: The Factors that Influence on Adoption of Cloud Computing for Small and
Medium Enterprises by Mahyar Amini : SSRN (2014)
25. Lin, H.F., Lin, S.M.: Determinants of e-business diffusion: A test of the technology diffusion
perspective. Technovation **28**, 135–145 (2008). https://doi.org/10.1016/j.technovation.2007.
10.003
26. Fan, Y.W., Wu, C.C., Der Chen, C., Fang, Y.H.: The effect of status quo bias on cloud system
adoption. J. Comput. Inf. Syst. **55**, 55–64 (2015). https://doi.org/10.1080/08874417.2015.116
45772
27. Senarathna, I.R.: Cloud Computing Adoption by SMEs in Australia (2016). https://doi.org/
10.1108/JEIM-09-2014-0094
28. Rauleder, S.: Cloud Computing As an Entrance for Start-Ups Into Erp Solutions. Karina
Cagarman, M.Sc (2016)
29. Johansson, B., Alajbegovic, A., Alexopoulo, V., Desalermos, A.: Cloud ERP adoption
opportunities and concerns: the role of organizational size," In: Proceedings of the Annual
Hawaii International Conference on System Sciences (2015) https://doi.org/10.1109/HICSS.
2015.504

30. Ali, O., Shrestha, A., Osmanaj, V., Muhammed, S.: Cloud computing technology adoption: an evaluation of key factors in local governments. Inf. Technol. People, **34**, 666–703 (2020). https://doi.org/10.1108/ITP-03-2019-0119

31. Shahzad, F., Xiu, G., Khan, I., Shahbaz, M., Riaz, M.U., Abbas, A.: The moderating role of intrinsic motivation in cloud computing adoption in online education in a developing country: a structural equation model. Asia Pac. Educ. Rev. **21**(1), 121–141 (2019). https://doi.org/10.1007/s12564-019-09611-2

32. Yang, Z., Sun, J., Zhang, Y., Wang, Y.: Understanding SaaS adoption from the perspective of organizational users: A tripod readiness model. Comput. Human Behav. **45**, 254–264 (2015). https://doi.org/10.1016/j.chb.2014.12.022

33. Mohammed, F., Ibrahim, O., Nilashi, M., Alzurqa, E.: Cloud computing adoption model for e-government implementation. Inf. Dev. **33**(3), 303–323 (2017). https://doi.org/10.1177/0266666916656033

34. Wilson, B.: A Framework to support cloud adoption decision-making by SMEs in Tamil Nadu (2017). http://shura.shu.ac.uk/23243/

35. Senarathna, I., Wilkin, C., Warren, M., Yeoh, W., Salzman, S.: Factors that influence adoption of cloud computing: An empirical study of Australian SMEs. Australas. J. Inf. Syst., **22** (2018). https://doi.org/10.3127/ajis.v22i0.1603

36. Asia Cloud Computing Association, "Cloud Readiness Index 2020," (2020)

37. Awa, H.O., Ukoha, O., Emecheta, B.C.: Using T-O-E theoretical framework to study the adoption of ERP solution. Cogent Bus. Manage. 3(1), 1196571 (2016).https://doi.org/10.1080/23311975.2016.1196571

38. Dincă, V.M., Dima, A.M., Rozsa, Z.: Determinants of cloud computing adoption by Romanian SMEs in the digital economy. J. Bus. Econ. Manage. **20**(4), 798–820 (2019). https://doi.org/10.3846/jbem.2019.9856

39. Gupta, S., Misra, S.C.: Compliance, network, security and the people related factors in cloud ERP implementation. Int. J. Commun. Syst. **29**, 1395–1419 (2016). https://doi.org/10.1002/dac.3107

40. AL-Shboul, M.A.: Towards better understanding of determinants logistical factors in SMEs for cloud ERP adoption in developing economies. Bus. Process Manage. J. **25**, 887–907 (2019). https://doi.org/10.1108/BPMJ-01-2018-0004

41. Gamage, T.C.: Determinants of cloud computing adoption among SMEs in Sri Lanka: a meta theoretical framework. Int. J. Asian Soc. Sci. **9**(2), 189–203 (2019). https://doi.org/10.18488/journal.1.2019.92.189.203

42. AlBar, A.M., Hoque, M.R.: Factors affecting cloud ERP adoption in Saudi Arabia: an empirical study. Inf. Dev. **35**, 150–164 (2019). https://doi.org/10.1177/0266666917735677

43. Bhatti, T.: Influences on adoption of cloud-based ERP systems in SMEs: the technological-organizational-environmental framework. Corp. Ownersh. Control **15**(1), 370–380 (2017). https://doi.org/10.22495/cocv15i1c2p6

44. Kinuthia, J.N.: Technological, organizational, and environmental factors affecting the adoption of Cloud Enterprise Resource Planning (ERP) systems. In: 2015 Americas Conference on Information Systems, AMCIS 2015 (2015)

45. Alsharari, N.M., Al-Shboul, M., Alteneiji, S.: Implementation of cloud ERP in the SME: evidence from UAE. J. Small Bus. Enterp. Dev. **27**(2), 299–327 (2020). https://doi.org/10.1108/JSBED-01-2019-0007

46. Al-Ma'Aitah, M.A.: The drivers of ERP cloud computing from an institutional prespective. J. Theor. Appl. Inf. Technol. **95**, 5142–5157 (2017)

47. Klein Woolthuis, R.J.A., Taminiau, Y.: Waves of change - The dynamics of Institutional Pressures, p. 44 (2017). www.rug.nl/cf/cse

48. "Countries in the EU and EEA," UK government. https://www.gov.uk/eu-eea#:~:text=. The European Union (EU) is, and people between member states

49. "Data Protection and Privacy Legislation Worldwide," United Nations Conference on Trade and Development. https://unctad.org/en/Pages/DTL/STI_and_ICTs/ICT4D-Legisl ation/eCom-Data-Protection- Laws.aspx
50. Saunders, M., Thornhill, A., Lewis, P.: Research Methods for Business Students, 7th ed. Pearson Education, Harlow (2016)
51. Statista. Forecast: global cloud ERP revenue 2018 and 2022 (2020). https://www.statista.com/statistics/681753/worldwide-cloud-erp-software-revenue/

Young Elderly DSS Users – Some Reasons for Sustained and Successful Adoption

Christer Carlsson[(✉)] and Pirkko Walden

IAMSR, Åbo Akademi University, Åhuset, 20500 Turku, Finland
{Christer.carlsson,pirkko.walden}@abo.fi

Abstract. There is consensus in health studies that regular physical activities of sufficient intensity and duration contribute to better health both in the short and long term. We have worked on getting young elderly, the 60–75 years age group, to adopt and include physical activities as part of their daily routines. One reason for addressing young elderly is large numbers – they are now 18–22% of the population in most EU countries (80–100 million citizens). A second reason is that regular health-enhancing physical activities (HEPA) can serve as preventive health care, which will improve and sustain quality of life and save health-care costs for the ageing population. We have learned that the adoption of digital services, which are modern implementations of DSS technology, can be instrumental for building sustainable HEPA programs. We also found out – a bit surprisingly – that digital applications on mobile phones are readily accepted and adopted by the young elderly (*"no problems with understanding and learning to use the application"*) when they are tailored to meaningful purposes and a context that is relevant for the young elderly.

Keywords: Young elderly users · Adoption of DSS · Self-efficacy

1 Introduction

The context we work out is the adoption and use of HEPA programs among young elderly with the guidance and support of digital tools for logging physical activity (PA loggers) that we show are implementations of classical DSS visions. HEPA is an acronym for health enhancing physical activity, which translates to physical activity (PA) of enough intensity and duration to give short- and long-term health effects. A HEPA program builds on one or several physical activities that individually or in combinations will give health effects in the short and/or long term.

In health recommendations regular PA at moderate intensity for at least 150 min per week is expected to have positive health effects (cf. [26]). The European HEPA network claims that thirty minutes a day of moderate-intensity activity is enough to benefit health. We carried out a research program that collected more than 1000 young elderly 2019–22 for HEPA activities; of these, 300–350 participants spent more than 24 months in the program. Our experience (cf. [11, 19]) is that the HEPA network guidelines are too

© The Author(s), under exclusive license to Springer Nature Switzerland AG 2023
S. Liu et al. (Eds.): ICDSST 2023, LNBIP 474, pp. 252–264, 2023.
https://doi.org/10.1007/978-3-031-32534-2_18

general and loose to actually produce HEPAs. A key part of the research program was the development, adoption, and use of modern DSS support.

The HEPA recommendations apply to healthy adults but show individual differences in the effects of PA programs. There are variations when we focus on young elderly, in terms of female/male participants, age groups, socio-economic background, physical demands from work, and HEPA capacity (decided by PA history and physical shape). We found the recommendations to be too vague to motivate sustained physical activity – "you cannot be sure that the time spent will actually give sufficient health effects" (cf. [12, 19]). Work with the young elderly showed that offered PA programs, (i) are not intensive enough, (ii) are not running regularly and for sufficient time, and (iii) are not interesting enough to become sustainable habits for young elderly. This often get young elderly to drop out of the PA programs. Thus, we decided to find another way to design, build and launch HEPA programs.

We used DSS methodology to develop digital service tools to support the participants in building and monitoring weekly HEPA programs. The tools collect daily data on actual PA exercises and combine it with data from follow-up surveys on perceptions of the effectiveness of PA exercises. Data is collected in cloud-supported databases for analysis - both cross-sectional and longitudinal - to trace progress and sustainability of HEPA programs (cf. [5, 13, 15, 25]). HEPA programs are important for young elderly; a renowned physician, himself part of the age group and research program, put it like this – "if you adopt and sustain systematic HEPA programs when you turn 60, then you get 10 more good senior years".

We have a general quest to find drivers that could get young elderly to adopt, to work with and to sustain the use of HEPA programs. We explore the role of DSS methodology in this quest, we are seeking answers to two research questions. RQ1 – can we get young elderly to adopt and use a DSS? RQ2 – will a DSS make a sustainable difference for young elderly?

In the next sub-sections, we will recall a few points in the DSS legacy, followed by an update of a modern DSS black box approach and an introduction to the DSS-based digital wellness services developed and used in the research program. Section 2 works out research results from a series of studies to understand the adoption and use of DSS-influenced digital wellness services. Section 3 is a summary and conclusions with answers to the research questions.

1.1 A Short History of DSS Legacy

In EURO Working Group on DSS. A Tour of the DSS Developments Over the Last 30 Years [20] we summarized some key contributions and features that formed the origins of Decision Support Systems and its fundamental technology in the early 1980's [8]. We have since seen 4–5 generations of technology introduced and used in the field, if we accept machine and deep learning as emerging new DSS technology (which offers some debate, cf. [6]). Nevertheless – quite a bit surprising – the basic principles for DSS are still viable and useful today. We will show – also quite a bit surprising – that DSS technology (in a 2020's generation, to be sure) is adopted and useful for young elderly; the young elderly has not been seen as a viable user group for the earlier generations of

DSS technology – at least they have not been given any prominent place in DSS studies or in the DSS literature (cf. e.g. [14]).

We will select some key features of the design and use of DSS technology, a more systematic study can be found in [24]. The DSS pioneers focused on the users' priorities and viewed the quality of a system as a function of the value it gives to the users [14] with less emphasis on the technology used (even if technology was actually a selling point in the early DSS days to offer a contrast to the mainframe systems [24]). Another key feature was to work with and support the users which is difficult if we do not know what they do, how they think and what they need to have [14]. Sprague wrote the first agenda for DSS [24]: (i) aim at less well-structured, underspecified problems; (ii) combine the use of models with data access and retrieval; (iii) focus on features to make systems easy to use by non-computer people in interactive mode; (iv) emphasize flexibility and adaptability; and (v) work with iterative design [24].

1.2 Modern DSS Black Box Approaches

It is of course the case that both the DSS technology and methodology have changed over the years; Delen and Ram [10] identified five changes in the analytics terminology that include changes in technology, methodology and models used, and how the implementation, use and support have evolved. It also appears that analytics has taken the role from DSS as a basis for applications in business and industry [6]. Analytics is introduced in three functional categories, (i) *descriptive* (business reporting, dashboards, scorecards, data warehousing), (ii) *predictive* (data mining, text mining, web/media mining, machine learning) and (iii) *prescriptive* (optimization, simulation, algorithms, network science), which tackle different types of problems and offer different but complementary forms of support.

Analytics (and DSS) is used in environments that offer *big data* and, in many cases, appears to make classical algorithms and database tools obsolete in the sense that the processing of data takes too much time and the results after a while are not of much use anymore. The large data sets have attracted *computational intelligence* algorithms that promise to be faster and more capable than the polynomial methods [6]; they include neural networks, support vector machines, genetic algorithms, genetic programming, swarm intelligence, software agents and soft computing. The faster processing comes at a price – there are much fewer users capable to use the more advanced tools than the classical DSS algorithms (cf. tailored Excel models). Modern DSS approaches turn out to become black boxes and users must accept on faith the results produced by the algorithms.

In [23] a modern-time DSS has knowledge representation as the starting point to deal with a problem area that requires a working solution and decision making. The basis for knowledge representation is an ontology which typically can be generated with the OWL API or SWARLAPI libraries. Imprecision and uncertainty are worked out in fuzzy ontologies that also form the basis for inferences that are constructed in linguistic terms and built using a fuzzy description logic. An inference system builds results from data and information on problems and problem complexes in a defined context; a fuzzy inference system (FIS) handles imprecision and uncertainty in concepts that for a specific problem area can be close to a natural language description. A FIS can be implemented with machine or deep learning, fuzzy knowledge base tools, or fuzzy controllers or simulators [23]. It quickly became apparent that the use of fuzzy inference systems cannot be the first choice if we want to get elderly users to adopt and use DSS-influenced HEPA support tools.

1.3 DW 3.0 – A Modern DSS Application

The research program *Digital Wellness Services for young Elderly [DigitalWells]*, which we run in Finland 2019–22, collected over 290 000 PA entries from more than 1000 participants in 24+ months. This was combined with cross-sectional and longitudinal studies with samples of 100–250 participants that were collected with 4–6-month intervals to show, (i) the acceptance and adoption of the DSS application, (ii) the support of HEPA programs, and (iii) the sustainability of accepted HEPA programs. A selection of results is reported in this paper. The DSS app (*DW 3.0*) went through several iterations with groups of users to improve the design and functionality. DW 3.0 composes and runs weekly PA programs and registers the actual activities (cf. Fig. 1). The DW 3.0 is a digital service for smart mobile phones (Android, iOS); digital services are architectures for data, information, and knowledge fusion [27, 28].

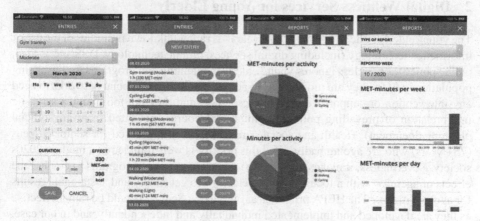

Fig. 1. DW 3.0 – A Modern DSS application.

The logging of activities on the smart phone is done in the left part of the screen (cf. Fig. 1): (i) the user selects the activity (*gym training*), (ii) the intensity (*moderate*), (iii) the *date* from the calendar, (iv) the duration (*hours, minutes*) after which the app (v) calculates and shows the effect of the PA exercise (*MET-min, kcal*).; a MET minute is the amount of energy spent during a minute while at rest; CPA [1] has calibrated more than 800 PA exercises in terms of MET (*metabolic equivalent of task*) to indicate their intensity). The MET-min measure uses the CPA [1] calibration. The most recent entries are collected in the second column. The user interface of DW 3.0 follows a descriptive design (cf. Sect. 1.2); the MET-min calculation uses algorithms to decide the effort and effect of PA exercises (efforts and effects are a function of the user's age, BMI and gender, with the type of PA activity, intensity, and duration).

The PA results are used to update a secure, cloud-based database with individual 8-digit pseudonyms for the participants and to produce reports on the users' integrated smart phone (the third and fourth columns): (i) a specified PA report (*weekly*), (ii) the reported week, (iii) the PA as *MET-minutes per week* and the (iv) *MET-minutes per day*. Graphical reports are shown in the third column to show *MET-minutes per activity* and *Minutes per intensity*.

The PA database invites further study and insight about what can be learned from the young elderly and what they learn from working out growing series of PA routines. In IS research the first choice for a conceptual framework to work out drivers that could give answers to both RQ1 and RQ2, would be the UTAUT2 (cf. [28]); UTAUT is an acronym for Unified Theory of Acceptance and Use of Technology; UTAUT2 is the second, extended version of the theory. Drivers for the adoption of digital services have been identified and studied with a basis in terms of [29]: (i) performance expectancy, (ii) effort expectancy, (iii) social influence, (iv) facilitating conditions, (v) hedonic motivation, (vi) price value and (vii) habit. We want to find out (as partial answer to RQ1 and RQ2) if UTAUT is a sufficient framework to trace drivers for the adoption, use and sustained use of PA programs among young elderly.

2   Digital Wellness Services for Young Elderly

The young elderly – the age group 60–75 years – is rather unknown in studies of the use of information technology (including digital services, mobile technology, DSS, etc.). Also, public policy more or less ignores young elderly in planning and programs for the ageing population in EU – they are too healthy, to active, with too good social networks to need any intervention or support from public resources; and they are too many, a sarcastic interpretation of prevailing political opinions (of course, not cited from any official planning document). Health and social care resources are reserved for senior citizens (75+ years) who are ageing badly – and this priority is well-founded in a modern 2020s society. Nevertheless, it makes good sense to create preventive programs to counter the effects of ageing – with a focus on young elderly - to get timely and sustainable results for ageing citizens. The HEPA programs as outlined in Sect. 1.3 could be rather effective as they are developed and implemented individually and independently, and in our case, activated with support technology.

In the following we will summarize a series of studies with the young elderly participants in the *DigitalWells* program to develop answers to research questions RQ1 and RQ2.

2.1   The UTAUT Framework and Constructs

In the studies we note that there are deviations from and variances in recommended HEPA standards when we focus on young elderly, in terms of female/male, age groups, socio-economic background, physical demands from work, and HEPA capacity (cf. [12, 19]). The young elderly cannot be expected to form any coherent HEPA group.

In the *DigitalWells* program, Makkonen et al. [18] first noted that there are rather few published studies of digital wellness technologies among the young elderly, which makes it difficult to compare and cross-validate research results. The study builds on a sample of 115 young elderly who used a PA logger to log, keep track of and get updates on their weekly PA exercises; daily activity data was analyzed with partial least square structural equation modelling (PLS-SEM) using UTAUT2 as the research model (cf. [28]). In UTAUT2 the behavioral intention to adopt and use a particular information technology is formed by seven constructs, of which three were found to be relevant [27]: performance expectancy, hedonic motivation, and habit had positive and statistically significant effects on behavioral intention to adopt and use the PA logger. The results differ from previous studies [9, 16, 29], which typically bring out performance expectancy as primary and hedonic motivation and habit as significant but secondary constructs.

In two further studies with the young elderly participants [18, 19] Makkonen et al. focus on how the adoption and use of the PA logger evolves after an initial acceptance. A longitudinal study captures "lapses" in the intention to use (and the use) for reasons which change and evolve over time. PA data was collected in three subsequent surveys, after four months (T1), after 12 months (T2) and after 18 months (T3) of using the digital PA logger (the final sample was 91 participants). The studies used UTAUT2 (cf. [28]) as the theoretical framework and two constructs, hedonic motivation and habit, had positive and statistically significant effects on the adoption and use of the logger; performance expectancy had a positive and statistically significant effect at T1 and T3, but not at T2; effort expectancy had a positive and statistically significant effect at T2, but not at T1 and T3.

The results are interesting: (i) the construct scores stabilized over time, and (ii) declined quite strongly between T1 and T2, but less so between T2 and T3. A likely explanation is the novelty effect of the PA logger, as the scores for habit also declined strongly between T2 and T3. The effects of performance and effort expectancy appear to switch places: performance expectancy as the main construct at both T1 and T3, and effort expectancy as the main construct at T2. This could explain lapses in the use of the PA logger.

It appears that the UTAUT2 constructs for which we found statistical support – habit, hedonic motivation, performance expectancy and effort expectancy – primarily explain intention to use a PA logger but not necessarily the adoption and use of HEPA programs. It is of course possible to argue that once a PA logger is adopted with an intention to use it, then the user has started PA exercises, which may gradually develop to a HEPA program. This type of cross-context influences is found as UTAUT extensions in several studies [28]; Venkatesh [28] also adds the hypothesis that behavioral intention has a significant positive influence on usage. On the other hand, he finds that computer self-efficacy - the confidence a user has in his/her ability and competence to use a computer (extended to any IT-device in later versions) - will not significantly influence behavioral intentions to use the information technology. In the 2020's computer self-efficacy serves a minor role in the use of information technology; smart mobile phone technology is a dominant platform – also among young elderly.

The studies carried out with the young elderly users show that they adopt and use the offered digital service tools (the PA logger, a modern times DSS) [RQ1].

2.2 Self-efficacy

Self-efficacy offers a conceptual framework for work on sustainable HEPA programs. Bandura [2] shows that self-efficacy beliefs affect the quality of human functioning through cognitive, motivational, affective, and decisional processes. He further finds that self-efficacy beliefs influence outcome expectations, and causal attributions for successes and failures. This fits quite well an intuitive understanding of what it takes to start, continue, and sustain HEPA programs.

Bandura finds that the sources of self-efficacy are developed in four ways [2]: (i) through mastery experiences, (ii) by social modelling, (iii) through social persuasion and (iv) through reliance on physical and emotional states.

Kari et al. [11] studied how effective the digital PA logger is in promoting PA self-efficacy in several groups of young elderly that had been 12 months or more with the DigitalWells program. The study traced changes in self-efficacy, at T1(+4 months), T2(+12 months) and at T3 (+18 months). A participant assesses his/her ability to exercise for 20 min three times per week and reports his/her personal confidence on a [0, 10] scale relative to nine statements on obstacles; an overall self-efficacy TS [0, 90] is the sum of the nine statement measures. A group of 165 participants responded to all three self-efficacy questionnaires and formed the sample. At the construct level, the total score (TS) showed a statistically significant change both at T1 and T2; the mean total score had increased from 56.0 (T1) to 62.0 (T2) and 61.5 (T3). The changes in self-efficacy were positive after 4 months and sustained after 12 months; the main explanation for the changes was found in improved mastery experience.

We also carried out a first screening of how well a selection of the participants reached 675 MET-min/week, which is a simple HEPA standard, at T1, T2, T3 and T4 (+4, +12, +18 and +24 months) (Table 1).

Table 1. PA exercise efforts at T1-T4 ($\geq$ 675 MET-min/week)

	T1	T2	T3	T4
N	238	192	181	147
Percentage	91.9	97.5	97.8	96.7

An interesting finding is that the PA exercise efforts appear to decline at the fourth follow-up (T4). We also tested if the changes in self-efficacy match with the changes in PA exercise.

Bandura suggested that self-efficacy could be raised or lowered by non-performance means (cf. [2]) as control variables: (i) age group ($\leq$69 years, $\geq$70 years); (ii) gender (male; female); (iii) education (4 levels); (iv) used apps ($\leq$3 years; 3–5 years; 6–10 years; $\geq$10 years); (v) BMI (normal; overweight; obese); (vi) residential environment (5 categories). The effects of the background factors were tested (with a multifactor variance analysis) on changes in self-efficacy and actual MET-minutes with difference variables (main effect model: MET1-MET2, MET2-MET3 and SE1-SE2, SE2-SE3). The METi is the total MET-min per week summed at T1, T2 and T3; the SEi is the self-efficacy total score summed at T1, T2 and T3. Bonferroni adjustments for multiple comparisons were used for pairwise comparisons. This appears to work as for MET1-MET2 there were three statistically significant factors: education (p = 0.009), BMI (p = 0.018) and residential environment (p = 0.027); the increase between T1 and T2 is larger among university educated than for those with vocational education; the increase is smaller in the obese group than normal weight and overweight groups; the increase is larger in the big city group than in small or medium-sized city and countryside groups; for MET2-MET3 there were no statistically significant factors.

For SE1-SE2 there were no statistically significant factors; for SE2-SE3 gender is a statistically significant factor – the increase T2-T3 is larger in the male than in the female group. Kari et al. [13] found that the self-efficacy total score had stabilized by T3 for the whole group, i.e., there probably is a decline in the female group. An interesting result is that experience of using applications on smartphones was not statistically significant for changes in neither self-efficacy nor PA exercise; the users' experience with both smartphones and applications are often mentioned as problems for the use of digital PA loggers (cf. [11, 15, 22]).

The present research design did not show the expected relation between positive changes in self-efficacy and PA exercise, which could have offered a more detailed analysis of the joint drivers. Future studies will probably find some joint driver mechanisms.

The increase in self efficacy for PA exercise is expected to be important for sustained PA (e.g., [19, 21, 22]) and for sustained HEPA when that is reached. Sustained improvement supports sustained adoption of PA exercise, which contributes to health benefits; when HEPA levels are reached, a reasonable proposal will be that sustained improvement secures long-term health effects. Self-efficacy will not increase indefinitely, mastering PA tasks and the PA application is typically accomplished in 1–2 moths, after which the novelty wears off (cf. [19, 22]) and no further increase in self-efficacy is expected.

Self-efficacy fits our storyline of drivers to get sustained adoption of HEPA programs among young elderly. The studies we carried out show that the digital PA logger (a modern times DSS) made a sustainable difference for the young elderly participants [RQ2].

2.3 ELM and UTAUT Extensions

The UTAUT2 served as a framework in several of the empirical studies summarised in Sect. 2; the UTAUT2 is a relevant framework [29] for the study of acceptance of digital services like the PA logger, which we call a modern times DSS. We had some doubt that drivers that motivate young elderly users to accept and use the PA logger also make them adopt and use HEPA programs; to test this doubt we added the Elaboration Likelihood Model (ELM) to our conceptual framework.

The ELM was constructed by Petty et al. [21], (i) to work out influence processes and their impact on human perceptions and behaviour, and (ii) to explain why a given influence process may have varying outcomes across different users in a given context. Influence processes can contribute to either intrinsic or extrinsic motivations and help build inherent satisfaction or instrumental outcomes that could motivate HEPA programs. The key part would be how an influence process is built and used to motivate young elderly. It appears that with a larger group we need a series of influence processes (one process never fits all).

The ELM has been used as a theory framework to describe and explain intention to use information technology (IT) (cf. [3, 4]). IT acceptance builds on social influence and the ELM offers instruments for studies of alternative influence processes, their effects, and the impact of (a set of) moderating factors. The logic appears to have some common ground with the UTAUT, and we have sketched out a joint conceptual framework.

The ELM builds on attitude as the key influence process and peripheral cues as moderating factors (cf. [4]). The moderating factors (when working with IT acceptance) include perceived usefulness, source credibility and argument quality, to which job relevance and user experience are added as more peripheral cues. In the framework, argument quality and source credibility decide the perceptions of perceived usefulness, which then is an extrinsic motivation for intention to use IT. The moderating factors – source credibility, job relevance and user experience - are extrinsic motivations for attitude, which is also influenced by the perceived usefulness; following the ELM descriptions, attitude is an intrinsic motivation. The ELM framework offers elements that make sense of intentions to use IT; it has been tested, its functionality verified and validated with users of a variety of IT applications (cf. [4]).

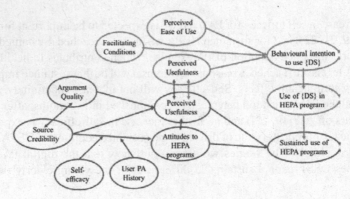

Fig. 2. Sustained HEPA programs - the ELM (blue) + UTAUT (green) frameworks.

We will try out the ELM constructs, with some modifications, to offer a simple way to describe how young elderly could develop intrinsic motivations for sustained use of HEPA programs.

In terms of the ELM (cf. Fig. 2), perceived usefulness and attitudes to HEPA programs are intrinsic motivations for sustained use of the programs; an argument can be raised for interaction - more perceived usefulness strengthens attitudes (and vice versa) – but this should be tested and verified as it refers to another context than IT. Some of the early studies (cf. [5, 7, 11]) showed that performance expectancy, hedonic motivation and habit have a statistically significant effect on behavioural intention to use a digital PA logger. The UTAUT constructs (cf. [28]) have some intuitive kinship with the ELM for HEPA programs: performance expectancy (~ perceived usefulness), hedonic motivation (~ attitudes), habit (~ sustained use). In [12] demographic backgrounds do not decide the effectiveness of the PA logger, but previous PA experience can be more decisive (~ user PA history). In [13] participants fall in three categories – low, moderate, and high-level PA activists (~ user PA history) – which is relevant to consider also for the ELM.

The perceived usefulness of HEPA programs builds on getting better and sustained health effects; "to get more good years" – is a short and to-the-point goal statement heard among young elderly. Argument quality and source credibility build on verifiable medical research results to show that HEPA gives health effects, both in the short- and long term. User PA history and self-efficacy, which we now propose as part of the ELM, decide the attitudes to HEPA programs.

The user PA history typically could identify, (i.1) regular PA users, who have been active for multiple years (even decades), (i.2) sporadic PA users who are active in an on-off mode, and (i.3) inactive PA users with on-off intentions to get active. The three categories (all found among the participants in *DigitalWells*) show different attitudes and different degrees of commitment to the HEPA programs. Self-efficacy brings out reasons to build mastery of HEPA programs, for instance, (ii.1) to lose weight and get in (much) better shape, (ii.2) to stay in sufficiently good shape to be able to carry out daily tasks, (ii.3) to enjoy life and (social) pleasures without HEPA pressures, and (ii.4) to relax in retirement with no HEPA requirements; the mastery could obviously cover both being active with and staying out of HEPA programs.

We propose that the PA logger (a placeholder for and generalised as a set of digital services, {DS}) contributes to a sustained use of HEPA programs; for this we need only three of the UTAUT drivers for behavioural intention (cf. [28]), (ELM will cover the rest of the drivers): (i) perceived usefulness ($\approx$ performance expectancy); (ii) perceived ease of use ($\approx$ effort expectancy) and (iii) facilitating conditions (FC). The FCs are determined by the context and include digital experience, trust, and technology readiness [28].

Figure 2 now shows how ELM and UTAUT combine conceptual frameworks (cf. [17] for similar arguments) to give a meaningful description of how young elderly adopt, use and sustain the use of PA programs, and aim to make progress towards HEPA programs. The {DS} should support the adoption and use of PA programs, should support the progress to HEPA programs and should help users to sustain programs. The {DS} is now a digital PA logger but can be developed to more advanced functionality (cf. coaching, personal trainer advice, knowledge support for advanced PA, etc.).

It is interesting to note that perceived usefulness now appears in both the ELM and the UTAUT frameworks (but they are not the same, they refer to HEPA programs versus digital services). In the ELM framework we work out the usefulness of HEPA programs from attitudes to sustained HEPA, and the self-efficacy and history of individual HEPA/PA for a user. In the UTAUT framework we work out what digital services will be useful and if and how they are easy to use for sustained use of HEPA programs. This approach, to use synergistic combinations of conceptual frameworks was used in [4] and [17], and offers innovative, new models for theory building that is not verifiable with the original conceptual frameworks. Combining ELM and UTAUT offers a better understanding of how digital services could be accepted and adopted among young elderly users.

3 Summary and Conclusions

The paper presents a selection of results from a research program that worked out methods to get young elderly to accept and adopt programs for health-enhancing physical activities (HEPA) and to make the programs sustainable. Regular health-enhancing physical activity programs can serve as preventive health care, which will improve and sustain quality of life and save health-care costs for an ageing population. The research program, called *DigitalWells*, collected more than 1000 young elderly 2019–22 for HEPA activities; of these, 300–350 participants spent more than 24 months in the program; data on more than 294 000 PA events were collected from the participants.

A key part of the research program was the development, adoption, and use of modern DSS support, which in our design is a digital PA logger. We tested the acceptance and intention to use the PA logger (which we called a modern times DSS) in several studies with groups of participants; the UTAUT served as the conceptual framework for the studies, and we could verify that *young elderly adopt and use a DSS* [RQ1]. We then shifted to use self-efficacy as a conceptual framework and carried out several studies with groups of participants to try to verify that the HEPA programs were sustainable; a large part of the participants stayed with the programs and the PA logger for 24 months and more, which shows that *a DSS makes a sustainable difference for young elderly* [RQ2].

Finally, we used the Elaboration Likelihood Model (ELM) as one more conceptual framework to work out the drivers for a sustained use of HEPA programs as they are supported with digital services that are motivated by UTAUT drivers. The combined frameworks offer a basis for enhanced HEPA programs.

Further and future studies will test the proposed framework (cf. Fig. 2) for sustained HEPA programs as they get support from multi-purpose digital services {DS} that are developed to correspond to user requirements for advice, guidance, and support.

An earlier version of the material used in this paper was presented as: "Self-efficacy improves UTAUT to describe adoption of health-enhancing physical activity programs. In: Pucihar, A., et al. (ed.) Proceedings of the 35th Bled eConference, Digital Restructuring and Human (Re)action, 26–29 June 2022, Bled, Slovenia, pp. 587–604 (2022). https://doi.org/10.18690/um.fov.4.2022.

References

1. Ainsworth, B.E., et al.: 2011 compendium of physical activities: a second update of codes and MET values. Med. Sci. Sports Exerc. **43**(8), 1575–1581 (2011). https://doi.org/10.1249/MSS.0b013e31821ece12
2. Bandura, A.: Self-efficacy: toward a unifying theory of behavioral change. Psychol. Rev. **84**(2), 191–215 (1977)
3. Bhattacherjee, A., Sanford, C.: Influence processes for information technology acceptance: an elaboration likelihood model. MIS Q. **30**(4), 805–825 (2006)
4. Brown, S.A., Dennis, A.R., Venkatesh, V.: Predicting collaboration technology use: integrating technology adoption and collaboration research. J. Manag. Inf. Syst. **27**(2), 9–53 (2010)

5. Carlsson, C., Walden, P.: Digital wellness services: key to better quality of life for young elderly. In: Pucihar, A., et al. (eds.) Proceedings of the 31st Bled eConference (Bled 2018), pp. 248–261 (2018)

6. Carlsson, C.: Decision analytics – key to digitalization. Inf. Sci. **460–461**(12), 424–438 (2018)

7. Carlsson, C., Kari, T., Makkonen, M., Frank, L., Walden, P.: Sustained adoption of systematic physical activity programs for young elderly – a developed UTAUT approach. In: Pucihar, A., et al. (eds.) Proceedings of the 33rd Bled eConference (2020)

8. Carlsson, C., Walden, P.: Decision support systems: historical innovations and modern technology challenges. In: Papathanasiou, J., Zaraté, P., Freire de Sousa, J. (eds.) EURO Working Group on DSS. ISIS, pp. 1–14. Springer, Cham (2021). https://doi.org/10.1007/978-3-030-70377-6_1

9. Davis, F.D.: Perceived usefulness, perceived ease of use and user acceptance of information technology. MIS Q. **13**(3), 319–339 (1989)

10. Delen, D., Ram, S.: Research challenges and opportunities in business analytics. J. Bus. Anal. **1**(1), 2–12 (2018)

11. Kari, T., Makkonen, M., Frank, L., Carlsson, J., Sell, A.: The effects of using a mobile wellness application on physical activity levels: a four-month follow-up study among aged people. In: Pucihar, A., et al. (eds.) Proceedings of the 33rd Bled eConference (2020)

12. Kari, T., et al.: Implementing a digital wellness application into use – challenges and solutions among aged people. In: Proceedings of the ITAP 2020, 6th International Conference on Human Aspects of IT for the Aged Population. 19–24 July 2020. Copenhagen, Denmark (2020)

13. Kari, T., Makkonen, M., Carlsson, J., Frank, L.: Using a physical activity application to promote physical activity levels among aged people: a follow-up study. In: Proceedings of the HICSS-54 Conference, pp. 1242–1251 (2020)

14. Keen, P.G.W.: Decision support systems: the next decade. Decis. Support Syst. **3**(3), 253–265 (1981)

15. Kettunen, E., Kari, T., Makkonen, M., Frank, L., Critchley, W.: Young elderly and digital coaching: a quantitative intervention study on exercise self-efficacy. In: Pucihar, A., et al. (eds.) Proceedings of the 33rd Bled eConference (2020)

16. Kettunen, E., Critchley, W., Kari, T.: Can digital coaching boost your performance? A qualitative study among physically active people. In: Proceedings of the 52nd Hawaii International Conference on System Sciences (HICSS). Grand Wailea, Maui. University of Hawai'i at Manoa, pp. 1331–1340 (2019)

17. Lallmahomed, M.Z.I., Ab Rahim, N.Z., Ibrahim, R., Rahman, A.A.: Predicting different conceptualizations of system use: acceptance in hedonic volitional context (Facebook). Comput. Hum. Behav. **29**(6), 2776–2787 (2013)

18. Makkonen, M., Kari, T., Frank, L.: Applying UTAUT2 to explain the use of physical activity logger applications among young elderly. In: Pucihar, A., et al. (eds.) Proceedings of the 33rd Bled eConference (2020)

19. Makkonen, M., Kari, T., Frank, L.: Changes in the use intention of digital wellness technologies and its antecedents over time: the use of physical activity logger applications among young elderly in Finland. In: Proceedings of the HICSS-54 Conference, pp. 1262–1271 (2020)

20. Papathanasiou, J., Zaraté, P., Freire de Sousa, J. (eds.): ISIS, Springer, Cham (2021). https://doi.org/10.1007/978-3-030-70377-6

21. Petty, R.E., Cacioppo, J.T.: Communication and persuasion: central and peripheral routes to attitude change. Springer, New York (1986). https://doi.org/10.1007/978-1-4612-4964-1

22. Reyes-Mercado, P.: Adoption of fitness wearables: insights from partial least squares and qualitative comparative analysis. J. Syst. Inf. Technol. **20**(1), 103–127 (2018)

23. Romanov, A., Stroeva, J., Filippov, A., Yarushkina, N.: An approach to building decision support systems based on an ontology service. Mathematics **9**(2946), 1–23 (2021)

24. Sprague, R.H.: Framework for the development of decision support systems. MIS Q. **4**(4), 1–26 (1980)
25. Stiggelbout, M., Hopman-Rock, M., Tak, E., Lechner, L., van Mechelen. W.: Droput from exercise programs for seniors: a prospective cohort study. J. Aging Phys. Act. **13**, 409–421 (2005)
26. THL – Finnish Institute for Health and Welfare (2019). National FinHealth Study
27. Venkatesh, V., Thong, J.Y.L., Xu, X.: Consumer acceptance and use of information technology: extending the unified theory of acceptance and use of technology. MIS Q. **36**(1), 157–178 (2012)
28. Venkatesh, V., Thong, J.Y.L., Xu, X.: Unified theory of acceptance and use of technology: a synthesis and the road ahead. JAIS **17**(5), 328–376 (2016)
29. Yuan, S., Ma, W., Kanthawala, S., Peng, W.: Keep using my health apps: discover users' perception of health and fitness apps with the UTAUT2 model. Telemed. e-Health **21**(9), 735–741 (2015)

Behavioral Studies for the Use of Visualization in Holistic Evaluation for Multicriteria Decision Problems Decision

Evanielle Barbosa Ferreira[✉], Tarsila Rani Soares de Vasconcelos,
Lucia Reis Peixoto Roselli[iD], and Adiel Teixeira de Almeida[iD]

Center for Decision Systems and Information Development (CDSID), Universidade Federal de Pernambuco, Recife, PE, Brazil

{evanielle.ferreira,tarsila.vasconcelos}@ufpe.br, {lrpr, almeida}@cdsid.org.br

Abstract. Several behavioral studies have been performed related to MCDM/A (Multi-Criteria Decision Making/Aiding) methods, although not many of them aim directly to modulate (transform) those methods. Some of the studies intended to modulate methods provide suggestions to improve the FITradeoff decision process and the design of its Decision Support System (DSS). In this context, this paper presents behavioral study which has been constructed during the Covid-19 Pandemic and has been applied until now. These studies are concerned with the use of visualization in holistic evaluation for multicriteria decision problems decision using online survey to compare bar graphics and tables during the holistic evaluation Although these studies are contextualized for the FITradeoff Method, their results can be applied to any other methods in the context of MAVT (Multi-Attribute Value Theory), with additive aggregation. This study tested how DMs use bar graphics and tables to perform the holistic evaluation of alternatives. The experiment considers two types of visualizations: bar graphics and tables. Also, it uses two decision processes: the selection of the best alternative and the elimination of the worst alternative. In the past, DMs can only select the best alternative during the decision process in the FITradeoff DSS. However now, the elimination process is also included in the DSS, providing flexibility for Decision-Makers. As result, the experiment suggests that for some types of visualizations, the DMs performed better on the elimination process than the selection process. Moreover, results also showed that most of DMs prefer to select the best alternative than to eliminate the worst, even performing better in the elimination process. Hence, this result reinforces the flexibility provided in the DSS, but recommend another experiment using neuroscience tools, permitting to compare cognitive efforts during both decision process.

Keywords: FITradeoff method · Elicitation process · Holistic evaluation · Multi-Criteria Decision Making/Aiding (MCDM/A) · Online survey

S. Liu et al. (Eds.): ICDSST 2023, LNBIP 474, pp. 265–276, 2023.
https://doi.org/10.1007/978-3-031-32534-2_19

1   Introduction

Decision Support Systems (DSSs) are designed to assist several Multi-Criteria Decision-Making/Aiding (MCDM/A) problems which intend to achieve different objectives of multiple Decision-Makers (DMs). A famous example of MCDM/A problem is the supplier selection problem in which conflicting objectives such as cost, and quality are presented [1–4].

In order to support Decision-Makers (DMs) to conduct a rational decision process several methods have been presented in literature [5–8]. These methods pretend to collect DMs preferences and insert them into mathematical models to obtain solutions which are in accordance with DMs preferences.

For instance, FITradeoff method [9, 10] is an MCDM/A method in the context of Multi-Attribute Value Theory (MAVT) [8]. This method can be used to support choice problems [9], ranking problems [11], sorting problems [12] and portfolio problems [13, 14]. Several applications have been done using the FITradeoff method [15–20].

In general, Multi-Criteria Decision-Making methods are implemented in Decision Support Systems. These DSSs intend to interact with DMs and capture the preferences during the decision process. However, even trying to conduct a rational decision-process, DSSs cannot capture behavioral aspects with are presented into the process, such as emotions [21, 22]. Thus, solutions obtained may not represent the real preferences expressed during the process.

In this context, in order to investigate behavioral aspects presented during the FITradeoff decision process, several studies have been performed supported with neuroscience tools [23–29]. These studies investigated the two perspectives of preference modelling: holistic evaluation [23–26] and elicitation by decomposition [27–29].

Hence, using neuroscience tools, aspects with are not controlled by DMs can be captured. Moreover, based on it, transformations (modulations) can be done in the FITradeoff decision process [30]. The studies aimed to modulate (transform) the FITradeoff method in two aspects: improve the decision process and improve the design of the FITradeoff DSS [31]. In addition, the studies bring advances to MCDM field, filled the gap of using neuroscience tools to investigate and modulate MCDM/A methods. [32].

In this context, this paper discusses a behavioral experiment performed using an online survey. The experiment aims to investigate the holistic evaluation process using graphical and tabular visualizations. The paper as divided as follows. Section 2 presents the FITradeoff method. Section 3 describes the Survey. Section 4 discuss the results and Sect. 5 presents the conclusions and remarks future studies.

2   FITradeoff Method

Flexible and Interactive Tradeoff (FITradeoff) method [9, 10] is based on the MAVT, presenting the same axiomatic structure as the Tradeoff procedure [5]. On the other hand, the FITradeoff uses concepts of partial information, considering only strict preferences between consequences. In other words, the FITradeoff method does not requires that Decision-Makers (DMs) express indifference relations between each pair of consequences.

The method also combines two paradigms of preference modelling – elicitation by decomposition, which has been based on the Tradeoff procedure, and holistic evaluation. The elicitation by decomposition considers the space of consequences, thus DMs express preferences over pairs of consequences. On the other hand, the holistic evaluation considers the space of alternatives, hence DMs express dominance relations between alternatives [10].

In the previous version of the FITradeoff method, DMs only express preferences during the decomposition process. The holistic evaluation was available only for choice problematic, being available when DMs wish to finalize the decision process by selecting the best alternative in the group of Potentially Optimal Alternatives (POA) [9].

Based on behavioral studies, several modulations (transformations – [30]) have been done in the FITradeoff method. One of the most important transformations is combining these two paradigms of preference modelling. Thus, the Linear Programming Problem (LPP) presented in the FITradeoff method has been updated to consider inequalities which represent preferences expressed in both paradigms of preference modelling.

Now, during the FITradeoff decision process, the DM can use both perspectives, altering between them in the middle of the process. DMs can express preferences using those that judge most appropriate with their cognitive style [10].

The FITradeoff method has been implemented in a Decision Support System (DSS), which is available on web at www.fitradeoff.org. An important transformation on the FITradeoff DSS is the inclusion of graphical and tabular visualizations to support DMs during holistic evaluations. Four visualizations have been included in the DSS for choice and ranking problematics [9, 11]. These visualizations are bar graphic, spider graphic, bubble graphic and tables. These visualizations have been tested in several behavioral experiments in order to improve the FITradeoff DSS [23–26]. Thus, the studies aimed to investigate how DMs used graphical and tabular visualizations to perform the holistic evaluation of alternatives.

This study presents a behavioral study which started during the Covid-19 Pandemic and continues until now. This study tested how DMs use bar graphics and tables to perform the holistic evaluation of alternatives. Moreover, it considers two decision processes: selection of the best alternative and elimination of the worst alternative. In the previous version of the method only selection process was considered [9].

3 Behavioral Experiment (Online Survey)

Given the Covid-19 Pandemic, behavioral experiments were suspended. In this context, an online survey has been developed in order to continue the studies which aimed to about the FITradeoff method.

This survey has been constructed to investigate the use of bar graphics and tables to perform the holistic evaluation. As discussed, the holistic evaluation is one of the perspectives for preference modelling presented in the FITradeoff method [10].

The survey considered two multi-criteria decision making (MCDM) problems. These problems do not have a specific context since was intended to generalize the results. The problems have three alternatives which were evaluated against five criteria. One of those has similar values for the criteria weights, and the other has different values for criteria weights. For the problem with different weights, the arithmetic progression was used to compute the weights.

Therefore, based on these two problems, eight visualizations have been generated. Four of them represent the problem with similar weights, being two bar graphics and two tables. In addition, these four visualizations have been divided in two groups: DMs should select the best alternative in two. For the others, DMs should eliminate the worst alternative. The same logic has been used with the visualizations constructed to represent the problem with different values for the criteria weights.

Figure 1 presents a flowchart to illustrate the survey. Also, Fig. 2 illustrates two bar graphics considered in the survey. It is worth noting that acronyms have been considered to represent each one of the visualizations. For instance, Sel 3A5C BS represents that DMs should perform the selection process in a bar graphic (B) with three alternatives (3A) evaluated in five criteria (5C) with similar values for the weight (S). Crit 1 had the highest weight value and Crit 5 had the lowest weight value.

In addition, these visualizations are exhibited in different screens of the survey, thus DMs cannot return to evaluated previous visualizations (i.e., which has been already evaluated). In other words, when one alternative was selected or eliminated, DMs cannot return to change the answered provided. Moreover, the sequence in which the visualizations were showed was defined previously. A random sequence was considered to avoid biases [24].

The survey has been applied to graduate and postgraduate students of Management Engineering in Federal University of Pernambuco (UFPE). The same conditions are regarded to the entire sample of students. In other words, the same visualizations and order of them have been considered. The survey had to be finished in fifteen minutes.

The survey was performed as an extra-activity of Multi-Criteria Decision-Making course. The students received the same instructions to perform the survey. The only task required has been to evaluate each one of the visualizations and select the best alternative or eliminate the worst alternative. To perform this task the students should follow the MAVT concepts to compute the alternatives global value V(A), as illustrated in Eq. (1). In (1), i represents each alternative, j each criterion, $v_j(a_{ij})$ the performance of alternative i in the criterion j, and kj the weight of criterion j.

$$V(A_i) = \sum_{j=1}^{m} k_j v_j(a_{ij}) \qquad (1)$$

4 Results

The survey has been applied to 117 students (75 men and 42 women). These students belong to different classes of Management Engineering course in Federal University of Pernambuco (UFPE). For instance, one of those groups represents the students who are in graduation, other represents students who are in post-graduation. The students in the same group present similar age and level of knowledge about Multi-Criteria Decision-Making field. All students received similar instructions to perform the experiment and done the experiment with the same conditions.

Hence, the first analysis compares the average of Hit Rate (HR). The HR has been computed comparing the answer provided for each student with the correct answer

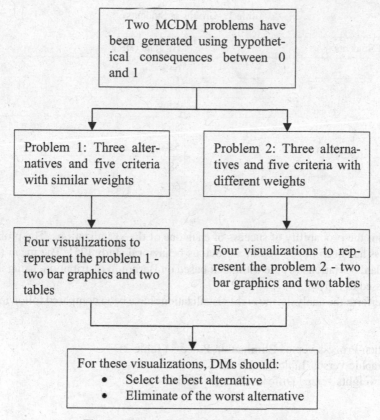

Fig. 1. Flowchart to describe the experiment

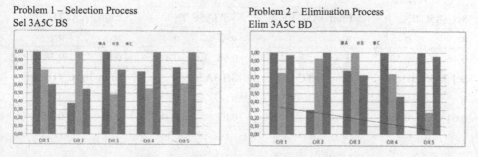

Fig. 2. Visualizations used in the experiment

computed previously by the authors, for each visualization. The HR values are between 0% and 100%, and represent the percentage of participants who correctly selected the best alternative. This metric has been discussed in a previous study [24].

Based on Table 1 it is possible to observe that the groups do not vary considerably. Hence, other analysis have been done considering all the students. An important result

Table 1. Groups of Students

Group of Students	Hit Rate (HR)
Group 1	64%
Group 2	57%
Group 3	57%
Group 4	56%
Group 5	55%
Group 6	58%
Group 7	66%

obtained is the probability of success of each one of the visualizations. The probability of success has been developed in a previous behavioral study [25]. The mean (π) and the standard deviations (σ) are estimated based on Bernoulli distribution, using the HR, as discussed in [25].

To perform the analysis, the eight visualizations have been compared following three aspects:

- Selection Process versus Elimination Process (Table 2).
- Bar graphic versus Tables (Table 3).
- Same weights versus Different Weights (Table 4).

Table 2. Selection Process versus Elimination Process

Sel 3A5C BS		Elim 3A5C BS		Sel 3A5C TS		Elim 3A5C TS	
π	σ	π	σ	π	σ	π	σ
0.46	0.50	0.70	0.46	0.64	0.48	0.82	0.38
Sel 3A5C BD		Elim 3A5C BD		Sel 3A5C TD		Elim 3A5C TD	
π	σ	π	σ	π	σ	π	σ
0.64	0.48	0.40	0.49	0.62	0.48	0.41	0.49

Based on Table 2 it is possible to observe that for visualizations with similar values for weights, the students (DMs) performed better when they had to eliminate the worst alternative. On the other hand, when different weights are considered, the DMs performed better in selecting the best alternative.

Table 3 compares bar graphics versus tables. Thus, for visualizations with similar values for weights, the students performed better using tables than using bar graphics. In addition, for different weights, both visualizations presented similar probability of success.

Table 3. Bar graphic versus Tables

Sel 3A5C BS		Sel 3A5C TS		Elim 3A5C BS		Elim 3A5C BS	
π	σ	π	π	π	σ	π	σ
0.46	0.50	0.64	0.48	0.70	0.46	0.82	0.38
Sel 3A5C BD		Sel 3A5C TD		Sel 3A5C TD			
π	π	π	σ	π	σ	π	σ
0.64	0.62	0.62	0.48	0.40	0.49	0.41	0.49

Table 4. Same weights versus Different Weights

Sel 3A5C BS		Sel 3A5C BD		Sel 3A5C TS		Sel 3A5C TD	
π	π	π	σ	π	σ	π	σ
0.46	0.64	0.64	0.48	0.64	0.48	0.62	0.48
Elim 3A5C BS		Elim 3A5C BD		Elim 3A5C TS		Elim 3A5C TD	
π	σ	π	σ	π	σ	π	σ
0.70	0.46	0.40	0.49	0.82	0.38	0.41	0.49

Table 4 compares visualizations with similar values for the weights versus those with different values for the weights. In general, the students performed better for visualizations with similar values for the weights.

In addition, preferential answered provided by the participants at the final of the survey have been evaluated. For instance, the students answered some questions:

- Which decision process did you prefer to perform?

  a) Select the best alternative.
     or
  b) Eliminate the worst alternative.

- Which visualization did you prefer to evaluate?

  a) Bar graphic
     or
  b) Table

- Which visualization did you should as be easier to evaluate?

  a) With similar values to the weights.
     or
  b) With different values to the weights

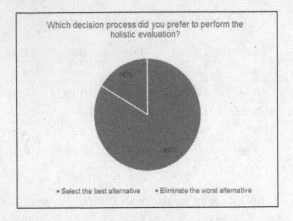

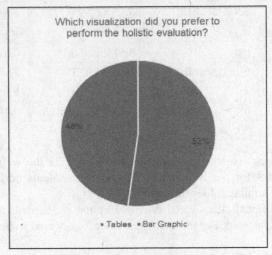

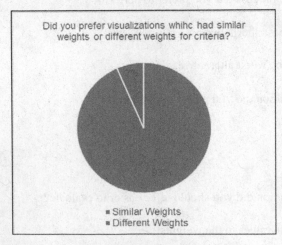

Fig. 3. Preferential survey

Figure 3 illustrates the answers provided by the students.

For instance, most of the students prefer to select the best alternative. However, when it is compared with the probability of success, it is possible to observe that they presented better performance in the elimination process.

Concerning to similar weights, the students truly presented better performance in problems with similar weights for the criteria. For the comparison of bar graphics and tables, similar probabilities of success and preferential percentage are observed.

Hence, the main difference regards the two-decision process. The selection process is more usual for DMs, which maybe suggested that most of them prefer to select the best alternative than eliminate the worst alternative. However, probabilities of success do not follow the same line.

The probability of success is an important result obtained in these studies since it can be by analysts and DMs during the holistic evaluation. For instance, if the visualization presents a lower probability of success, the analysts can advise the DM to not use this kind of visualization to express a dominance relation between alternatives in the holistic evaluation and proceed to the elicitation by decomposition in order to continue the decision process [25].

For future studies, experiments can be performed using neuroscience tools to collect physiological variables in order to compare cognitive effort in these two decision processes. In addition, the groups can be treated separately in order to compare it performance with specific characteristics of the groups.

5 Conclusion

The paper presents a behavioral experiment performed to investigate the holistic evaluation in the FITradeoff method. Several behavioral studies have been performed to modulate (transform) the FITradeoff method [23–30]. Some of the studies intended to improve the FITradeoff decision process and the design of the FITradeoff Decision Support System (DSS).

The behavioral study discussed in this paper used an online survey to investigate how DMs use visualizations to perform the holistic evaluation of alternatives. The experiment considers bar graphics and tables. Also, it uses two decision processes: the selection of the best alternative and the elimination of the worst alternative.

An important aspect of this study is the evaluation of two decision processes: selection of the best alternative and the elimination of the worst alternative. In the previous version of the FITradeoff method DMs can only select the best alternative during the decision process [9].

Now, the opportunity to eliminate the worst alternative has been included in the DSS in order to provide flexibility. Hence, DMs can use the decision process which judges most adequate to perform the holistic evaluation.

This flexibility is also reinforced by this study which suggested that for some visualizations, DMs presented a better performance in the elimination process. This process is not so usual for them but can be explored by the analyst. Also, the analyst can use the probability of success to advise DMs during the holistic evaluation, not only to use or not use some visualization to express a dominance relation, but also to conduct the process selecting the best alternative or eliminating the worst alternatives.

It is worth to mention that although these studies are contextualized for the FITradeoff Method, their results can be applied to other methods in the context of MAVT [5].

Acknowledgment. This work had partial support from the Brazilian Research Council (CNPq) [grant 308531/2015–9;312695/2020–9] and the Foundation of Support in Science and Technology of the State of Pernambuco (FACEPE) [APQ-0484–3.08/17].

References

1. Santos, I.M., Roselli, L.R.P, da Silva, A.L.G, Alencar, L.H.: A supplier selection model for a wholesaler and retailer company based on FITradeoff multicriteria method. Math. Probl. Eng. **2020**, 1–14 (2020)
2. Frej, E.A., Roselli, L.R.P., Araújo de Almeida, J., de Almeida, A.T.: A multicriteria decision model for supplier selection in a food industry based on FITradeoff method. Math. Probl. Eng. **2017**, 1–9 (2017)
3. Chai, J., Liu, J., Ngai, E.: Application of decision-making techniques in supplier selection: a systematic review of literature. Expert Syst. Appl. **40**(10), 3872–3885 (2013)
4. Barla, S.B.: A case study of supplier selection for lean supply by using a mathematical model. Logist. Inf. Manage. **16**, 451–459 (2003)
5. Keeney, R.L, Raiffa, H.: Decisions with Multiple Objectives: Preferences, and Value Tradeoffs. Wiley, New York (1976)
6. Belton, V., Stewart, T.: Multiple Criteria Decision Analysis. Kluwer Academic Publishers, Dordrecht (2002)
7. Figueira, J., Greco, S., Ehrgott, M. (eds.): Springer, Berlin (2005)
8. de Almeida, A.T., Cavalcante, C., Alencar, M., Ferreira, R., de Almeida-Filho, A.T., Garcez. T.: Multicriteria and Multi-Objective Models for Risk, Reliability and Maintenance Decision Analysis. International Series in Operations Research & Management Science, vol. 231. New York: Springer (2015). https://doi.org/10.1007/978-3-319-17969-8
9. de Almeida, A.T., Almeida, J.A., Costa, A.P.C.S., Almeida-Filho, A.T.: A new method for elicitation of criteria weights in additive models: flexible and interactive tradeoff. Eur. J. Oper. Res. **250**(1), 179–191 (2016)
10. de Almeida, A.T., Frej, E.A., Roselli, L.R.P.: Combining holistic and decomposition paradigms in preference modeling with the flexibility of FITradeoff. CEJOR **29**(1), 7–47 (2021). https://doi.org/10.1007/s10100-020-00728-z
11. Frej, E.A., de Almeida, A.T., Costa, A.P.C.S.: Using data visualization for ranking alternatives with partial information and interactive tradeoff elicitation. Oper. Res. Int. J. **19**(4), 909–931 (2019). https://doi.org/10.1007/s12351-018-00444-2
12. Kang, T.H.A., Frej, E.A., de Almeida, A.T.: Flexible and interactive tradeoff elicitation for multicriteria sorting problems. Asia Pac. J. Oper. Res. **37**, 2050020 (2020)
13. Frej, E.A., Ekel, P., de Almeida, A.T.: A benefit-to-cost ratio based approach for portfolio selection under multiple criteria with incomplete preference information. Inf. Sci. **545**, 487–498 (2021)
14. Marques, A.C., Frej, E.A., de Almeida, A.T.: Multicriteria decision support for project portfolio selection with the FITradeoff method. Omega-Int. J. Manage. Sci. **111**, 102661 (2022)

15. Kang, T.H.A., Júnior, A.M.D.C.S., de Almeida, A.T.: Evaluating electric power generation technologies: a multicriteria analysis based on the FITradeoff method. Energy **165**, 10–20 (2018)
16. Alvarez Carrillo, P.A., Roselli, L.R.P., Frej, E.A., de Almeida, A.T.: Selecting an agricultural technology package based on the flexible and interactive tradeoff method. Ann. Oper. Res. **314**, 1–16. (2018). https://doi.org/10.1007/s10479-018-3020-y
17. Monte, M.B.S., Morais, D.C.: A decision model for identifying and solving problems in an urban water supply system. Water Resour. Manage. 33(14), 4835–4848 (2019)
18. Fossile, D.K., Frej, E.A., da Costa, S.E.G., de Lima, E.P., de Almeida, A.T.: Selecting the most viable renewable energy source for Brazilian ports using the FITradeoff method. J. Cleaner Prod. **260**, 121107 (2020)
19. Dell'Ovo, M., Oppio, A., Capolongo, S.: Decision Support System for the Location of Healthcare Facilities SitHealth Evaluation Tool. PoliMI SpringerBriefs. Springer, Switzerland (2020). https://doi.org/10.1007/978-3-030-50173-0
20. Pergher, I., Frej, E.A., Roselli, L.R.P., de Almeida, A.T.: Integrating simulation and FITradeoff method for scheduling rules selection in job-shop production systems. Int. J. Prod. Econ. **227**, 107669 (2020)
21. Eagleman, D.: The Brain: A story of you. Pantheon Books, New York (2015)
22. de Almeida, A., Rosselli, L., Costa Morais, D., Costa, A.: Neuroscience tools for behavioural studies in group decision and negotiation. In: Kilgour, D.M., Eden, C. (eds.) Handbook of Group Decision and Negotiation, 1st edn., pp. 1–24. Springer, Dordrecht, Netherlands (2020)
23. Roselli, L.R.P., de Almeida, A.T.: Use of the alpha-theta diagram as a decision neuroscience tool for analyzing holistic evaluation in decision making. Ann. Oper. Res. (2022). https://doi.org/10.1007/s10479-021-04495-1
24. Roselli, L.R.P., de Almeida, A.T., Frej, E.A.: Decision neuroscience for improving data visualization of decision support in the FITradeoff method. Oper. Res. Int. Journal **19**(4), 933–953 (2019). https://doi.org/10.1007/s12351-018-00445-1
25. Roselli, L.R.P., de Almeida, A.T.: The use of the success-based decision rule to support the holistic evaluation process in FITradeoff. Int. Trans. Oper. Res. **2021**, 1299–1319 (2023)
26. Roselli, L.R.P., Pereira, L., da Silva, A., de Almeida, A.T., Morais, D.C., Costa, A.P.C.S.: Neuroscience experiment applied to investigate decision-maker behavior in the tradeoff elicitation procedure. Ann. Oper. Res. **289**(1), 67–84 (2019). https://doi.org/10.1007/s10479-019-03394-w
27. Carneiro de Lima da Silva, A.L., Cabral Seixas Costa, A.P., de Almeida, A.T.:Analysis of the cognitive aspects of the preference elicitation process in the compensatory context: a neuroscience experiment with FITradeoff. Int. Trans. Oper. Res. **31** (2022)
28. da Silva, A.L.C.D.L., Costa, A.P.C.S., de Almeida, A.T.: Exploring cognitive aspects of FITradeoff method using neuroscience tools. Ann. Oper. Res. 312, 1–23 (2021).https://doi.org/10.1007/s10479-020-03894-0
29. Carneiro de Lima da Silva, A.L., Cabral Seixas Costa, A.P.: FITradeoff decision support system: an exploratory study with neuroscience tools. In: Davis, F., Riedl, R., vom Brocke, J., Léger, P.M., Randolph, A., Fischer, T. (eds.) Information Systems and Neuroscience. Lecture Notes in Information Systems and Organisation, vol. 32, pp. 365–372 Springer, Cham (2020). https://doi.org/10.1007/978-3-030-28144-1_40
30. Roselli, L.R.P., de Almeida, A.T.: Neuroscience behavioral studies for modula-tion of the FITradeoff method. In: Morais, D.C., Fang, L. (eds) Group Decision and Negotiation: Method-ological and Practical Issues. GDN 2022. Lecture Notes in Busi-ness Information Processing, vol. 454. Springer, Cham (2022). https://doi.org/10.1007/978-3-031-07996-2_4
31. Korhonen, P., Wallenius, J.: Behavioral Issues in MCDM: Neglected research questions. In: Clímaco, J. (eds) Multicriteria Analysis. Springer, Heidelberg (1997). https://doi.org/10.1007/978-3-642-60667-0_39

32. Wallenius, H., Wallenius, J.: Implications of world mega trends for MCDM research. In: Ben amor, s., De Almeida, A., De Miranda, J, Aktas, E. (Eds.). Advanced Studies in Multi-Criteria Decision Making, pp. 1–10 New York: Chapman and Hall/CRC, Series in Operations Research, 1st Ed (2020)

A Digital Distance Learning Critical Success Factors Model for Conducting Learning Analytics Research

Sean Eom(✉) (iD)

Southeast Missouri State University, Cape Girardeau, MO 63701, USA
sbeom@semo.edu

Abstract. A recent EDUCAUSE horizon report describes that learning analytics is one of the leading technologies and practices that will impact the future of teaching and learning. The growing presence of online delivery modes has accelerated the advancement of learning analytics (LA) and the use of data in education. Despite huge volumes of LA research publications, a systematic literature review reveals that LA research faces several challenges, including a lack of good pedagogical models that will further advance theoretical development in understanding relationships between the effectiveness and learning outcomes and the complexity of learning processes.

Recently, Guzmán-Valenzuela et al. claimed that LA tends to underplay the complexity of Learning processes. Their bibliometric analysis of recent literature identified several critical concerns of LA research, including oversimplification of the learning process and lack of good pedagogical models to illuminate students' learning processes and outcomes. This paper aims to tackle these critical concerns. The complexities of teaching and learning processes are due to multiple interdependent factors that affect learning outcomes directly and indirectly. This paper aims to provide an integrated, foundational pedagogical model that is complete and parsimonious for further advancing e-learning analytics research.

Keywords: Learning Analytics · Learning Outcomes · Learning Processes · Systems View · Distance Learning · Critical Success Model

1 Introduction

A recent EDUCAUSE horizon report states that learning analytics (LA) is one of the leading technologies and practices that will impact the future of teaching and learning [1]. Further, recent COVID-19 phenomena worldwide have changed how educational institutions deliver education, including HyFlex, a new delivery model in which the instructor teaches students simultaneously in a physical classroom and synchronously online through videoconferencing software [2]. The growing presence of new delivery modes has accelerated the advancement of LA and the use of data in education [3]. Consequently, LA has become a growing field and a significant trend in the current

S. Liu et al. (Eds.): ICDSST 2023, LNBIP 474, pp. 277–286, 2023.
https://doi.org/10.1007/978-3-031-32534-2_20

educational environment. LA has become the critical decision tool for enhancing data-driven education learning outcomes [4].

Using Proquest databases, approximately 95% of learning analytics research publications (12592 papers) were published over the recent 13 years (2010–2022). Higher education institutions worldwide produce massive amounts of data through online and offline learning. Despite huge volumes of LA research publications, a systematic literature review concluded that there is still a shortage of research addressing the effectiveness and consequences of learning processes and outcomes [5]. Recently, Guzmán-Valenzuela et al. [6] claimed that LA tends to underplay the complexity of Learning processes and their bibliometric, and a content analysis of recent literature identified several critical concerns, including the following [6, p.13]:

* LA oversimplifies the learning process by making it equivalent to observable behaviours (for example, the number of times students download documents or access the LMS).

* LA is focused on collecting and analysing large sets of data in the light of educational and pedagogical theories. The LA literature rarely identifies instances where educational or pedagogical paradigms are drawn upon in illuminating students' learning processes.

The purpose of this paper is to take on these two challenges.

Challenge 1. How can LA tackle improving learning outcomes in digital distance learning?

Challenge 2. How can LA tackle improving the learning process in digital distance learning?

The paper is organized into the following sections. The first section provides basic definitions and a snapshot of the dynamic trend of business intelligence (BI) and LA research publications from January 2015 through November 2022. The second section introduces the fundamental concept of LA research in digital distance learning systems. The third section is devoted to a brief introduction of the critical success model of digital distance learning systems based on the results of past decades of continuing empirical e-learning research. The following section describes how LA research contributes to digital distance learning processes and outcomes. The complexities of teaching and learning processes are due to multiple interdependent factors that affect learning outcomes directly and indirectly. To understand the CSF model, it is necessary to introduce a systems view of the distance learning success model.

2 Basic Definition of LA the Relationship Between DA and LA

Over the past decades, we have witnessed the emergence of new terms such as decision support systems (DSS), business intelligence (BI), data analytics (DA), business analytics (BA), and learning analytics (LA). All these terms are to deal with the same problems in different organizations. Different organizations may need additional tools and techniques to manage the same issues.

LA is a subset of DA to deal with problems in learning systems. DA has been applied in many domains, such as business, education, city management, military, healthcare, energy, and many other miscellaneous areas [7]. Along with DA, academic analytics

(AA) is another frequently used similar term in education (see Table 1). DA has been widely applied to business, education, healthcare, government, the energy industry, and the military. The 1st International Conference on Learning Analytics and Knowledge defined LA in this way. "learning analytics is the measurement, collection, analysis, and reporting of data about learners and their contexts, for purposes of understanding and optimizing learning and the environments in which it occurs." LA focuses on course and department-level analysis of critical success factors affecting learning outcomes and student satisfaction. Learning analytics focuses on the learning process, such as the interaction among students and the interaction between students and the instructor. On the hand, academic analytics' focus moves one or higher organizational levels to institutional, state, national, and international.

Table 1. Academic analytics and Learning analytics Source: [8, p.34]

TYPE OF ANALYTICS	LEVEL OR OBJECT OF ANALYSIS	WHO BENEFITS?
Learning Analytics	**Course-level:** social networks, conceptual development, discourse analysis, "intelligent curriculum"	Learners, faculty
	Departmental: predictive modeling, patterns of success/failure	Learners, faculty
Academic Analytics	**Institutional:** learner profiles, performance of academics, knowledge flow	Administrators, funders, marketing
	Regional (state/provincial): comparisons between systems	Funders, administrators
	National and International	National governments, education authorities

3 Theoretical Foundation

3.1 System's View of Digital Distance Learning Success Model

The systems view of the e-learning success model helps us view e-learning systems as a dynamic set of interdependent sub-entities interacting together, and e-learning systems are not explainable from characteristics of isolated sub-entities. The components of a systemic model consist of inputs, processes, and outputs (Fig. 1). The inputs of the distance learning systems consist of the human and design dimensions. The human dimension is concerned with two human entities (students and instructors) and their various attributes, and the design dimension includes learning management systems (LMS) and communication and information technology (CIT). The process is the bridge that connects input and output. There are two outputs: learning outcomes and student satisfaction. Learning outcomes are the results of three inputs working together. The primary actor in the learning process is students who interact with the instructor (student-student dialogue), with other students (student-student dialogue), and with learning systems (student-system dialogue). The other crucial element of the e-learning success model is self-regulated learning (SRL). Students are using self-regulated Learning (SRL) to achieve learning outcomes. The SRL process includes motivational, metacognitive, and behavioral processes. Due to space limitations, readers are referred to Eom and Ashill [9, 10] for details of the process variables and the interactions among input, process, and output.

Two characteristics distinguish this system's view (Fig. 1): The significant reduction of constructs and the use of moderating process variables to incorporate the interdependent (not independent) process nature of e-learning success. The proliferation of dependent and independent variables measures has been one of the bottlenecks of empirical e-learning research that prevents us from building good theories. For example, studies such as [11] show more than 100 criterion and predictor variables and measures used in empirical e-learning research.

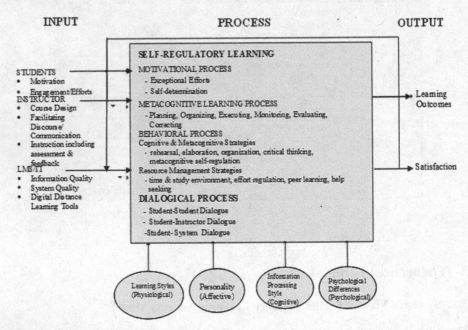

Fig. 1. A Systems View of the E-learning Success Model (Adapted from Eom and Ashill 2018)

4 Literature Review

The literature review is conducted using ProQuest Research Library covering the period of January 2016 through December 2022 to report publication trends of peer-reviewed and full-text articles on learning analytics using the following three descriptors: (Learning analytics) AND (learning process) AND e-learning. The first step retrieves 1196 articles with source type = "scholarly journals," and document type = "article" and language = "English." Each article is manually examined to finalize the LA research publication. We clustered the selected papers into four broad categories: personalization, adaptive learning, predictive learning, and monitoring learning progress. All previous literature on personalized learning reviewed is based on different dimensions of personality, including physiological, affective, cognitive, and psychological. Adaptive learning is the other side of the same coin, and its aim is enhancing learning outcomes and learnability by adjusting the learning /teaching processes with the recommender systems.

4.1 Personalization

- LMS personalization based on Multi-Attribute Decision Making T [12]
- Supporting SRL and personalization using ePortfolios: a semantic approach based on learning paths [13]
- Individual learning preferences based on personality traits [14]
- Designing a pedagogical strategy based on learning itineraries based on learners' characteristics [15]
- Identifying Students' Learning Patterns with Ebook Systems to provide timely intervention as well as to predict learning outcomes [16]

4.2 Adaptive Learning

- Adaptive E-learning System to Monitor the Learner's Activities [17]
- Adaptive learning management expert system with evolving knowledge base and enhanced learnability [18]
- An adaptive intelligent system to improve online learners' performance [19]

4.3 Predictive Learning

- Predicting learner performance via analyzing video clickstream data using deep learning model in MOOCs [20]
- Early Prediction of Students' Academic Performance in Blended Learning [21]
- Identifying, using clickstream data, student self-regulatory behavioral patterns for predicting learning outcomes [22]

4.4 Development of Learning Analytics Dashboards

Learning analytics dashboards [23] are developed to analyze data generated from the user's usage patterns to give educators insight into their students' performance. With that, they can apply early intervention and modification of their delivery method to suit the student's needs, increase the quality of the content, and can improve learning outcomes.

The literature reviewed points out that significant trends in LA research over the past seven years between 2016 and 2022 are personalization, adaptive learning, and predictive learning. These three research subspecialties are rooted in differential psychology

[24]. Another topic different from the three closely related topics is the LA dashboard development research to monitor the learning progress.

We pointed out in the beginning that a systematic literature review conducted in the past concluded that there is still a shortage of research addressing the effectiveness and consequences of learning processes and outcomes [5].

Another research based on LA based on bibliometric research asserted that "learning analytics tends to underplay the complexity of teaching-learning processes." Further, LA research focuses "more on analytics than on learning more on analytics than on learning" [6]. Therefore, this has been considered a complex challenge to LA research. This research aims to take on these challenges and critical concerns raised by Guzmán-Valenzuela, et al., as described early.

5   Two Challenges and Responses

5.1   Challenge 1. How Can LA Tackle Improving Learning Outcomes in Digital Distance Learning?

A primary challenge around Learning Analytics in Higher Education is improving learning outcomes and their imprecise focus on learning processes. LA research trivialized the complexity of learning processes and that LA oversimplifies the learning process. We need good pedagogical models that are complete and parsimonious, as described by DeLone and McLean [25, p.87].

To fully tackle this problem, we introduce the system's view of the e-learning success model (Fig. 1.) as an example of a pedagogical model for empirical e-learning studies, rooted in the educational theories (constructivism and collaborativism) and empirically tested to be widely accepted by e-learning empirical researcher. This CSF model is based on the review of past decades of empirical e-learning research and effectively supports the interdependent learning process and improves learning outcomes [9, 10, 26, 27]. The system's view of the CSF model is based on the input, process, and output sequence. It not only encompasses all necessary constructs but also is parsimonious. It has evolved over the past decades. The initial model [26] has been recognized as one of the top 10 most cited papers in empirical e-learning research [28]. Since then, several other updated, follow-up models have firmly established themselves as the leading e-learning pedagogical exemplar that provides theoretically and historically grounded conceptualization that has demonstrated e-learning key predictor of perceived e-learning outcomes and learner satisfaction [29].

Building a holistic success model with a system's view has been a critical issue that must be tackled to make progress toward building robust e-learning theories. This CSF model is built to guide future empirical research in building robust e-learning theories. Most e-learning empirical research studies of critical success factors over the past decade built models of disconnected constructs. This model focused on building a holistic success model of interconnected constructs with a system's view [27, 30]. With the holistic CSF model, e-learning analytical studies can invalidate the harsh criticism such as the following,

LA oversimplifies the learning process by making it equivalent to observable behaviours (for example, the number of times that students download documents or access the LMS).

The CSF model we presented can help foster two core learning processes that connect major inputs (students, the instructor, and LMS/IS) to outputs (learning outcomes and learner satisfaction). As Fig. 1 shows, the number of times students download documents or access the LMS indicates the degree of student-system interaction/dialogue. This indicator only represents a very tiny fraction of e-learning success factors, along with other constructs, including other parts of process constructs [interaction (student-student and student-instructor), and SRL], other input constructors [students, instructor, and LMS/information systems]. Some [30] found little evidence for the roles of LA to improve learning outcomes. Therefore, academics should utilize LA to support, not simply measuring, the learning process that will result in improved learning outcomes. In other words, applying system's view of e-lerning success model to LA means that e-learning outcomes must be analyzed as an output produced by two dynamic processes (interaction and self-regulated learning) taken by a set of interdependent subcentities (students, the instructor, and LMS/IT) interacting together. Student-system interaction/dialogue is a small element in Fig. 1 and it was used by Guzmán-Valenzuela et al. [6] as an example of LA critical shortcomimg (oversimplification of the learning process). Systems view of CSF model of e-leraning success strongly refutes those harsh criticism.

5.2 Challenge 2. How Can LA Tackle Improving Learning Processes in Digital Distance Learning?

Learning analytic dashborad has been important tools for positively affecting learning outcomes, student satisfaction, and reducing dropout rates. We reviewed an essential contribution of LA from developing the LA dashboard [23]. The system's view of the e-learning success model guides us in developing learning analytics dashboards (LADs). In Fig. 1, there are three human and non-humen entities (Students, the instructor, andLMS/IT). Our literature review below shows that LADs have been developed to monitor student performances.

A systematic literature review of learning analytics dashboards (LADs) research with a specific focus on the self-regulated learning process is conducted by Matcha et al. [31]. They examined 29 empirical studies on LADs and synthesized the literature to propose a comprehensive model for user-centered learning analytics systems (MULAS). The MULAS model comprises four interconnected dimensions: theory, design, feedback, and evaluation.

Adaptive intelligent LA dashboards are developed to monitor learning activities, analyze each student's performance, and give early intervention. An Intelligent Nudging System by Rodriguez et al. [32] monitors students' lesarning activities, collects and analyzes their performance data with AI-enabled predictive capability, and provides learners with personalized nudges. Sunstein [33, p.2] defined nudges as "interventions that preserve freedom of choice that nonetheless influence people's decisions."

LMS such as Moodle has built-in learning analytics allowing the instructor and students to access students' performance. Due to the limited functionality, more research has been conducted to enrich learning progress reporting via the LA Dashboard [23] development that complements and strengthens existing analytics dashboards available on the market. The fundamental function of LA dashboards is to provide surface-level descriptive analytics to inform learners of their progress. Some advanced LA dashboards added one more layer with predictive analytic components. This predictive functionality is due to the machine learning algorithm embedded in LA dashboards. The advanced LA dashboards enable learners to interpret the predictive model behavior and, therefore, could trigger behavioral changes in the learning process [34]. A similar LA dashboard in terms of functional capabilities and embedded tools are developed [35] to be used with Moodle learning management systems. These dashboards provide specific advice and feedback [36] to the users so they can change their study behavior or enhance self-awareness [37]. Further, with the use of BigData and BigData Processing Tools such as (Hadoop, MapReduce, and In-database analytics), higher education institutions can predict the probability that students are likely to fail/drop-out [38].

6   Conclusion and Future Research Direction

Using LA supports the learning process and increases student satisfaction and learning outcomes. The literature review concluded that over the most recent seven years (January 2016 through December 2022), prevailing LA research trends have been in personalization, adaptive learning, predictive learning, and the development of LA dashboards. Looking at the big picture of the CSF model of distance learning (Fig. 1), most of the recent LA research concentrated on the differential psychology-based LA: personalization, adaptive Learning, and predictive Learning. However, in empirical e-learning studies, individual difference-related variables are rarely included. They are treated as control variables in empirical e-learning research conducted over the past decades [9, 27, 29, 37, 38].

LA helps educators and researchers use their judgments and conscientious efforts to achieve their goals: increase learning outcomes and student satisfaction. We provided a foundation for improving learning processes that consist of self-regulation and motivational process.

Despite the broad definition of LA, our review of the literature clearly showed that differential psychology-based LA is the dominant theme. Therefore, this research makes a worthy contribution to the LA research area that has been overlooked. As the literature review indicated, recent LA research emphasized too heavily individual difference-based research subspecialties. This research urges LA researchers to redirect their LA research focus to each area of the CSF e-learning arena. We provided an integrated, foundational pedagogical model that can guide and facilitate further e-learning analytics research.

References

1. Kelly, B., McCormack, M., Reeves, J., Brooks, D.C., O'Brien, J.: 2021 EDUCAUSE Horizon Report: Information Security Edition. EDUCAUSE, Boulder, CO, USA (2021)
2. Kohnke, L., Moorhouse, B.L.: Adopting HyFlex in higher education in response to COVID-19: students' perspectives. Open Learn.: J. Open Distance e-Learn. **36**, 231–244 (2021)

3. Penrod, J.: staying relevant: the importance of incorporating hyflex learning into higher education strategy. EDUCAUSE Review (2022)
4. Domínguez Figaredo, D., Reich, J., Ruipérez-Valiente, J.A.: Learning analytics and data-driven education: a growing field. RIED. Revista Iberoamericana de Educación a Distancia **23**, 33–43 (2020)
5. Veira, C., Parsons, P., Byrd, V.: Visual learning analytics of educational data: a systematic literature review and research agenda. Comput. Educ. **122**, 119–135 (2018)
6. Guzmán-Valenzuela, C., Gómez-González, C., Rojas-Murphy Tagle, A., Lorca-Vyhmeister, A.: Learning analytics in higher education: a preponderance of analytics but very little learning? Int. J. Educ. Technol. High. Educ. **18**, 1–19 (2021)
7. Eom, S.: DSS, BI, and data analytics research: current state and emerging trends (2015–2019). In: Moreno-Jiménez, J.M., Linden, I., Dargam, F., Jayawickrama, U. (eds.) ICDSST 2020. LNBIP, vol. 384, pp. 167–179. Springer, Cham (2020). https://doi.org/10.1007/978-3-030-46224-6_13
8. Long, P., Siemens, G.: Penetrating the fog: Analytics in learning and education. Educause Rev. **46**, 31–40 (2011)
9. Eom, S.B., Ashill, N.: The determinants of students' perceived learning outcomes and satisfaction in university online education: an update. Decision Sci. J. Innov. Educ. **14**(2), 185–215 (2016)
10. Eom, S.B., Ashill, N.: A system's view of e-learning success model. Decis. Sci. J. Innov. Educ. **16**, 42–76 (2018)
11. Arbaugh, J.B., Hwang, A., Pollack, B.L.: A review of research methods in online and blended business education: 2000–2009. In: Eom, S.B., Arbaugh, J.B. (Eds.) Student Satisfaction and Learning Outcomes in E-Learning: An Introduction to Empirical Research, IGI Global, Hershey, PA, pp. 37–56 (2010)
12. Luna-Urquizo, J.: Learning management system personalization based on multi-attribute decision making techniques and intuitionistic fuzzy numbers. Int. J. Adv. Comput. Sci. Appl. **10**, 669–676 (2019)
13. Romero, L., Saucedo, C., Caliusco, M., Gutiérrez, M.: Supporting self-regulated learning and personalization using ePortfolios: a semantic approach based on learning paths. Int. J. Educ. Technol. High. Educ. **16**(1), 1–16 (2019). https://doi.org/10.1186/s41239-019-0146-1
14. Kamal, A., Radhakrishnan, S.: Individual learning preferences based on personality traits in an E-learning scenario. Educ. Inf. Technol. **24**(1), 407–435 (2018). https://doi.org/10.1007/s10639-018-9777-4
15. Pérez-Garcias, A., Ferrer, G.T., Moral, S.V., Darder-Mesquida, A.: Flexible learning itineraries in digital environments for personalised learning in teacher training alternate title: itinerarios de aprendizaje flexibles en entornos digitales para un aprendizaje personalizado en la formación docente. Revista Iberoamericana de Educación a Distancia. **25**, 173–193 (2022)
16. Yang, C.C.Y., Chen, I.Y.L., Ogata, H.: Toward precision education: educational data mining and learning analytics for identifying students' learning patterns with ebook systems. Educ. Technol. Soc. **24**, 152–163 (2021)
17. Janati, S.E., Maach, A., Ghanami, D.E.: Learning analytics framework for adaptive e-learning system to monitor the learner's activities. Int. J. Adv. Comput. Sci. Appl. **10** (2019)
18. Sridharan, S., Saravanan, D., Srinivasan, A.K., Murugan, B.: Adaptive learning management expert system with evolving knowledge base and enhanced learnability. Educ. Inf. Technol. **26**(5), 5895–5916 (2021). https://doi.org/10.1007/s10639-021-10560-w
19. Guerrero-Roldán, A.E., Rodríguez-González, M.E., Bañeres, D., Elasri-Ejjaberi, A., Cortadas, P.: Experiences in the use of an adaptive intelligent system to enhance online learners' performance: a case study in Economics and Business courses. Int. J. Educ. Technol. High. Educ. **18**, 1–27 (2021)

20. Mubarak, A.A., Cao, H., Ahmed, S.A.M.: Predictive learning analytics using deep learning model in MOOCs' courses videos. Educ. Inf. Technol. **26**(1), 371–392 (2020). https://doi.org/10.1007/s10639-020-10273-6
21. Lu, O.H., Huang, A.Y., Huang, J.C.H., Lin, A.J.Q., Ogata, H., Yang, S.J.H.: Applying learning analytics for the early prediction of students' academic performance in blended learning. J. Educ. Technol. Soc. **21**, 220–232 (2018)
22. Baker, R., et al.: The benefits and caveats of using clickstream data to understand student self-regulatory behaviors: opening the black box of learning processes. Int. J. Educ. Technol. High. Educ. **17**(1), 1–24 (2020). https://doi.org/10.1186/s41239-020-00187-1
23. Xin, O.K., Singh, D.: Development of learning analytics dashboard based on moodle l learning management system. Int. J. Adv. Comput. Sci. Appl. **12**, 838–843 (2021)
24. Revelle, W., Wilt, J., Condon, D.M.: Individual differences and differential psychology: a brief history and prospect. In: Chamorro-Premuzic, T., Stumm, S.V., Furnham, A. (eds.), The Wiley-Blackwell Handbook of Individual Differences, Wiley Blackwell, pp. 3–38 (2011)
25. DeLone, W.H., McLean, E.R.: Information system success: the quest for the dependent variable. Inf. Syst. Res. **3**, 60–95 (1992)
26. Eom, S.B., Ashill, N., Wen, H.J.: The determinants of students' perceived learning outcome and satisfaction in university online education: an empirical investigation. Decis. Sci. J. Innov. Educ. **4**, 215–236 (2006)
27. Eom, S.: Online learning empirical research on the learning process and its impact on learning outcomes: review of literature and a future research direction. In: MENACIS2021, AIS, Agadir, Morocco (2021)
28. Ortega Azurduy, M.: A bibliometric analysis of the adoption and use of e-learning in higher education. Un análisis bibliométrico sobre el uso y la adopción de la educación en línea en la enseñanza superior. Educación Superior 49 – 65 (2021)
29. Eom, S.B., Ashill, N.J., Arbaugh, J.B.: guest editors' introduction to the special issue. Decision Sci. J. Innov. Educ. **14**, 124–127 (2016)
30. Eom, S.B.: A system's view of e-learning success model and its implications to e-learning empirical research. In: The 2020 SIGED International Conference on Information Systems Education and Research, AIS SIGED Association for Information Systems Special Interest Group on IS Education (2020)
31. Matcha, W., Uzir, N.A.A., Gašević, D., Pardo, A.A.: Systematic review of empirical studies on learning analytics dashboards: a self-regulated learning perspective. IEEE Trans. Learn. Technol. **13**, 226–245 (2020)
32. Rodriguez, M.E., Guerrero-Roldán, A.E., Baneres, D., Karadeniz, A.: An intelligent nudging system to guide online learners. Int. Rev. Res. Open Distrib. Learn. **23**, 41–62 (2022)
33. Sunstein, C.R.: Which nudges do people like? A national survey. Soc. Sci. Res. Netw. (2015)
34. Teo, S., Suganya, R.G., Anuradha, M.: Learning analytics dashboard: a tool for providing actionable insights to learners. Int. J. Educ. Technol. High. Educ. **19**, 12 (2022)
35. Peraić, I., Grubišić, A.: Development and evaluation of a learning analytics dashboard for moodle learning management system. In: et al. HCI International 2022 - Late Breaking Papers. Interaction in New Media, Learning and Games. HCII 2022. Lecture Notes in Computer Science, vol. 13517, pp. 390–408. Springer, Cham (2022). https://doi.org/10.1007/978-3-031-22131-6_30
36. Bodily, R., Ikahihifo, T.K., Mackley, B., Graham, C.R.: The design, development, and implementation of student-facing learning analytics dashboards. J. Comput. High. Educ. **30**, 572–598 (2018)
37. Teasley, S.D.: Student facing dashboards: one size fits all? Technol. Knowl. Learn. **22**, 377–384 (2017)
38. Caspari-Sadeghi, S.: Applying learning analytics in online environments: measuring learners' engagement unobtrusively. Front. Educ. **7**, 21 (2022)

Scientific Authorship in DSS Research: Past Trends and Future Opportunities

Peter B. Keenan[1]($\boxtimes$) and Ciara Heavin[2]

[1] UCD School of Business, University College Dublin, Dublin 4, Ireland
Peter.keenan@ucd.ie
[2] Business Information Systems, Cork University Business School, University College Cork, Cork, Ireland

Abstract. Over a period of almost 60 years, Decision Support Systems (DSS) research has focused on supporting managerial decision-making, drawing on contributions from diverse fields including Economics, Operations Research/Management Science (OR/MS), Information Systems (IS), and Management. To better understand the DSS landscape, this article uses a bibliometric analysis to investigate current publishing trends in DSS as a research area, co-authorship by gender, and location. By leveraging Scopus, we identify notable patterns and developments in DSS research authorship from 2018 to 2022. We present initial recommendations to guide the future research efforts of both DSS academics and practitioners.

Keywords: Decision Support · Decision Support Systems · DSS · bibliometric analysis · gender · author · location

1 Introduction

1.1 Decision Support Systems

The field of Decision Support Systems (DSS), a sub-domain of the Information Systems (IS) discipline, has a history of looking to the past to prepare for the future. DSS is the area of the IS discipline that has traditionally focused on supporting and improving managerial decision-making [1]. Power [2] defined a DSS as "…an interactive computer-based system or subsystem intended to help decision makers use communications technologies, data, documents, knowledge and/or models to identify and solve problems, complete decision process tasks, and make decisions". These are computer-based solutions that may be used to support difficult decision-making and problem-solving [3]. Existing research characterises DSS in terms of (i) database management capabilities, (ii) modelling functions, and (iii) simple, accessible user interface designs that facilitate engagement by an end user [3].

Building on the tradition of Blanning's [4] and Keen's [5] work predicting the trajectory of DSS research, IS scholars such as Shim et al. [3], Arnott and Pervan [1, 6] and Hosack et al. [7] considered the successes of DSS, the nature of the problems solved and

S. Liu et al. (Eds.): ICDSST 2023, LNBIP 474, pp. 287–301, 2023.
https://doi.org/10.1007/978-3-031-32534-2_21

the approaches deployed to tackle existing and new challenges. Just over ten years ago, Bryan Hosack and colleagues [7] examined the relevance of DSS as a research area. At that time, DSS was viewed as a mature domain where many difficult problems had been solved [7]. Although DSS had reached maturity in traditional areas of application, they highlighted the growth of DSS in new disciplines, notably that the Shim et al. [2] paper had been widely cited in several domains outside the traditional business area [7]. Since the publication of this seminal article, there has not been a widely cited contribution central to the DSS area [8].

Extensive accessible data resources are now available capturing data about academic article citations and references. These data can help the DSS research community understand how knowledge has been disseminated and shared, but screening and assessing search results and citations can be cumbersome. A quick search on Google Scholar in January 2023 shows that the term DSS, or decision support systems, appeared in the academic literature 394 in the 1970s, 5,830 times in the 1980s, 11,500 times in the last decade of the previous century, 14,700 times from 2000 to 2010, and since 16,300 times to 2023. These rudimentary measures provide us with an interesting sense of the DSS research landscape, these data reveal that in this new "era of Analytics" DSS continues to persist and grow as an area of research.

This study builds on previous work [9] which leverages WOS scientific data resources to uncover an aggregated view of the authors publishing on the research subjects of DSS globally between 2011 and 2020. Further, recent research-in-progress work identifies the geographic differences in DSS interest in these areas across the Association for Information Systems (AIS) regions and the application areas in which DSS research is conducted [8]. The need for an ongoing global research conversation on gender in academic publishing has been increased by trends in publishing observed during the COVID-19 pandemic [10, 11], this has prompted us to further consider gender as one characteristic of authors publishing in the DSS field. The implications of gender-based differences in IS-related contexts are under-researched in the IS domain and more specifically in IS-based decision-making research [9].

There has been continuing academic interest since the 1970s in the changing trends in publishing, particularly in the sciences. It is recognised that existing challenges continue to have negative implications for the career progression of women academics and researchers globally [12]. Female academics have significantly shorter career lengths and lower publication rates than their male counterparts [13–15]. An increased focus on research performance in the form of national and international research audit regimes, for example the REF (Research Excellence Framework) in the UK and ERA (Excellence in Research for Australia) in Australia, have intensified unequal outcomes for women who experience tensions between demands for greater volumes of research publications, commitment to academic research excellence and other commitments such as family/caring responsibilities [16]. Nevertheless, there have been considerable gains in terms of the volume and visibility of female academic authorship over the last 50 years [12]. Yet, many research fields continue to be dominated by men [11]. Existing research has identified that the "field of research" is the most important factor influencing international authorship collaborations [17]. With this in mind, our research extends previous work [8] by conducting further analysis to better understand the geographic distribution of DSS research and the gender of DSS authors. We aim to investigate the publication trends in the DSS domain, paying particular attention to trends in co-authorship.

The next section presents the research approach, the dataset, and the techniques used to complete the bibliometric analysis. As such, the remaining text in this section presents the research approach undertaken, and details of the Scopus dataset analysed. Further sections characterise the DSS landscape by research area, the use of Scopus to present a bibliometric analysis of recent DSS research and examine the co-authorship patterns by gender and geographical distribution of DSS research output. The final section presents a discussion of the data presented and considers the limitations of this approach. Finally, we offer conclusions and consider opportunities for future research.

1.2 Research Approach

Bibliographic databases such as Scopus and Web of Science (WOS) provide valuable insight into the evolution of academic disciplines as they contain both the articles published and the articles cited [18]. In conducting this study, the researchers took advantage of the strengths and limitations of Scopus. Scopus indexes scientific journals, allows the download of abstracts and cited articles for aggregate sets of papers and there are bibliographic tools to analyse this data. Scopus indexes more publications than WOS, and allows the download of aggregate information, but has limitations in terms of the availability of older research publications, so is more useful for recent periods [19]. In 2022, Scopus had over 87 million records drawn from over 27,000 serial publications. In May 2022, Scopus introduced the facility to download bibliographic data including the authors' full names instead of the author initials previously available. In December 2022, we conducted a preliminary investigation of the DSS literature using this enhanced feature of Scopus. Our focus was on investigating DSS article authorship where we relied on the authors' first names to determine their gender.

We used a search following Keenan [18], searching the titles, abstracts, and keywords in Scopus for the search terms "decision support systems" "decision support software" and "decision support tool" and the combination (DSS and "decision support"). We have only included journal articles, as the Scopus indexing of book chapters and conference proceedings is less consistent than that of journals. Our search returned 19,363 records representing journal articles for five years from 2018 to 2022. We used the full record download from Scopus, this contained a field containing full names with the required information available for most authors.

1.3 Bibliographic Dataset and Techniques

There were 106,866 authors in the dataset, an average of 5.52 authors per paper, and papers had from 1 author to 388 authors per paper. Papers with many authors were not typical and were difficult to process reliably, so we decided to process only the first 12 authors, as 95% of articles in the dataset had this number of authors or less. Some records had formatting issues which meant that certain author names could not be processed. The limit of 12 authors meant the removal of 11,664 authors from 972 records. After this adjustment and other issues with record formatting, we were able to process 82,374 author names drawn from 17,860 articles published in 3,790 journals.

Although Scopus now provides the full name of authors, not all full names were recorded and only initials were available in some cases. This reflects journal publisher policies on collecting full names and the widespread use of multiple initials to identify people in some cultures, for instance in South Asia. In our dataset, 6% of author records had only initials available. This is comparable to earlier work using WOS data where 8% of records in 2020 only had initials [9], which was a substantial decline from earlier years, reflecting the improvement in the quality of bibliographic databases and amended journal policies requiring the full name of authors.

For a variety of reasons, such as personal choice, cultural practice and the limitations of these databases, this research approach cannot always accurately determine the gender identity of an individual author, but it can still provide a useful overview of the aggregate landscape of the DSS research area. To identify gender, we matched the author's first name against the World Gender Name Dictionary version 2.0 [20]. Version 2 of this database has enhanced coverage when compared to the first version, with over four million Asian names having been added [21]. In general, we only used the first name of the author but used a second name instead if the first name was only an initial. This initial process matched 62,341 names or 80.7% of the records with full names. This is a higher matching rate than earlier work with WOS [9], reflecting the use of the extended gender database. While the new database has improved coverage of Asian names, matching was still higher for European-originated names compared with Asian ones. Some names remained unmatched owing to features such as hyphens in names, addressing these issues would have required substantial further processing. The aggregate nature of our work means that the absence of an individual name should not adversely affect the research and extra processing would have a very limited effect on the value of the insight from the research.

1.4 Gender of Authors

The process of associating a gender to the first 12 authors of the overall dataset indicated that 64.5% of authors were male and 35.5% were female. This proportion is similar to the proportion in the later years of the previous WOS-based analysis [9]. In this dataset, the journals with the highest number of articles are: Sustainability, IEEE Access, Journal Of Cleaner Production, Plos One, Decision Support Systems and Expert Systems With Applications. These reflect DSS in the twenty-first century. Where the traditional areas of applications in business and engineering have been extended by newer environmental and medical applications. These top journals represent traditional sources of DSS output from technical areas, journals set up specifically to publish DSS content, a journal concerned with the environment and a journal substantially concerned with medical applications (Table 1).

Figure 1 presents a graphical representation of authors by co-authorship position during the years 2018 through 2022. Notably, female authors make up a higher proportion of first authors than their proportion generally.

A first author may be the only author or the first of multiple authors, and other author positions may be in the middle or at the end of an author list. We can also look at the gender proportion by the number of authors on a paper. Figure 2 shows the gender proportions for articles with a particular number of authors. It is notable here that while

Table 1. Gender proportions in journals with the highest number of DSS papers

Journal	Articles	Authors	Authors per paper	Male	Female
Sustainability	299	1223	4.1	62.8%	37.2%
IEEE Access	295	1336	4.5	77.2%	22.8%
Journal of Cleaner Production	203	890	4.4	70.7%	29.3%
PLoS ONE	194	1269	6.5	59.0%	41.0%
Decision Support Systems	175	562	3.2	77.8%	22.2%
Expert Systems with Applications	155	602	3.9	77.3%	22.7%

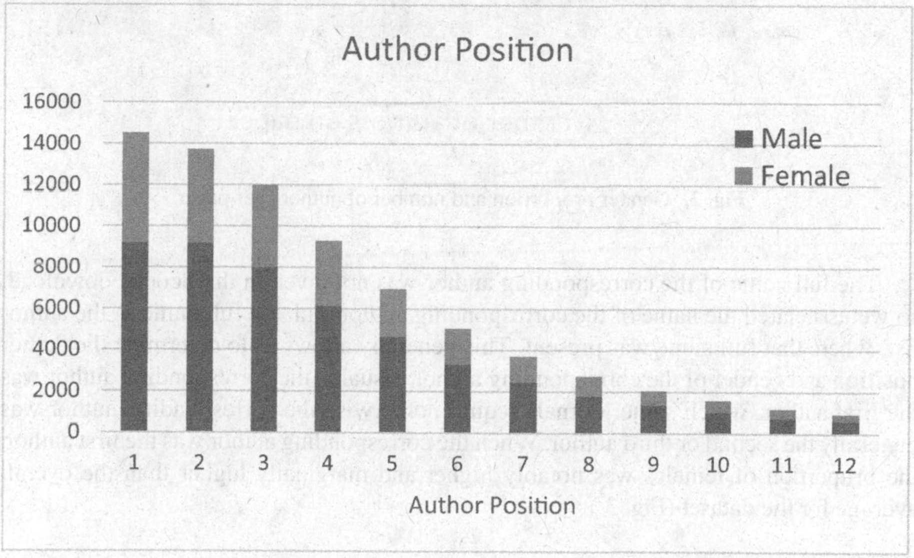

Fig. 1. Gender proportions by author position in Scopus (2018–2022)

male authors predominate in every category, reflecting the overall proportion, there is a higher proportion of male single-authored papers than you would expect from the overall ratios. For papers with two authors, there are more papers with two male authors than you would expect from a random process, but about the number of papers that you expect with two female authors or with a female as the first author. There are fewer two author papers with a male first author and female second author than you would expect from a random process. These aggregate conclusions need further investigation by discipline, for instance single author papers may be more common in disciplines with a higher proportion of males. In the case of papers with three authors, the proportion of papers with all authors of the same gender is higher than you would expect if this was a random process, and this is broadly true for all discipline groupings. The more complex patterns for papers with more than three authors also warrant future investigation.

Fig. 2. Gender proportion and number of authors per paper

The full name of the corresponding author was not given in the Scopus download, so we associated the name of the corresponding author with the full name in the author list, where that full name was present. This generally allows us to determine the author position and gender of the corresponding author. Usually, the corresponding author was the first author, which some journals require, otherwise the corresponding author was generally the second or third author. When the corresponding author was the first author, the proportion of females was notably higher and marginally higher than the overall average for the dataset (Fig. 3.)

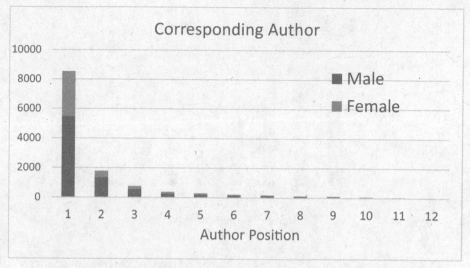

Fig. 3. The gender proportion and number of papers for corresponding authors.

2 Exploring DSS in the Wider Scientific Research Landscape

Scopus has its own groupings of disciplines, namely the All-Science Journal Classification Codes (ASJC) schema. This is grouped into 31 subject areas, which are organised by Scopus into four major areas: Life Sciences, Social Sciences, Physical Sciences, and Health Sciences. Analysis using these research areas creates complexity because a given publication may be included in one or more classifications and in up to three top-level groupings. Frequently, a DSS publication can be in two top-level groupings, typically combining a computer science classification with an application area. For instance, the journal Decision Support Systems is in both the Social Sciences and Physical Sciences categories and the journal International Journal of Environmental Research and Public Health is categorised both in Physical Sciences and Health Sciences. While these overlaps complicate the analysis, this research is interested in the patterns of gender and co-authorship in different disciplines; these comparisons are possible notwithstanding these challenges [9].

Across the dataset, 15% of the papers are in Life Sciences, 17% are in Social Sciences, 50% in Physical Sciences and 40% in Health Sciences, note that the overlapping categorisation means that this totals more than 100%. However, if we look at authors then we see that the number of authors differs by generic discipline, with health sciences dominating papers with a larger number of authors. Note that a journal may be in two categories, so the total number of papers is increased, and the effect of different authorship norms may be less clear as some journals are counted as both Health Sciences and another disciplinary grouping (Figs. 4 and 5).

To illustrate the difference, the figure below shows the distribution of discipline groupings for papers with two authors and papers with ten authors (Fig. 6).

We examined the frequency of keywords in the abstract for articles with 2, 3 or 4 authors of the same gender. In the total dataset, there are some differences between

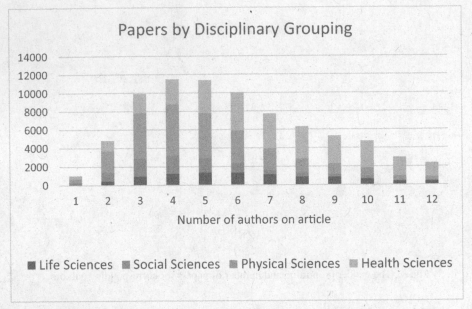

Fig. 4. Disciplinary grouping for papers with different numbers of authors.

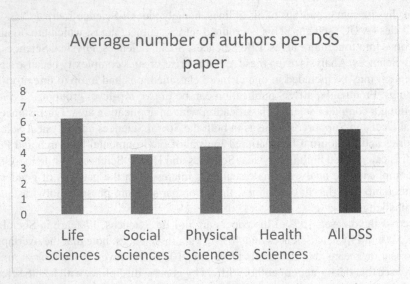

Fig. 5. Average number of authors for different disciplinary groupings.

the all male-authored papers and the all-female-authored papers. However, most of that variation reflected the differing proportions of males and females in different disciplines. When we looked only at papers published in journals classified in the Physical Sciences grouping then there was little difference in the word frequency in abstracts between

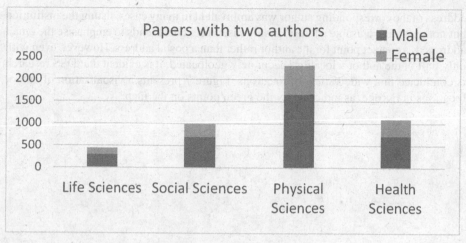

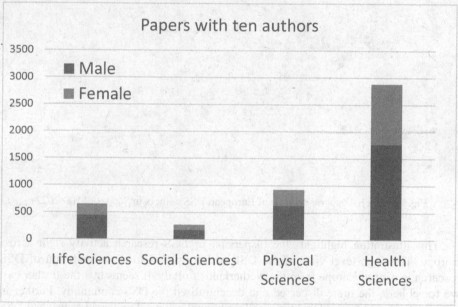

Fig. 6. Disciplinary groups for papers with two and ten authors.

papers with all-male authors and those with all-female authors. This analysis did not provide evidence of different research themes for males and females.

3 Geographic Structure of DSS Research

In this research, we attempted to examine the geographic location of the authors. Initially, we attempted to geolocate the author addresses using the ArcGIS geocoding service. While this is a very comprehensive geocoding database, this process was only partly successful as recorded author affiliations often did not give a precise location. Even the address of the corresponding author was ambivalent in many cases, listing the institution but not providing a usable address. In this case, recent data tends to emphasise the email address as a contact point for the author rather than a postal address. However, even with only half of the author's locations accurately geolocated, it is evident that DSS research is conducted in a wide variety of locations. Figure 7 presents a visualisation of author locations in Europe, as indicated by the green points on the map.

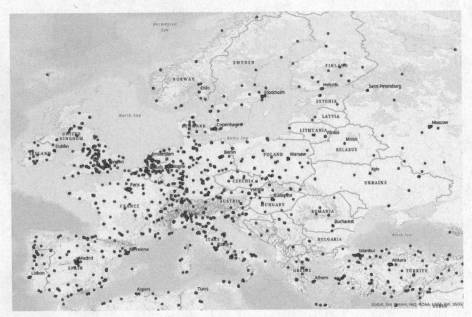

Fig. 7. Detailed geographic map of European DSS authors in Scopus (2018–2022)

This illustration highlights the dispersion of DSS research activity right across Europe. This high-level view of the DSS activity points to a concentration of DSS research in central Europe from the Netherlands to Italy. It seems that the further east we travel here, the more dispersed and decentralised the DSS community. Further in the Irish context, we noted that the smaller regional technical universities also had DSS output in the dataset, indicating that DSS research output was not limited to the larger institutions.

While precise geolocation proved challenging for many authors, we sought to identify their countries from the text affiliation data provided by Scopus. This was successful in most cases, although variations in the naming of countries meant that some records were not matched. There was a particular problem identifying the country of authors with two affiliations, as Scopus does not distinguish these two affiliations clearly in its records.

At a country level, the gender ratio can differ significantly owing to the relatively small number of papers in some countries [8]. Therefore, it is more useful to look at world regions. We grouped countries into regions and continents and matched corresponding author information with the gender of those authors. Table 2 presents this analysis, it confirms a pattern noted in Keenan and Heavin [8] of female authorship being high in Oceania and Africa, although these regions together represent only 6% of DSS papers.

Table 2. Corresponding authors of DSS papers by location by Gender in Scopus (2018–2022)

Location	M	F
Western Europe	66.7%	33.3%
Southern Europe	67.1%	32.9%
Eastern Europe	75.2%	24.8%
Northern Europe	65.1%	34.9%
Europe	**67.0%**	**33.0%**
Western Asia	77.3%	22.7%
Southern Asia	75.7%	24.3%
South-eastern Asia	71.7%	28.3%
Eastern Asia	69.6%	30.4%
Asia	**72.2%**	**27.8%**
Northern America	65.0%	35.0%
Central America	86.0%	14.0%
South America	73.2%	26.8%
Caribbean	66.7%	33.3%
Americas	**66.0%**	**34.0%**
Africa	**60.6%**	**39.4%**
Oceania	**60.4%**	**39.6%**

While the aggregate totals are a useful guide, these proportions may vary slightly owing to data quality issues and the challenges in determining the gender of author first names. We have selected countries located in the respective continents to reveal insights on the DSS authorship by gender breakdown. In the subset of larger countries in each continent presented in Table 3, we highlight that Australia has the most representative balance of publishing authors with around 60% men and 40% women, while India presents a less representative landscape by gender.

The pattern represented in Table 3 broadly translates to two male authors to every one female for articles in a DSS-related area during this period of analysis. Following, Table 4 presents a high-level view of the extent of international co-authorship considering the number of co-authors on a single published article. The matching column reflects whether the country was determined for each author, the more authors there are on a paper the more likely it is that one author could not be assigned. Notably, the lower the number of co-authors the more likely authors are to be in the same country.

As highlighted in Table 4, some of the records remain unmatched. For example, any author with two affiliations is not matched, plus some countries might have variations

Table 3. Author gender for countries in different regions for DSS papers in Scopus (2018–2022)

Country	M	F
Australia	60.1%	39.9%
China	68.5%	31.5%
Germany	73.0%	27.0%
India	74.8%	25.2%
United Kingdom	66.3%	33.7%
United States	65.7%	34.3%

Table 4. Corresponding authors of DSS papers located in the same country in Scopus (2018–2022)

Number of Authors	Same Country %	Matched %
2	86.7%	80.4%
3	84.4%	69.6%
4	83.0%	61.9%
5	77.1%	57.0%
6	74.0%	56.6%
7	72.1%	53.9%
8	67.7%	53.4%
9	68.5%	49.3%
10	67.7%	54.4%
11	63.8%	49.0%
12	64.9%	53.5%

in their names that are more complex to process. The more authors collaborating on a paper, the increased likelihood that one country could not be determined using our analysis techniques. The "same country" column is therefore conservative. If you had 7 authors and one country was not determined, then they would not be regarded as the same country in this percentage, even though those that were determined were in the same country. It is noteworthy that the greater the number of authors on an authorship team, the more likely it is that one or more authors are located in another country.

4 Discussion and Conclusion

This research uses a bibliometric analysis of articles drawn from Scopus published from 2018 to 2022. We aim to investigate current trends in DSS publishing with a particular focus on co-authorship by gender by geographic location. Our findings suggest that in DSS-related papers approximately one-third of authors are female, and two-thirds are male with male authors leading on the majority of published papers. However, we have shown that this proportion varies by discipline and that expanding areas of DSS application have a somewhat more balanced ratio. This analysis is just a starting point, we recognise that there is still a great deal of work to be done to defeat gender disparity in scientific publishing in the DSS domain. Through our analysis of this recent Scopus dataset, we highlight the volume and diversity of DSS research and collaboration opportunities that currently exist, and the potential opportunities given the trends identified.

It is important to acknowledge the limitations of the analysis presented. The sample of papers could be expanded to include a longer period and by improving our techniques for matching names. In our analysis, 97.3% of the articles are in English; the inclusion of additional languages may alter the DSS authorship by location presented in Fig. 7. Further, this map focuses on DSS research in Europe, additional work might include a more in-depth analysis of DSS in other continents. Our analysis includes the period of the global pandemic, this initial rudimentary analysis does not account for the likely "Covid effect" on DSS research output from 2020 to 2022.

Following our bibliometric analysis, it is useful to revisit the Hosack et al. [7] question "Is Decision Support Research alive and well?". This research investigating academic publication patterns during the most recent five-year period reveals that scholars continue to publish scientific research in DSS. More than ten years later, we continue to highlight "the plethora of DSS research and collaboration opportunities that currently exist or are within our reach in the near future given the trends" [7]. Indeed, Hosack and colleagues acknowledged the variety of decisions that confront users daily presenting "limitless" new research opportunities to understand socio-technical interaction. These possibilities have brought DSS research into areas of environmental science and medical applications which have different academic traditions compared with the business and engineering disciplines that provided the bulk of DSS research in its earlier years [8]. In this research, these traditions are reflected in the number of authors per paper, but further research may also reveal less obvious differences.

However, the pervasiveness of DSS in modern organisations, emphasises the need for researchers, designers, and builders of DSS technologies to reflect the underlying characteristics and diversity of their users [9]. Given this diversity, there is also a need for the traditional DSS research community to interact with DSS researchers in newer areas of application, to avoid a fragmented field.

It is important to note that the period from 2018 to 2022 was not a "typical" period in scientific publishing. Future research could consider how this period and the subsequent opportunities and challenges for scientific researchers have impacted publication in terms of gender imbalance and geographic jurisdiction considering lockdowns, school closures etc. in DSS research output. A new phase of this research might further explore opportunities for academic collaborations across these diverse locations. Further research considering various contributing factors that may affect scientific productivity is necessary, particularly in terms of co-authorship relationships (e.g., childcare resources, caring responsibilities, type of authorship). Novel research is required to better understand the intrinsic and extrinsic factors that influence this phenomenon in the DSS research domain.

References

1. Arnott, D., Pervan, G.: A critical analysis of decision support systems research revisited: the rise of design science. J. Inf. Technol. **29**(4), 269–293 (2014). https://doi.org/10.1057/jit.2014.16
2. Power, D.J.: A brief history of decision support systems. DSSResources.com (2007). http://dssresources.com/history/dsshistory.html. Accessed 03 May 2011
3. Shim, J.P., Warkentin, M., Courtney, J.F., Power, D.J., Sharda, R., Carlsson, C.: Past, present, and future of decision support technology. Decis. Support Syst. **33**(2), 111–126 (2002). https://doi.org/10.1016/S0167-9236(01)00139-7
4. Blanning, R.W.: What is happening in DSS? Interfaces **13**(5), 71–80 (1983). https://doi.org/10.1287/inte.13.5.71
5. Keen, P.G.: Decision support systems: the next decade. Decis. Support Syst. **3**(3), 253–265 (1987). https://doi.org/10.1016/0167-9236(87)90180-1
6. Arnott, D., Pervan, G.: Eight key issues for the decision support systems discipline. Decis. Support Syst. **44**(3), 657–672 (2008). https://doi.org/10.1016/j.dss.2007.09.003
7. Hosack, B., Hall, D., Paradice, D., Courtney, J.F.: A look toward the future: decision support systems research is alive and well. J. Assoc. Inf. Syst. **13**(5), 315–340 (2012). https://doi.org/10.17705/1jais.00297
8. Keenan, P.B., Heavin, C.: Understanding the evolving frontier of DSS: an empirical investigation. In: Proceedings of the 2022 Pre-ICIS SIGDSA Symposium, Copenhagen, vol. 19. Association of Information Systems (2022)
9. Keenan, P., Heavin, C.: DSS research: a bibliometric analysis by gender. J. Decis. Syst. **31**(sup1), 107–116 (2022). https://doi.org/10.1080/12460125.2022.2070953
10. Abramo, G., D'Angelo, C.A., Mele, I.: Impact of Covid-19 on research output by gender across countries. Scientometrics **127**, 6811–6826 (2022). https://doi.org/10.1007/s11192-021-04245-x
11. Son, J.-Y., Bell, M.L.: Scientific authorship by gender: trends before and during a global pandemic. Humanit. Soc. Sci. Commun. **9**, 348 (2022). https://doi.org/10.1057/s41599-022-01365-4
12. Shen, H.: Inequality quantified: mind the gender gap. Nat. News **495**(7439), 22–24 (2013). https://doi.org/10.1038/495022a
13. Long, J.S., Allison, P.D., McGinnis, R.: Rank advancement in academic careers: sex differences and the effects of productivity. Am. Sociol. Rev. **58**(5), 703–722 (1993). https://doi.org/10.2307/2096282
14. Nakhaie, M.R.: Gender differences in publication among university professors in Canada. Can. Rev. Sociol./Revue Canadienne Sociologie **39**(2), 151–179 (2002). https://doi.org/10.1111/j.1755-618X.2002.tb00615.x
15. Zeng, X.H.T., et al.: Differences in collaboration patterns across discipline, career stage, and gender. PLoS Biol. **14**(11), e1002573 (2016). https://doi.org/10.1371/journal.pbio.1002573
16. Baker, M.: Choices or constraints? Family responsibilities, gender and academic career. J. Comp. Fam. Stud. **41**(1), 1–18 (2010). https://doi.org/10.3138/jcfs.41.1.1
17. Aksnes, D.W., Piro, F.N., Rørstad, K.: Gender gaps in international research collaboration: a bibliometric approach. Scientometrics **120**(2), 747–774 (2019). https://doi.org/10.1007/s11192-019-03155-3

18. Keenan, P.B.: Thirty years of decision support: a bibliometric view. In: Papathanasiou, J., Zaraté, P., Freire de Sousa, J. (eds.) EURO Working Group on DSS. ISIS, pp. 15–32. Springer, Cham (2021). https://doi.org/10.1007/978-3-030-70377-6_2

19. Crowley, J., Heavin, C., Keenan, P., Power, D.: CDSS and DSS: shared roots and divergent paths. J. Decis. Syst. **29**, 71–78 (2020). https://doi.org/10.1080/12460125.2020.1811446

20. Raffo, J.: WGND 2.0. DRAFT VERSION edn. Harvard Dataverse (2021). https://doi.org/10.7910/DVN/MSEGSJ

21. Martínez, G.L., et al.: Expanding the world gender-name dictionary: WGND 2.0. World Intellectual Property Organization, Geneva, Switzerland (2021). https://doi.org/10.34667/tind.43980

Correction to: Multi-actor VIKOR Method for Highway Selection in Montenegro

Boris Delibašić⦿, Draženko Glavić ⦿, Sandro Radovanović ⦿,
Andrija Petrović ⦿, Marina Milenković ⦿, and Milija Suknović

Correction to:
Chapter 1 in: S. Liu et al. (Eds.): *Decision Support Systems XIII*, LNBIP 474, https://doi.org/10.1007/978-3-031-32534-2_1

In the original version there is a correction in the city name in chapter 1. The city name Andrijevica should be changed to Berane wherever necessary in the chapter.

The updated version of this chapter can be found at
https://doi.org/10.1007/978-3-031-32534-2_1

Author Index

S. Liu et al. (Eds.): ICDSST 2023, LNBIP 474, pp. 303–304, 2023.
https://doi.org/10.1007/978-3-031-32534-2

Printed in the United States
by Baker & Taylor Publisher Services